Data in Depth

Exploring Mathematics with **Fathom**™

Tim Erickson

Key Curriculum Press
Innovators in Mathematics Education

Project Editor:	Mary Jo Cittadino
Editorial Assistants:	Jeff Gammon, James A. Browne
Software Development:	KCP Technologies
Software Coordination:	Denise Howald, Jill Binker
Reviewers:	Karen Radcliff, Murray Siegel, James Swick
Production Editors:	Jason Luz, Kristin Ferraioli
Copy Editors:	Judith Abrahms, Joan Saunders
Production Director:	Diana Jean Parks
Production Coordinator:	Ann Rothenbuhler
Text Design, Composition, and Art:	Kirk Mills
Art and Design Coordinator:	Caroline Ayres
Cover Designer:	Jenny K. Somerville
Front Cover Art:	Precision Graphics
Prepress and Printer:	Data Reproductions
Publisher:	Steven Rasmussen
Senior Scientist:	Bill Finzer

Portions of this material are based upon work supported by the National Science Foundation under award number III–9400091. Any opinions, findings, and conclusions or recommendations expressed in this publication are those of the author(s) and do not necessarily reflect the views of the National Science Foundation.

Key Curriculum Press
1150 65th Street
Emeryville, CA 94608
510-595-7000
editorial@keypress.com
http://www.keypress.com

Printed in the United States of America
10 9 8 7 6 5 4 3 2 1   05 04 03 02 01   ISBN 1-55953-517-2

Contents

1 Come to Your Census 1

Using U.S. Census microdata to study univariate data and representations; writing Boolean filters; making conjectures and testing them informally

Data in Depth
© 2001 Key Curriculum Press

8 Under a Cloud

Studying variability in one and two dimensions, beginning with a random walk; measures of spread and work with correlation and association

9 Probability Through Simulations

Constructing simulations to study probability; sampling from a population; using random numbers and functions to generate data

Data in Depth

Mathematics Topics Grid

Key: √ = main focus
　　　+ = addressed

	Linear Functions, Slope	Nonlinear Functions	Proportion	Using Symbols	Geometry	$f(t)$	Probability	Representations	Inference	Estimation
1: Come to Your Census										
Turning Numbers into People								+		
The Card People								+	√	√
Exploring Census Data								+		
Two Graphs and Selection								+		
Out of Many, Fewer I and II				+						
Making Categories			+	+				+		
Investigating a Conjecture			+	+				√	√	√
Features Buffet:										
Plot Value										
Summary Tables								+		
Display Attributes										
Sorting				√						
Percentile Plots										
Ntigrams										
The Switch Function										
2: Lines and Data										
Reading the News, Parts I and II	√					+		√		√
The Coast Starlight I and II	√		+			+		√		√
Sonatas About Linear Data:										
The Prisoner Sonata	√		√							√
Tall Buildings	√									+
Airliners and Fuel Costs	√		√							√
Batter Up!	√		√					√		√
Sonatas About Lines and Geometry:										
What R π?	√		√		+					√
The Book Cover	√		√		+					
Everybody's Favorite Rectangle	√		√		+					
Explaining Patterns	√			√				√		
The World Is Linear	√			√	√	√		√		

Key: √ = main focus
     + = addressed

3: Per Portions

	Linear Functions, Slope	Nonlinear Functions	Proportion	Using Symbols	Geometry	f(t)	Probability	Representations	Inference	Estimation
A Return to Prison			+	√				√		
The Geography of U.S. Cars I, II, and III			+	√						
Saved by the Belt			+	+			+	√		+
"Per" Sonatas and Investigations:										
Counting the Cars			+	√						
Extreme Capital			+	√						
The Best Drivers			+	√						
The Wide-Open Spaces			+	√						
More Car Stuff			+	√			√	√		
Per in the World			+	√				√		

4: Straighten Up!

	Linear Functions, Slope	Nonlinear Functions	Proportion	Using Symbols	Geometry	f(t)	Probability	Representations	Inference	Estimation
Fitting the Planets										
Fitting a Curve to the Planets		√		√				√		√
Straightening the Planets with Logs	+	√		√						
Moore's Law:										
Moore's Law Logs	+	√		√		+				
Moore's Law Redux		√		√		+		√		√
Area and Perimeter: A Study in Limits		√		√	+			√		
How Much Tape Is Left?		√		√	+	√				+
Nonlinear Geometrical Sonatas:										
The Great Toilet Paper Mystery		√		√	+					+
Printing Paragraphs		√		√	+					√
Incredible Shrinking Text		√		√	+					√
Measuring the Bass		√		√	+					
Puff Puff Puff Puff Pop		√		√	+		√			
More Ideas for Nonlinear Data		√		√	+			√		√

5: Lines and Leverage

	Linear Functions, Slope	Nonlinear Functions	Proportion	Using Symbols	Geometry	f(t)	Probability	Representations	Inference	Estimation
Introducing the World Population Clock	+		√	√		+				+
Predict-a-Pop	+			+		+				+
World Population: A Little Leverage	+			√		√				+
Jupiter's Moons			+	√	+	√	+	√		+

Data in Depth
© 2001 Key Curriculum Press

Key: √ = main focus
+ = addressed

6: Describing and Modeling Change

	Linear Functions, Slope	Nonlinear Functions	Proportion	Using Symbols	Geometry	f(t)	Probability	Representations	Inference	Estimation
Mauna Loa	+	+				+		√		√
Carbon Dioxide: The Whole World			+	√		+				
Carbon Dioxide by Region			√	√		+		√		
Change Playground				+		√		√		
Consumer Price Index			+	√		+		√		
Radiosonde				+		+		√		√
Generation by Generation and Generation II: Limits to Growth		+	√	+		+	√			
Building the Weather Machine			√	+		+	+	+		√
Change Sonatas and Investigations:										
Sequences of Squares				√	√					
Fibonacci		√	√	+				√		
Change Challenges			√	√		+	√	√		

7: What to Do with Leftovers

	Linear Functions, Slope	Nonlinear Functions	Proportion	Using Symbols	Geometry	f(t)	Probability	Representations	Inference	Estimation
Introduction to Residuals:										
I: Residuals Playground		+	√	√	√			+		
II: Heating Water	+			√		+		+		
III: Radiosonde Residuals						+		+		
Estimating Parameters Using Residuals		+		+				+		+
Exercises: Inverting Residual Plots	+	+		√				+		
British Couples	+			+				√		√
Modeling Mauna Loa	+	+		+				√		√
Residual Investigations:										
Cooling Off		+		+		+				+
Out on a Limb with Jupiter		+		+		+				

Key: √ = main focus
     + = addressed

8: Under a Cloud

	Linear Functions, Slope	Nonlinear Functions	Proportion	Using Symbols	Geometry	f(t)	Probability	Representations	Inference	Estimation
Random Walk: Inventing Spread				+		√	+			
SATs and GPAs				√				√		+
Exploring the Normal Distribution		√		√			+			
Exploring Correlation				+			√			
Building a Cloud from Scratch	√			√			√	√		
Straight or Curved?		√		+			√	√		√
Cloud Sonatas:										
Predicting Spread		√		+		√	+			√
Additional Random Walk Sonatas				+		√	+			
Pre-Proto-Yahtzee				√			+			
Proto-Yahtzee				√			+			
The Error in the Sum		√		√			√			√
Combined SAT Scores				√						√

9: Probability Through Simulations

	Linear Functions, Slope	Nonlinear Functions	Proportion	Using Symbols	Geometry	f(t)	Probability	Representations	Inference	Estimation
Rolling Dice			+	√			+			
Exploring Sampling, I and II			+				+	√		
Just You Wait!				√			+			
Great Expectations			√	+		√	+			
HIV Testing:										
HIV Testing I			+	√			+	√		
HIV Testing II: Be an Epidemiologist			+	√			+			+
Simulation Problems and Sonatas:										
Grubs Again?			√	+			+			
A New Birthday Problem				+			+			
Dice Probability Problems			√	√			+	√		
Sampling Challenges			√	√			+	√		

10: Inference with Fathom

	Linear Functions, Slope	Nonlinear Functions	Proportion	Using Symbols	Geometry	f(t)	Probability	Representations	Inference	Estimation
Constructivist Dice			√	+			+	√	√	
Pennies and Polling, I and II			√	+			+		√	+
Pennies and Polling III		√	√	+			+		√	+
Orbital Express				+		√	√	+	√	√
Inferring the Mean, I and II									√	+
Inference Sonatas and Other Challenges:										
Aunt Belinda			√	+			+		√	
Hot Hoops				+		√	+		√	√
Beyond Constructivist Dice				√			+		√	√

Data in Depth
© 2001 Key Curriculum Press

Preface

Data in Depth: Exploring Mathematics with Fathom is filled with activities to use with Fathom—a computer learning environment for data analysis and statistics. This book helps you, the teacher, use Fathom with your students in your mathematics and statistics courses. *Data in Depth* is organized as much as possible around using real data to do data analysis and statistics, and to illuminate mathematical concepts. It contains student activity pages and suggestions for lessons. Ordinarily, the software determines what you can do in curriculum. In this case, it has been more of a partnership, and both Fathom and *Data in Depth* are better as a result.

This book has hardly been a solo effort. I cannot adequately express my gratitude to Steve Rasmussen, President of Key Curriculum Press, and Bill Finzer, Director of Educational Technology, for their faith in me and in this project. The project could not have begun without the National Science Foundation, and it could not have been completed without Jerry Lyons of Springer-Verlag. The Fathom programming team, led by Kirk Swenson, made our dreams real. Denise Howald, Jill Binker, and Sharon McBride contributed criticism, ideas, and much needed organization throughout the project. Howard Amerlan wrote the solutions, thank goodness. Dudley Brooks checked us for accuracy, but don't blame him for mistakes that remain. Mary Jo Cittadino and the editorial and production staff of Key have been creative and patient in the face of this project's unusual constraints. And Meg and Anne—my family—did their best to keep me sane.

But the real heroes of this effort are the hundreds of teachers who braved the perils of pre-release software to attend workshops, review the manuscript, field test activities with students in their classrooms, and give us feedback. Some provided detailed comments on the entire manuscript and others participated in monthly study groups to try out new activities before they were used in the classroom. We appreciate their contributions and those of Gretchen Davis, whose care and wisdom have been indispensable. We dedicate this book to their students and acclaim the good fortune of these students in learning from such professionals.

Tim Erickson

Introduction

These activities help students in middle grades, high school, and college teacher-preparation programs learn mathematics and statistics.

We believe strongly that students learn best when they themselves develop concepts and tools in response to some need. This does not mean that we expect students to invent everything or find the "best" way alone. But we'll try, for example, to put students in a situation where they *need* a measure of spread. Then we give them time to invent one that fills their need. Will they invent the standard deviation? No, but once they have their own measures, their first encounter with standard deviation will not be so traumatic. They will have already solved the problem of "Why would anyone ever invent this?"

What You Will Find in This Book

Each of the ten chapters begins with an overview followed by activities. Each activity consists of Teacher Notes, followed in most cases by blackline masters for student handouts. The additional material includes "What's Going On Here?" pages, usually about the mathematics or the statistics in nearby activities, and collections of additional problems or ideas for small investigations. Pages ix–xii contain a "topics grid" you can use to judge which activities might fit with your mathematics curriculum. As with any designation like this, it's somewhat inexact. For example, you may see a great geometrical application for something the author only recognized as having to do with functions. But the grid should give you some idea of what to expect where.

Teacher Notes

You can recognize Teacher Notes by the shaded stripe on the outside edge of the page. Teacher Notes begin each activity, and here is a partial example of one for a detailed explanation of the information contained in its activity box:

Generation by Generation

> - Two structured computer activities
> - Data generated in simulation
> - Student pages 162–166
> - Guided, medium features

- **Two structured computer activities.** Most of these pages introduce only one activity, but sometimes two or more activities are related so closely that they use the same notes. In some activities, you will see *open-ended* instead of *structured*; the former give students more latitude, the latter give students more explicit instructions. Finally, some activities are labeled *offline* instead of *computer*. These typically precede a related computer activity.

- **Data generated in simulation.** The source of data sometimes defines the character of an activity. In this book, much of the data comes from computer files, but some comes from the Internet, or from physical measurements, or, as in this case, from simulation.

- **Student pages.** These are blackline masters for the student handouts.

- **Guided, medium features.** The first indicates the level of detail found in the instructions. The second indicates the level of complexity of Fathom features you will use to do the activity. There are four levels of detail regarding instructions:

    Starter means that the instructions help you at every step of the way. They tell you where to click and what to type.

    Guided means that the instructions tell you the harder things explicitly, and remind you of the basics. Some exposure to Fathom is beneficial.

    Intermediate means that the instructions assume you know how to do some things in Fathom, and they do not explain those skills. The specific skills are listed on the teacher page.

    Independent means that the instructions generally give you little help with the program, but rather pose a problem and ask you to address it.

- There are three levels of complexity:

    Basic features include making graphs, putting lines on scatter plots, and writing formulas to define attributes and filters.

    Medium features include using sliders, using formulas to draw functions, using nested if-statements, and writing measures.

    Complex features include using derived collections, for example, for sampling, collecting measures, and designing simulations.

The subheadings on each Teacher Notes page vary from activity to activity, but they always include "What's Important Here," a list of the main points of the activity, and "Discussion Questions," a set of questions or topics to use as probes for your discussions during or after the activities themselves.

What's Going On Here?

The "What's Going On Here?" pages go into extra detail about the mathematics or statistics (or physics), giving some of the derivations and equations that underlie the activities. A few are background pages that describe, for example, where the data come from. These are intended primarily for the teacher, but you may give them to students as you think appropriate.

Student Pages

You can recognize student pages by the "name" line and the absence of a shaded stripe on the outside edge.

In general, we expect students to respond to the step-by-step questions by writing directly on the pages themselves, using the backs of the sheets as necessary. The "Going Further" sections at the end, if present, should be answered on separate sheets, since these questions generally require more elaboration to explain and justify. They're also separated out from the activities because they do not follow in sequence, but, as their name suggests, apply and extend what students have learned in the activity.

Homework

Some of the background pages may be assigned as reading, depending on the experience of your class. There are also occasional problem sets which may be good for homework or open lab time, depending on your students' access to computers. The "Going Further" questions in the student pages are also natural homework assignments. Finally, many Sonatas need out-of-class time, if only for planning (see *Sonatas for Data and Brain,* page xx).

Timing

These activities are designed to be completed in a fifty-minute class period. We split extremely long activities into smaller ones. Occasionally, you will find activities short enough that two can be done in a period. Those are noted on their teacher pages.

That said, timing computer activities in statistics for students that may range from middle-schoolers to college students is challenging. We recommend that you try the first activity you plan to present with a few colleagues beforehand. After you and your students are more comfortable with the software and the logistics at your site, things should go even more smoothly.

A Paradox About Learning Mathematics with Data

On the one hand, working with data makes mathematics easier. Data make mathematics more concrete because they are tied to some reality, and more connected because data often come from a context that have some meaning for students outside the math class.

On the other hand, working with data makes mathematics *harder.* Data have variability, which means that—unlike the rest of mathematics—there is often no "answer" when you ask a question of any depth. And as you become more experienced with data, the underlying questions become increasingly conditional and hypothetical, which is hard just from the language point of view, much less working out the logic. Consider the confidence-interval mantra, "If I were to repeat this experiment and repeatedly calculate confidence intervals using this procedure, 95% of those intervals would contain the [unknown] population mean. . . . " It may take ages to have that make sense. And anything having to do with conditional probability is hard before you start.

How do we address the hard parts of data while benefiting from the easy ones?

- First, address variability head-on. Develop a class culture that does away with the question, "What's the answer?" and replaces it with "What do we know about the answer?" This begins informally, and gradually becomes more quantitative.

- Second, be visual and use graphics often to answer questions about data—especially when information isn't obvious from the numbers alone. Good graphs are at the root of prediction and inference.

- Third, connect within the discipline. Moving beyond simple description in statistics requires mathematical manipulations. Therefore use algebra—starting with very simple algebra—in your statistics instruction. The most important consequence of this is that students see a need for what they're learning with all those symbols. And when you connect geometrical ideas to algebra through data, students can begin to see that these subjects are really all stars in the same constellation.

- Finally, predict, predict, predict. Insist, often, that students make explicit written conjectures about the data, what the data will show, and what one might conclude. Do this *before* the students study the data. Then, after the analysis, explicitly compare the results to the predictions.

The activities in this book try to take this approach. Some activities will be pretty hard if completed to the fullest. But we have tried to design these so that they can be approached by students with varying levels of experience and tenacity.

More Food for Thought

Following are some short pieces of pedagogical advice about teaching statistics with technology in general, and using this book in particular. Any one of these tidbits could be a chapter on its own. So do not consider them to be comprehensive on any subject, but rather food for thought.

- **Think developmentally.** First, allow fooling-around time with new ideas and tools. Just as most first-graders need to play with pattern blocks before they start exploring symmetry, so do most of the rest of us need to play with computers and data before we are ready to buckle down and be systematic. Second, build ties to the concrete. Data analysis gets abstract fast. The more you can represent the data or its manipulation using physical materials, the better. We know teachers who have their students build human histograms and box plots. This is a good idea.

- **Offline activities** are part of the design—and part of being concrete. We've tried to make the offline activities applicable to many different topics in data analysis, so that you can get multiple uses out of the time it takes to do them. For example, if you're planning a course in statistics, look in the last chapter especially, and do some of the inference offline activities early—when you're doing exploratory data analysis, say—and save the data so you can revisit it when you do inference.

- **Have students work in pairs.** Students working in pairs solve many problems for you, especially having to do with learning to drive the program. But they also stand a better chance of understanding the mathematics because they're talking to each other. Besides, pairs use only half as many computers.

- **You can use Fathom with few computers.** This can work two ways. First, projection systems are getting better and better. For example, you can use Fathom as a demonstration platform to show many concepts in data analysis, the effect of outliers on least-squares lines, or the effect of changing bin size in a histogram. Second, having only a few computers does not preclude student work on them. Most of these assignments can be done with little teacher intervention at the computer itself; students in pairs or groups can cycle through the machines, even over a period of weeks.

- **Your role in the lab.** The student sheets provide questions to answer, so you can look over students' work and listen to them as you circulate about the room. You can tell which pairs are on task and moving along, as well as where you may have to help students overcome problems. Do not hesitate to have students help each other. While you do this, think about your wrap-up. You may not have time for a thorough discussion right there: so what is the one best question to ask the class? It will depend on what you have seen and heard.

For example, you might do the offline part of *Orbital Express* (page 276) early in a course when you're doing box plots and discussing experiment design informally. You can return to it to do the on-line part, designing statistics and creating sampling distributions. Then you can do it again when you use a *t*-test to compare two means.

About Conjectures

In this book, we help students make *conjectures* and evaluate them. When we watch students making their own conjectures, we see them building their understanding more quickly and securely than if we feed them only predigested mathematics.

What do we mean by a conjecture? We have identified three different kinds:

We use the word *conjecture* here because *hypothesis* has a specific meaning in statistics.

- **A generalization from a sample to a population.** Students look at a few cases and get an idea (the conjecture) about what might be true for all cases. For example, looking at a small amount of census data, students might suggest (as a group of teachers did) that people of German ancestry tend not to get divorced. That's a conjecture. To evaluate the conjecture, you may look at more data and/or perform statistical (hypothesis) tests.

- **A proposal for a model.** By analyzing the situation—with or without actual data—students propose mathematical models (for example, a proportion, function, or a simulation) that predict what additional data will look like. For example, a student might suggest that the heights of ball bounces decrease exponentially. To evaluate this conjecture, students get more data and compare it to the model.

- **A proposal for a cause.** Separating correlation from causation is crucial in statistics education, but that doesn't mean we should ignore cause. For example, a student might think that the southbound *Coast Starlight* goes faster in Oregon and suggest that it is because the California track is in worse shape. To evaluate this conjecture, she must figure out other consequences beyond her initial observation. She must ask what other data might refute the conjecture (for example, data from the northbound train). She must also take a look at other attributes (for example, time of day— maybe the trains run slower at night) to see whether they follow the pattern her conjecture predicts. And she should look at more data (for example, other trains) and other data sources.

It is not good enough for students simply to make any of these three types of conjectures. Students also have to compare their predictions to the data and evaluate what they find. In general, they will discover that no matter how detailed their conjectures, they will uncover unanticipated subtleties. Insist that students report on these discrepancies and propose explanations if they can— essentially starting a new round of conjecture.

Challenging students to be specific when making their conjectures makes them dig deeper. Even if there is no exact answer in statistics, there are better answers and worse answers. We may not have *the* answer, so our goal is to learn more *about* the answer.

Assumptions and Definitions

It's important that students be careful about making assumptions or implicitly defining something. The more they can make explicit the better.

For example, suppose students are looking at census data and come up with this conjecture: "Rich people live in bigger houses." They make a 2 × 2 table with income (> 35,000 and ≤ 35,000) on one axis and house size (> 6 rooms and ≤ 6 rooms) on the other.

In doing this, they have made definitions: "rich" means earning more than $35,000 income; and "big house" means more than six rooms. They have also made an assumption, namely, that income is the sole indicator of wealth. (There is another assumption: that number of rooms is the sole indicator of house size.)

While we don't want our students to become mired in legalese as they describe the assumptions they make (after all, these seem like reasonable assumptions), we still want them to make recognizing their assumptions a habit. One way students can deal with this problem is to add sentences near the beginning of their responses that describe the assumptions and definitions, for example, "Our income figures include people 22 years and older; we define *rich* to mean earning more than $35,000." Another is to change the conjecture to speak only to the facts. For example, "A greater proportion of people earning more than $35K live in houses of more than six rooms than those who earn $35K or less." This makes the conjecture hard to read and less interesting, but it does serve to make assumptions and definitions explicit.

Students do need to work up to being inventive and tenacious about conjectures, and are not expected to be able to immediately articulate the details. Consistently challenge students to improve their conjectures.

In these activities, students have many chances to make conjectures. One of the most pervasive is in a type of assignment that occurs throughout the book, at the ends of most chapters. We call these assignments *Sonatas for Data and Brain*.

Sonatas for Data and Brain

Tasks for students can range from highly structured, where students get step-by-step instructions or examples followed by problem sets, to extremely open-ended, where students find data that interests them and do projects based on this data.

Students who know only the structured end of this spectrum can have trouble with an open-ended assignment. They ask, "But what do you want us to *do?*"

To help deal with open-endedness, we have developed a type of task we call a *Sonata for Data and Brain.* A Sonata is longer than a problem or a worksheet, but much shorter than a project—maybe at most an hour or two of work. And while a Sonata lets students use a variety of methods to come to a conclusion, it provides structure by describing the task, identifying relevant attributes, and giving instructions on how to get the data.

A *Sonata for Data and Brain* (like its musical analog) is defined by its structure. It has three parts:

- **Conjecture**—in music, the *exposition*—in which students hypothesize, or make a prediction, or propose a model for some phenomenon

- **Measurement or Analysis**—the *development*—in which students record the data if necessary and analyze the data to see if their conjecture is true

- **Comparison**—the *recapitulation*—in which students explicitly compare their conjecture to the results of the analysis, possibly developing a new conjecture

There is also an introduction that identifies the relevant attributes and describes the situation where the data arise.

The key is to realize that students will approach an activity like this at different levels and to figure out how to encourage everyone to try to meet a higher standard.

What is a sonata in music? And why use this metaphor?

In music, a sonata is a *form.* It's a structure composers use to organize their musical ideas. It's not the only reasonable structure, but it's an important one. Here's how it works:

The sonata begins with the *exposition.* During the exposition, you hear all of the main themes of the piece. In the second section, the *development,* you hear the themes elaborated, taken apart, and put together in interesting ways. In the final section, the *recapitulation,* you hear the themes whole again, but subtly different—reorganized, improved, and informed by the development that came before.

Modelmaking and Simulation in Sonatas

Many of the Sonatas are really about making mathematical models, for example, coming up with a function that will describe a set of data. This kind of data analysis task is increasingly important in statistics education, but it also fits well into the rest of the mathematics and science curriculum. In the Sonatas, students often have to try to figure out the function before they see the data. Frequently this means predicting the form of the function but not its specific parameters.

In some Sonatas, such as the Sonatas addressing probability, we ask students to develop a simulation to demonstrate some principle or solve a problem. In these Sonatas, we change the labels on the three parts of the assignment. *Conjecture* changes to *Design,* where the student designs the simulation. In *Construction,* the middle section, the student builds the simulation. Finally, the student evaluates the results of the simulation to answer the original question.

Students have a problem with the eternal distinction between constants and variables. Remember the old slogan: "Constants aren't; variables won't." It can be hard for students to imagine parameters of the situation (such as means or medians) before they can calculate them, but doing so (for example, in estimating how much more z is going to be, on average, than x) is good for their data sense.

Sonata for Data and Brain Summary Sheet

You will find many pages in the book—typically after the Sonata pages in each chapter—that have ideas for Sonata-sized problems. We have not made separate Sonata pages for each of these problems. Instead, students who are familiar with the form can use separate sheets.

But if you want a little more structure, and a little more connection to already-made Sonatas students have done—or if you want to pose problems of your own and have students respond to them using the structure they are familiar with—we provide the "blank" Sonata form on the following page. This form may also be useful to help students remember what sorts of things could go in each section.

Fantasia for Unaccompanied Brain

Experiment design is an important part of a course about data. It connects math and science, and forms a foundation for understanding what we really know when we get results. We have an activity about experiment design, based on an idea of Denise Howald.

Fantasia for Unaccompanied Brain, page xxiii, doesn't require computers (though we've seen teachers actually use Internet data to answer the questions), and it's a whole lot of fun (though it has a serious purpose).

There's a terrific book about experiment design by George W. Cobb: *Introduction to Design and Analysis of Experiments,* 1998, Springer-Verlag.

Sonata for Data and Brain

Summary Sheet

Name(s): _____

Turn this sheet in when you're done with your Sonata. You may attach other sheets as necessary.

Exposition: The Conjecture

Describe what you think will be true about your data.

Include some or all of the following:
> What are your cases?
> What are their attributes?
> What values do you expect the attributes to have?
> How will they be distributed?
> What can you say about their center and spread?

Especially: How will the attributes be related to one another? A *clear* conjecture is better than a *correct* one!

Make a guess as to the mathematical form of the relationship, for example, *the mean of x will be about twice the mean of y; or as k goes up, p will go down; or (best of all) g will be something like t^2 minus a constant.*

Development: Measurement and Analysis

Describe how you made your measurements and/or analyzed your data.

Make a plan for getting the data, and then carry it out.

Be sure you get the attributes you need!

Enter your data into Fathom.

Sketching graphs is a good idea.

Recapitulation: The Comparison

How did your conjectures compare with the data?

Analyze your data, seeing whether your conjectures hold.

If they do hold, describe how you know and how well the data fits.

If the conjectures do not hold, try to describe why it did not work out and what conjecture might be true.

Pick carefully what you include. Find what's most important.

Data in Depth
© 2001 Key Curriculum Press

Fantasia for Unaccompanied Brain

Name(s): _____

Have fun with this activity, but take it seriously. Don't let its silliness deceive you! Even though everything in this activity is made up, try to make it as detailed and realistic as you can.

1. Pick a saying from the list in the right-hand column.

2. Imagine what observations or measurements you would have to make in order to evaluate whether the statement is true. You may even have to design an experiment. Write down what you would do.

3. Sketch a display of data you might get if you did the observations or experiment.

4. What kind of data analysis could you do on these data? What sort of result would you get?

5. What could you conclude based on your data and analysis?

The early bird catches the worm.

The bigger they are, the harder they fall.

Haste makes waste.

Money can't buy happiness.

If March comes in like a lion, it will go out like a lamb.

A bird in the hand is worth two in the bush.

If wishes were horses, beggars would ride.

A picture is worth a thousand words.

A fool and his money are soon parted.

A little knowledge is a dangerous thing.

Honey attracts more flies than vinegar.

Too many cooks spoil the broth.

Pride goeth before a fall.

When the cat's away, the mice will play.

It's always darkest just before the dawn.

Absence makes the heart grow fonder.

Out of sight, out of mind.

Only the good die young.

Some Technical Notes on Using Fathom in the Classroom

We've tried to anticipate some technical questions you may have.

Windows versus Macintosh

Fathom runs nicely and looks nearly identical on both Windows and Macintosh computers. But there are a few differences in the interfaces for each platform—keyboard shortcuts, the look of windows, and so on.

The instructions in this book apply to both Windows and Macintosh users. When necessary, two sets of commands are given, with the Windows command listed first. The screen shots will look much the same as what students see on their own screens, regardless of the type of computer they are using. Where there are differences, we've alternated examples of Windows and Macintosh screens.

Also, bear in mind that while a Windows mouse has two buttons, left and right, a Macintosh mouse usually has only one button. With a Windows mouse, right-clicking on an object, such as a graph, will cause a menu of commands appropriate to that object to appear. Macintosh users can simulate this shortcut by holding down the **CTRL** key while clicking. To avoid confusion in the instructions, we do not mention the right-click shortcut, leaving it to your students to discover on their own.

To Save or Not to Save . . .

All sample Fathom documents are locked in order to preserve them for subsequent use. If students want to save their changes, they will need to use the Save As dialog and rename or move their files before saving them.

As with any computer work, students should be encouraged to save frequently, especially when they have entered data. This way, if they later change their data (say, by dragging points on a graph), they can use the **Revert Collection** command to get their original data back. Although Fathom has nearly infinite undo capabilities, it may be inconvenient to undo all changes to get data back. Using **Revert Collection** makes the attributes and values revert to the last saved version, without undoing other changes, such as plotted lines on graphs or calculations in summary tables.

Sample Documents

When installing Fathom, by default, you get a folder of **Sample Documents**. Fathom files referred to in this book can be found in the **Data in Depth** folder within **Sample Documents**. Census files have their own folder in the **Sample Documents** folder.

Within the **Data in Depth** folder is a folder of solutions to some of the problems in the book. You may want to restrict students' access to these files. (The Student Edition does not include this folder.)

Come to Your Census

1

Welcome to data, data analysis, and Fathom. This chapter introduces students to interesting data in an engaging way and helps them see technology as a tool for getting things done. In addition, these materials lay the foundation for an idea that runs throughout this book: *making conjectures.* We want students to state explicitly what they believe may be true, and then to look critically at data to see whether their statements are true or not.

We use some intriguing data: microdata from the 1990 U.S. Census. This material is not about states or towns; it's about *individuals*—and that makes all the difference. Individuals are fascinating because they're us.

The individuals are also important because every statistic you read, every graph you see, comes from individual pieces of data. When you hear that 35 million households watched the big game, or that 25% of all children grow up in poverty, or that you double your risk of melanoma if you don't put on sunblock, it's not about a wedge of some pie chart. Those numbers are made of people, and each one counts. Once we know this, two important things happen: We become more interested in the data, looking for ourselves and those we know, and we become more skeptical about the conclusions.

Here are some goals for this chapter:

- Students learn about and use *proportion.* It's critical mathematics. Although its foundations were laid in elementary school, every student (and most of us teachers) can use some practice and may learn some new things.

- Students learn (or remember) some basic statistics skills: how to make and interpret a box plot; how to make and interpret a histogram; how to calculate mean and median.

- Students make and define conjectures—statements that may be true or false about the data. Making conjectures also means making *good* conjectures—that is, conjectures that we can actually investigate. (One job of statistics is to help us judge—but not to prove—whether a conjecture is true.)

For more about conjectures see page xviii.

- Finally, students take steps along the road to skepticism. We mean this in a positive way. When students are presented with a conclusion, we want them to ask, "Is that right? What data might support that? And are there any other explanations for these data?"

Correlation, Causation, and Multiple Explanations

Students must not confuse correlation with causation. Our conjectures may have causal components ("people with college degrees make more money because they have more options"), but our job, for now, is to concentrate on the data ("people with degrees earn more"). To the second conjecture, our response will be to produce the evidence—the data and their display—that supports or refutes or qualifies the conjecture.

Thus we separate the causal parts of the statements from the purely descriptive ones. But that does not make causation unimportant, especially in discussion. For example, when students make a histogram of age (*Exploring Census Data,* page 16, Step 8), you might ask them to identify features of the distribution. They'll notice the hump in the middle and the fact that it trails off at high ages. It's worth asking, "Why do you suppose the distribution does that?"

Students will immediately point out that some people have died. But if you ask for additional explanations, they'll come up with some—for example:

- Older people move out of our community.

- The overall population was smaller when older people were born, so there have always been fewer people in that group than in younger groups.

- Some older people may not fill out census forms.

Once students see that there are always multiple explanations for phenomena, they will be less likely to assume that their data "prove" the obvious cause. With more experienced students, you can ask what additional information they might need to decide how much the various proposed causes explain the data.

The Census Data

The activities in this chapter use census microdata—data about individuals. The Census folder contains many Fathom files of microdata from all over the United States. You probably want to use a file for an area near where you live, though you can look at any of them. The files are in the Sample Documents folder within the Fathom folder. Each file name describes where the file is from. See the "Read Me (census)" file for more information.

For background on microdata, see page 6.

Level

This chapter deals with counting groups of people and finding proportions. Students need to know something about mean and median; concepts such as standard deviation are not discussed in this chapter. And our evaluation of conjectures is strictly informal. The problem is to make a display that shows whether a conjecture *looks* reasonable. We're making no statistical tests.

Middle-schoolers can do much of this work. It requires nothing more than a sense of proportion. Yet proportion is hard and needs reinforcement, especially when it applies to real data instead of book problems. We have seen graduate students challenged by some of this material.

The Activities

- **Turning Numbers into People.** An offline activity in which students decode U.S. Census microdata by hand.

- **The Card People.** Another offline activity that uses census data. In this activity, students use pre-decoded cards for real people to construct graphs, answer questions, and begin to make conjectures.

Then we introduce the software. These activities begin with exploration and lead to making conjectures and evaluating them informally.

- **Exploring Census Data.** This activity gives students practice using various Fathom features. The questions are a set of exercises you (and the students) can use to assess how well they know their stuff. See "Tech Note: Axes" in the Teacher Notes to this activity.

- **Two Graphs and Selection.** We continue exploring census data and learning Fathom features, this time using multiple graphs to see what is going on. Again, you can use the questions to assess student progress. Students may be able to do this page on the same day as they do *Exploring Census Data.*

- **Out of Many, Fewer.** *Filters* are mathematical expressions that define subsets of our data. These expressions are *Boolean*—they are either **true** or **false**. So the expression **age > 20** chooses people who are 21 or older. Students learn how to make filters and use them to answer questions about the data.

  This activity introduces students to Fathom's formula editor.

- **Making Categories.** Students use the formula editor to create new categorical attributes; for example, they use **age** to classify people as **old** or **young**.

- **Investigating a Conjecture.** Students use Fathom to investigate a conjecture, just as they may have done during *The Card People.* There is no student page for this, but all is explained in the Teacher Notes.

- **Features Buffet.** A collection of one-page introductions to specific features of Fathom with mathematical connections. You could use them as "menu" activities, as homework, or in a jigsaw format.

Objectives

In these activities, we hope students will

- Become secure in basic Fathom skills: opening files, making graphs, using various graph options, and reading data.

- Write filter expressions to look at only a subset of their data.

- Use Fathom to draw reasonable conclusions from data, in particular, to assess informally whether conjectures are true or not.

- Make connections between their off- and online experiences.

Turning Numbers into People

- Structured offline activity
- Data from handout
- No student instruction pages
- No Fathom skills required

This introductory offline activity introduces students to data. We use published 1990 U.S. Census *microdata*—data about individuals.

What's Important Here

Ideally, you will see that the dizzying array of numbers becomes, for the students, a real collection of people. But this activity also lays a foundation for important statistical understanding—understanding we often (mistakenly) take for granted.

- Data is composed of *cases*—the individual elements we will soon summarize with statistics such as means and proportions. Here, a case is one person (or, in some situations, one household).

- Each case may have several *attributes* (a.k.a. *variables*), which can be *continuous* (numeric, such as **age** or **income**) or *categorical* (nonnumeric, such as **sex** or **ancestry**).

- While we use our personal experience to help us interpret data, we must distinguish our *conjectures* (the stories) from the data themselves. See more about conjectures on page xviii.

Topics
  introduction to data
  attributes and cases
  stories and data

Materials
  Turning Numbers into People
    Data 1
  pencils
  scratch paper
  optional: rulers

Students will also admit that though the activity is fun for a period, it could get tedious fast. This is a chance to underscore an advantage of using technology.

Step by Step

1. To prepare, copy page 5; make enough copies so that you have one sheet per pair of students. If you can, make a transparency of the page so you can explain to the whole class how to read it.

2. In class, discuss the census briefly. Ask students, what is the census? What kinds of questions are asked? Why do we have a census? Explain that we'll look at 1990 census data. (When year-2000 data are available, you can get them at **www.keypress.com**.)

3. Pass out copies of page 5, one per pair. Explain, using the transparency if you can, that each line is a person and each set of lines delimited by shading is a household—a group of people living together.

4. Show students how to find the age of the top person as an example, explaining how to use the legend and the column numbers.

5. Explain that each pair of students will choose one household: "Find out as much as you can. What are these people like? Try to make up a story about the numbers you find."

6. Let each pair study a household while you watch and answer questions. See page 6 for some background if you need it.

7. Let the class share some stories about their households. Encourage fantasy.

8. Make the point that some of what we've said is from the data, but some is from our imaginations. The material from our imaginations may be true, but we have to distinguish it from data.

9. Choose one interesting story students came up with and ask for alternative hypotheses: What other story can explain the data?

Cols. 15–16 (age): The first person is 40; the second is 39, etc. A shaded band indicates a new household. So, the first household has two adults and three children.

```
.........1.........2..
12345678901234567890 12
P008927700000140000130
P008927701100139000110
P008927702000110400100
P008927702000106400100
P008927702000104400080
P008927800100119000180
P008927801000147000180
```

Note: You do not have to define everything beforehand, for example the meaning of **poverty**. Let it come up in discussion. You can learn about these issues on page 6.

Data in Depth
© 2001 Key Curriculum Press

A few people from Berkeley, Albany, or Emeryville, according to the 1990 U.S. Census

A grid of census data records, each beginning with a person identifier (e.g. P0089277, P0089278, …), listed above a numbered column ruler (1…9 repeating across the page width). Gray shading highlights several record rows.

Col.	Contents
9–10	Relationship to "householder": (00 = self, 01 = spouse, 02 = child, 03 = stepchild, 08 = roomer, 09 = housemate, 10 = unmarried partner)
11	Sex (0 = M, 1 = F)
12–14	Race (001 = White, 002 = Black, 006 = Chinese, 009 = Japanese, 024 = "other" Asian)
15–16	Age
17	Marital Status (0 = married; 1 = wid, 2 = div, 3 = separated; 4 = never married)
41–43	Poverty (% of poverty value, i.e. 100 = the poverty line)
50	School (0 = N/A, 1 = no, 2 = yes, public, 3 = yes, private)
51–52	Years schooling (05 = 8th grade, 10 = HS grad, 14 = bach, 15 = mast, 17 = doct)

Col.	Contents
89–90	# of children ever born to you (00 = N/A, otherwise subtract one, i.e. 02 = 1 kid)
91	Employed? (0 = < 16 years, 1 = employed, 6 = not in labor force)
93–94	Hours worked last week
102–03	Get to work… (01 = in a car, 04 = subway/EL, 10 = walk)
104	# of riders
105–08	Departure time for work (24-hour clock)
127–32	Person's total earnings

Background on Census Microdata

We made the census data files that come with Fathom from a CD-ROM published by the U.S. Bureau of the Census. We were amazed when we found out that the Bureau publishes microdata (data about individuals) as well as the familiar *aggregate* data (for example, the distribution of white- and blue-collar employment across the country).

Access to data about individuals is wonderful because it is so interesting and immediate. It brings home the fact that every bar chart is made up of real, breathing, quirky people. But isn't the census supposed to be completely anonymous? Why might that be important? And how does the census try to ensure anonymity?

The census statisticians divide the country into areas whose populations are at least 100,000. These are called PUMAs (Public Use Microdata Areas). Within each PUMA, they take a sample of 5% of the population (at least 5,000 cases), keeping households intact. Then they scramble those households and remove any identifying data (such as addresses). Nevertheless, anonymity has its limits. While it is wonderful to use data from your own PUMA if you can, you should avoid selecting a thin, specific slice of people from that anonymous sample (for example, all the high school teachers) and looking at them as individuals.

A big city such as Chicago has many PUMAs; in rural areas, a PUMA might cover several counties.

Here are definitions of some of the attributes on the sheet:

poverty   This is the percentage above the poverty line, so 125 means 125% or 1.25 times. The "poverty line" depends on the number of people in the household—the more people living there, the higher it is. And 501 is a "topcode." This means that if you earn 700% of the poverty line, your value on the sheet is still 501.

Interestingly, the Census Bureau does not include Hispanic or Latino under the attribute **race**. There is a separate attribute for Hispanic heritage.

children born   This is the number of children born to the person whose line it is, plus 1. If you see "00," that translates as "does not apply," which means that you are male or that you are a female under age 16. So "03" means the female has two children born alive.

role   "Householder" is the person who filled out the form for the household. Everyone else's **role** code reflects his or her relationship to the householder.

income   The census has eight income categories. We have grouped them into two: earned income and unearned. Unearned income includes investment income such as interest or rent; public assistance; child support and alimony; Social Security; and pension income.

Must the census be done by direct enumeration? For the 2000 census, the Bureau proposed sampling as a way to adjust the counts in rural areas and impoverished inner-city areas. The issue is which method gives a more accurate result *for the same investment*. Political squabbles ensued; the result was that direct enumeration was required for reapportionment, but that sampling could be used for other purposes, such as the allocation of funds. This controversy will undoubtedly last for decades.

Thus, another lesson is this: Whenever you use any data at all, whoever recorded the data had to make decisions. Why 501? Why age 16? Why do they record motherhood and not fatherhood? In 2000, people chose up to two races, but in 1990, there was only one choice. These decisions are necessary, and not malevolent, but they have political consequences; they reflect and shape our view of the world.

Data in Depth
© 2001 Key Curriculum Press

The Card People

This offline activity is about making categories and conjectures. Along the way, students will get to use additional statistics skills, such as calculating means or proportions and making different kinds of displays. Again, we use microdata from the 1990 U.S. Census.

- Structured offline activity
- Data from handouts
- No student instruction pages
- No Fathom skills required

What's Important Here

- Students develop criteria for dividing their data into two groups. Even more important, they have to be explicit and mathematical about these criteria.

- This activity gives students a chance to develop conjectures. They're so important that there's a whole page about them—page 27.

- In evaluating conjectures, students distinguish unanswerable questions from those they can answer with the available data, and from those for which they need additional information.

- Social stereotypes are sometimes supported by data, sometimes not. But you can always come up with an alternative explanation for the data.

Topics
    categorization
    conjectures
    representing data

Materials
    The Card People Data Pages 1–4
    scissors (one pair per pair of students)
    butcher paper
    tape
    markers

Preparation

- Copy the materials. There are four originals to copy, pages 10–13. You need one page per student, so if you have 32 students, you should copy eight of each page. In class, each student will work in a pair with someone who has a *different* sheet (so they'll have new data). Thus, if you can copy the pages onto different colors, you can simply say, "Make sure your partner has a different color from you."

- Assemble the other materials listed in the margin. You may be able to adapt the activity to use different materials.

Step by Step

There is no student handout except the pages you will have photocopied. These steps represent only one path through the material; you may follow it, or, as you get to know the landscape, depart from it as you see fit.

1. **Familiarization.** Pass out one sheet to each student. Make sure each pair has two different sheets. Explain that each page has 30 people on it. Have students find the most unusual person on their sheet and tell their partner about that person.

2. Ask for questions about the sheets and what the attributes mean.

3. **First Categories.** Have the pairs cut the "people" out so that each pair will have 60 small rectangles.

4. Ask each pair to work together to separate their 60 people into two groups (they don't have to be of equal size) according to some criterion they choose. The criterion has to reliably place people in one group or the other. Maybe it's about age, maybe ancestry, maybe something else—but the pair must agree.

Students will ask, "Does it have to be two groups?" These instructions assume two groups of cards, but it's up to you. Having more than two groups makes it harder but richer. Adapt as needed.

Teacher Notes

5. Have a few pairs report their criteria; ask for more and different criteria from other pairs. **Language Note:** Remind students that *criteria* is the plural and *criterion* the singular.

6. Have each pair write a mathematical expression that describes the rule that puts cards into the two groups. The rule should be in a form that has a Boolean expression—one that is true or false. For example, students might say, "We separated them by income." They need to make that really explicit; for example "If income > $35,000, they're in the rich group; otherwise, they're in the poor group."

You may even prepare them for future mathematics (and Fathom) use by insisting on a more compact, symbolic form, for instance

$$if\,(income > 35000)\begin{cases}\text{"rich"}\\\text{"poor"}\end{cases}$$

7. **Fishing for Relationships.** Have pairs look again at their two groups, and ask them to look at what's similar within each group *besides the criterion itself.* For example, you might have the groups separated by income, as above. You may notice that, in general, the rich people are older. That's what we're looking for.

8. **Making the Conjecture.** Each pair writes a statement that expresses the relationship only as a generalization that's either true or false. It's also a statement about the data, *not about the causes* of the relationship. In the preceding example, you might write, "Richer people are older." Other statement "starters" include "The more _____, the more _____" and "People who _____ also _____." The word *because* is forbidden.
   Note: If you're going on to do *Exploring Census Data,* and especially *Investigating a Conjecture* (page 27), record these conjectures for the whole class, as well as other conjectures that come up—no matter how imprecise—for students to study later on.

Some students are reluctant to write such bold statements. They want to hedge and hide. Don't let them. Tell them the assignment is to write the statement clearly. It doesn't matter if it is true.

9. **Second Categories.** Have the students develop a new criterion (and its mathematical expression) that will split their piles a second time. This second criterion should capture whatever they found to be similar about the groups in Step 7. They might split by age, for example "age > 25."

A more open-ended presentation can skip this step.

10. **Making the Display.** Have each pair write their conjecture on the butcher paper as a title. Then have them make a display that illustrates their conjecture by making an arrangement of the "people" on the butcher paper and taping or gluing them down. Finally, the display has to include the pair's conclusion: whether they think the conjecture is true, and why.

If you've done Step 9, you might have students make a two-by-two table and calculate proportions.

What Makes a Good Display

You can use these criteria to let students know what you expect:

- A clear, concise conjecture.
- Clear criteria for the categories (e.g., *old* means *age* > 25).
- It's clear how the arrangement of people is related to the conjecture.
- The conclusion is supported *mathematically.*
- The data and analysis logically support the conclusion.

A typical good "mathematical support" at a ninth-grade level is "Ninety percent of the rich people are old, but only 55% of the poor people are old. This supports our conjecture that rich people are older."

The Card People

Discussion Questions

➲ What other conjectures can you think of for these data? (Write them down!)

➲ Looking at the whole list of conjectures, which of them can we really use data to investigate? Which of them can we study with data we already have? Are there any we need more data for? What data?

➲ Looking at the displays, are there any conclusions you think might appear true just because we have an unusual sample of people?

➲ (If you have differences in proportions.) How big a difference in proportions do you think it takes to support a conjecture?

➲ Do you see any displays showing that some social stereotypes are true? Any showing that some may not be true?

➲ (Choose a display with a plausible conjecture.) Why do you think this conjecture is true? Now think up another reason why the data might turn out this way.

➲ Why might it be important for the census to be anonymous?

Subsidiary Goals

Depending on your students' experience, you can use this activity to introduce, reinforce, or assess many statistics skills that ideally were taught to them in middle school, but that may need reinforcement. You can easily include work on

- Identifying a case (here, a person) and its attributes (or variables—here, *age, sex, ancestry,* etc.).

- Distinguishing a categorical attribute from its values (e.g., *sex* from *male* and *female*). This sounds simple and pedantic, but it causes no end of trouble when you try to express ideas with the precision that computers demand.

- Calculating means or medians.

- Making two-by-two tables.

- Calculating proportions.

- Making box plots (you could have students take samples of 15 and make box plots of *age* or *income*).

- Making histograms (you could have students make histograms of *age,* with *ages* binned in decades: 0–9, 10–19, 20–29, etc.).

The Card People

Married (German) White F age 63
Immigrated before 1950
High school graduate, diploma or GED
Unearned income: $2028

Single Black M age 19
Immigrated 1975 to 1979
Some college, but no degree (in public school)
Administrative support worker earning $367

Married (Irish) White F age 77
Some college, but no degree
Unearned income: $21770

Married Laotian M age 30
Immigrated 1985 to 1986
Speaks Thai at home
Some college, but no degree
General office clerk earning $25000

Single (German/Irish) White M age 20
Some college, but no degree (in public school)
Cashier earning $1250

Married (Russian) White F age 41
Master's degree
Auctioneer earning $807

Divorced (Italian/German) White M age 52
Bachelor's degree
Engineer earning $130000
Unearned income: $700

(German/Irish) White F age 5
Nursery school (in public school)

Single Chinese M age 28
Immigrated 1985 to 1986
Speaks Chinese (Cantonese) at home
Bachelor's degree (in public school)
Postsecondary teacher/subject not specified
earning $27600

Single Korean F age 23
Speaks Korean at home
Bachelor's degree
Architect earning $400

Single (Honduran) Latina F age 26
Immigrated 1985 to 1986
Speaks Spanish at home
High school graduate, diploma or GED
Child care worker (private household)
earning $9800

Single (Welsh/German) White F age 39
High school graduate, diploma or GED
(in public school)
Manager, properties/real estate
earning $6500

Married (English/Danish) White F age 45
Bachelor's degree
Bookkeeper/accounting/auditing clerk
earning $11001

Single Chinese M age 22
Speaks Chinese (Cantonese) at home
Some college, but no degree (in private school)
Technician earning $1300

Single White F age 22
Some college, but no degree (in public school)
Clinical laboratory technologist/technician
earning $7800

(Italian) White F age 11
1st, 2nd, 3rd, or 4th grade (in public school)

Married (English/French) White F age 42
Doctorate degree
Archivist/curator earning $39000

Divorced (English) White F age 59
Immigrated 1950 to 1959
Speaks Spanish at home
Professional degree
Registered nurse earning $38000
Unearned income: $424

Single (Irish) White F age 49
Immigrated 1987 to 1990
Speaks French at home
Master's degree (in private school)
Teacher earning $20400.

Single Black F age 44
Associate degree in college, academic program
Accountant or auditor earning $38048

Single Black F age 18
Some college, but no degree (in public school)
Manager or administrator earning $2236

(British/Swedish) White M age 16
9th grade (in public school)
Waiter/waitress assistant earning $700

Married (German/Irish) White F age 29
Some college, but no degree (in private school)
File clerk (except financial) earning $900

Married Chinese M age 64
Bachelor's degree
Manager or administrator earning $90000
Unearned income: $10000

Single (Italian) White M age 19
Some college, but no degree (in public school)
Mechanic/repairer earning $4000
Unearned income: $200

Divorced White M age 42
Doctorate degree
Management analyst earning $86000
Unearned income: $1500

Divorced Black F age 80
9th grade
Unearned income: $16612

Married Chinese F age 65
Immigrated 1970 to 1974
Speaks Chinese (Cantonese) at home
Some college, but no degree
Cook, but no earnings

Black F age 1

(Polish) White M age 7
1st, 2nd, 3rd, or 4th grade (in public school)

The Card People

Widowed Black F age 64
Associate degree in college, academic program
Unearned income: $6800

Widowed (Danish) White M age 73
Bachelor's degree
Unearned income: $32204

Single Black F age 25
High school graduate, diploma or GED
Other busines services salesperson, but no earnings
Unearned income: $8160

Single (Irish) White F age 23
High school graduate, diploma or GED
Cashier earning $20000

Single Japanese F age 26
Immigrated 1987 to 1990
Speaks Japanese at home
High school graduate, diploma or GED
(in private school)
Teacher, but no earnings

Single Taiwanese M age 22
Speaks Formosan at home
Some college, but no degree (in public school)
Computer programmer earning $960

Married Chinese F age 79
Immigrated 1970 to 1974
Speaks Chinese (Cantonese) at home
Bachelor's degree (in public school)
Unearned income: $11832

Single Black F age 46
High school graduate, diploma or GED
Guard/police, except public service, but no earnings
Unearned income: $5708

Single (Scotch Irish/English) White F age 23
Bachelor's degree
Earning $3300

Married (German/English) White M age 43
Bachelor's degree
Engineering technician earning $81000
Unearned income: $1500

Black M age 2

Single Filipino F age 20
Immigrated 1970 to 1974
Some college, but no degree (in public school)
Cashier earning $1170

Single (Scotch Irish/German) White M age 35
Some college, but no degree
Computer programmer earning $50801
Unearned income: $2731

Married Black M age 56
Speaks Spanish at home
Master's degree
Postsecondary teacher/subject not specified earning $50000

Single Chinese F age 35
Immigrated 1987 to 1990
Speaks Chinese (Cantonese) at home
Bachelor's degree
Physician earning $50000
Unearned income: $200

(English/German) White F age 7
1st, 2nd, 3rd, or 4th grade (in public school)

Widowed (English/Welsh) White F age 77
Bachelor's degree
Unearned income: $14940

Widowed other race Latino M age 79
High school graduate, diploma or GED
Unearned income: $3700

Married (English) White F age 63
Immigrated 1950 to 1959
Master's degree

Single (German) White M age 22
Some college, but no degree (in public school)
Sales worker (apparel) earning $4200

Single Filipino F age 21
Immigrated 1970 to 1974
Speaks Tagalog at home
Bachelor's degree (in public school)
Amusement/recreation facilities attendant, but no earnings

Divorced (German/Irish) White M age 43
Some college, but no degree
Stationary engineer earning $25600
Unearned income: $2000

Married (Scottish) White M age 26
Bachelor's degree
Drafting occupation earning $39000
Unearned income: $200

Widowed Black F age 80
Some college, but no degree
Unearned income: $12000

Divorced (American) White M age 64
Professional degree
Postsecondary teacher/subject not specified earning $105000
Unearned income: $10000

Vietnamese F age 4
Nursery school (in private school)

Single (United States) White M age 32
Bachelor's degree
Data processing equipment repairer earning $37306
Unearned income: $4554

Single (British/French) White M age 38
Bachelor's degree
Editor/reporter earning $49000
Unearned income: $300

Widowed (Portuguese) White F age 83
10th grade
Unearned income: $9150

Divorced (English/Irish) White F age 28
Some college, but no degree (in public school)

The Card People

Married (Russian) White M age 51
Doctorate degree
Teacher earning $67594
Unearned income: $1438

Divorced (Polish) White F age 66
Master's degree
Psychologist, but no earnings
Unearned income: $18323

Single (Danish/German) White F age 35
Bachelor's degree
Secretary earning $6000

(United States) Black F age 16
10th grade (in public school)

Widowed (German) White F age 85
High school graduate, diploma or GED
Unearned income: $47574

Black F age 2

(German/Scottish) White F age 9
1st, 2nd, 3rd, or 4th grade (in public school)

Married (Spanish/Irish) White F age 69
High school graduate, diploma or GED
Unearned income: $3924

Single Black M age 27
Some college, but no degree
Laborer (except construction) earning $23000

Married (Irish/Russian) White M age 32
Some college, but no degree
Garage/service station worker earning $33442

Single (German/French) White F age 19
Immigrated 1970 to 1974
Some college, but no degree (in public school)
Sales worker (radio, TV, hi-fi/appliance)
earning $2000

Single Chinese F age 20
Immigrated 1975 to 1979
Speaks Chinese (Cantonese) at home
High school graduate, diploma or GED
(in public school)
Cashier, but no earnings

Single (Scotch Irish) White F age 34
Bachelor's degree
Secondary school teacher earning $24000
Unearned income: $1500

(Russian/English) White F age 6
Kindergarten (in public school)

Separated (Welsh/English) White F age 52
Immigrated 1970 to 1974
Bachelor's degree
Elementary school teacher earning $8298
Unearned income: $14400

Single (German/Danish) White M age 20
Some college, but no degree (in public school)
Technician earning $4100
Unearned income: $50

Married (Norwegian) White F age 37
Speaks Spanish at home
Bachelor's degree (in public school)
Elementary school teacher earning $22000
Unearned income: $200

Married (Italian) White M age 36
Master's degree (in public school)
Sales worker (hardware/building supplies)
earning $5455
Unearned income: $2000

Married (English/German) White M age 31
Bachelor's degree
Elementary school teacher earning $24634

Married Black M age 51
Bachelor's degree
Stock handler/bagger earning $60000

Married (Iranian) White M age 38
Immigrated 1975 to 1979
Speaks Farsi at home
Bachelor's degree
Accountant or auditor earning $35000
Unearned income: $20

Divorced (Hungarian/Slovak) White F age 53
Bachelor's degree
Unearned income: $69091

Single (German) White M age 20
High school graduate, diploma or GED
(in public school)
Teacher's aide earning $900

(English/Italian) White M age 16
10th grade (in public school)

Married (German) White F age 37
Master's degree
Manager or administrator earning $52523

Single (British/Swedish) White F age 19
Some college, but no degree (in public school)
Sales worker earning $7000

Single (French/English) White M age 37
Some college, but no degree
Agricultural/food scientist earning $31600

Divorced (English) White M age 61
Bachelor's degree
Administrator / official earning $10000
Unearned income: $25000

Married Japanese F age 48
Bachelor's degree
Secretary earning $9343

Single (Russian/German) White F age 32
Bachelor's degree
Cook earning $6000

Single White F age 38
Master's degree
Farmer, except horticultural earning $12000

Married Black F age 57
Some college, but no degree
General office clerk earning $23736

Married (German) White M age 72
Immigrated before 1950
Some college, but no degree
Sales representative in mining/
manufacturing/wholesale earning $18000
Unearned income: $23852

Separated (Irish/French) White M age 42
Associate degree in college, occupational
program
Taxicab driver/chauffeur earning $12000

Single (Welsh/English) White F age 30
Master's degree
Physical scientist earning $37968
Unearned income: $68

(Eastern European) White M age 2

Married (Pennsylvania German) White M
age 41
Bachelor's degree
Manager, service organization earning $27800
Unearned income: $3650

Married Black F age 73
11th grade
Unearned income: $7270

Divorced (German/Russian) White F age 37
Master's degree
Elementary school teacher earning $26696

Single Filipino F age 19
Some college, but no degree (in public school)
Drafting occupation earning $3900

Single (German/Irish) White M age 22
Some college, but no degree (in public school)
Unearned income: $18000

Married Black M age 48
High school graduate, diploma or GED
Truck driver earning $30000
Unearned income: $840

Black F age 1

Married (Scottish) White F age 39
Immigrated 1950 to 1959
Some college, but no degree
Teacher's aide earning $6000

Divorced Black M age 37
Some college, but no degree
Bus, truck/stationary engine mechanic
earning $2000

Married (Scottish/English) White F age 31
Bachelor's degree
Technical writer earning $9822
Unearned income: $563

Single (German/Irish) White F age 34
Some college, but no degree
Health diagnosing practitioner earning $14000

Married Korean F age 61
Immigrated 1950 to 1959
Speaks Korean at home
Master's degree

Married (Latin American/Colombian)
Latina F age 45
Speaks Spanish at home
Master's degree
Psychologist earning $115000

Divorced other race Latino M age 41
Immigrated 1975 to 1979
Speaks Spanish at home
5th, 6th, 7th, or 8th grade
Cook earning $20000
Unearned income: $12821

(Albanian/Basque) White M age 6
Nursery school

Married Black M age 67
5th, 6th, 7th, or 8th grade
Unearned income: $8600

Single (Irish) White M age 56
Immigrated 1950 to 1959
Master's degree
Elementary school teacher earning $40000

Married (Irish/Welsh) White M age 58
Master's degree
Computer system analyst/scientist
earning $77500
Unearned income: $14000

Married (German) White F age 47
Bachelor's degree
Postsecondary teacher/subject not specified
earning $40000
Unearned income: $3000

Single Black F age 30
Some college, but no degree
Sales worker earning $25000

Single Black M age 47
Master's degree
Social worker earning $38800

Married White M age 43
Professional degree
Physician earning $100000
Unearned income: $500

Single (Swedish/Spanish) Latina F age 25
Some college, but no degree
Truck driver earning $32000

Married (Irish/Swedish) White M age 45
High school graduate, diploma or GED
Manager or administrator earning $70000
Unearned income: $2000

Exploring Census Data

- Structured computer activity
- Data from census data file
- Student pages 15–16
- Starter, basic features

Your students may have looked at census data by hand and generated some conjectures (e.g., in the activity *The Card People,* page 9). But working "by hand" is hard when you have even more cases to investigate, and is a pain when you change your mind as to exactly what you're investigating.

The end of the second student page has questions for them to answer. In later activities, questions like these are spread throughout the computer instructions.

What's Important Here

- This and the next few activities give students both an introduction to exploratory data analysis and a grounding in the way Fathom works. Both will serve them well.

- Different representations are good for answering different questions.

- Some representations show differences and similarities between groups.

Discussion Questions

At the end of class, you could go over some of the answers from the "Answer These" section (which may vary from group to group) and ask how the students figured them out. This is not a test, after all, but a way to get familiar with the software and the data.

You can use questions like these to check for understanding during the exploration or as questions for class discussion at the end.

↪ What's the difference between **race** and **ancestry**?

↪ When you zoom in on the **age**s, why do the points seem to have gaps between them? (The **age**s are only integers.)

↪ If you zoom in to find median **age**, why is the median line right on one of the points (probably), while the mean is between them? (The median is usually one of the values in the set, whereas the mean probably isn't.)

Tech Note: Axes

There is no direct instruction here about how to scale axes in Fathom. Given encouragement, students will figure out the axes themselves and tell each other how they work. Axes are hard to explain on paper, but if you just show somebody, they'll get it. Students can look in **Help** as well.

If students need help getting started with axes, tell them they can change the scale by dragging parts of the axes. The cursor changes to give a hint.

To check for understanding, ask something like, "How do you zoom in to a part of the graph?"

Topics

learning about Fathom
multiple representations

Materials

census data file

Preparation Note

Before you turn the students loose on the Census file, try opening it yourself. Each file has 500 cases in it. Depending on the speed of your machines, that may be too many. Therefore, please go through this first activity, *Exploring Census Data,* yourself *on a school machine* ahead of time as a test.

If it's too slow, select about half the cases and delete them. Repeat as necessary. (To select many cases, click on the first row number in the case table—the thing that looks like a spreadsheet. Then scroll halfway down and **SHIFT**-click on another row number. All the cases in between will be selected. To delete them, choose **Delete Cases** from the **Edit** menu.)

You can also double-click on an axis, which brings up some text you can edit to adjust the axis bounds. Delete the text object using the **Delete Object** command in the **Edit** menu.

Exploring Census Data

Name(s): _____

If you did activities like *Turning Numbers into People,* you probably saw some interesting data but realized you'd get tired of decoding numbers. Computers make it easier.

1. Start up Fathom.

2. Choose **Open** from the **File** menu. Your teacher will tell you the name of your census data file (something like **AZ_Central112**). Select it. A "collection" appears—a box with gold balls in it.

3. We need a table to see our data. Choose **Case Table** from the **Insert** menu. A case table appears.

4. If it is empty, you need to make the data flow from the collection into this table. Put the mouse pointer over the title tab in the collection. It turns into a hand.

5. With the mouse button down, drag the hand over the empty case table and let go ("drop" it). The table will have a thick black border when you're in the right place. The table should fill up with data. If it doesn't, try it again.

Your window should look something like the one shown here.

Before we make graphs, let's talk about screen space.

About Screen Space

Fathom takes up a lot of room on your screen. Here are some techniques for making the most of the space you have:

- Make your window as large as possible by clicking in the zoom box.

- You can resize the *objects* (collections, tables, etc.) that live inside the window. Make them larger or smaller by dragging on their edges. If you make them small enough, they turn into icons.

- You can rearrange these components; you can even overlap them. Drag on the top to move the whole component.

- You can delete a component by pressing **DELETE** when it's selected. Don't delete your collection if you need your data.

You will probably develop your own style for managing your screen space. Now, on to graphs!

Sidebar

You need to know
   how to start up Fathom
   what a box plot is

You'll learn how to
   connect collections to tables and graphs
   make lots of graphs

Drag from the title tab of the collection . . .

. . . to the body of the case table.

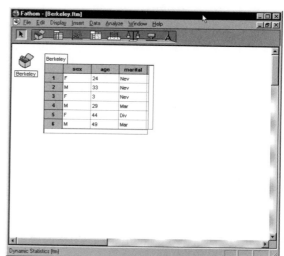

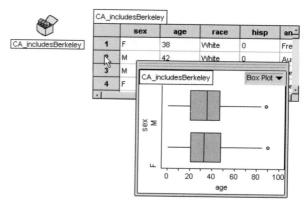

Save space by rearranging your components.

Name(s): _____

Making Graphs

We'll start with a graph of **age**.

6. Choose **Graph** from the **Insert** menu. An empty graph appears. (If it's in an inconvenient place, move it.)

7. Drag the column heading for **age** from the case table (with the "grabber" hand, just as before) to the axis of the graph, where it says **Drop an attribute here.** Presto! You get a dot plot of the ages of the people in your collection. It may not be terribly useful because there are so many people. So let's change it . . .

8. Choose **Histogram** from the popup menu in the graph itself.

9. Change the widths of histogram bars by dragging on their edges.

10. Choose **Box Plot** from that same popup menu. Now you get a box plot of **age**.

11. To zoom in to a particular part of the graph, try dragging on the axis numbers. Choose the type of graph again (e.g., **Box Plot**) to zoom back out.

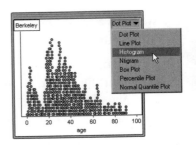

Answer These

becomes

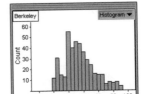

To answer these questions, do not look up exact numbers in a table. Just read the graphs and write your estimates after the questions.

1. How old is the oldest person in your file? What kind of graph did you use?

2. What is the median age of the people in your file? Again, what kind of graph did you use?

3. How many people in your data set are between 15 and 20 years old? (Try making a histogram and move the edges of a bin to 15 and 20. Point at the bin. The number of cases appears somewhere. Find it!)

4. Drag the attribute **sex** onto the vertical axis of your **age** graph. It should split into two graphs, one for males and one for females. What is the median age for males? What is the median age for females?

5. With the graph active (it has a border), look in the **Graph** menu. Choose **Plot Value**. In the box that appears (the formula editor), enter **mean(age)**. Close the editor by clicking the **OK** button. What are the mean ages for males and females in your file?

Enter formulas in the formula editor by typing or by double-clicking items in the formula list, the pane in the lower-right part of the formula editor.

6. For most communities, the mean age is greater than the median. Why is that? Is that true for your data file?

Two Graphs and Selection

- Structured computer activity
- Data from census data file
- Student page 18
- Guided, basic features

This is a simple "aha!" activity that practically explains itself. It is written to follow the preceding activity, *Exploring Census Data*—in fact, you may be able to do both activities in one sitting.

What's Important Here

The central idea is so brilliant that we have to acknowledge that we first saw it in *Data Desk,* by Paul Velleman: Whenever you select cases in one view, they appear selected in all views of the data. This one feature allows a universe of exploratory data analysis without your having to learn anything about fancy statistics.

Discussion Questions

Besides going over the questions students answer on the sheet itself, you can use these ideas for discussion questions:

➲ How did you decide who was "really rich"?

➲ What do you think a graph of **age** versus **income** would look like?

Also, if you have done *The Card People* (page 7), you can refer to conjectures the students have come up with: "How can we use this selection feature to see how **age** is related to **income**?" and so forth.

Topics

exploring relationships among attributes

graphs and multiple representations

Students need to be able to

make a graph

Materials

census data file

Two Graphs and Selection

Name(s): _____

You know how graphs work—you drag attributes to axes to tell graphs *what* to display. The popup menus on the graph tell Fathom *how* to display the data.

   You can make more than one graph at a time to help you compare different groups or to look at the data in different ways. Selecting people in any graph or table selects them everywhere.

1. Open your census data file. Make a histogram of **age**.
2. If your **age** graph has the attribute **sex** (or some other attribute) on the vertical axis, select the graph and choose **Remove Y Attribute** from the **Graph** menu.
3. Choose **Graph** from the **Insert** menu. A new, empty graph appears.
4. Drag the attribute **marital** (marital status) from the case table to the horizontal axis of the new graph. A **Bar Chart** appears. (Now you have two different graphs.)
5. Click on the bar that says **Nev** (for "never married"). It turns red. Notice that red regions appear in the **age** graph as well. You may even see cases in the collection or the case table that are highlighted.

Whenever you select cases, those cases appear selected in all views of the data. You can use this feature to show relationships among attributes. For example, in the two graphs shown here, the people who have never married are, in general, younger than the others. It's nice when something obvious makes sense.

6. How many people in your data set are married? (Select them, then point at the collection—the box of balls. The number is in the status bar at the bottom of the window.)

7. What percentage of the people in your data set are female? How do you know?

8. Make a new graph of **income**. Select all the really rich people—those few people who earn the most money. See who is selected in the other graphs. Are the rich people predominantly from one group? That is, are they mostly male? Are they mostly old? Look for patterns. What do you find?

9. You don't have to use selection to study relationships. Make box plots for **age**, split by **marital** status, as shown in the illustration (that is, five box plots of **age**: one each for never married, married, divorced, separated, and widowed). Estimate the median ages of these five groups. Do they make sense? Why or why not?

You need
   census data file

You need to know how to
   make graphs

You'll learn how to
   use selection to study relationships

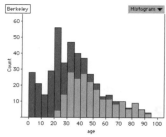

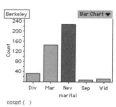

These graphs illustrate how Fathom shows selected data in all views.

Use **SHIFT**-click to select more than one bar, or drag a rectangle around the bars you want to select.

Also, when you point at a bar in a graph, the status bar shows how many cases are in that bar.

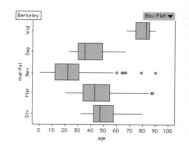

Out of Many, Fewer

- Two structured computer activities
- Data from census data file
- Student pages 20–22
- Guided, basic features

This idea of filters is tricky; if you have a projection system, do the first page as a demo. If you don't, use the pages as separate student handouts to introduce filtering.

At the end of the second page, students use filters to answer a whole slew of questions (they can turn them in; there's probably enough room on the sheet itself). These exercises gradually use more and more features of the formula editor. This is suitable for homework or open lab time.

Topics
filters and subsets
Boolean expressions
exploring data

Students need to be able to
make a graph

Materials
census data file

What's Important Here

- Formulas permeate Fathom, and this is an excellent introduction.

- Students who are used to using formulas or otherwise constructing mathematical expressions sometimes forget that Boolean expressions are legitimate mathematics as well. They are some of the most useful mathematics in our information-drenched society.

- The concept of using filters to reduce the scope of your data is important in data analysis.

- This same concept is important for suitably skeptical citizens. When we are presented with some conclusion, we must always ask, "For whom is this true?" Filters address this issue.

Discussion Questions

➲ If you see a Boolean expression without parentheses, such as **age > 20 and age < 30**, what do you suppose is the order of operations? (Generally, the comparison operators >, <, and = take precedence over the Boolean operators **and**, **or**, and **not**. Usually, **not** takes precedence over **and** and **or**.)

➲ If you just type the above Boolean expression into Fathom, what does Fathom do? (It puts in parentheses.)

➲ If you're trying to "find yourself" in the file (task at the end of *Out of Many, Fewer II*), does it matter which filters you put in first?

➲ Generally, in this class, which filter did we use first? What does that say about how we view people?

Out of Many, Fewer I

Name(s): _____

Suppose we were going to investigate the conjecture that males earn more than females. Here's what we could do:

1. Open a saved census data set.
2. Drag **income** from the column heading in the case table to the horizontal axis of a graph. (You get a dot plot.)
3. Drag the attribute **sex** to the vertical axis. (The dot plot splits.)
4. Choose **box plot** from the popup menu on the graph. Each dot plot becomes a box plot.

It certainly looks as if males earn more, but looks can be deceiving. Study the boxes. The lower end of each box is at about zero. That's the lower quartile. That is, for both males and females, fully one quarter of the population earns nothing at all!

Things like this should make you suspicious of your first conclusions. Maybe there's something going on that we haven't taken into account. What do you suppose it might be?

In this case, one problem is that we've included all the children. (There may be other fishy things; think of as many as you can.) To take care of the children, we really want to look at the incomes of all the people over a certain age. You'll have to decide what age is appropriate. For our purposes, we'll use 20.

5. Click in the collection to activate it.
6. Choose **Add Filter** from the **Data** menu.
7. A filter area appears below the collection and the formula editor opens.
8. Type **age > 20**. Close the editor.

When you close the editor (or click **OK** or **Apply**), the table and graph change so that now they include only cases where **age > 20** is true. Fathom calls these expressions *filters*.

Now we look at the box plots and see that the lower quartile is not zero; these people are finally earning! You probably still see that males earn more than females. But you may also suggest that elderly people shouldn't be counted as we investigate our conjecture. So we really want a new filter, like this one:

(age > 20) and (age < 65)

Here's how to get it:

9. Open the formula editor by double-clicking the filter on the screen.
10. Use the keypad in the formula editor to enter the **and** (or type an ampersand). You can't type "and."
11. Type **age < 65** and close the box by clicking **OK** to make Fathom apply your filter. How did the graph change?

Note: The rest of the cases haven't been deleted; you just can't see them. To get them all back, choose **Remove Filter** from the **Data** menu.

If all the cases vanished, you probably mistyped. You have to type the names of the attributes (variables) exactly. Capital letters don't count, so **age = Age**.

Out of Many, Fewer II

Name(s): _____

Use the census data to answer these questions. For each one, give your answer and write the filter (the logical expression, such as **age > 17**) that you used to help answer it.

1. How many people in your file make more than $50,000 per year?

2. How many of them are females? What kinds of jobs do they have?

3. How many teenagers are there in your file?

4. Estimate the median income of teenagers.

Estimate medians by looking at a box plot.

If an attribute doesn't have numbers for values (such as **sex** or **race**), you can still write filters, but you have to put the values in quotes. So

(age > 80) and (sex = "M") and (race = "White")

*Remember: Use ampersand (&) or the keypad for **and**.*

finds all the white males over 80.

5. How many males like these are in your data set?

6. Estimate the median age for people of some heavily represented race in your file who earn more than $30,000.

7. Estimate the median income for people of some heavily represented ancestry in your file who are over age 30.

Some attributes (such as **eduText**) are really decoded versions of numerical attributes (in this case, **eduCode**). You probably don't want to type in all of an **eduText** category to make a filter, but you can use the table to figure out what the **eduCode** numbers mean. (Do not think of **eduCode** as "years of schooling"!) For example,

eduCode = 10

means "high school diploma." So **eduCode > 9** means "high school diploma *or more.*"

8. Who is the oldest person in your data set without a high school diploma?

9. Estimate the median income of people with four-year college degrees.

10. Estimate the median income of people with a high school diploma but no degree from a four-year college or university.

11. Find people like yourself. Keep adding phrases to your filter until there are only a few people left. What filter did you use? Did you find yourself? Did you find people like yourself?

Codes for Education

eduCode	eduText
1	No school completed
2	Nursery school
3	Kindergarten
4	Grades 1, 2, 3, 4
5	Grades 5, 6, 7, 8
6	Grade 9
7	Grade 10
8	Grade 11
9	Grade 12, no diploma
10	High school graduate
11	Some college, no degree
12	Associate, occupational program
13	Associate, academic program
14	Baccalaureate
15	Master's degree
16	Professional degree
17	Doctorate

Making Categories

In this activity, students use formulas to create new categories for their census data set. On the surface, this is about Fathom skills, but underneath, it's all about using mathematics to accomplish something. It's a good "practice analysis," showing them one way—though hardly the only way—to look at their own conjectures.

<table>
<tr><td>

- Structured computer activity
- Data from census data file
- Student pages 24–26
- Guided, basic features

</td></tr>
</table>

What's Important Here

This activity has a lot in it. If you are looking for a single activity that teaches a lot of Fathom and still has a lot of math, this is a good one. But it's dense, so you may have to make choices—and you'll certainly have to stay on your toes. These notes describe some of the issues your students will deal with.

- Having multiple ways to represent the same data lets you discover more about the data than any single technique.

- Making a new attribute is critical to creative data analysis. While we give students an example using the **if( )** function to produce categorical (text) values, Fathom also lets them make continuous formulas.

- This activity involves *conditional probability*. If students seem confused, don't despair; it's just plain cognitively hard. Even if they don't completely "get it," this work will lay a foundation for later understanding.

- While making new attributes is important, it can also be misleading. Bring up with students the potential problems of stereotyping people with incomes under $25,000 (or whatever) as "poor."

Topics
exploring data
multiple representations
recoding data using Booleans
conditional statements
probability

Students need to know how to
open files
make graphs

Materials
census data file

Discussion Questions

➲ If you wanted just as many **rich** people as **poor**, how would you choose an **income** to separate **rich** from **poor** in exactly that way? (Find the median.)

➲ When we made the ribbon chart for **wealth** and **college**, we put **college** on the axis and **wealth** in the middle. What would it look like if we did it the other way around? What would it tell us that's different from what the original graph told us?

Answer: We have created two such graphs, shown here. Basically, the one with **wealth** on the horizontal axis tells us the difference in education for people with different incomes: Rich people generally have degrees. The one with **college** on the horizontal axis tells us the difference in income for people with different educations: People with degrees tend to be rich.

While both graphs display the same information, the one on the right will generally be better if you're trying to persuade students to stay in school. It implies that education *causes* wealth. On the other hand, if you want to make the case that rich people have more access to education, use the one on the left.

Note: This kind of plot, in which the area of the rectangle is proportional to the size of the group, and the whole group becomes a single large rectangle, is also called a *mosaic plot*.

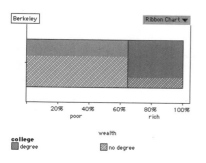

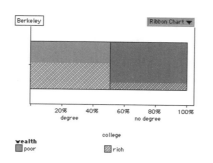

Making Categories

Name(s): _____

Sometimes you have too much information. Suppose you believe that college graduates are more likely to be wealthy than people who are not college graduates. But when you plot **income** against **eduCode** it's a mess. There are too many different bins.

Let's make it simpler. First, let's divide people into wealthy and not wealthy.

1. Make sure your census data file is open in Fathom. You should be able to see the collection and the case table.

2. Choose **Graph** from the **Insert** menu (if there isn't one already). Put **income** on the horizontal axis. You should see that there are a whole lot of people earning not very much and a few earning a lot.

3. With your partner, decide how much income will define what you mean by wealthy. Don't make it too high; that is, you want enough people to fall into that category. Write that value here:

4. Select the **income** column in the case table (as shown).

5. Choose **New Attribute** from the **Data** menu. A box asks you for the name of the new attribute.

6. Enter **wealth**. Click **OK** to tell Fathom you're finished with that. A new, empty column appears for the new attribute.

Now we have a new *attribute,* but the attribute has no *values.* We could go through and label everyone by hand, but that would be too much trouble (and we'd mess up). We'll make the computer do it for us . . . .

7. Click in the box labeled **wealth** and choose **Edit Formula** from the **Edit** menu. You can see the cursor in the picture. The formula editor appears. Enter the formula so it looks like the one shown here. We're using $20,000 for "rich" here.

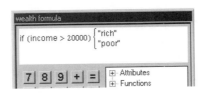

In Fathom's **if( )** function, if the expression in parentheses is true, the result is the expression on top after the bracket. Otherwise, it's the expression on the bottom. Put text results in quotes.

If you press **ENTER**, you'll see the values for **wealth** appear in the empty column. **Note: wealth** is the attribute's name. The *values* of **wealth** are **rich** and **poor**. Click **OK** to close the editor.

You need
census data file

You need to know how to
open a Fathom file
make a case table
make graphs

You'll learn how to
make new attributes
define new attributes with a formula
make a ribbon chart
make a summary table

Here are the keystrokes to make the formula. Press the **TAB** key where you see **TAB**:

> if (income>20000 **TAB**
> "rich **TAB** "poor

Note 1: You do not have to close your parentheses or double quotes. Fathom does it for you.

Note 2: It's OK to close them if you want.

Note 3: When you're in the formula editor, pressing **TAB** eventually moves you to an empty question mark.

8. Now make a new graph with **wealth** on the horizontal axis (only). Sketch the graph at right; be sure to label and scale your axes.

9. How many **rich** people are there in your data set? How do you know?

10. Change **Bar Chart** to a **Ribbon Chart** in the popup menu. Now what percent of the people in your data set are **rich**? How do you know?

Now we'll do the same thing for college graduates.

11. First, determine what value of **eduCode** means someone is a college graduate. (Answer: We'll take that to be an associate degree, which begins where **eduCode** = 12.) If we didn't tell you, how could you figure that out?

12. Make a new attribute, **college**, with two values, **degree** and **no degree**. Make the formula just as you did for **wealth**. Write the formula here.

13. Drag college onto the horizontal axis of your wealth graph, replacing wealth. Now drag wealth to the middle (not the axis) of that graph. Sketch the graph at right.

14. The display in the preceding step probably shows a relationship between getting a college degree and being wealthy. Explain what the relationship is and how the data show it.

15. Choose **Summary Table** from the **Insert** menu. An empty table appears. Drag **college** to the space at the side and drag **wealth** to the top. Sketch what you see at right.

16. Make a new graph and put **college** on the horizontal axis. It will make a bar chart. Now drag **wealth** to the middle. Sketch it at right.

17. Now you have three representations of the same data: a ribbon chart, a bar chart, and a summary table. Explain, in words, why you would use a summary table in some cases, a ribbon chart in others, and a bar chart in still others.

Name(s): _____

Going Further

1. The analysis we just did includes all the young children and retired people. Add a filter to the collection to exclude them. One filter that would work is **inRange(age, 18, 65)**. How does adding the filter change the results?

2. What is the chance that someone chosen at random would be labeled **rich**?

3. What is the chance that someone **rich** has a college degree?

4. What is the chance that someone with a college degree is **rich**?

5. When we turn a number into a category—for example, when we turn **income** (a number) into **wealth** (a variable with two categories, **rich** and **poor**), there are advantages and disadvantages. What are some of them?

Investigating a Conjecture

Now students are ready to use Fathom to investigate conjectures like the ones they may have generated during *The Card People*. You may even have posters with conjectures on them. Brainstorm new conjectures to add to the old ones that you could investigate using Fathom.

> • Open-ended computer activity
> • Handout of data from census data file
> • No student instruction sheets
> • Independent, basic features

Whole Class: A Sample Conjecture

If you wish, you can work with the whole class to begin a sample investigation of a conjecture:

> Women live longer than men.

Do you think it's true? We can't get the information directly; the only people we have in our data set are still alive, so we don't know how long they'll live. So first we list some consequences that follow from the conjecture. If the conjecture is true, then

- The average age of women will be older.
- The oldest people will be mostly women.

Discuss what graphs or filters you might use. Consider the choices you have to make. (Is "average" mean or median? How old are "the oldest people"?) Note that there are questions you cannot answer with this information alone, for example "*How much* longer do women live?"

Topics
   conjectures
   proportion

Students need to be able to
   use selection to study
     relationships
   use filters
   make many kinds of graphs

Materials
   census data file

Working in Pairs

Have students investigate their conjectures. This can be quick-and-dirty or pretty elaborate, depending on your assessment needs. In any case, listen to them as they work and leave time for class discussion at the end.

Have students create a brief written report, make a display, or give a presentation. You can evaluate this presentation using the same criteria you may already have used in *The Card People*. (See the notes on page 8.)

Discussion Questions

- ➲ Do you think your conclusion (about whether the conjecture is true or false, say) is generally true for people in this state, or just in this community?
- ➲ What other questions do you have? What other data would you like to see?
- ➲ Do you think your conclusion is so strong that it couldn't be "just by chance," or could it have been caused by random fluctuations?

Features Buffet

- Seven structured computer activities
- Data from census data file
- Student pages 29–35
- Guided, basic features

Each of the seven pages that follows gives a short introduction to one Fathom feature and some solutions to common problems. You can give students a choice of what to look at or simply deal out different pages to the pairs of students; then, at the end of the period, they can demonstrate what they've learned to the class or to members of a small group.

There are often so many different ways to do things that it's hard to make a coherent set of worksheets that develops all the paths students might want to use. So this "buffet" is designed to give students a few more options than the sequence of activities would otherwise introduce.

Topics
various Fathom features
problem-solving strategies
multiple representations

Students need to know how to
open files
make graphs

Materials
census data file

The Activities

- **Plot Value.** Students already have used this command once, to get the mean to appear, but this worksheet takes them further.

- **Summary Tables.** Summary tables let you display numerical statistics such as the count, mean, and standard deviation. We emphasize graphs, but numbers are still important.

- **Display Attributes.** Students may wonder why each person looks like a little gold ball. By using display attributes, you can change the picture and the caption, and see how that might be useful in data analysis.

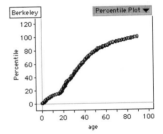

- **Sorting.** You can sort in the case table; this activity shows how and lets students investigate this feature more fully.

- **Percentile Plots.** Students may not be familiar with this kind of plot; it's another powerful way of displaying distributions.

- **Ntigrams.** These are a type of histogram—yet another way of displaying distributions. It turns out that our common histogram, with bins of equal width, is only a special case. Ntigrams are another special case: They have bins of equal *population* instead of equal *width*. As a consequence, Ntigrams have a **Density** axis rather than a **Count** axis. For an **age** Ntigram, for example, the units of the other axis would be *people per year*. This may seem odd at first, but histograms are actually defined with this density axis.

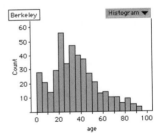

- **The Switch Function.** This is a way to divide cases into more than two categories.

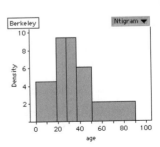

Discussion Questions

↪ What is the most useful feature you've heard about from someone else? How would you use it?

↪ Suppose somebody who knew mathematics but didn't know Fathom asked for an introduction to the program. What would be the most important thing to tell this person?

Data in Depth
© 2001 Key Curriculum Press

Features Buffet: Plot Value

Name(s): _____

This "menu" activity shows you how to use Fathom's **Plot Value** command. It's great for visualizing quantities on graphs, and comparing those quantities across groups. You can plot any quantity you like, but you have to write a formula to express it.

1. Open your census data file.
2. Make sure you have a case table open.
3. Make a new (empty) graph.
4. Drag the **age** attribute to the horizontal axis. A dot plot appears.
5. Choose **Plot Value** from the **Graph** menu. The formula editor opens.
6. Enter **mean()** in the box and close it. You'll see a vertical line, probably red, in the dot plot where the mean of the ages is. You'll also see the numerical value and your formula below the graph.
7. Drag the **marital** attribute from the case table to the vertical axis of the graph. The graph splits by marital status. What are the mean ages for the various marital statuses?

8. You probably had to estimate them from the graph. What does the calculated number at the bottom of the graph indicate?

9. Plot two more values: **mean( ) - s** and **mean( ) + s**. These are the mean minus (and plus) one sample standard deviation. Standard deviation is a common measure of *spread*.

10. Using the mouse pointer, draw a rectangle around a group of the youngest points in the **Nev** (never married) category to select them, as shown in the illustration. They will highlight.
11. Now drag those points to the right. Describe what happens to the values you plotted.

12. When you're finished, close the file without saving—you have, after all, changed their ages.

You need
 census data file

You need to know how to
 open a data file
 make graphs

You'll learn how to
 write formulas to plot values on graphs

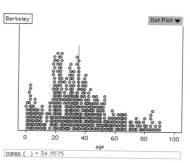

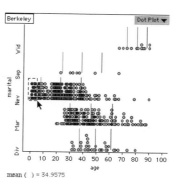

Features Buffet: Summary Tables

Name(s): _____

This "menu" activity shows you how to use Fathom's *summary tables*. They're perfect for getting the numerical values for statistics such as the mean and standard deviation. But you can get any quantity you like with a summary table, as long as you can write a formula to express it.

You need
census data file

You'll learn how to
use summary tables
enter formulas in summary tables

1. Open your census data file.

2. Make sure you have a case table open.

3. Choose **Summary Table** from the **Insert** menu. A blank, empty summary table appears. Now we have to tell Fathom what attribute to summarize.

4. Drag the **age** column header from the case table to the right arrow at the top of the table. The table shows the mean **age**.

5. We want more! With the table selected, choose **Add Formula** from the **Summary** menu.

6. You have to tell Fathom what summary statistic you want. Enter **median(**. Fathom will supply the close parenthesis. In your mind, but not on the screen, fill in the blank with the head of the column, namely **age**. When you close the box by clicking **OK**, the median **age** appears in the table.

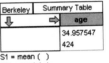

7. What is the median age for people in your collection?

8. Now we'll add another attribute. Drag the attribute **sex** and put it on the down arrow. The table will split. On the average, who is older, males or females? And by how much?

9. Let's add one more attribute. Drag **income** to the right arrow. Now you'll see **age** split by **sex** and **income** split by **sex**. Which sex earns more? By how much?

10. Other functions you can put into that formula box include **min( )**, **max( )**, **stdDev( )** (standard deviation), and **iqr( )** (interquartile range). You can look them up in **Help**. Try them out. Use **max( )** to tell how old the oldest male and female are.

11. You can also do arithmetic. What is the mean age minus the standard deviation of age for males? For females?

Data in Depth
© 2001 Key Curriculum Press

Features Buffet: Display Attributes

Name(s): _____

This "menu" activity shows you how to use Fathom's *display attributes*. They're perfect for changing the way the open collection displays your data. Here, we'll focus on the *captions,* that is, the words that appear under the gold balls, and the *x*- and *y*-positions of the balls in the window. You can learn more about display attributes by checking out **Help**.

You need
census data file

You need to know how to
use a formula editor

You'll learn how to
use the inspector
change the labels in the collection
change the positions of the icons in the collection

1. Open your census data file.

2. Open the collection (the little box of gold balls) by dragging a bottom corner out and down.

3. Double-click in your collection. The *inspector* window appears.

4. Click on the **Display** tab. You'll see new attributes such as **x**, **y**, and **caption**. You can see that **caption** has a simple formula, **sex**. That's why the gold balls in the collection are labeled by sex.

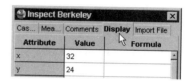

5. Let's change the captions. Double-click to the right of **caption** in the **Formula** column. The formula editor appears.

6. Enter **concat(sex, " age ", age)**. Click **OK** to close the formula editor. Look in the collection; it should look something like the one shown here. The function **concat( )** concatenates (sticks together) whatever you give it. Separate the elements by commas, and put literal strings (such as **" age"**) inside quotation marks. If you need spaces in your text, put them inside the quotation marks as well.

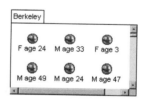

7. The attributes **x** and **y** control the positions of the gold balls. Change the 24 for **y** in the first case to 32. What happens to the position of the gold ball in the collection?

8. Experiment with values for both **x** and **y**. Where is the origin of the coordinate system in the collection? Which ways do the axes point? How do you know?

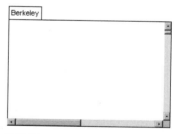

9. Change the formula for **x** to **age + 50** (just the number). Change the formula for **y** to **caseIndex * 32**. Sketch what you get in the empty collection shown above.

10. Make a formula for **caption** that produces a collection like the one shown here. Write your formula below:

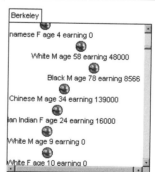

11. Make a scatter plot of **income** as a function of **age**. Point with the mouse at an interesting case in the plot. Your **caption** will show up in the status bar at the bottom of the window (as in the illustration). Who is the richest person in your file? The oldest?

Data in Depth
© 2001 Key Curriculum Press

Features Buffet: Sorting

Name(s): _____

This "menu" activity shows you how to sort data in Fathom's case table. This technique is useful for finding specific cases.

1. Open your census data file.
2. Make sure you have a case table open. Make sure you can see the **age** attribute.
3. Select the attribute by clicking on its name once. The column of data highlights.
4. Choose **Sort Ascending** from the **Data** menu. Describe what happened.

5. What happens when you sort an attribute that is not numeric? Describe what you did and what happened.

6. Tell about the oldest person in your file and how you sorted to find her or him.

7. How many people in your file earn between $15,000 and $17,000? Use only sorting and the case table (no filters this time). Tell the answer and how you sorted.

8. What person who has completed only high school (but no college) earns the most? Sort by **income** and by **eduText**. But in what order? Describe the person and tell how you sorted.

You need
census data file

You'll need to know how to
make a case table

You'll learn how to
sort the case table

Features Buffet: Percentile Plots

Name(s): _____

A *percentile plot* is a kind of plot that shows you the distribution of a *continuous* attribute (one whose values are numbers, not words). In this "menu" activity, we'll make a percentile plot and see what it has to tell us.

1. Open up your census data file.
2. Make sure you have a case table.
3. Make a new graph by choosing **Graph** from the **Insert** menu.
4. Drag the attribute label **age** from the case table to the horizontal axis of the graph. A dot plot appears.
5. Choose **Percentile Plot** from the popup menu in the upper-right corner of the graph. The plot for 133 cases from Berkeley, California, looks like the one shown here. It's like a dot plot, but with the dot positions stretched out vertically. Sketch yours here.

You need
census data file

You need to know how to
open a file
make graphs

You'll learn about
percentile plots

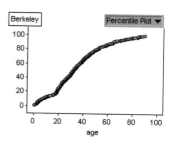

The vertical axis shows the *percentile*. That is, if a point is at 40, then 40% of the cases are less than or equal to this one.

6. Place the mouse pointer on a point. Don't click. When the arrow points straight left, you'll see the coordinates of the point in the status bar at the bottom of the Fathom window. Find the point as close to 50% as you can. What is the age of that case?

7. How old do you have to be to be in the oldest 10% of the population? Also, describe how you used the percentile plot to find out.

8. The Berkeley graph in the illustration is shallow at the beginning, steep in the middle, and shallow at the end. What does that mean for the distribution of people?

9. Make a new percentile plot of **income**. Sketch it at right and tell what its shape means for the distribution of incomes.

Features Buffet: Ntigrams

Name(s): _____

This "menu" activity shows you how to use Fathom's Ntigrams. They're a kind of graph that shows a distribution. Basically, an Ntigram (pronounced EN-ti-gram) is a histogram whose bin widths are not equal.

1. Open your census data file.
2. Make sure you have a case table open.
3. Make two new graphs (pull them off the shelf or choose **Graph** from the **Insert** menu).
4. Drag **age** to the horizontal axis of each. You'll get dot plots.
5. Make one a histogram by choosing **Histogram** from the popup menu in the graph.
6. Make the other an Ntigram by choosing **Ntigram** from that popup menu. Your two graphs should look something like the ones shown here.

In any histogram, each rectangle represents the number of people in a particular range. The *area* of the rectangle is proportional to the *number* of people it represents. In a regular histogram (the one on top), the bins are all the same width, so they represent different numbers of people. In an Ntigram (the bottom), each bin represents the same number of people, so they are different widths.

7. How many are in each bin? Position the mouse pointer over one of the bins. You don't have to click. Look in the status bar; it will tell you (as in the picture). How many are in each of your bins?

You need
census data file

You'll need to know how to
make a graph

You'll learn how to
make an Ntigram
interpret an Ntigram

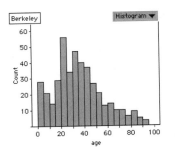

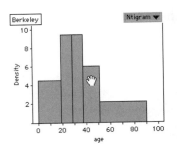

`37 <= age <= 51 : 85 cases`

8. Drag on the edges of the bins to change their widths (and therefore the number of bins). Try to make exactly ten bins. Sketch your result.

9. How much do you have to earn to be in the top 10% of incomes? Sketch the graph and explain how you know.

10. Drag the attribute **sex** onto the vertical axis of your graph. Answer the preceding question for males and females separately.

Features Buffet: The Switch Function

Name(s): _____

In the activity *Making Categories,* you used an if( ) function to change a continuous value (such as **income**) into two categorical values (**rich** and **poor**). But what if you want to make three or more categories? You could put if( )s inside of if( )s, but sometimes the **switch( )** function is better.

We'll investigate income that is split among young people, working-age people, and older people.

1. Open your census data file.
2. Make sure you have a case table open.
3. Select the **age** attribute by clicking once on it. The column highlights.
4. Choose **New Attribute...** from the **Data** menu. You can name the new attribute. Call it **ageCategory**. Close the new-attribute box by clicking **OK**.
5. Select the **ageCategory** label and choose **Edit Formula** from the **Edit** menu to bring up the formula editor.
6. Begin by entering **switch( )**. You'll see the formula in the first picture.
7. Press **TAB** to move inside the first parenthesis. Enter **age < 19**.
8. Press **TAB** to move to the question mark. Enter **"young"**. You should see the second picture.

Right now, we have two possibilities, but we need three.

9. Press **INS** (Windows) or **OPTION-RETURN** (Mac). A new possibility opens up. Fill in the question marks (you may tab between them) to make a formula like the third picture.
10. Click **OK** to close the editor.

Two things to note:

- These conditions are checked in order from top to bottom, so a 13-year-old girl will be assigned **young**. Because she is younger than 19, Fathom will never check the (true) second condition, **age < 65**.

- You don't need to fill in the parentheses immediately following the **switch(?)** itself. (That's for a different use of the **switch( )** function.)

11. Let's use our attribute! Make a new summary table by choosing **Summary Table** from the **Insert** menu.
12. Drag the attribute **income** from the case table to the right arrow on the summary table. You'll see the mean income.
13. Now drop the new attribute, **ageCategory**, onto the down arrow on the summary table. This tells Fathom to split the table. Copy the table from your screen in the space here and tell what it means.

You need
census data

You'll need to know how to
make a new attribute
use the formula editor

You'll learn how to
use the **switch()** function

Lines and Data

2

If you could choose ten things from first-year algebra for students to understand thoroughly, the slope-intercept form of the equation of a line—or perhaps just the concept of slope—would be one of them. Too often, however, "$y = mx + b$" becomes a mindless response. It earns partial credit—but what does it mean?

The activities and exercises in this chapter help students approach slope and the equation for a line from the "data" side. Giving a face to the slope and intercept—a meaning in context—will help some students understand these crucial quantities more clearly. At the same time, students will learn new skills using Fathom.

This chapter begins with two fairly elaborate, structured activities (*Reading the News* and *Coast Starlight*), for which we have produced student pages with spaces for responses and step-by-step instructions.

Then there are Sonatas, which are less-structured assignments that help students explore various aspects of lines and data. For more information about Sonatas in general, see *Sonatas for Data and Brain,* page xx.

There are also several "What's Going On Here?" pages, intended primarily for your benefit. Even so, you may want to copy some of these for some students.

Level

Since these activities are all about lines and their equations (usually in slope-intercept form), they are appropriate for students who are taking algebra or have taken it.

The Activities

- **Reading the News, Part I** is an offline activity that generates data that probably fall in a pretty straight line. They should be good for talking about slope.

- **Reading the News, Part II** is its online continuation: we enter the data into Fathom and investigate them more fully.

- In **The Coast Starlight,** students look at the schedule of a train in order to study its speed. In order to do so effectively, however, they need a formula to convert the time on the schedule into an elapsed time.

- **Sonatas About Linear Data** is a collection of five mini-investigations. The first is more structured and step-by-step than those that follow.

- **Sonatas About Lines and Geometry** is a pair of more open-ended investigations, this time in a geometrical context.

- **Explaining Patterns** is an open-ended task, with suggestions for existing data sets that will work with the assignment.

- **The World Is Linear** is a collection of ideas for assignments and small projects in which students collect their own data.

Objectives

- Students become comfortable using scatter plots in Fathom.

- Students use lines and their equations to model linear data.

- Students figure out real-world meanings of slope and intercept in context.

- Students use linear models to draw conclusions about data.

Where We're Heading

This chapter focuses on data that students can model easily with lines. There are four chapters immediately related to this one.

Chapter 3, *Per Portions,* focuses on the idea of making a new attribute (such as per capita income) to help the student understand the relationships of its components (in this case, total income and population) to other attributes.

Chapter 4, *Straighten Up!,* discusses data that students can model using nonlinear functions. They learn to change "curvy" plots into straight ones by applying functions to the data; they also use Fathom to draw the curves themselves.

Chapter 7, *What to Do with Leftovers,* introduces residuals and residual plots. Students learn to use them to assess the quality of linear models.

Chapter 8, *Under a Cloud,* deals with data whose relationships are obscured by noise and randomness. Students learn about correlation and the correlation coefficient.

Curriculum Connections

Algebra. Scatter plots, lines, slope, the Cartesian coordinate system. Also, when students use Fathom to do the work in these activities, they have to use algebra to create formulas—for example, to convert hours and minutes into decimal hours.

Geometry. Similarity can give rise to linear data. When students study those data—and come up with the linear functions that model them—they gain new insight into the geometrical issues.

Advanced Algebra. Juniors are supposed to know all about lines. But in a field test, some of them couldn't interpret a function whose variables were not *x* and *y*. These activities help students develop "function sense."

Calculus. Slope, especially instantaneous slope, defines the derivative. The work in this chapter is a good foundation for Chapter 4 *Straighten Up!*, in which we study nonlinear bivariate data and, therefore, more sophisticated functions.

Physics. Uniform motion is thoroughly entangled with slope. If you put time on the horizontal axis and distance on the vertical—a common choice—slope is speed. Also, as physicists recognize, the *dimension* of the slope—its units—is critically important to understanding.

Reading the News, Parts I and II

- Offline and online structured activities
- Data from measurements
- Student pages 41–45
- Starter, basic features

How long would it take to read the newspaper aloud? Two activities address this question. In the first, students collect data and do analysis offline. In the second, students use Fathom to help them do further analysis.

Collecting the Data

Students read aloud from the newspaper. They record how much they read during set intervals of time ranging from 10 to 60 seconds. They measure the vertical distance (in column-centimeters) they were able to read during the interval (this is how we measure the total amount of text rather than, say, counting words or letters).

There are many interesting sources of variation in this project. Here are some issues:

- This is not a race. They should just read as if they were radio announcers.
- Every reader should read new material each time, because rereading is faster.
- Every reader should read from columns of the same width. Pictures don't count. Students may also have to decide about headlines, changes of font size, and so on.
- Students vary in their ability to measure time accurately. You may want to measure it for them, or let them practice beforehand.

Finally, you may want to collect the various slopes (reading speeds) on the board so students can see the variation in the data.

Topics

slope, rate, and proportion

No Fathom skills required

Materials

centimeter rulers
newspapers
clock with a second hand
(or a stopwatch)

What's Important Here

This is all about slope and the equations of lines. Students must be able to explain why, in this setting, the slope is the speed, in centimeters per second.

We assume students have calculated slopes of lines before as "rise over run" or "the amount y increases when x increases by one."

Discussion Questions

Use the questions for students to answer at the end of each activity as springboards for discussion.

Tech Tips

- Choose **Movable Line** from the **Graph** menu to make the line appear. If you move the line manually, the equation changes. How it changes depends on where you grab it.
- The equation of the line (complete with slope) appears below the graph.
- When you try to move the line, you may accidentally grab a data point and change your data. Remember: Fathom has "multiple undo." If you mess up, undo repeatedly until everything is OK. **Undo** is in the **Edit** menu. You can also press **CTRL-Z** (Windows) or **⌘-Z** (Mac).
- If you have more than one graph, you can have separate movable lines in each.

If **Movable Line** is missing or disabled, it means the graph is not *active;* that is, it doesn't have a border. Click on the scatter plot to make it active.

Shortcut: Right-click (Windows) or **CTRL**-click (Mac) in the graph to get the **Graph** menu in place.

Reading the News, Part I (Offline)

Name(s): _____

Somebody once said that listening to a half-hour news broadcast on the radio was the same as reading the front section of the paper. Is that true? We're going to find out.

Get a newspaper and a partner. One person is the timer, the other is the reader. The reader picks a place to start reading. When the timer says "Go," the reader reads until the timer says "Stop." (**Note:** If necessary, your teacher can be the timer for everyone.) You'll see on the chart below that you get to read six times—for different lengths of time. Each time you read, record the number of *centimeters* you were able to read. That will be the vertical distance in the column. Reading faster doesn't matter. Read as if you were a news announcer on the radio. This is not a race!

Pick columns to read that are (a) all the same width and (b) pretty narrow.

You switch roles, too. Each partner will be a reader six times (for six durations: 10 seconds, 20 seconds, and so forth) and a timer six times. Do not read the same paragraph twice. If you've already seen it, you'll read it differently.

You need

newspaper
ruler
clock with a second hand (or a stopwatch)

You need to know how to

calculate the slope of a line

You'll learn about

reading speed
how slope is connected to speed

Name:		Name:	
Time (seconds)	Centimeters read	Time (seconds)	Centimeters read
10		10	
20		20	
30		30	
40		40	
50		50	
60		60	

Answer These

Write your answers on this page.

1. How many centimeters of text are there on a typical page of your newspaper? It will depend on how many columns there are and how many pictures and ads.

2. How long would it take you to read one page? Calculate an answer using your data.

3. How many pages could you read in 30 minutes? Is that more than the number of pages in the first section?

Making a Scatter Plot

Now plot the data on the graphs given here (one graph for each of you). Be careful to scale your vertical axis to match your data; that is, make sure you use up as much of the grid as you can without going outside the grid. We've scaled the horizontal axis for you.

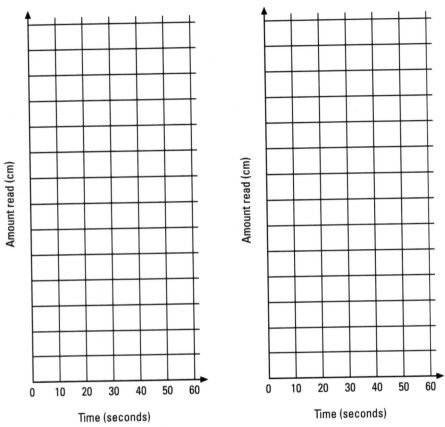

Next, you should each draw a single straight line with your ruler that approximates your data. It should (probably) go through the origin (0, 0) of your graph.

Finally, calculate the *slope* (rise over run) of each of your lines.

Answer These

Answer these questions with your partner. Write your answers after each question; continue on the back of the page if you need more space.

1. Why should the line go through the origin?

2. Which of you read faster? Can you tell from the graphs? Can you tell from the slopes?

3. Did you read at a constant rate? How can you tell?

4. Your slope's units are centimeters per second (rise was in centimeters, run was in seconds). That sounds like a speed. What does it mean in connection with reading?

5. Quick! Use your slope to calculate how many centimeters you would read in 100 seconds.

6. What is the range of slopes in the class? What do you think is the steepest slope anyone could possibly have?

Reading the News, Part II (Online)

Name(s): _____

Now you'll enter the data you collected into Fathom. Use one of your individual data sets. When you're finished, you can repeat the process with the other data if you have time.

1. Start up Fathom. You'll have an empty document. Choose **Case Table** from the **Insert** menu. An empty case table appears.

2. Click the word **<new>** at the top of a column in the table.

3. Type **time** and press **ENTER**. A collection appears (it looks like a box).

4. Make another new attribute: **cm** for centimeters. (You can choose **New Attribute** from the **Data** menu or click in the **<new>** box.)

5. Enter the data from *Reading the News, Part I (Offline)*. To enter a new case in your table, just add the data to the empty line at the bottom of the table. (You can move to the next cell with the **TAB** key.) You'll have six cases when you're finished. You should save and name your file.

6. Now make a scatter plot. First, make a new (empty) graph by choosing **Graph** from the **Insert** menu.

7. Next, drag the column heading **time** from the top of the case table (you'll see a grabbing-hand cursor) and drop it on the horizontal axis of the graph. You can drop it when the black box appears next to the axis. This makes a dot plot.

8. Drag the **cm** column heading to the vertical axis. The graph changes to a scatter plot. Sketch it here, with scaled and labeled axes.

You need
> data from *Reading the News, Part I*
> computer running Fathom

You'll learn how to
> make new attributes
> make a scatter plot
> add a line to a scatter plot

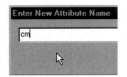

Compare the scatter plot the computer made to the one you made. The one from the computer should show the same information. If you entered any of the numbers incorrectly, you can change them in the case table and the points in the graph will move to the right places.

Answer These

Answer these questions in the space provided.

1. **Movable Line.** Choose **Movable Line** from the **Graph** menu (you may have to click on the graph to activate the **Graph** menu). The line and its equation appear. Get comfortable with changing the line's intercept and slope. Move the line to try to approximate the points. What is its slope? What was the slope when you drew the line by hand?

2. **Locking the Intercept.** Suppose you have reason to believe that the correct equation of the line is not **cm = slope * time + intercept** but really only **cm = slope * time**. That is, you believe that **intercept = 0**. You can force the movable line to have zero for an intercept: choose **Lock Intercept at Zero** from the **Graph** menu. Lock the intercept and continue to play with the line. Do you think it's right to have a zero intercept in this situation? Why or why not?

3. **Least-Squares Line.** Choose **Least-Squares Line** from the **Graph** menu (you may have to click on the graph to activate the **Graph** menu). The line and its equation appear. The computer calculates a line to fit the points. What equation does it have? How does this line look different from the movable line (besides its color)?

The equation for the least-squares line also shows a quantity called *r*-squared. It's a measure of how well the line "explains" the data.

4. **Dragging Data Dangerously.** Click on a point on the graph. See how the case gets selected in the table? Now drag the point. Watch how the values for that data point change. Also watch the values for the slope of the least-squares line. What are the largest and smallest slopes you can get by dragging that point to different locations?

Note: This is dangerous; you want to avoid inadvertently changing your data. Fortunately, you can always retype it, or choose **Undo** in the **Edit** menu or press **CTRL-Z** (Windows) or ⌘-Z (Mac) to undo what you've done. Fathom will let you undo more than one thing.

5. **Switcheroo.** Make another graph but with **cm** on the horizontal axis and **time** on the vertical. Make a line to fit the points. What does its slope mean?

The Coast Starlight

- Structured computer activity
- Data from handout
- Student pages 47–50
- Starter, basic features

Students will look at the schedule for the Coast Starlight, a West coast train. Students get practice entering data and using formulas. They use lines on a scatter plot of the data to answer questions about the train's speed.

We have split this activity into two parts. Some classes do both in a day. The first, *The Coast Starlight I: Entering Data,* involves only entering data. *The Coast Starlight II: Studying Train Speed* is more mathematical. Students

- Make a formula for total time (the trip spans two days, so clock time alone is not enough)

- Make a scatter plot of distance as a function of time (so that slope is speed)

- Use the graph and slopes to answer questions about the train's speed

Topics
slope, speed

Math required
some exposure to slope

Materials
train schedules (one per group)
optionally, a pre-made file with the schedule in it

What's Important Here

- Students actually make formulas in order to accomplish something here— to convert **days**, **hours**, and **minutes** into a useful **time** measure.

- With these graphs, slope is the same as speed, *as long as the right variables are on the right axes.* You might get in the habit of pointing to the vertical axis, saying "per," and pointing to the horizontal. Slope is rise over run, and speed is distance over time, so **miles** goes on the vertical axis and **time** on the horizontal.

- The *absolute* time is irrelevant to the calculation; it's only the *difference* between times that matters.

- *Being careful pays.* The computer can help you see subtle trends in the data that you'd be unlikely to catch with a handmade graph.

To omit data entry, you may use the pre-made file, **CoastStarlight** on the CD, and begin with part II.

Preparation

- If you're doing *The Coast Starlight I: Entering Data,* photocopy the schedules. To save paper, we put two copies of the schedule on the page. Copy half as many as you need, then cut them in half.

- Be sure you know how to enter formulas and change axis scales in Fathom so you can help students. Choose **Help Topics...** from the **Help** menu.

- Decide which of the questions and tasks at the end of *The Coast Starlight II: Studying Train Speed* you want students to write up and hand in.

In general, "Going Further" questions are too elaborate to leave as fill-in-the-blank questions. They could be assessments, or even homework, depending on access to equipment.

Discussion Questions

↪ Why does the formula **24 * day + hour** work for **time**?

↪ If we wanted **time** in **days**, what would the formula be?

↪ If we had time in **days** (you may want to demonstrate this), what would the slope of the line for the train be? What are the units of that slope—the speed? (Miles per day.)

Data in Depth
© 2001 Key Curriculum Press

The Coast Starlight: The Amtrak Schedules

11 Daily ReadDown	Mile ▼		◄ Train Number ► / ◄ Days of Operation ►	Symbol	▲	14 Daily Read Up
			🚌 *Amtrak Thruway Connection—Vancouver, BC/Seattle, WA*			
6 00A	0	Dp	*Vancouver, BC*–Pacific Central Sta. ✹ (PT)	●	Ar	11 50P
6 15A	12		*Richmond, BC*–Delta Pacific Resort			11 20P
6 45A	29		*Surrey, BC*–Tudor Inn			10 50P
9 15A	144	Ar	*Seattle, WA* ✹ 🚌	⊘	Dp	8 30P
10 00A	0	Dp	Seattle, WA ✹ (PT) (Victoria, BC ⛴)	📷⊘♿	Ar	7 50P
10 57A	40		Tacoma, WA	📷♿		6 53P
11 43A	72		Olympia-Lacey, WA	●♿		6 09P
12 06P	94		Centralia, WA	📷♿		5 47P
12 52P	137		Kelso-Longview, WA	●♿		5 01P
1 35P	176		Vancouver, WA	📷♿		4 18P
1 55P	186	Ar	Portland, OR ✹	📷♿	Dp	3 55P
2 30P		Dp			Ar	3 20P
3 45P	239		Salem, OR	📷♿		1 20P
4 17P	267		Albany, OR (Corvallis)	📷♿		12 45P
5 07P	310		Eugene, OR (Springfield) ✹	📷♿		12 00N
8 07P	431		Chemult, OR	●♿		8 55A
10 07P	505		Klamath Falls, OR (Crater Lake ✹)	📷♿		7 42A
12 31A	611		Dunsmuir, CA (Mt. Shasta)	●♿		4 39A
2 19A	668		Redding, CA	●♿		2 52A
3 33A	742		Chico, CA	●♿		1 29A
4 16A	785		Marysville, CA (Yuba City)	●♿		12 46A
6 30A	837		Sacramento, CA ✹	📷♿		11 42P
6 50A	850		Davis, CA	📷♿		10 48P
7 45A	894		Martinez, CA	📷♿		9 58P
8 30A	921		Emeryville, CA	📷♿		9 20P
9 20A	926	Ar	Oakland, CA–Jack London Sq.	📷♿	Dp	8 30P
9 35A					Ar	8 15P
			🚌 *Amtrak Thruway Connection—Emeryville/Oakland/San Francisco—Schedule Below*			
10 30A	966	Dp	San Jose, CA (CalTrain)	📷♿ 🚌		7 20P
12 01P	1034		Salinas, CA (Monterey 🚌 ✹)	📷♿		5 45P
			🚌 *Amtrak Thruway Connection—Salinas/Monterey/Carmel—Schedule on Reverse*			
1 41P	1140		Paso Robles, CA	●♿		3 55P
3 30P	1167		San Luis Obispo, CA (Hearst Castle ✹)	📷♿		2 55P
67	1278		Goleta, CA	●	67	
6 17P	1286		Santa Barbara, CA ✹	📷♿		12 00N
7 10P	1323		Oxnard, CA	📷♿		11 02A
7 48P	1352		Simi Valley, CA	●♿		10 29A
8 30P	1384		Glendale, CA	31		9 48A
9 05P	1389	Ar	Los Angeles, CA ✹	📷♿	Dp	9 30A
			🚌 *Amtrak Thruway Connection—Emeryville/Oakland/San Francisco*			
8 35A	0	Dp	Emeryville, CA–Amtrak Sta. (PT)	🚌♿	Ar	8 55P
			San Francisco, CA ✹ 🚌			
D 9 05A	9	Ar	–Ferry Bldg., Amtrak Sta.	🚌♿	Dp	8 30P
D 9 15A	10		–Fishermans Wharf, Pier 39	●		8 10P
9 30A	11	Ar	–S.F. Shopping Ctr., 835 Market	●	Dp	7 55P
8 00A	0	Dp	–S.F. Shopping Ctr., 835 Market	●	Ar	9 20P
8 15A	1		–Fishermans Wharf, Pier 39	●		D 9 05P
8 45A	2	Dp	–Ferry Bldg., Amtrak Sta.	🚌♿	Ar	D 8 50P
9 15A	11	Ar	*Oakland, CA*–Jack London Sq. ✹ (PT)	📷♿	Dp	8 25P

11 Daily ReadDown	Mile ▼		◄ Train Number ► / ◄ Days of Operation ►	Symbol	▲	14 Daily Read Up
			🚌 *Amtrak Thruway Connection—Vancouver, BC/Seattle, WA*			
6 00A	0	Dp	*Vancouver, BC*–Pacific Central Sta. ✹ (PT)	●	Ar	11 50P
6 15A	12		*Richmond, BC*–Delta Pacific Resort			11 20P
6 45A	29		*Surrey, BC*–Tudor Inn			10 50P
9 15A	144	Ar	*Seattle, WA* ✹ 🚌	⊘	Dp	8 30P
10 00A	0	Dp	Seattle, WA ✹ (PT) (Victoria, BC ⛴)	📷⊘♿	Ar	7 50P
10 57A	40		Tacoma, WA	📷♿		6 53P
11 43A	72		Olympia-Lacey, WA	●♿		6 09P
12 06P	94		Centralia, WA	📷♿		5 47P
12 52P	137		Kelso-Longview, WA	●♿		5 01P
1 35P	176		Vancouver, WA	📷♿		4 18P
1 55P	186	Ar	Portland, OR ✹	📷♿	Dp	3 55P
2 30P		Dp			Ar	3 20P
3 45P	239		Salem, OR	📷♿		1 20P
4 17P	267		Albany, OR (Corvallis)	📷♿		12 45P
5 07P	310		Eugene, OR (Springfield) ✹	📷♿		12 00N
8 07P	431		Chemult, OR	●♿		8 55A
10 07P	505		Klamath Falls, OR (Crater Lake ✹)	📷♿		7 42A
12 31A	611		Dunsmuir, CA (Mt. Shasta)	●♿		4 39A
2 19A	668		Redding, CA	●♿		2 52A
3 33A	742		Chico, CA	●♿		1 29A
4 16A	785		Marysville, CA (Yuba City)	●♿		12 46A
6 30A	837		Sacramento, CA ✹	📷♿		11 42P
6 50A	850		Davis, CA	📷♿		10 48P
7 45A	894		Martinez, CA	📷♿		9 58P
8 30A	921		Emeryville, CA	📷♿		9 20P
9 20A	926	Ar	Oakland, CA–Jack London Sq.	📷♿	Dp	8 30P
9 35A					Ar	8 15P
			🚌 *Amtrak Thruway Connection—Emeryville/Oakland/San Francisco—Schedule Below*			
10 30A	966	Dp	San Jose, CA (CalTrain)	📷♿ 🚌		7 20P
12 01P	1034		Salinas, CA (Monterey 🚌 ✹)	📷♿		5 45P
			🚌 *Amtrak Thruway Connection—Salinas/Monterey/Carmel—Schedule on Reverse*			
1 41P	1140		Paso Robles, CA	●♿		3 55P
3 30P	1167		San Luis Obispo, CA (Hearst Castle ✹)	📷♿		2 55P
67	1278		Goleta, CA	●	67	
6 17P	1286		Santa Barbara, CA ✹	📷♿		12 00N
7 10P	1323		Oxnard, CA	📷♿		11 02A
7 48P	1352		Simi Valley, CA	●♿		10 29A
8 30P	1384		Glendale, CA	31		9 48A
9 05P	1389	Ar	Los Angeles, CA ✹	📷♿	Dp	9 30A
			🚌 *Amtrak Thruway Connection—Emeryville/Oakland/San Francisco*			
8 35A	0	Dp	Emeryville, CA–Amtrak Sta. (PT)	🚌♿	Ar	8 55P
			San Francisco, CA ✹ 🚌			
D 9 05A	9	Ar	–Ferry Bldg., Amtrak Sta.	🚌♿	Dp	8 30P
D 9 15A	10		–Fishermans Wharf, Pier 39	●		8 10P
9 30A	11	Ar	–S.F. Shopping Ctr., 835 Market	●	Dp	7 55P
8 00A	0	Dp	–S.F. Shopping Ctr., 835 Market	●	Ar	9 20P
8 15A	1		–Fishermans Wharf, Pier 39	●		D 9 05P
8 45A	2	Dp	–Ferry Bldg., Amtrak Sta.	🚌♿	Ar	D 8 50P
9 15A	11	Ar	*Oakland, CA*–Jack London Sq. ✹ (PT)	📷♿	Dp	8 25P

The Coast Starlight I: Entering Data

Name(s): _____

You have the schedule for the Coast Starlight, an Amtrak train that runs from Seattle down to Los Angeles. The train trip actually takes two days. If you leave Seattle on Monday morning, you get to Los Angeles Tuesday night.

You need
   a schedule for the Coast Starlight

You'll learn how to
   add new attributes
   add new cases

Understanding the Schedule

Train schedules can be confusing. The schedule for our train is in the clear white area; the gray represents connecting trains and buses. This schedule shows both the northbound and southbound trains. We'll just go south, which means we'll take train #11—on the left side of the schedule.

Work with a partner to understand how to find the answers to these questions (the answers themselves are in parentheses; your job is to know how to get the answers):

1. When does the train leave Seattle? (10:00 a.m. on the first day.)
2. How many miles is it from Seattle to Portland? (186.)
3. What's the first stop after midnight on the trip? (Dunsmuir, 12:31 a.m.)
4. What's the next stop after Oakland? (San Jose.)
5. How many miles between Santa Barbara and Los Angeles? (103.)

Entering Data

Use Fathom to enter data from the schedule. Look at the columns of the train schedule and decide what information you might need. We'll be studying speed, so time and distance are important. Recording the names of the stations is useful, too.

At a minimum, you need attributes for

   station   (the station name)

   miles   (the next column—the number of miles from Seattle)

   hour   (the hour the train arrives)

   minute   (the minute the train arrives)

You may add any additional attributes you like. If you don't know how to add attributes, check the online **Help** menu.

Once you have those attributes, put your cursor in the first row. Now enter the data. Put the name of the city in **station**, the number of miles in **miles**, and the time in **hour** and **minute**. You should use a 24-hour clock for the time so that 5 p.m. is 17:00 (12 + 5). Your table should look something like the one shown here.

When you've finished, save your work.

One way to begin is to make a new document and then choose **Case Table** from the **Insert** menu.

To get a new attribute, click on the **<new>** box at the head of a column in the case table.

CoastStarlight			
	station	**miles**	**hour**	**minute**
9	Albany	267	16	17
10	Eugene	310	17	7
11	Sacrame...	837	6	30
12	Emeryville	921	8	30

Don't enter all the cities. Use all the stops from Seattle to Portland. Then focus on major cities: Salem, Eugene, Sacramento, Emeryville, Oakland, Santa Barbara, and Los Angeles. You don't have to enter the stations in order.

Data in Depth
© 2001 Key Curriculum Press

The Coast Starlight II: Studying Train Speed

Name(s): _____

You'll be studying a train called the Coast Starlight, which runs from Seattle, Washington, south to Los Angeles. How fast does it go? And does it go faster during some parts of its route and slower during other parts?

    You can figure out the speed by hand, but it will get tedious. For example, between Albany and Eugene, the train goes 43 miles in 50 minutes, which is 51.6 miles per hour. Is that typical? To find out, we'd have to do a lot of these calculations. Instead, we'll get the computer to help.

1. Choose **Open** from the **File** menu, select the name of the file you saved in *The Coast Starlight I: Entering Data* (e.g., **CoastStarlight**), and click **OK**. Be sure your file has the attributes for **station**, **miles**, **hour**, and **minute**. We'll use a scatter plot to help us study train speed.

2. Be sure a case table is showing. If not, select the collection and choose **Case Table** from the **Insert** menu. The table should appear and fill with data.

3. Make a new (empty) graph by choosing **Graph** from the **Insert** menu.

4. Drag the names of attributes from the table headers to the axes of the graph. Drag **hour** to the horizontal axis and **miles** to the vertical. You should see something like the graph shown here.

5. Why are there two lines of dots? The reason is because we didn't account for the fact that the train trip takes more than a single day. Notice: The bottom "line" of points is day 1; the top one (**miles** is larger) is day 2.

6. Make a new attribute and call it **day**. (Click the column heading **<new>** to the right of **minute**. Type **day** and press **ENTER**.)

7. For each station, put in **1** if the train arrives on the first day of the trip, and **2** if it arrives on the second. What is the first station of day 2?

8. Make another new attribute. Call it **time**.

9. Select the **time** label. Choose **Edit Formula** from the **Edit** menu. You'll get the formula editor, a window called **time formula**.

Notice that you didn't have to get it all perfect in order to start working with the data. With Fathom, you can mess up (e.g., forget that you needed the **day**) and fix it later.

10. Enter a formula that takes the **day** attribute into account. It will be good to have time in hours, so try this: **day * 24 + hour**. Do not enter the left-hand side of the equation, which would be **time =** .

11. To close the formula editor, click **OK**.

Prerequisite
The Coast Starlight I: Entering Data

You need
  a schedule for the Coast Starlight
  your data from that schedule

You'll learn
  about slope and speed
  how to write a formula for an attribute
  how to make a scatter plot
  how to add a line to a scatter plot

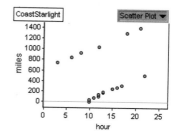

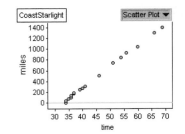

12. Replace **hour** on the graph with **time**: Drag the table header for **time** onto the (horizontal) axis where **hour** is now. The graph will be redrawn, and you will see a set of points that lie more along a line, as in the picture.

13. Optional: Note that **time** starts at thirtysomething hours. Adjust the formula so that it still gives hours, but starts at zero.

14. Get a movable line for the graph. Select the graph by clicking on it and then choose **Movable Line** from the **Graph** menu. Move the line to match the points as best you can.

15. Sketch your graph in the margin at right. Label the axes and scale the graph. Label Seattle, Oakland, and Los Angeles. Be sure to include the line and the equation for the line (it's at the bottom of the graph).

16. A train's average speed in miles per hour is the *slope* of the line its points lie on. That is, the equation looks like this: *miles* = *m* · *time* + *b*. The *m* is the slope (the speed). The *b* is the intercept. What is your slope? What are the units of that slope? Is that a reasonable speed?

Going Further

These tasks let you explore these data more deeply and challenge you further.

1. Verify (with a calculator or by hand, not with the computer) that the train's speed between Albany and Eugene is 51.6 miles per hour. Show that you know why that is the case.

2. Make a convincing argument that the slope of the line is the average speed. Consider, for example, what the slope would mean if you reversed the axes (i.e., if you put the time on the vertical axis and the miles on the horizontal one). Suggestion: Actually make that graph for comparison so you can see the two graphs side by side. See what slope you get, and figure out what it means.

3. In some places, the graph is vertical (e.g., between Seattle and Tacoma). That's an infinite (or undefined) slope. Surely that doesn't tell us the train's speed. The problem is that we've measured time only in hours—we haven't used the **minutes** attribute. Change the formula for **time** to take the minutes into account. Write down what you changed it to and why.

4. It looks as if the graph may be steeper at the beginning (near Seattle) and shallower at the end. If that's the case, the speed changes. Measure the speed in the two areas and see if it's really different. Describe how you measured the speeds—and include, for example, the range of cities your measurements cover.

5. According to the schedule, the train arrives in Portland at 1:55 and leaves at 2:30. That's a long time to be sitting there! Do this: Give your collection *two* cases for Portland, one when the train arrives and one when it leaves. How does that affect the graph? Sketch the graph in the vicinity of Portland. How does it affect your decisions about the train's speed?

Sonatas About Linear Data

Please read the more extensive description of this kind of assignment in *Sonatas for Data and Brain* on page xx. This page gives specific advice about the four Sonatas that follow.

The main idea in Sonatas is for students to predict or make conjectures. *Insist that students commit to their predictions and write them down before they see the data.* This is a great way to use class or homework time *before* you go to the lab. You can even assess the "prediction" work—as long as you assess it only in terms of its being sensible, not necessarily correct. Help students make *simple* mathematical models (i.e., all linear) but *daring* ones (i.e., imagining data they have not seen). Consider the first Sonata—predicting states' prison populations from the total state populations. Here are several levels of model, all acceptable depending on the students' experience:

- Qualitative: the more people, the more prisoners.

- Functional: the graph will be a straight line (it's proportional). The slope will be less than 1, because there are more people than prisoners.

- Functional with quantity: the above is true, and the slope is probably about 0.01.

- With context: the above is generally true, but some states (such as Georgia) will be on the high side, while others (such as Vermont) will be on the low side.

The Rehearsal

Sometimes students have a hard time getting started. For *The Prisoner Sonata*, we have created *Rehearsal: The Prisoner Sonata*—a step-by-step approach to finishing the Sonata. Students should get both pages—the rehearsal and the Sonata. The rehearsal tells them what to fill in on the Sonata page itself.

The Activities

- **Sonata 1: The Prisoner Sonata**—predicting the number of prisoners in a state given the population.

- **Sonata 2: Tall Buildings**—predicting the height of a tall building given the number of stories.

- **Sonata 3: Airliners and Fuel Cost**—predicting the hourly cost of fuel (in dollars per hour) given the rate at which fuel burns in gallons per hour.

- **Sonata 4: Batter Up!**—explaining a limit in the graph of at-bats as a function of games. **Note:** The first part of this Sonata must be done offline.

- Four open-ended computer activities
- Data from files
- Student pages 54–58
- *Independent, basic features

Topics
slope in nonspeed contexts
reading scatter plots

Math required
exposure to slope

Materials
data files, as listed

Students need to be able to
open files
make graphs
use movable lines

In fact, the first part of the first four Sonatas is called "Prediction" instead of "Conjecture" because the assignment tells the students what to predict rather than letting them come up with their own ideas.

*No Fathom experience needed if you use the "rehearsal."

Units epiphany: The slope of the line is the price of fuel in dollars per gallon.

Teacher Notes

Discussion Questions

↻ What do you think constitutes a good response to this kind of assignment? (You can go on to have students help develop an assessment rubric.)

↻ This kind of assignment is more "open" in that it doesn't tell the student, step by step, how to get it done. What do you like or dislike about assignments like this?

Why Lines and Not Just Ratios

We spend a lot of time in this chapter making scatter plots and the lines that model the data. For example, in *The Prisoner Sonata*, pages 54–55, we graph number of prisoners against population. The line we fit to the data is a model of the number of prisoners as a function of the population. The function helps us predict: We can plug in the population and get a number of prisoners. We can also use the formula to tell whether a state has an unusually high or low number of prisoners compared to the model (and therefore compared to other states). In this case, the formula (for a least-squares line that passes through the origin) is **Prisoners = 0.0051 * Persons.**

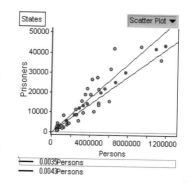

But why use a scatter plot? We could, instead, make a new attribute, **PercentInPrison**, and just look at that percentage. The average value for the states is 0.40%, so if we had 10,000,000 people in a state, we'd expect it to have 40,000 prisoners. A histogram of these percentages is an interesting and useful representation, and it gives a perspective that the scatter plot can't give.

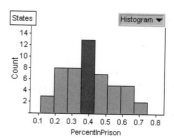

If you look at the graphs, the lines in the scatter plot are lines of equal *ratio*. They're at slopes of 0.0035 and 0.0043. These are the same as the boundaries for the tall bin in the histogram. So you can think of each bin in the histogram as representing a wedge-shaped slice of the scatter plot. Great, right?

Yet this histogram is, by its nature, a summary. When you take the ratio and create the histogram, you are leaving out information—that's why it looks simpler than the scatter plot. So we begin with the scatter plot: It is a *case plot*—that is, it represents each case separately—and it shows all the information.

What can make an analysis based on ratios go wrong? Here are two dangers:

- Plots of ratios work well only if the intercept is zero. If there is a meaningful intercept (e.g., in the **Buildings** data), plotting the ratios will mask that fact.

- A plot of ratio alone does not show how that ratio might depend on the attributes. In the prison data, for example, the histogram doesn't show you how the most populous states have a greater proportion of prisoners (as well as a greater absolute number).

Therefore, at least look at the scatter plot before you change everything to a proportion.

That said, making proportions is a valuable tool. It's especially useful when you compare things whose sizes are unequal—such as these states. We'll explore proportion and per-unit attributes more extensively in Chapter 3, *Per Portions*.

Rehearsal: The Prisoner Sonata

Name(s): _____

Use this page to guide you in how to fill out the Sonata page that follows. Future Sonata pages will not have these helpful hints!

The instructions say we'll study the relationship between population and the number of prisoners in the states. A good first step is to make a graph. Each state (and the District of Columbia) is a case. The two attributes are **Persons** and **Prisoners**.

1. Before you touch the computer, think about the situation. First, make a prediction. Predict exactly what the relationship will be. Write the entire equation in the Prediction section of the Sonata page. Also sketch a graph—with labeled axes—that shows the relationship. Put **Persons** on the horizontal axis and **Prisoners** on the vertical axis.

2. According to your relationship, how many prisoners would there be in a state of 10,000,000 people? Write that in the Prediction section too. *This is a conjecture. You don't have to be right—just reasonable.*

3. Open the file **States.**

4. Make a new graph by choosing **Graph** from the **Insert** menu.

5. Drag the attribute name—the column header—**Persons** to the horizontal axis and **Prisoners** to the vertical. A scatter plot should appear.

6. Add a movable line and adjust it to fit the data. Choose **Lock Intercept at Zero** from the **Graph** menu to get the "no-intercept" form.

7. Write what you just did ("I made a scatter plot with . . . ") in the middle section of the Sonata.

8. How is the graph like—and unlike—the one you predicted in Step 2? Write your answer in the Comparison section, and sketch the actual graph there.

9. Go further. Impress your teacher by pursuing questions like these:

- Which states have the highest and lowest *rates* of incarceration? You may need a new attribute, **PercentInPrison**, to study this.

- What other attributes (if any) are related to incarceration?

- What other relationships among attributes do you see or suspect?

- How accurate do you think your estimate for the number of prisoners in a state with 10,000,000 people is? (That is, how large or small could it be before you were surprised?)

Keep it simple: In general, states with bigger populations will have more prisoners. Now we make our prediction quantitative. The number of prisoners will be smaller than the population, so the relationship may be something like this:

Prisoners =
Persons * (number between 0 and 1)

To make it specific, you have to choose a number between 0 and 1. What fraction of the people do you think are in prison?

You can also make a graph by dragging one off of the shelf.

Choose **Movable Line** from the **Graph** menu. If you don't see the **Graph** menu, click on the graph.

Sonata 1: The Prisoner Sonata

Name(s): _____

In this Sonata, you'll study data about the 50 states plus the District of Columbia. You'll find the data in the file **States.** These data come from the 1990 U.S. Census.

You need
   States

The Question

How is the population of a state related to the number of people in its prisons?

You'll show that you can
   make a prediction about a
      numerical relationship
   make scatter plots

Prediction

The relevant attributes are **Persons** (which is the total population) and **Prisoners** (which is the number of incarcerated people in the state). How do you predict the two quantities will be related? And about how many prisoners would you predict for a state with 10,000,000 people?

Draw a scatter plot of your prediction. Put **Persons** on the horizontal axis and **Prisoners** on the vertical axis.

Measurement

Do the analysis in Fathom. Describe *briefly* what you did:

Comparison

Use Fathom to compare your prediction to the data. Report what you found out. Refine your description of the relationship between population and prisoners. Describe the relationship as you see it now.

It's OK if your predictions weren't exact! This is the place where you describe any surprises in the data and any additional considerations you think people should take into account. Sketching another graph that illustrates your points is good.

Sonata 2: Tall Buildings

Name(s): _____

In this Sonata, you'll study data about the tallest buildings in Minnesota and Florida. You'll find the data in the file **Buildings.** These data come from the World Wide Web.

The Question

How is the height of a building related to the number of stories it has?

Prediction

The relevant attributes are **height** (which is the height of the building in feet) and **stories** (the number of stories). How do you predict the two quantities will be related? In particular, about how many feet do you think there are per story?

Measurement

Analyze the data using Fathom. Be sure to use a movable line. Describe *briefly* what you did:

Comparison

Use Fathom to compare your prediction to the data. Report what you found out. Refine your description of the relationship between height and number of stories. Develop a rule of thumb (a simple calculation) you can use to predict the height of a building from the number of stories. Describe that rule:

You need
Buildings

You'll show that you can
make a prediction about a numerical relationship
make scatter plots
use a movable line
develop a rule of thumb

This is a good place to describe anything else you noticed or can explain. For example, is there any difference between Minnesota and Florida? Can you explain both the slope and the intercept of any line you used?

Sonata 3: Airliners and Fuel Cost

Name(s): _____

This Sonata uses data about commercial airliners and their fuel use. You'll find the data in the file **Airplanes.** These data come from the World Wide Web.

You need

Airplanes

You'll show that you can
   make a prediction about a
     numerical relationship
   make scatter plots
   use a movable line
   develop a rule of thumb

The Question

How is fuel use (in gallons per hour) related to fuel cost (in dollars per hour)? Clearly, the more you use, the more it will cost in general. But what exactly will the relationship be?

Prediction

The relevant attributes are **fuelgph** (which is the fuel use in gallons per hour) and **costph** (the fuel cost in dollars per hour). How do you predict the two quantities will be related?

Eventually, you'll create a rule of thumb for predicting the cost per hour if you know the fuel use.

Measurement

Analyze the data using Fathom. Make a scatter plot and consider using a movable line. Describe *briefly* what you did:

Comparison

Use Fathom to compare your prediction to the data. Report what you found out. Refine your description of the relationship between fuel cost and fuel use. Develop a rule of thumb (a simple calculation) you can use to predict the hourly fuel cost for an airliner given the number of gallons it burns in an hour.

This is a good place to describe anything else you noticed or can explain. For example, do any other attributes seem to be correlated with each other? What is the meaning of the slope of the line that you get? Can you explain why the relationship is not a completely straight line?

Sonata 4: Batter Up!

Name(s): _____

These data are from the 1996 National League baseball season. There is one case for each hitter. In the graph, the vertical axis is **AB**, or the number of times at bat. This is roughly the number of times the player is "up," except that walks (bases on balls) and sacrifices (e.g., bunts) don't count as at-bats. The horizontal axis is the number of **games** the player was in.

You need
Baseball96

You'll show that you can
interpret the edge of a cloud of points
make scatter plots
use a movable line

The Task

Looking at the graph, you can see that the upper edge of the cloud of points seems to fall along a straight line. Your job is to predict, and then find out, as much as possible about that line. What is its slope? Its intercept? What are the scales of the axes? What kind of player is right on the line? What kind of player lies below it? And why does that line exist? While some knowledge of baseball can help, you can still figure out what's going on even if you know little of the game.

Conjecture

Below, write your best guess for the equation of the line in terms of **games**, the attribute on the horizontal axis. Explain it as best you can. Sketch the graph of the line *on the graph of the data* in the margin. Before you see the data on the computer, label and scale the axes, and make a conjecture about why the "limit" line exists in the graph.

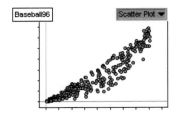

Measurement

Open **Baseball96** (or a more recent file). Explore the data. Make the scatter plot. Use a movable line to find the actual equation for the line. Record that equation here:

Comparison

How did your predicted graph compare to the actual graph? How did you do on the equation? Having seen the actual data, how would you modify what you wrote about them? In particular, why do you think the line exists?

Data in Depth
© 2001 Key Curriculum Press

Sonatas About Lines and Geometry

- Three open-ended computer activities
- Data from measurements
- Student pages 60–62
- Independent, basic features

Here are more open-ended, conjecture-oriented Sonatas. They are also more geometrical. For each Sonata, students can either use physical objects (round tables and jar lids for circles; rectangles cut from strips of paper) or dynamic geometry software, such as *The Geometer's Sketchpad®*, to make and measure the figures that become the cases in their collections.

The situations—the relationship of circumference to radius and the proportions of pleasant-looking rectangles—have a good chance of producing proportional data.

Sonata 5: What R π?

This activity is accessible to younger students, but watch out for several things:

First, be sure that students use the string to measure the circumference directly. If they measure the diameter and then *calculate* the circumference, they will see a proportional relationship—but they will have missed the point!

Finally, as mentioned in *Why Lines and Not Just Ratios*, page 53, students might simply make a new attribute that is the ratio of one to the other. In that case, it's more appropriate to make a *univariate* plot, such as a histogram or box plot, and calculate the mean or median. While that analysis makes some sense, a histogram of these π-ratios doesn't tell you whether the ratio is the same for circles of all sizes. This is especially important if you follow this activity with *What R π, the Cool Version,* page 67, where doing the ratio alone obscures the importance of the intercept. So, honor the ingenuity of the histogram or box plot, but insist on the scatter plot and the line.

Sonata 6: The Book Cover

The Book Cover is straightforward and is an exercise in informal similarity, made more formal through measurement.

Sonata 7: Everybody's Favorite Rectangle

Everybody's Favorite Rectangle is more subtle. Some think that people will generally pick golden rectangles, in which case the slope of **length** vs. **width** will be either about 1.6 or 0.6. The suggestion of using rectangular strips at least four times as long as they are wide is to keep subjects from being influenced by the shape of the strip.

The admonition in *What R π?* to create the scatter plot (and not just the ratio) holds here as well.

This activity is connected to the *Fibonacci* Sonata, page 172, since the ratio of two adjacent Fibonacci numbers approaches this same golden ratio, Φ (the Greek letter phi).

Topics
circles
proportion
similarity
interpreting slope
measurement

Materials
varied—see student sheets

Students need to be able to
make collections
make graphs
add lines to graphs

The Answer!

For **circumference** and **diameter**, the proportion is π, of course; if students plot **circumference** on the vertical axis, π will be the slope of the line. If they do it the other way (**diameter** on the vertical) they will get a slope of 1/π, or about 0.318. If they use **radius** instead of **diameter**, they will get correspondingly different slopes: about 6.28 or 0.159.

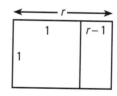

A golden rectangle is one that, if you cut the largest possible square out of it, leaves a rectangle similar to the original one.

$$\frac{r}{1} = \frac{1}{r-1}$$

$$r^2 - r - 1 = 0$$

$$r = \frac{1 + \sqrt{5}}{2}$$

Many math books use a capital Greek phi (Φ) for this value.

Sonata 5: What R π?

Name(s): _____

What is the relationship between circumference and diameter? If you already know, predict how well real measurements will conform to your understanding. If not, just try to predict what will happen.

You need

paper and compass or
The Geometer's Sketchpad or
many circular objects of
 different sizes;
rulers and string or measuring
 tapes

Conjecture

What is the relationship between the circumference and the diameter of various circles? Sketch the way you think the graph of **circumference** as a function of **diameter** will look. Be sure to scale your axes.

You'll show that you can

measure carefully
enter data
make scatter plots
interpret slope

Measurement

Either construct (e.g., with a compass or with *The Geometer's Sketchpad*®) or find and measure a variety of circles. For each circle, measure its **circumference** and its **diameter.** Those are the two essential attributes. Enter the data in Fathom. Make the scatter plot. Try to model the data with a line. Briefly describe what you did (how you got your circles, how you measured circumference and diameter, what you plotted, and so on) and sketch the scatter plot and its line:

To measure the circumference of a circular object, lay the string around its circumference, then straighten the string to measure.

To get the movable line in Fathom, select the scatter plot and choose **Movable Line** from the **Graph** menu.

Comparison

How did your conjecture hold up? Describe and explain any surprises. Does a single line fit all the data? What is the slope of the line (or lines)?

Sonata 6: The Book Cover

Name(s): _____

This Sonata is about shape. We want to find out how well people can draw a rectangle similar to a given rectangle. Recruit at least one person to be in your study. Each person is a "subject." You also need one book (any book).

Prepare one sheet of paper for each subject. (If enough people are doing this, prepare one sheet and have copies made.) About 2 cm from the left edge, carefully draw line segments 10 mm, 30 mm, and 50 mm long. Then, about 2 cm from the right, draw segments 60 mm, 40 mm, and 20 mm long.

Give the book and this sheet of paper to the subject. Tell the subject to draw six rectangles, using each of the segments you have drawn as one of the sides of a rectangle. Each rectangle should be the same shape as (i.e., similar to) the cover of the book. The subject may *not* use a ruler.

Thus, each case will be a rectangle. The important attributes will be the **length** and **width** of the rectangle. You may also want to record the name of the **subject** (so you can identify the subjects later).

You need
paper, prepared as described
ruler
people for your study
a book (any book)

You'll show that you can
measure
enter data
make scatter plots
make lines
interpret slope

Conjecture

Before you begin, imagine the results. What will a scatter plot of **length** versus **width** look like? Sketch it. Is there a pattern? Can you find a formula relating **length** and **width** for most points? Decide how many subjects you want to use (one may be plenty, depending on how experienced you are).

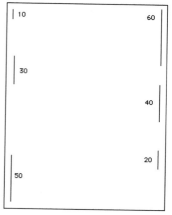

Your sheet of paper will look something like this (without the numbers written on it).

Measurement

Now collect data. Take the book and sheet to your subject(s). Then measure the results and enter them into Fathom. Sketch the scatter plot to the right and summarize any immediate results.

Comparison

Compare your results to your conjecture. What did you get right? What did you miss? What additional considerations did you uncover? Make some conclusions: What can you say about people's ability to draw similar rectangles?

Sonata 7: Everybody's Favorite Rectangle

Name(s): _____

This Sonata is all about shape and proportion. We want to find out what rectangle shape people prefer. (Some people think that we naturally prefer a shape called the "golden rectangle.")

You need
  paper, cut into strips
  ruler
  scissors
  people for your study

You'll show that you can
  measure
  enter data
  make scatter plots
  make lines
  interpret slope
  interpret variability

Procedure

Prepare strips of paper of different widths. Each strip should be at least four times as long as it is wide. They should be at least 2 cm wide. Find people (you have to choose them) to be subjects in your study. Ask each subject to cut a rectangle off the end of one strip. They should cut the rectangle to have as pleasant a shape (to them) as possible.

Each case will be a rectangle. The important attributes will be the **length** and **width** of the rectangle. You may also want to record the name of the **subject** (so you can identify the subject later on).

Conjecture

Before you begin, imagine the results. What will a scatter plot of **length** versus **width** look like? Sketch it. Is there a pattern? Can you figure out the math behind it (e.g., is there a formula relating **length** and **width** for most points)?

Measurement

Before you collect data, decide *exactly* how you are going to ask the subject to do the task. Write it down. Now collect data. Take the strips and scissors to your subjects. Then measure the results and enter them into Fathom. Sketch the scatter plot here and summarize any immediate results:

Comparison

Compare your results to your conjecture. What did you get right? What did you miss? What additional ideas did you uncover? Make some conclusions: What can you say about people's favorite rectangle shape?

Look up *golden ratio* or *golden rectangle* in a math book or on the Web. Did the people you asked clip out golden rectangles?

Explaining Patterns

• Open-ended computer activity
• Data from files
• Student page 64
• Independent, basic features

This assignment is simple to explain and hard to do. Students look for patterns in data, and try to explain the patterns that they see.

One kind of explanation is to model the data with lines (or, eventually, some other function); another is to propose explanations telling why the pattern exists.

The assignment page lists many possible tasks for the students. You may not want them to do all of these, so look them over ahead of time and tell students which you will be collecting.

These are appropriate as homework assignments depending on access to technology.

Students can read descriptions of the files in the documents themselves. Sometimes the comments are in the comments pane of the inspectors. These comments often include interesting questions and directions to pursue.

These files are particularly relevant to this chapter; they include the ones used in the Sonatas we have seen. For the Sonata files (e.g., **Airplanes** or **Baseball96**), students are to look for different patterns from the ones they may already have investigated as Sonatas.

Topics
proportion
interpreting slope
interpreting intercepts
relationships among attributes

Materials
various files

Students need to be able to
make collections
make graphs
add lines to graphs
make new attributes
define attributes by formula
define filters

What's Important Here

- Students become increasingly comfortable using lines to model data.
- Students become increasingly skilled at interpreting the slope of a model line: they give it units; they can reason about slope; they can invent problems using the slope.

Discussion Questions

Besides exploring the questions on the assignment sheet further—especially any you decided *not* to collect—here are some ideas for discussion questions:

➲ What would the units of the slope be if you switched the axes on your plot? What would the slope mean?

➲ What would the numerical value of the slope be if you did that?

What's the Difference Between These and the Sonatas?

There's an intentional trade-off here for students who have done some Sonatas. These are less demanding in that they don't require making conjectures. Instead, they present much stranger and more difficult data—difficult in different ways. Sometimes the data are not really well correlated, or there's a "limit" line, or the data are linear for a while and then are not.

Of course, you can make these data sets and questions into Sonatas easily, if your students know the form from previous assignments—just insist on a write-up in the appropriate form, especially including a conjecture written before they look at the data.

Explaining Patterns

Name(s): _____

In this assignment, you look for patterns in data and try to explain the patterns you see. One way to "explain" a pattern is to model the data with lines. Another way is to propose explanations telling why the pattern exists.

    Choose one of the data sets that follow and investigate it with Fathom. Turn in the following tasks. You will need to use your own paper.

1. For at least one pair of attributes, sketch the scatter plot that Fathom makes when you graph them against one another.

2. Sketch in a good "movable line" you used that models the data (or something about the data) and record its equation.

3. Using coordinates of points on the line, calculate the slope by hand and show that the computer's slope is correct (if it is).

4. Interpret the slope. What does the slope mean? For example, when you timed your reading, the slope was the number of centimeters you read each second.

5. Is your intercept zero? If so, why? If not, why not—and what does your intercept mean?

6. Write a math question you can answer easily if you know the slope.

7. Explain why the two attributes are related the way they are. If you have any doubt about your explanation, include an additional, different explanation.

8. Sometimes a good line goes through the data; sometimes it's a limit—a line that goes along the edge of the data. Which is yours and why? (You can see a good example of the "limit" situation in the baseball data.)

The Files

Airplanes.ftm	Data on airliners.
Baseball96.ftm	1996 National League hitters.
Buildings.ftm	The tallest buildings in Minnesota and Florida.
CACounties.ftm	Education and more in the 58 California counties.
HeatingAndCooling.ftm	Temperature as a function of time.
SATGPA.ftm	SAT scores and GPAs for 1000 college freshmen.
States.ftm	Demographic information on the states.
States-Traffic.ftm	Information about cars and driving in the states.
States-SAT.ftm	For a negative correlation, look at SAT as a function of percentage of students taking the test; for a positive one, look at Math vs. Verbal.
Radiosonde.ftm	Balloon ascent data: temperature vs. height.
ModelWeightMPG.ftm	About cars. Look at weight vs. MPG.

The World Is Linear

- Six open-ended computer activities
- Data from students
- Student pages 66–67
- Independent, basic features

It is good to mix data files from out in the world with data students measure and enter themselves. We hope that it will make the data more real, and also support a healthy skepticism—after all, the data you download may be no better than your own.

These are different from the *Explaining Patterns* materials in that students get the data themselves instead of reading computer files. These, therefore, are more appropriate as Sonatas, since students may have experiences that will lead to more plausible conjectures. Thus, you may think of these as "Sonata starters," though write-ups of other kinds will work equally well.

Topics
proportion
interpreting slope
interpreting intercepts
relationships among attributes
measurement

Materials
these vary—see student pages

Students need to be able to
make collections
make graphs
add lines to graphs
make new attributes
define attributes by formula

What's Important Here

- As with other assignments in this chapter, slope and linear models are central.

- Measurement—the process of going out into the real world and finding out how big, how long, how many—*always* presents us with unexpected challenges. Dealing with these appropriately is part of being mathematically powerful. Students need to be able to decide what to do about hard-to-measure situations. They also need to develop a reflex about documentation—describing in writing what they did and what assumptions they made.

Discussion Questions

➲ What did you plot against what? What did that graph tell you?

➲ What line did you find in your data? What does its slope mean?

➲ What problems did you have collecting your data?

➲ What decisions or assumptions did you have to make in deciding what numbers to use?

➲ Did you modify the original assignment in any way? If so, how—and why?

Tech Note

As with any more open-ended assignment, students may need Fathom skills you haven't covered. Encourage them to use the help system and share what they learn.

Additional Note on What R π, the Cool Version

Make sure students actually tie the knot, or they will lose the "coolness" of this activity (some students, for example, tape the ends together).

The World Is Linear

Name(s): _____

Here are ideas for measurements that will result in data that are more or less linear.

Library Research

Measure the **thickness** of books in millimeters and count the number of **pages.** How are they related? Are there any other relevant attributes? Extension: Use this relationship to estimate the number of pages in the library altogether. You may want to record the **titles** of the books as well so you can identify strange outliers.

You need
library or varied books
millimeter rulers

Here are some extensions and follow-up questions:

- How did you count the pages? Did you count pages or sheets? Why?

- How did you decide how many measurements to make?

- In what kinds of jobs would this information be useful?

- Predict the number of pages in the biggest dictionary you can find. Then check. How good was your prediction? If it was bad, explain why.

- Is the relationship between the attributes different for different kinds of books?

- In your measurements, did you include the covers? Why or why not?

In Hot Water

Measure the **temperature** of water as a function of **time** while it is being heated to boiling. This has many interesting extensions that go beyond the limited scope of this chapter. For example:

You need
kitchen or chem lab
saucepans or beakers
thermometers
clocks or watches

- Measure the temperature as it cools (see *Cooling Off,* page 194).

- Make similar measurements for different volumes of water.

- Measure volume as a function of time as water boils away (the challenge is to measure volumes of boiling water) or evaporates.

In Cold Water

Measure the **temperature** of water as a function of the number of ice **cubes** you put in it. Stir briefly after each addition. This has the virtue of being one of the few situations we could find that produces a straight line of negative slope.

You need
water and a container
ice cubes
thermometer

What R π, the Cool Version

Cut string into various lengths. For each string, measure the length to get an attribute, **length**. Then, tie the ends together to make a loop. (Just make a knot; don't be fancy.) Next, make a circle out of each loop. Measure its **diameter**. Predict, then study, the relationship between **length** and **diameter**. How will it be different from the geometrical version?

Note: This is more interesting if you measure the string before you tie the knots. See if you can explain why.

You need
string
rulers or tape measures

Pencil Sharpener

This requires the sacrifice of a few pencils. Measure a pencil, then put it in a pencil sharpener for ten cranks (manual) or five seconds (electric). Record the new length. Do the same for different numbers of cranks or seconds. In this scheme, you have three attributes: **before, after,** and **cranks** (or **seconds**). How will they be related? A final task might be predicting how many cranks (or seconds) it takes to devour a new pencil.

There may be other ways to set up the attributes, or other ways to look at the problem, and other questions you can ask. Do different people sharpen pencils at different rates? Do different kinds of pencils sharpen differently? Is there a way to relate how dull a pencil is to how many cranks are needed to sharpen it?

You need
pencils (not for writing)
pencil sharpener
ruler

Miler

Go to a quarter-mile track with someone who is willing to run a mile. (Extension: You can have more than one runner and compare data if you wish.) You will probably need more than one person to collect the data. Devise a system for observing the runner and counting strides. The goal is to record the total, *cumulative* number of strides since the beginning of the mile at each sixteenth of a mile, that is, each quarter of the way around the track. (So if it takes 100 strides to go 1/16 mile, you get 100 at the first point and 200 at the second, and so forth.) Naturally we expect something fairly linear, but what will its slope be? If it's not linear, will it get shallower at the end or get steeper? Predict first!

Of course, there are other potential investigations here having to do with time. If you invent one, you'll need clocks or stopwatches.

You need
track
runner
helpers

Per Portions

3

Why do we have percentages? One reason is to compare populations of unequal size.

Whether we're doing data analysis or just being skeptical citizens, the question of whether to compare proportions or absolute numbers comes up all the time. For example, suppose your school and another school (Eastside, say) compare their student body budgets. You get a budget of $10,000 per year, while Eastside gets only $5,000. Does that mean you're the richer school? Maybe. But you have 2000 students in your school, while Eastside has only 500. Now what do you think? Your budget is $5 *per student,* while Eastside's is $10 *per student.* The $10,000 is an *absolute* quantity. "$5 per student" is a *proportion.*

Both quantities—the absolute and the proportion—are important. Can you pay $6,000 for a band? You have to look at the absolute. Can you afford food that costs $5.50 per person? Better look at the proportion.

One thing we often forget: When we make a per-unit quantity, we're taking an average. We're throwing information away. If the per-capita income is $22,000, does that mean that the person walking down the street is likely to earn that much? No way. It doesn't even mean that $22,000 is *typical.* It's just an average. It ignores the distribution, and it ignores individual cases. If you're the one in a car accident in Rhode Island, it doesn't matter that Rhode Island looks pretty safe on the average.

Nevertheless, these quantities are always convenient, and often the most relevant way to characterize and compare groups.

Level

Studying proportion is appropriate even for students in the middle grades. Some of the activities in this chapter are suitable for seventh- or eighth-grade mathematics, and certainly for the traditional ninth-grade algebra class. However, many third year students have problems with proportion; these activities are not too easy for them.

The Activities

- **A Return to Prison** looks again at the data about prisoners in the 50 states. You could use it as a follow-up to *The Prisoner Sonata* page 55. Students make a new, proportional attribute (the proportion of prisoners in each state) for the first time. This activity includes a "warm-up" offline sheet, *Introduction to "Per" Quantities,* that you may want to assign before any of the activities in this chapter.

The Geography of U.S. Cars is really three activities.

- **The Geography of U.S. Cars** introduces some of our car data. Students study vehicles per person and miles per vehicle.

- **The Geography of U.S. Cars II: Total It Up** introduces Fathom's summary table. Students use it to find means and sums of attributes, among other things. We use this to demonstrate that the mean of a group of proportions is not the same as the overall proportion. ("You can't average averages.")

- **The Geography of U.S. Cars III: Unsafe in Any State** introduces the ghoulish but fascinating car accident data file. In it, we compute proportions (such as miles driven per fatality) and their reciprocals (fatalities per mile driven). Usually, one of the two is more understandable than the other.

- **Saved by the Belt** asks how many people were saved by seat belts in the U.S. in 1992. This is an estimation question that requires serious, brain-numbing thinking, even though seventh-graders could do the arithmetic. Good thing there's a page of hints . . .

- **Car Sonatas.** This is a series of four relatively open-ended activities, all based on the automobile data from earlier in the chapter. Some have surprising results.

- **More Car Stuff** is a collection of rich questions and ideas for Sonatas or short projects.

- **Per in the World** is a chance to escape from cars (at last) and see a few other contexts where these per-unit quantities help you think about problems. Like *More Car Stuff,* these questions are less structured and could become Sonatas or small projects.

Objectives

- Students hear "per" quantities all the time, especially *per capita,* but they may not know how to use them. This chapter gives them plenty of practice creating various per quantities—many of them in an automotive context.

- Students can use per-unit quantities to compare groups of different size and learn that the consequence of this is that proportion (or percentage) is often more important and interesting than absolute number.

A Return to Prison

• Structured computer activity
• Data from file
• Student pages 72–75
• Intermediate, basic features

Teacher Notes

Depending on your students' experience, you may want to give them *Introduction to "Per" Quantities* as a reading and homework assignment. This is too easy for more advanced students; you may want to skip that—or this activity—altogether. On the other hand, many teachers have been surprised at what their "advanced" students still do not know!

What's Important Here

- We use rates and proportions to compare things of unequal size—especially when comparing magnitudes directly is unfair. For example, the fact that California has the most prisoners doesn't make it the most jail-happy state. Its high incarceration *rate* tells that story more accurately.

- This is a "ratio" perspective on the prisoner data, illuminated somewhat in the "What's Going On Here?" page on ratios (page 53).

- A *rate* is not always a speed. Here we calculate per-capita rates—or percentages—that are very common in statistics about our world.

Discussion Questions

➲ How did you use Fathom to find the states with the largest and smallest rates of incarceration? (This is a chance to let students inform one another of different techniques. Some will have just looked, others may have sorted, and so on.)

➲ Point out that many "per capita" rates are per 100,000 people (this is especially true of mortality and disease data). Have students make a new attribute, **PrisonersPer100K**, that produces that figure for each state. Discuss how to make the formula and what it means. Then discuss how the original proportions (about 0.005), the percentages (about 0.5), and these new values (about 500) all really mean the same thing. What are the advantages and disadvantages of using one over the other?

➲ Did what you found out about the states fit your impressions of them? Did you notice any regional differences in incarceration rates?

Extensions

- Have students look on the Internet to find incarceration rates for other countries. Enter them into Fathom, or simply compare those values to the range of values for the U.S.

- Have students make a new attribute, **region**, and code each state for the part of the country it's in. Then do regional comparisons.

Topics
proportion
interpreting rates
relationships among attributes
U.S. states

Materials
States

Students need to be able to
open files
make scatter plots
make histograms

Connection
These are the same data we studied in *The Prisoner Sonata*.

Introduction to "Per" Quantities

Name(s): _____

For each of the situations below, you get data. Make proportions and compare what is indicated.

You need
calculator

1. Last year, Dave drove 8700 miles in his 1985 Lada and spent $1,950 on gas, maintenance, and insurance. Thalia spent only $1,675 on her Yugo, but she drove only 6950 miles. Compare the amounts they spent per mile.

2. Out of the 52 weeks of the year, Thalia's Yugo was being worked on for 6 weeks. She also didn't drive it for 6 weeks when she was away during the summer. Dave's Lada was out of commission only 2 weeks, and he stayed in town. Compare the numbers of miles they drove per week.

3. Dave's insurance costs $1,000 per year, while Thalia's costs only $800. Dave spent $300 on maintenance, while Thalia spent $500. Compare the amounts they spent per mile on gas alone.

4. Gas costs $1.40 per gallon. Compute the number of miles per gallon each car gets.

5. Looking back on the "miles per week" question (#2) above, describe a situation or pose a question where the total, absolute mileage is most relevant.

6. Do the same, but where the per-week mileage is most relevant.

Data in Depth
© 2001 Key Curriculum Press

A Return to Prison

Name(s): _____

In this activity, we'll study data about the number of prisoners in each state. If you have done *The Prisoner Sonata,* you have already seen these data. We'll treat the data differently here. If you haven't done that Sonata, don't worry— it's not a prerequisite.

This activity helps you learn to use Fathom to calculate per-unit quantities (such as per-capita amounts and other rates). Later activities in this chapter will give you practice using these skills in other contexts.

You need to know how to
make a scatter plot
make a histogram

You'll learn how to
make a new attribute
use the formula editor

1. Open the file **States.** You'll see a data set of the states, their populations, and the number of prisoners each has incarcerated. You'll also see other attributes. These data are from the 1990 U.S. Census.

2. Make a scatter plot of the number of **Prisoners** (vertical axis) as a function of the population (**Persons**—put it on the horizontal). As you can see, in general, the more people in the state, the more prisoners.

But what's the proportion of people in prison in each state? We need a new attribute to figure it out.

3. Make a new attribute by clicking in the **<new>** box at the top of the last column in the case table. Name it **PrisonProp** for "prisoner proportion."

4. Make a formula for the attribute. Select it and choose **Edit Formula** from the **Edit** menu. In the formula editor, enter **Prisoners / Persons**. It will look like the picture. Click **OK** to close the formula editor. Fathom calculates the values.

5. Make another new attribute, **PrisonPct** (for "prisoner percentage"). Give it the formula **100 * (Prisoners / Persons)**. That will move the numbers into a more convenient range, as shown.

Note that the numbers you get—for example, 0.47 for Alabama—are *percentages* because of the **100 *** we put in the formula. That is, 0.47 people are in prison for every 100 in the population. So that's 4.7 per 1000, 47 per 10,000, and so forth.

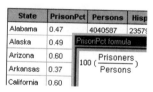

State	PrisonPct	Persons	Hisp
Alabama	0.47	4040587	23579
Alaska	0.49		
Arizona	0.60		
Arkansas	0.37		
California	0.60		

In this picture, we have moved the new attribute to a more convenient place in the table by dragging its name—the column head—in the case table.

6. Find the states with the highest and lowest values for incarceration rates (that is, highest and lowest **PrisonPct**). What are the states and the rates?

7. Write the names of the states with the highest and lowest *numbers* of prisoners below.

Name(s): _____

8. Comment on whether the states in the last two questions are the same or different. How can that be?

9. Make a histogram of the incarceration rates. Sketch it (with labeled axes) at right. What is a typical value for an incarceration rate? How did you choose it?

10. Make a scatter plot of **PrisonPct** (vertical) as a function of the population (**Persons**). Sketch it at right.

	Low population	**High population**
High incarceration rate		
Low incarceration rate		

11. Put the names of two or three states in each of the cells in the table above. One of the cells should be empty (there are no such states). What does that mean?

12. Brenda says, "Big states not only put more people in prison, they put a bigger percentage of people in prison." Below, describe the ways in which Brenda is both right and wrong.

Practice on a Different Attribute

13. Make a new attribute that shows the percentage of the population aged 85 or over. Write its formula.

14. Make a box plot of it. Sketch the box plot below. Which state is the outlier?

15. Suggest an explanation for why that state is an outlier.

Data in Depth
© 2001 Key Curriculum Press

Going Further

HTI, a think tank, publishes a report that says, "These data on the states confirm what we know by common sense: Crime is worst in low-income areas."

1. Make a graph with the data in this file that refutes HTI's claim. Sketch it (with labeled axes) and write a one-sentence refutation.

2. Explain how their claim could still be true despite your evidence to the contrary.

The Geography of U.S. Cars

- Structured computer activity
- Data in files
- Student pages 78–83
- *Experience, basic features

This collection of activities makes up the bulk of the chapter. It is all about cars and the 50 states (plus the District of Columbia). Students use ratios to compare the states, making many different per-unit quantities. You don't have to do all these activities, and you don't have to do them in order, though they are presented roughly in order of difficulty.

Topics
proportion
interpreting rates
relationships among attributes
U.S. states

What's Important Here

This is about proportion, but let's highlight a few issues:

- Remind students to see whether their answers make sense. Assess them through other assignments or by including sense-making in the rubric. This could easily be a sentence that begins, "0.42 cars per person makes sense because . . ." followed by an explanation or calculation, or "5.7 cars per person is surprising because in the city hardly anyone has a car . . ."

- Any "per" quantity is an average. It represents the whole group (especially in comparisons), but individuals may differ greatly. Per capita income, for example, may not represent many people's actual earnings.

- Help students use what they know about the states. Encourage geographical speculation. For example, New England states are often clustered together in the attributes we will study. Why? California, known for its "car culture," is unexceptional in these data except for being large. Why is that?

Materials
    States – CarsNDrivers
    States – Accidents

Students need to be able to
    open files
    make graphs, including
      box plots
    create new attributes
    use the formula editor

The Geography of U.S. Cars I

*Guided

Here are some suggestions for discussion topics:

➲ Ask students how they found out which state had the maximum or minimum of some quantity. Have them explain their methods (e.g., looking at a point plot or sorting the table) so the whole class can build its repertoire of skills.

➲ Ask students if they know how far their family cars (if any) drive in a year. Compare each distance to your state's **milesPerVeh**. Explain any discrepancies you come across. (This technique, for example, ignores commercial travel.)

The Geography of U.S. Cars II: Total It Up

*Starter

This activity introduces Fathom's summary tables if students have never met them before. In the process, it highlights a common misstep students can make about the mean (or any aggregate function), namely, that the mean of a quantity for a set of groups (in this case, the states) is not necessarily the same as the mean for the whole population.

Here are some discussion topics:

➲ Students have calculated how many vehicles there are per mile of road in your state. Have them calculate how many miles there are per vehicle—and then the number of *feet* per vehicle. Ask if the results seem reasonable.

The Geography of U.S. Cars

- ⊃ Have students explain, as clearly as possible, how it can be that the average of averages among the states is *not* the same as the average for the whole country.

- ⊃ Ask students to come up with an example in the context of the school where the same mathematical effect takes place. (For example, how can it be that the average of the average heights in the classes is not the average height of the school population? It's because the populations are different in the groups.)

The Geography of U.S. Cars III: Unsafe in Any State

*Intermediate

This is about units and looking at ratios both ways. By that we mean looking at both A/B and its reciprocal, B/A. Here are two good discussion topics:

- ⊃ Discuss students' explanations of why certain states are "best" or "worst" in their ratios. Ask the class if the answers sound reasonable. Ask for and discuss alternative explanations. Probe into whether we can use any of the other data we have to test the ideas. For instance, in the example about Rhode Island (they drive less because they're in a small state, so they have fewer accidents), we could look in **States – CarsNDrivers** to see whether Rhode Islanders do in fact drive fewer miles.

- ⊃ The task asks students to make numbers more convenient (e.g., by multiplying them by 1,000,000) as well as to choose which direction of the ratio (deaths per million drivers or drivers per death) is better for them. This helps them learn to make the numbers more meaningful and accessible. Discuss what makes a number convenient. Can the students generate a rule of thumb to help them understand how to make a set of numbers more meaningful?

Extensions

- Students may ask, "What do they mean by a motor vehicle?" or "Do motorcycles count?" The answer is that motor vehicles include everything that's licensed for the road. So motorcycles and trucks count, but All Terrain Vehicles (ATVs) do not. So if students are trying to calculate something and it matters how many trucks there are, for example, they have a great chance to do a survey to figure it out. Of course, it will not be a simple random sample, but you can do your best to make your count representative.

- Another fun question: Suppose we each had to take care of some length of roadway. If we split up the roadway evenly among all the licensed drivers in a state, how much roadway (in feet or miles) would each person have to take care of? Which states would give you the biggest and smallest shares?

For this and other related questions, it's fine to ignore the fact that some roads are multilane.

The Geography of U.S. Cars I

Name(s): _____

This activity is about driving in the various states of the U.S. The file is called **States – CarsNDrivers**. For each state, it records these attributes:

PopThou	Population of the state (in thousands)
DriversThou	Number of licensed drivers (in thousands)
VehThou	Number of registered vehicles (in thousands)
MilesMill	Number of miles driven (in millions)
RoadMiles	Number of miles of roadway in the state (as of December 31, 1994)
AreaSqMi	Area of the state in square miles

You'll learn how to
make new attributes
define attributes by formula

You need
States – CarsNDrivers

These data come from the U.S. Department of Transportation and are for 1992 except where noted.

You will be computing and comparing various per-unit quantities. We'll start in a very step-by-step way, and quickly move to asking you the big questions and just letting you use Fathom to respond.

1. **Open States – CarsNDrivers.** First we're going to ask what percentage of the population in each state drives. For that, we'll divide the number of drivers by the population, then multiply by 100 to get the percent. But first . . .

2. Predict! Which states do you think will have the highest and lowest percentage of licensed drivers? Guess the three highest and the three lowest.

3. Onward! Click on the heading for **PopThou**. The column is highlighted.

4. Choose **New Attribute** from the **Data** menu. When the attribute name box appears, name it **PctDrivers** for "Percent Drivers" and close the box.

5. Select the new attribute. Choose **Edit Formula** from the **Edit** menu. The formula editor appears.

6. Enter **100 * DriversThou / PopThou.** Close the editor by clicking **OK.** You should see numbers like the ones in the picture.

7. Figure out which states have the highest and the lowest percentages of licensed drivers. Report the three highest and the three lowest.

8. How did you figure out which were the highest and lowest?

9. Why do you suppose those states are the highest and lowest?

You can also scroll to the **<new>** column, but this technique puts the column closer to the other attributes you need in this activity.

Data in Depth
© 2001 Key Curriculum Press

Per Capita Vehicles

10. Use the same procedure to figure out which states have the largest and smallest numbers of vehicles per capita in the population. First predict which states will have the most and the fewest vehicles per capita.

The Latin phrase per capita means "per person."

11. How many vehicles per person were there for the highest and lowest states?

12. Write the name of your new attribute and the formula that you used to calculate it.

13. Sketch the box plot of that attribute.

14. Again, propose an explanation for why those states are the ones that are highest and lowest.

Miles per Vehicle

15. Do the same thing you did above, only this time compute the average number of miles each vehicle travels per year in each state. In the formula for your new attribute, use the attribute **MilesMill**, which is the total number of miles driven that year *in millions of miles*. Be careful! The number of vehicles, **VehThou**, is in *thousands* of vehicles. Include responses to the preceding five items (but for the new attribute).

16. Look at the states that had the highest values of vehicles per person. Where do they fall in miles per vehicle? Explain that. See if the same pattern holds true for the states with the smallest numbers of vehicles per person.

This is easiest if you make two dot plots or box plots, one for each of the last two new attributes. When you select states in one, they are highlighted in the other.

The Geography of U.S. Cars II: Total It Up

Name(s): _____

Now we'll step away from proportions to do some adding up. As usual, we'll start with a simpler step-by-step example and then move on to subtler problems.

You'll learn how to
use a summary table
use the formula editor
use built-in functions such
as **mean( )**

You need
States – CarsNDrivers

How Many Miles?

We'll begin by computing the total number of miles of roads in the U.S.

1. Open the file **States – CarsNDrivers.** It contains the number of miles of roads in each state. We're going to add them up to get the total for the U.S. population.

2. Choose **Summary Table** from the **Insert** menu. The new, empty summary table appears. Drag the attribute **RoadMiles** to the right arrow at the top. The table will look like the one shown here. You can see that the mean of these road-mile figures is 76,599.

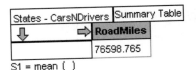

3. Choose **Add Formula** from the **Summary** menu.

4. Enter **sum(** . The close parenthesis appears automatically. You can leave the space between the parentheses blank; it gets **RoadMiles** from the column heading.

5. Close the editor. The sum of **RoadMiles** appears in the table: about 4,000,000. Four million miles of roads! Wow!

6. Using a calculator, divide **sum( )** by **mean( )**. Explain your answer.

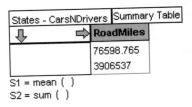

Now we'll investigate the total number of vehicles. Fortunately, we can use the same summary table—we'll just add onto it.

7. Drag the attribute name **VehThou** (thousands of vehicles) onto the right arrow at the top. The table expands. Sketch it to the right.

8. What does the number (the **sum( )** of **VehThou**) in the summary table mean? That is, is it vehicles, thousands of vehicles, or millions, or what? How do you know?

9. Create a new attribute, **VehPerMile**, in the data. Give it a formula so that the value for each state is the number of vehicles per mile of roads. Write the formula here, and sketch a histogram of that new attribute. Label and scale the axes.

Create a new attribute either in the case table or in the Inspector. Choose **Help Topics...** from the **Help** menu if you don't know how. Your results should range from about 7 to about 230.

10. Drag that attribute, **VehPerMile**, onto that same right arrow in the summary table. Now you can see the sum of the vehicle-per-mile values (it should be about 3000). That is not a particularly meaningful number. Why not?

Data in Depth
© 2001 Key Curriculum Press

11. The average—or mean—number of vehicles per mile is more interesting. What is that average, and what does it mean?

12. There are different ways of computing averages. Using a calculator, find the total number of vehicles divided by the total number of miles that we found earlier. Write that here.

13. The preceding two figures are not the same. Each is a way of computing the average number of vehicles per mile on U.S. roadways (if everyone were driving). Decide which of them you prefer and explain why.

14. Which "average" number is larger? Again, try to explain why. It will have to do with the shape of the distribution or with which states have which values.

Other Totals

Finally, for practice, compute the following:

15. The total land area of the United States

16. The total number of drivers

17. The total number of miles driven each year

Be careful of those thousands!

Going Further

1. In this activity, we calculated the number of vehicles per mile two different ways: by averaging the individual states' **VehPerMile** numbers, and by taking the total number of vehicles divided by the total number of miles. Another technique is to take a *weighted average* of the states' **VehPerMile** numbers. Compare the original two results to (a) the average of **VehPerMile** weighted by number of vehicles, (b) **VehPerMile** weighted by the number of miles of road, and (c) the same thing weighted by the number of drivers. Explain the relationship between these numbers and the original two, and what meaning these numbers might have (that is, when might it be appropriate to use them?).

To do this task, you have to know what a weighted average is.

The Geography of U.S. Cars III: Unsafe in Any State

Name(s): _____

Any time you have a ratio of two quantities, you have to decide which one is on top. Frequently, either way will work—but the two ways have a different "sense." The numerical values of the two ratios are *reciprocals*—if one is 6, the other is 1/6.

In addition, sometimes numbers are inconvenient. If a disease occurs in 0.025% of the population, the fact may be easier to grasp if you say the disease occurs in 25 people out of every 100,000.

In this activity, you'll produce ratios that compare states in a number of different ways. For each ratio, you'll also make its reciprocal—the other side up. And if the numbers are not convenient, you'll fix them so they are.

You need to know how to
make new attributes
define attributes by formula
edit formulas to make the numbers more "convenient"
make graphs

You need
States – Accidents

The Task

Use the file **States – Accidents.** For each pair of attributes, you have to do each of the nine things listed below.

1. Make a new attribute that is the ratio with the first number on top: **Fatal92 / PopThou.**

2. Make a ratio with the other number on top: **PopThou / Fatal92.**

3. Convert the formulas to give you convenient numbers if necessary. For example, the first one ranges from 0.08 to 0.29. If we multiplied by 1000, the numbers would be easier to grasp. So we change the formula to **1000 * Fatal92 / PopThou** and get a range from 79 to 293.

4. Report the names of the attributes and the formulas you used in Fathom.

5. Describe in words what the ratios mean. This first attribute's formula is given above. Before we multiplied by 1000, this number was the number of fatalities in 1992 *per thousand people.* After multiplying, it's the number of fatalities *per million.* We might call it **DeathsPerMillion.** The reciprocal will be something like **PeoplePerDeath.**

6. Sketch a histogram of one of the attributes so we can see its distribution.

7. Find the best state, the worst state, and the value of the ratio for each (with units). The best state is Rhode Island, with only 78.61 deaths per million people ("deaths per million people" are the units), or 12,722 people per death (that is, there was one death for every 12,700 people). Do the worst, too.

8. Speculate as to why one of the states is the best or worst in whatever we're measuring. We might think, "Maybe Rhode Island is best because it's small and people don't drive much?" You can do better.

9. Explain why you might prefer one sense of the ratio over the other. You may like the "people per death" version because we can picture a town with 12,700 people, but we can't picture 79 out of a million. You may prefer the other.

As an example, we have sketched responses you might make if we gave you **Fatal92** (the number of vehicle fatalities in 1992) and **PopThou** (the population of the state in thousands).

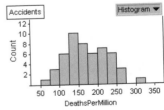

This histogram is a response to Step 6. It shows the distribution of **DeathsPerMillion.**

Data in Depth
© 2001 Key Curriculum Press

The Assignment

Use **Fatal92** and **DriversThou**

Use **Fatal92** and **VehThou**

Use **Fatal92** and **RoadMiles**

Use **DriversThou** and **RoadMiles**

Saved by the Belt

- Open-ended computer activity
- Data from file
- Student page 85 (optionally pages 86–87)
- Independent, basic features

Everybody agrees that *Saved by the Belt* requires really hard thinking, even though the arithmetic is simple. A student who can make a clear, correct response to that task deserves a good grade in anybody's class.

Although the reasoning is hard, many students will be able to do it themselves given this context. It's really about expected values and conditional probability; it has some of the same feel as figuring out expected values in a chi-square situation. There is a "hints" page (see page 86) about the reasoning itself that you can pass out beforehand or make available as you see fit.

The author's answer: About 14,500 lives saved, though we can't fully use the data for Wyoming.

Topics
proportion
interpreting rates
conditional probability

Materials
States – Seat Belts
optionally pages 86–87

Students need to be able to
open files
make graphs
use summary tables
create new attributes
use the formula editor

What's Important Here

- The idea that we can compute the number of people who *would have* died if they had *not* been wearing belts is confusing. While it takes sophisticated thinking, it's approachable—by looking at one state and simpler, hypothetical numbers.

- When students extend their solution from one state to the whole country, they have to be sure not to "average the averages" inappropriately.

Discussion Questions

- ⮑ How did you deal with Wyoming? (Delete it; ignore it because it's so small; make up a plausible number for **BeltUsePct**.)

- ⮑ How did you deal with the fatalities that were listed as "unknown"? (Remove them from the data; divide them in the same proportion as **BeltPct** and **NoBeltPct**; divide them in the same proportion as **BeltUsePct**.)

- ⮑ How do you suppose these data are collected? Do you think the procedures vary from state to state? How do you think the "unknown" data can get into the system?

Tech Notes

- If students have trouble, encourage them to make more than one new attribute in order to solve a problem. They do not have to make one huge formula that takes care of everything. Instead, they should make an attribute that represents the results of each step in the process (e.g., *number of people killed not wearing a belt*) and ensure that it makes sense. Fathom recomputes everything it needs to, so it's easy to make adjustments. If you redefine one formula, Fathom recomputes everything.

- Students should be careful to distinguish **BeltPct**—the percentage of people killed who were wearing belts—from **BeltUsePct**—the percentage of drivers observed to be wearing belts. Perhaps **KilledWearingBeltPct** would have been a better name for the first, but it was too long.

Saved by the Belt

Name(s): _____

How many lives were saved by seat belts in the U.S. in 1992?

You always hear that seat belts save lives. It's probably even true. In this activity, you'll estimate how many. In statistics, *estimate* doesn't mean *guess*. It means using data to calculate something you can't know for sure.

The arithmetic in this activity is easy, but the reasoning can be hard. Consider spending time away from the computer thinking about this.

The file **States – Seat Belts** has a group of useful attributes for each state, listed in the file itself. Here is some advice about them:

- **Fatal92** is the total number of fatalities; **KilledInCars** is the number killed as occupants (drivers and passengers) of passenger vehicles.

- Three belt attributes (**BeltPct**, **NoBeltPct**, and **UnkBeltPct**) are the *percentages* of the people counted in **KilledInCars** who had been wearing belts, who had not been wearing belts, and whose belt-wearing status is unknown.

- **BeltUsePct** is the *percentage* of all persons in cars who wear seat belts in that state. Figuring out the right way to use this attribute is the key to your success.

Warm-up

Use a calculator to answer these questions. They're all about Alabama (answers are in parentheses; show how you got them):

1. How many people were killed in cars not wearing a belt? (427.)

2. For how many people do we *not* know whether they were belted? (34.)

3. If the same fraction of those people wore belts as in the general population, how many more non-belt-wearers were among the unknowns? (14, for a total of 441.)

4. Out of the whole population of Alabama, how many people do not wear belts (at a given instant)? (1,737,000.)

5. If you picked one of those beltless people at random, what is the chance that he or she got killed in a car crash in Alabama in 1992? (About 1 in 4000, or 0.00025.)

If you got those right, you can probably calculate the chance that a person *with* a belt got killed; you'd expect that probability to be smaller. That may or may not be useful in answering the question. Remember, you must calculate *how many* people were saved—not just verify that you're safer if you buckle up.

In your write-up be sure you state the problem and your assumptions, describe your reasoning and how your work makes sense, make your conclusions clear, and explain why and in what way the real answer might be different from the one you give.

A really great graphic may help you show your reasoning and conclusions.

You need to know how to
make new attributes
define attribute formulas
use summary tables

You will need to
write this up and turn it in using separate sheets

The difference between them represents pedestrians, people in trucks or on buses, motorcycles, and so on.

In this activity, belts refers to seat belts, shoulder harnesses, child safety seats, and so forth—the normal restraints you're supposed to wear in a car.

Note: In the file, there is no value for **BeltUsePct** for Wyoming. You will have to decide how to deal with that.

And remember: You have to do the whole U.S., not just Alabama. A summary table will help; use the function **sum( )**.

Saved by the Belt: Two Ways to Think About It

Name(s): _____

In *Saved by the Belt,* it's easy to get completely mixed up. The problem is neither data nor technology—it's just a problem with thinking about the situation. There may even be more than one answer.

If you want to figure it out entirely on your own, don't read this. But if you're stumped, or if you're finished and need another perspective, check this out.

How many lives were saved? In order to figure that out, the key question is "How many people would have died if **none** of them had been wearing seat belts?"

George Pólya, that famous problem solver, advises us to make it simpler. So we'll make it simpler by choosing smaller and nicer numbers.

We also need to make our assumptions explicit (you know that, right?). One of them is that people who wear seat belts are exactly as likely to get in accidents as those who do not. It's just that belts save some of them once they're in the accident.

So here's a simpler, clearer setup for the problem.

In a town of 6000 people, researchers decide to do a somewhat macabre experiment. On January 1, everybody rolls a die. The ones and twos don't wear belts for the year, but the rest do. The chance of wearing a belt is 2/3, so about 4000 wear belts and 2000 do not.

In one year, 7 people were killed: 2 with belts and 5 without. How many would have died if no one had worn belts? One third of the population (the no-belt people) had 5 deaths, so the other two thirds would have had 10 deaths, for a total of 15. Since 7 really died, 8 lives were saved.

In general,

> the number of belted people who would have died = the number of unbelted deaths · (the number of belted people / the number of unbelted people).

In the case we just discussed,

$$10 = 5 \cdot \left(\frac{4000}{2000} \right) = 5 \cdot \left(\frac{\frac{2}{3}}{\frac{1}{3}} \right).$$

People argue about whether this assumption is true. We don't have data, so we will simply acknowledge the assumption. You may state your opinion in the write-up, of course, and discuss how it affects the outcome.

Saved by the Belt: Another Way to Think About It

Does that ratio seem a little strange? Find an explanation that makes sense to you. Here's another way to see where it comes from.

You can also do this problem by looking at rates (or probabilities). What's the chance that an unbelted person gets killed in a car crash? Empirically, it's 5/2000.

If the belted people had gone unbelted, their chance would have been the same. So the number that would have been killed is

the number of belted people · the chance that they get killed if unbelted

$= 4000 \cdot (5/2000)$

$= 10$ people.

Since two belted people really got killed, eight lives were saved.

"Per" Sonatas and Investigations

- Eleven open-ended computer activities
- Data from files
- Student pages 89–94
- Independent, basic features

The next four pages are in the Conjecture-Measure-Compare form of the *Sonata for Data and Brain.* Page xx provides a more extensive description of this type of assignment. The two pages that follow the Sonatas have seven ideas you can use as Sonatas, problems, or other projects.

Sonata 8: Counting the Cars

Your debriefing should help students check in with reality. After all, their calculation is an *average* and may not represent reality very often.

- What if we counted cars in front of the school for five minutes? How would that fit with the number we got?
- What do you think the range of intervals between cars is over the course of the day on the street where you live? On the busiest street in town?

Consider calling up the traffic department in your town. They actually put sensors down so you can find out what kinds of rates they get and compare them to the students' calculations.

Sonata 9: Extreme Capital

In this Sonata, students should try many different ratios to get lots of practice as they search for the District of Columbia at its strangest. Here's a question to ask them; you can decide how hard-nosed you want to be about it.

How do you measure whether one graph is more extreme than another?

Sonata 10: The Best Drivers

This activity asks students to buttress an opinion with data. If students get into a rut, encourage them to come up with alternative hypotheses (i.e., make up better excuses). For example, "Those New England states are so small; the people probably spend a lot of time driving—and getting killed—in other states. There should be a correction factor based on square miles in the state."

Sonata 11: The Wide-Open Spaces

This Sonata has students produce two different ratios and look at the relationships between them. Once students have eliminated the District of Columbia as an outlier, encourage them to look at the more unusual states that remain, such as Rhode Island, Hawaii, and California.

- Ask students to explain what Hawaii's position means. One way to start is, "Compared to a state with a similar population density . . ."
- Point to a blank place on the graph and ask, "What kind of place would this be?"

More Car Stuff and Per in the World

These are project starters or "Sonata seeds" that you can use as you see fit. The first page uses data from the same files we've been using; the second leaves the files behind and asks students to go out and get data on their own.

Topics
   proportion
   interpreting rates
   measurement and dimension
   outliers

Materials
   States – CarsNDrivers
   States – Accidents
   States

Students need to be able to
   open files
   make graphs
   use summary tables
   create new attributes
   use the formula editor

Note: In any of these Sonatas, students should state their assumptions. In *Counting the Cars,* for example, they might decide to assume that all roads have one lane in each direction.

Sonata 8: Counting the Cars

Name(s): _____

On the average, how often does a car go over a given spot on a road?

Imagine that you stretch one of those sensor lines across the road and attach a counter and a timer to it so you can record when cars go over it. How often will that happen? Of course, it depends on many things: what road, what time of day, and so forth. But you can use data we already have to find at least an average value.

You need
States – CarsNDrivers

You'll show that you can
use proportion and rates
make new attributes
define formulas

Conjecture

For this Sonata, give your answer (how much time passes between vehicles) in units of time: for example, milliseconds, seconds, minutes, or days.

Without looking at the data, figure out how you will calculate the answer for each state. You can see what attributes are in the file—**States – CarsNDrivers**—by referring to *The Geography of U.S. Cars I* on page 78. You may use only those attributes. Make estimates for your own state, and predict which states will have the highest and lowest values, and why.

Be sure to write down your assumptions!

Measurement

Make the calculation. You will need at least one new attribute. Write down its name and formula. Sketch a labeled and scaled display of its distribution. Identify the most extreme states and their values.

Comparison

How did your conjectures measure up? Describe the way additional considerations explain how the data differ from your prediction. Now, given that you know your statewide average, how fast does this recording device have to work to record real traffic? Going to a busy street and counting is a really good idea for this activity.

Sonata 9: Extreme Capital

Name(s): _____

In what quantities do you expect the District of Columbia to be extreme?

Data about the states usually include an entry for the District of Columbia. The District of Columbia ought to be unusual when compared with the states—after all, it's really small and it's entirely filled by a city. Often, if you plot an attribute—either a given one or one that you make (for example, by making a ratio such as "people per car")—as a box plot, the District of Columbia will show up as an outlier when compared to the states.

You need
 States – CarsNDrivers
 States – Accidents

You'll show that you can
 use proportion and rates
 work with outliers
 make new attributes
 define formulas

Conjecture

Before you look at the data, make a conjecture about which per-unit quantity having to do with traffic deaths or roads or drivers will show the District of Columbia as the most extreme outlier. State which one you think will be extreme and why.

Measurement

Using **States – Accidents** and **States – CarsNDrivers,** make many "ratio" attributes and plot them using box plots. Find the one for which the District of Columbia is the most extreme. Sketch a plot of the attribute and give its formula; also sketch the plot for the attributes you thought would be most extreme. Be sure the District of Columbia is clearly labeled in both plots.

Comparison

What happened? Did you guess right? If not, why is the other one even more extreme? Describe, in retrospect, what gives one of the most extreme ratios such an unusual value.

Sonata 10: The Best Drivers

Name(s): _____

Which state has the best drivers in the country? Your job is to make a conjecture, and then present data to back it up. You may use data from any of the **"States"** files we have been using in this chapter.

You need

    States – CarsNDrivers

    States – Accidents

    States

You'll show that you can

    back up an argument with data

    use proportion and rates to compare states

    make new attributes

    define formulas

Conjecture

The data include information on state population, number of drivers, number of vehicles, miles traveled, miles of roads, numbers of traffic fatalities, and seat belt use. You can get any other data you like as well.

Before you look at the data, you must not only say which state you think will have the best drivers, but (more important) *how you will determine which state has the best drivers* and why that is a good way. Your method should include creating at least one new attribute and its formula.

Measurement

Analyze the data; write your results here. Be sure to sketch a graph of your new attribute and give its formula. Explain how the formula works.

Comparison

Did the results match what you thought? Were there any surprises? What additional considerations would you take into account if you could? Speculate where you would get the data and how you might change your mind in the light of new information.

Sonata 11: The Wide-Open Spaces

Name(s): _____

Consider two ratio quantities: the number of people per square mile and the number of cars per mile of road. How do you suppose these two are related? Use **States – CarsNDrivers.**

Conjecture

Before you look at the data, try to answer the question above. Give reasons—perhaps things you remember from your travels or from other assignments. Show any calculations you do in your predictions.

Measurement

Describe how you use Fathom to answer the question. In this case, you probably have at least two new attributes. Be sure to give their formulas and explain why the formulas work and what they mean. State any assumptions you make. There's also a serious outlier you might consider getting rid of—but if you do, you need a reason.

Comparison

Explain what you found out and compare it to your conjecture. Were there any surprises? What else can you figure out from these data? What implications do your findings have?

You need
    States – CarsNDrivers

You'll show that you can
    make predictions about the relationship between two rates
    use proportion and rates to evaluate your prediction
    make new attributes
    define formulas

Remember—**RoadMiles** includes all of the roads in the state, from the smallest city street to the Interstates to the county roads. But you have to put all the vehicles on them—every car, truck, bus, and motorcycle.

Be sure to sketch a labeled graph that shows your data.

More Car Stuff

Name(s): _____

This page presents ideas for questions you can answer that all have to do with per-unit quantities. They can be starters for Sonatas, of course (see *Sonatas for Data and Brain*, page xx, and also *Sonata for Data and Brain Summary Sheet*, page xxii), or ideas for more open-ended projects. You will need to write them up on separate sheets.

Percent Paved

Many environmentally conscious people cry out that the whole country is being paved over. Using data in **States – CarsNDrivers,** estimate the percentage of each state (and of the whole country) that is paved. Be sure to state your assumptions!

You need

States – CarsNDrivers

The key is estimating the *area* of the roads. Try taking the total length and multiplying by an estimated (or measured) width. This does not account for different widths, so you'll have to compromise. It also does not account for intersections. Do you think that matters? If so, in what direction does it distort the analysis?

Acres of Cars

Suppose the cars in the states were spread evenly over the area of each state. How many cars per acre (or acres per car) are there? What's the national average? Which states are extreme? Predict before you calculate.

You need

States – CarsNDrivers

You may have to figure out how big an acre is. There are 640 acres in a square mile. How big is that compared to a football or soccer field, for example? Include this in your write-up.

Age and Drivers

Before you look at the data, what do you think: Do states with a greater number of older people have a higher or lower percentage of drivers than others? You will need data from two files, **States** and **States – CarsNDrivers,** to answer this question.

You need

States – CarsNDrivers

States

If you do not know how to combine data from two files, look in the online Help under "moving data from one collection to another."

Dropping a Meteor

Suppose you dropped a small (say 1-cm-diameter) meteor on your state. What's the chance that it would hit a vehicle? Estimate, then figure it out. You'll need to make well-documented assumptions about the sizes of vehicles.

You need

States – CarsNDrivers

Compare the states. (Tricky question—be careful!) If you were really scared of meteors hitting your car, which state would you move to? Why?

Per in the World

Name(s): _____

Not all data come from files you already have. Sometimes you have to go out and get it—from the Internet or from the world.

These "Sonata seeds" can turn into *Sonatas for Data and Brain* (see page xx) or just projects you do on your own. You will have to write them up on separate sheets.

The Final Frontier

Do you have more space at school or at home? How much do you get in each place? Estimate first, and then count, measure, and so forth, to compute the area—the number of square feet (or square meters)—per person in each location. That is, the measured attributes are **people** and **area**. **Density** (in people per square whatever) is computed.

Extension: Work with other class members to create a Fathom collection of data from different locations. Some suggestions: the supermarket at 9 a.m. Saturday; the gym during basketball practice; the gym during a home basketball game; the block where you live (including the outside parts, if any); a fast-food place, every hour for as long as you can stand it; a cemetery . . .

You need
> estimates or measurements of the size of your home and school

Libraries

What's the smartest town in your area?

Call up public libraries in several (at least five) towns or cities in your area. Find out how many books each one has in its collection. While you're at it, find out the town's population. Compute the number of books per person each library has.

You might also call a college and compare its collection to the number of people studying and working there. How will your answer compare with the one for a town?

Instead of making phone calls, you may be able to get this information from the Internet.

You need
> information on local libraries

Your class can share basic information about libraries, such as the number of books. Consider splitting up the libraries you have to call.

Walking Fingers

First, estimate: In your community, how many people are there per restaurant? How many restaurants per person? Which number makes more sense? How do your numbers compare with those you get from another community?

Now measure the ratio. Get your phone books. Count the restaurants and figure out how to count the residential listings. Divide to get your answer. Do the same for another community (sometimes there's more than one community in a phone book, or maybe you can get a different book).

Once you have that phone book, consider other ratios you might predict and compute, such as attorneys per hospital, the fast food/slow food ratio, and so on. Again, compare these values to those from other towns. What do the numbers tell you about the communities?

You need
> phone books

Straighten Up!

4

An enormous body of understanding in data analysis revolves around linear models. Unfortunately, few things in life are linear. Why, then, do we study lines so much?

Because lines are easy. We understand them thoroughly, so we can solve for anything. But as soon as we study nonlinear data, we're in trouble: We only know how to solve a few of the myriad possible nonlinear equations—often by transforming them into something linear. Therefore, until recently, people who looked at data tried, as often as possible, to see what was linear in it—and hoped they could disregard the rest.

But now we have computer technology. What was once impossibly hard is within our reach. In this chapter, we'll use traditional "straightening" techniques, as well as informal curve-fitting, using Fathom's powerful formula editor coupled with using sliders for variable parameters.

This chapter's activities approach nonlinear data in different ways. Some focus on straightening; others use curve-fitting. Some are just modeling; others use modeling to predict. More than those in some earlier chapters, these activities have richer contexts and fewer step-by-step instructions. As a teacher, you will need to judge what kind of extra support—if any—your students need.

Level

In this chapter, the opening activities, *Fitting the Planets* and *Moore's Law,* use logarithms. You can use them as a first application of logs or as a review of logs, but they don't teach logs—so if your students have never inverted an exponent before, don't start here.

Later in the chapter, however, we visit parabolas (*Area and Perimeter, Incredible Shrinking Text*) and other more accessible curves, so they may be appropriate for students who have algebra experience but have not yet mastered the elementary functions.

The Activities

- **Fitting the Planets** is really two activities with the same purpose: to determine the relationship between the planets' orbital periods and the radii of their orbits. The first activity fits the curve; the second uses a log-log transformation.

- **Moore's Law** consists of two more activities, parallel to the *Planets* activities except that it's a semilog transformation, the fit requires two parameters instead of one, and the context is Moore's law—the pattern of exponential growth in the semiconductor industry.

- **Area and Perimeter** has (as you might suspect) a geometrical context. What is the relationship between the areas and perimeters of randomly constructed rectangles? Fathom makes the rectangle data for us in an elementary simulation; when we analyze it, we find that a curve—whose equation we find—forms the *boundary* of a cloud of points.

- **How Much Tape Is Left?** is an investigation using measurement, geometry, algebra, and common sense. Basically, the task is to know how much is left on a roll of adding machine tape if you can measure only the diameter.

Now we have a series of more open-ended Sonatas in nonlinear, geometrical contexts.

- **The Great Toilet Paper Mystery** is similar to *How Much Tape Is Left?* but, since it uses toilet paper, has a harder measurement problem.

- **Printing Paragraphs** and **Incredible Shrinking Text** are two Sonatas that explore how the characteristics of type affect the space a given piece of text will take up on the page.

- **Measuring the Bass** is a Sonata about scale and size in musical instruments. Students find an exponential function.

- **Puff Puff Puff Puff Pop** is another Sonata, this one about the relationship of volume to circumference in balloons. Students find a power law.

- **More Ideas for Nonlinear Data** is a collection of ideas for additional Sonatas or short projects.

Objectives

In this chapter, in the various activities, students will

- Use straightening techniques (especially using logarithms) to linearize data and interpret it

- Use Fathom to fit nonlinear functions by eye, using sliders as variable parameters

- Use algebra to make sense of situations and the data that arise from them

Connections with Chapter 7, What to Do with Leftovers

What to Do with Leftovers is all about residuals. And one of the primary functions of residuals is to tell you when your linear fit is bad because you see something systematic in the residual plot. This means you may be dealing with a nonlinear function. Several of the activities in Chapter 7 (e.g., *Estimating Parameters, Using Residuals* or *Modeling Mauna Loa*) could just as easily have been presented here.

Curriculum Connections

Physics. Most things in nature are nonlinear. Several of the activities (notably *Fitting the Planets*) come right from physics. Even the physics of music is represented here in *Measuring the Bass*.

Calculus and Advanced Algebra. These disciplines are all about functions. Nonlinear data give students a chance to see "when we'll ever have to use this," because they see that the functions they study—polynomials, power laws, logarithms, sinusoids—show up in real data. But that's not all. In order to get the most out of these activities, and to make the best conjectures possible, they have to actually use algebraic manipulations to accomplish something.

Geometry. Any time we can connect data, symbols, and shape, we're doing the students a service. And just as similarity gives rise to interesting linear relationships, differences in dimension create nonlinear relationships. Thus, when you look at area and distance, you get quadratics, as in *How Much Tape Is Left?* or *Area and Perimeter.* The "typographic" activities (e.g., *Incredible Shrinking Text*) are fundamentally geometrical.

Beginning Algebra. Some people would say that beginning algebra students should not work with nonlinear functions until they have mastered lines and acquired more mathematical baggage. We agree that beginners may not understand exponentials (for example) as fully as more experienced students—but does that mean they shouldn't use them? It's a tough question. One thing is certain: Without technology, students wouldn't have any way of getting the access to logs, sines, or even polynomials, that computers and graphing calculators give them. So here's some advice: try it. But don't expect the kind of understanding you'd get from students in more advanced classes. Beginning algebra students will not master logarithms because of an activity on the computer, but the experience will give them exposure so that logs will be easier for them to learn. Also, look for ways the computer can help make the logic more concrete—for example, by creating more "intermediate-step" attributes.

Straightening Data

Suppose you have a scatter plot that shows a relationship, but it's curved. How do you figure out the form of the function?

One way is to *straighten* it. That means transforming one or both of the attributes in a way that makes the resulting scatter plot straight. You can use that to figure out the untransformed relationship. As a problem solver, you have two hurdles: finding the right transformation and then undoing its effects.

A Simple Example

Suppose you have these data: (1, 2), (2, 8), (3, 18), (4, 32). Suppose you don't recognize these as $y = 2x^2$. You plot them and see the data curving up.

"Maybe it's quadratic," you think. You decide, therefore, to transform the data. You want to take the square of something, but of which variable? One strategy is to try it each way (you have a computer), but let's think instead. If it were quadratic, it would be like $y = x^2$. That means that if we squared the x, we'd get a straight line. So let's make a new variable, z, which is x^2.

Now our points are $(z, y) = (1, 2), (4, 8), (9, 18), (16, 32)$.

They line up! In fact, it's clear that $y = 2z$—and we could see this easily on a scatter plot. When we substitute back in, we get $y = 2x^2$.

Why do we plot x^2 against y instead of x against $\sqrt{y}$? Both would work, but we do it this way for two reasons: First, the computation is easier; second, most people understand "squared" before they understand its inverse, "square root."

A Less Simple Example

Sometimes you know the form of the equation you expect and need to see whether the data fit it. If the data fit when you transform the data the right way, the transformed plot will be straight.

In *How Much Tape Is Left?*, pages 116–117, the situation gives rise to this equation:

$$T - P = B\,(d^2 - c^2)$$

T and B are (unknown) constants, c is a measurable constant, and P and d are our measured variables—the amount of tape pulled off and the diameter of the remaining cylinder of tape.

If we plot d as a function of P, we'll see a curved graph of this form:

$$d = \sqrt{\frac{T - P}{B} + c^2}.$$

This is a mess. But if we change the equation around, to

$$d^2 = \left(-\frac{1}{B}\right)P + \left(c^2 + \frac{T}{B}\right),$$

we find the form $y = mx + b$! If we plot d^2 as a function of P, we should get a straight line—even if we don't know the constants. Then we can *derive* the value of B from the slope of the line we get, and having measured c, we get T from the intercept.

The trick, of course, is being facile enough with algebra to see how to transform an equation into something in slope-intercept form.

That Log Thing

Some of the most important transformations are logarithmic. In this book, we have a number of activities about logarithms for four reasons:

- Logarithms are all about ratios, and proportion is hugely important in statistics and in everyday life.

- Logarithms help us deal with sets of data that span many orders of magnitude, and data from science (and increasingly from everyday life) do just that.

- Logarithmic transformations of data straighten some nonlinear relationships, in particular, exponential functions and power laws.

- Some students (and adults) seem to fear logs—possibly because they never understood how useful logs are.

We'll focus on the third of these points. In particular, we'll go over what kinds of relationships logs straighten, in what circumstances, and why.

Exponential Functions: The Semilog Transformation

These have the form $y = C \cdot D^x$. They occur often in exponential growth (such as the growth of populations, money in accounts, or successful businesses) or decay (such as in radioactivity or temperature decreasing into equilibrium). Functions that start small and then explode are good candidates for exponential growth; those that come zooming down and then pull out of their dive for a smooth landing might represent decay.

In decay, D is less than 1.

You can also write exponentials as $y = Ae^{kx}$ where it is decay if k is negative.

If you look at the equation and take the log of both sides, you get

$$\log y = \log C + x \log D$$

This looks like a mess, but C and D are constants; therefore, so are $\log C$ and $\log D$. Let's make up new constants $b = \log C$ and $m = \log D$. Now we substitute to get

$$\log y = b + mx,$$

which is our familiar slope-intercept form, as long as you plot the log of y instead of y but leave x the same. In that case, the intercept is the log of the "coefficient out front" and the slope is the log of the base of the exponent.

Power Functions: The Log-Log Transformation

These have the form $y = C \cdot x^D$. They occur from time to time in physical-science situations, and are often used as models for other phenomena. The familiar quadratic function $y = x^2$ is a great example of a power law, but power laws include x-to-the-anything—and the exponent is frequently *not* an integer.

Straightening Data

Again, we take the log of both sides. But this time, we get

$$\log y = \log C + D \log x.$$

Making the same substitutions, $b = \log C$ and $m = \log D$, we get

$$\log y = b + m \log x.$$

Again it's the slope-intercept form, but this time you have to plot the log of y against the *log* of x. Here, the intercept is again the log of the "coefficient out front," but the slope is the log of the exponent itself (instead of the log of the base).

Author's Confession

Having said all that, I have to admit that even with a pretty good understanding of functions, I never really thought about what was confusing about semilog and log-log transformations until I began working on this book. So I offer here some of my perspectives.

Why do we take the log of both sides in both situations? Don't you take the log of only one side in the semilog case?

No. You take the log of both sides in both cases because that's how you ensure that both sides remain equal. (The Golden Rule of Algebra: Do unto one side what you do unto the other.) The equation after you take the log of both sides is an equation for *exactly the same function*, just expressed differently.

The difference is in what you *plot*. With the exponential, you get a line in slope-intercept form if you plot the log of y against plain old x. In the power-law case, you get a line only if you plot log x against log y.

Why does taking the log work on two functions of different form?

Thinking "typographically," it works because they both have exponents, so logs bring the exponents down from the shelf and onto the floor. Because the *variable* is in the exponent in the exponential case, and it's the base of the exponent in the power law, the two x's look different: one winds up logged and the other does not.

Thinking graphically, both kinds of functions blow up similarly, but the specific shape is different. A log transformation along an axis compresses higher values more than lower. Compressing the y-axis that way is perfect for an exponential—it squeezes the blowing-up large values just enough to make it a line. But that squeezing is too much for a power law because any exponential (with a base > 1) blows up faster than any power law (with an exponent > 1). The resulting graph droops over. So to make it a line, you have to prop it up by doing this "differential compression" in the x-direction (taking the log of x), which turns out to be just right.

Three Views of $y = 1.8^x$

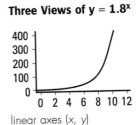
linear axes (x, y)

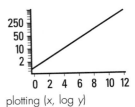
plotting (x, log y)

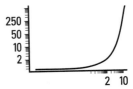
plotting (log x, log y)

Three Views of $y = x^{2.5}$

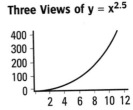
linear axes (x, y)

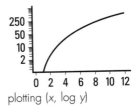
plotting (x, log y)

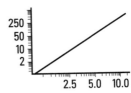
plotting (log x, log y)

Data in Depth
© 2001 Key Curriculum Press

Straightening Data

What about other terms in the functions, such as the 1 in $y = x^2 + 1$?

If you have other terms, and you take the log, it won't work. When you take $\log(x^2 + 1)$, you can't reduce it by bringing the 2 down. Therefore, even if the function is as nice as $y = x^2 + 1$, *the result after the transformation will not be straight.* But you can use an additional transformation, for example subtracting 1 from each side before you take the log and plotting $\log(y - 1)$ against $\log x$.

If you don't know what number to subtract, you can try to fit a third constant to your data (besides the slope and the intercept), or, if you're using Fathom, just hook up a slider to the constant and slide it until the data straighten.

If x is large enough, the difference is inconsequential and the data appear linear.

Fitting the Planets

- Two structured computer activities
- Data from file
- Student pages 104–107
- Intermediate, medium features

In these activities—*Fitting a Curve to the Planets* and *Straightening the Planets with Logs*—students look for relationships in data about the planets. The data are simple—there aren't many cases, and everybody has heard of the planets—but the numerical relationships are complex.

The handouts prompt students to study the relationship between the length of the year (called **year** in our collection, measured in Earth years—so Earth is 1.00) and the distance from the planet to the sun (called **orbit_AU**, measured in "Astronomical Units" or Earth-orbital-radii—so Earth is again 1.00).

What's Important Here

- **Fitting nonlinear functions.** The relationship between year and orbital radius is extremely reliable, but curved. Students get to see that there can be noninteger exponents.

- **Straightening data.** "Straightening" data is an important skill. It works really well with these data.

- **Logarithms.** While you don't have to use a logarithmic transformation to straighten these data, (a) it works and (b) the data do encompass many orders of magnitude. They're profoundly skewed, so taking the log is the only way to see them all on the same screen. We strongly recommend that teachers take the time to see the effect of the log transformation here; if you ever had doubts about its legitimacy, this should help allay them.

Discussion Questions

➲ With planetary distances, taking the log spaces data more evenly. Why?

➲ Look at your original plot of **year** versus **orbit_AU**. What would it look like if you reversed the axes?

➲ Why do you suppose astronomers frequently use Astronomical Units (AUs) instead of expressing quantities in kilometers using scientific notation?

Extensions

- There are important differences between the Jovian planets (Jupiter, Saturn, Uranus, and Neptune) and the terrestrial ones (the rest). Create a new attribute you can use to split the data.

- There is a relationship among a planet's radius, its mass, and its surface gravity. We don't have data for surface gravity, but you can compute density. Even mass/r^3 is a good stand-in; you can discover that the Jovians are less dense and that Saturn is the least dense of all the planets.

- If you take the log of the orbital radius, there's an obvious hole in the pattern. What is that hole? Answer: the asteroid belt. If someone looks up the orbit and period data for Ceres (the largest asteroid), you can add it as a case and see if it fits.

Topics
the planets
straightening data
fractional exponents
logarithms
power-law relationships

Materials
Planets

Students need to be able to
add new attributes
write formulas for attributes
make scatter plots
add lines to scatter plots

In case no one finds Ceres, its period is 4.6 years, and its distance from the sun is 381 million km, or 2.56 AU.

Orbital Mechanics for Math Teachers

(and Why Log-Log Straightening Works)

If you're a physics teacher, this is part of the bread and butter of your existence.

The problem is to predict the relationship between the orbital period of a planet and its distance from the sun. We'll assume a circular orbit, which means that the gravitational force pulling the planet in is equal to the centrifugal force trying to make it go out. (Centrifugal force is not a real force but a so-called pseudoforce, but it's real enough to make this argument correct.)

Let's let

R be the radius of the orbit

T be the period (the amount of time it takes for the planet to complete one revolution)

M be the mass of the sun

v be the velocity of the planet on its orbit

G be the gravitational constant

Then

$$A_g = \frac{GM}{R^2}$$

is the gravitational acceleration, and

$$A_c = \frac{v^2}{R}$$

is the centrifugal acceleration. These two are equal in a circular orbit, so

$$\frac{GM}{R^2} = \frac{v^2}{R}.$$

But what's v? The distance the planet travels in a year is $C = 2\pi R$. Since rate = distance / time, it must be true that

$$v = C/T = 2\pi R/T$$

Substituting, you get

$$\frac{GM}{R^2} = \frac{4\pi^2 R^2}{RT^2},$$

or, rearranging,

$$T^2 = \left(\frac{4\pi^2}{GM}\right)R^3.$$

The terms in parentheses are all constants. So the square of the period is proportional to the cube of the orbital radius. If you measure R in AU and T in years, the constant is 1 (it must be to make the Earth correct). Anyway, that also means that

$$T = R^{1.5}$$

and that $\log T = (3/2) \log R$,

which form the basis for our two ways of figuring out the relationship.

Why does $A_c = v^2/R$?

If you don't teach physics, you may not be familiar with this one. One way to look at it is with calculus. Consider circular motion. We'll look at the x-coordinate:

$$x = R\cos\omega t$$

where $\omega = v/R$ is the angular frequency of the motion (in radians per second).

The question is, what acceleration is inherent in circular motion? Acceleration is a second derivative; substituting and taking two derivatives, we get

$$\dot{x} = -R(v/R)\sin\omega t$$
$$\ddot{x} = -R(v/R)^2\cos\omega t.$$

Similarly,

$$\ddot{y} = -R(v/R)^2\sin\omega t.$$

So the total acceleration is

$$a = \sqrt{\ddot{x}^2 + \ddot{y}^2}$$
$$= v^2/R$$

(using $\sin^2 + \cos^2 = 1$).

There's an even prettier demonstration with vectors and geometry, which we will leave as an exercise for the reader.

Fitting a Curve to the Planets

Name(s): _____

You have data about planets in our solar system. You'll now study the relationship between the attributes **orbit_AU** and **year**.

orbit_AU   is the distance from the planet to the sun: the radius of its orbit in *Astronomical Units* (AU). One AU is the radius of Earth's orbit, about 150,000,000 kilometers or 93,000,000 miles.

year   is the planet's period in Earth years. It's how long the planet takes to go around the sun.

We want to understand the relationship between these two variables as accurately as possible. In practical terms, we want to be able to predict either one accurately given the other. That means finding a *function* that relates them. Here's what to do:

1. Make a scatter plot showing **year** (vertical) as a function of **orbit_AU** (horizontal). You should see an arc of points—the relationship is curved upward. We want to know what that function is. One way is to fit a curve directly to the points.

2. Before we do that, however, select points on the graph to verify which planets you're looking at—they're Jupiter and the ones beyond. Earth and its neighbors are jammed together down in the lower left. Expand the axes to see how the inner planets form a similar arc. Note how *far* you have to expand them.

Hint: You can always return to viewing the whole data set by reselecting **Scatter plot** from the popup menu in the graph.

Now we'll draw a curve and make it match the points. Our first guess—because it's curved upwards—is that it's a parabola. We'll try $y = x^2$, or, in the language of this activity,

> **year = orbit_AU^2**.

3. Be sure the graph is active. Then choose **Plot Function** from the **Graph** menu.

4. Enter the formula **orbit_AU^2**. Enter only the right-hand side (no **year =**). Click **OK** to close the formula editor and make the function appear. Sketch what you get at right.

It doesn't fit the points! We're going to change the exponent until it does. We'll use one of the most important Fathom tools: a slider.

5. Choose **Slider** from the **Insert** menu. A slider, which is mostly an axis with a little rectangle and a pointer on it, appears with text reading something like **V1 = 5.00**.

6. Drag the pointer on the slider. What do you observe?

You need to know how to
    add a new attribute
    write a formula for an attribute
    make a scatter plot
    adjust the bounds of axes

You'll learn how to
    add a function to a scatter plot
    use a slider

In the 1600s, Johannes Kepler, a German astronomer, figured out a lot of things about the motions of the planets that paved the way for Isaac Newton's understanding of gravity, which, with a few modifications from Einstein, we still use today. One of Kepler's biggest contributions was the relationship you're about to discover using Fathom.

Note: We could also work on changing a coefficient, that is, make it $y = kx^2$. That's a good thing to try, though it won't help this time.

You can also make a new slider by dragging one from the shelf.

7. Edit the **V1** to read **exponent**.

8. Now double-click the formula for the function at the bottom of the graph. The formula editor appears.

9. Edit the formula so it reads **orbit_AU^exponent** instead of **orbit_AU²**. Close the editor.

10. Now drag the pointer on the slider. Again, what do you observe? (The curve should change. How?)

11. What value for the exponent fits the points best?

To get a really precise **exponent**, we're going to make a residual plot.

12. Select the formula for the curve by selecting it (single-click) at the bottom of the graph.

13. Choose **Make Residual Plot** from the **Graph** menu. A residual plot appears, showing how far each planet is from the curve. Unless you're fantastically lucky, the residuals will show a systematic drift. That is, the curve doesn't actually hit the points. Yet it looks as if it does in the main graph. Explain here how this is possible.

14. Adjust the exponent slider until the planets' residuals are as small as possible. You may have to zoom in to the slider axis to get enough control. We find that Pluto doesn't fit too well, but the rest do. What is your new exponent value? Report all of Fathom's figures here.

> Zoom in on an axis either by pushing the axis numbers "off the end" or by **CTRL**-clicking (Windows) or **OPTION**-clicking (Mac) to make a magnifying glass on the axis itself.

Going Further

1. If you square both sides of your equation, you'll get another form, namely,

   year² = orbit_AU³.

   Use Fathom to demonstrate more directly that this relationship also holds.

2. Suppose, after you tried the simple parabola, you thought it would be better to change a coefficient instead of the exponent. You would make a slider called **coefficient** and put it into the formula. Try that, play with it, and explain how you can tell that just changing the coefficient is not going to provide a good fit for the data.

3. Suppose you didn't think it was a parabola at first, but an exponential: namely,

   year = 2^(k · orbit_AU).

   Try that and other exponentials (use a slider for **k**), and then describe, in words, how the graphs convince you that the relationship does not have an exponential form.

Straightening the Planets with Logs

Name(s): _____

You have data about planets in our solar system. Now you'll study the relationship between the attributes **orbit_AU** and **year**.

orbit_AU   is the distance from the planet to the sun: the radius of its orbit in *Astronomical Units* (AU). One AU is the radius of Earth's orbit, about 150,000,000 kilometers or 93,000,000 miles.

year   is the planet's period in Earth years. It's how long the planet takes to go around the sun.

You need to know how to
add a new attribute
write a formula for an attribute
make a scatter plot
adjust the bounds of axes
add a line to a scatter plot

You'll learn how to
use a log transformation to straighten data

We want to understand the relationship between these two variables as accurately as possible. In practical terms, we want to be able to predict either one accurately given the other. That means finding a *function* that relates them. Here's what to do:

1. Make a scatter plot showing **year** (vertical) as a function of **orbit_AU** (horizontal). You should see an arc of points—the relationship is curved upward. We want to know what that function is. We're going to find out by *transforming* the data.

2. Before we do that, however, select points on the graph to verify which planets you're looking at—mostly you can see Jupiter and beyond. Earth and its neighbors are jammed together down in the lower left. Expand the axes to see how the inner planets form a similar arc. Note how *far* you have to expand them.

Hint: You can always return to viewing the whole data set by reselecting **Scatter Plot** from the popup menu in the graph itself.

It turns out that in situations like these—where points are all crowded together—it sometimes helps to take the logarithm of one or both of the attributes. Try it . . . .

3. Make two new attributes, **logOrbit** and **logYear**. These are not formulas, just the names of the attributes.

4. Assign formulas to those attributes: **log(orbit_AU)** and **log(year)**. The values appear when you close the formula editor.

5. Make a scatter plot showing **logYear** as a function of **logOrbit**. Wow! It's a straight line! And notice: You can see all the points, nicely separated, in a single screen. Sketch the scatter plot, label and scale the axes, and label the positions of Earth and Saturn.

Notice that Earth has a value of zero for both. That's correct, since its original value was 1.00 and log1 = 0. For outer planets, the logs are positive; inner planets are negative. The value of the log is the exponent (base 10) of the value in terms of Earth. So, for example, **logOrbit** for Saturn is 0.98 (close to 1), which means that the distance from Saturn to the sun is about ten times the Earth's (which is correct).

6. Find the equation for the line. (You could use the least-squares line.) Write it here:

Data in Depth
© 2001 Key Curriculum Press

7. Time for some algebra. Take "10-to-the" of both sides of the equation. What do you get? (Remember: $10^{(\log \text{ of anything})}$ = that thing. For example, $10^{\log x} = x$.)

8. Look back at the least-squares line you fitted to the transformed data (Step 6). What does the slope mean?

9. Suppose there was another planet exactly twice as far from the sun as Earth. How long would its year be?

10. Suppose there was a planet whose year was exactly 20 years long. How far would it be from the sun?

Going Further

1. In the log method, you see all the points, which is good. You also see a pattern. The planets seem more or less evenly spaced (in the log) except that there's a gap. If there was a planet there, how far from the sun would it be? How long would its year be? What is in that spot in our solar system, anyway?

2. Earth is at (0, 0) because we're measuring everything in Earth units and log1 = 0. But when you fitted a least-squares line to the planet's data (in Step 6 above), there was still a tiny intercept. How can that be? Explain what that intercept means.

3. Redo this section, but using **orbit_mKm** (radius of the orbit in millions of kilometers) and its log instead of the **orbit_AU** variables. The slope should be the same, but the intercept is not zero. Explain that.

Moore's Law

- Two structured computer activities
- Data from file
- Student pages 109–110
- Intermediate, basic features

The goal of these two activities—*Moore's Law Logs* and *Moore's Law Redux*—is to predict the number of transistors that will be on a chip in the year 2005. These two activities use the same data, but different strategies. Just as with the *Planets* (pages 102–107), one is an activity about using a log transformation in order to straighten data; the other fits a curve to the points.

You may choose which activity to do. If you do both, it might be worth comparing groups' predictions across the two strategies. Which strategy gives a tighter distribution of results?

Topics
history of technology
straightening data
exponential relationships
logarithms
semilog transformation

Materials
Moore

Students need to be able to
add new attributes
write formulas for attributes
make scatter plots
plot functions on a scatter plot

What's Important Here

- The data are exponential, so you apply the log only to the vertical (dependent) axis. (This is called a "semilog" plot, as opposed to the "log-log" transformation that straightens power-law data as in the *Planets*.)

- Each of these fits really requires two parameters (e.g., slope and intercept if you straighten the data); in the *Planets'* fit, working in Earth units eliminated the need for one parameter (the intercept was effectively zero). If you use sliders, this means that you have to adjust two sliders to get the fit, as opposed to the single (exponent) slider we used in the *Planets*.

Discussion Questions

⟳ How did you go about fitting the curve? (Listen for multiple strategies. Students may use formulas, sliders, computation, or things we never anticipated.)

⟳ When you fit a line to the logarithms of data, what does the slope mean? What's the intercept? (For a quantitative answer, many students will need the algebra demonstrated—preferably by another student.)

⟳ Both techniques give similar answers because underneath, they're the same mathematical model. Why is that the case?

Tech Notes

We have avoided much of the round-off problem by using the attribute **since1970** instead of **year**. But be warned: The equation for a line shows the number of significant figures needed to describe the line unambiguously *as it appears on the screen*. Therefore, to get more significant figures, you may need to zoom in to a small part of the scatter plot (near a right-hand point is good). The prudent teacher will explore this issue before class, the better to help students who need guidance; the issue is also discussed more thoroughly in Chapter 5, *Lines and Leverage* (page 127).

It looks to the author as if the exponent of the data changes for about the last four data points, as if the increase is not as fast. If students focus on the last four points when making their fit, they will be more consistent. Whether to suggest this to students or to let them point it out depends on your situation.

Hint: If a curve is a little bit off, tweak the formula (or the sliders controlling coefficients).

Also: If you're a long way from the axis, a small change in the slope (the exponent) will make a big difference in the curve.

Developments in chip technology have inspired claims that the density of transistors will be even higher than Moore's law predicts. So maybe the "flattening" we see is just a phase we're going through.

Data in Depth
© 2001 Key Curriculum Press

Moore's Law Logs

Name(s): _____

Several "Moore's laws" are attributed to Gordon Moore, who was the first CEO of Intel, a company known for making computer CPUs (central processing units). The gist of these laws is that computers keep getting more powerful *exponentially.*

In this activity, you'll *predict the number of transistors in a CPU chip in the year 2005.* We'll use a logarithmic strategy for making the prediction.

1. Open **Moore.** There is one case for each major Intel CPU since 1970. The attributes are the name of the chip; **year,** the year it was released; **KTransistors,** the number of transistors in thousands (kilotransistors); and **since1970,** which is like **year,** except that it's years since 1970 instead of since the beginning of the Common era.

2. If it is not already made, make a graph with **since1970** on the horizontal axis and **KTransistors** on the vertical. Sketch the graph here, with scaled axes.

You need
    a scientific calculator

You need to know how to
    transform data using logs
    make a new attribute and define it with a formula
    fit a line to data

You'll learn how to
    straighten data
    use logarithms
    make predictions

If the function is exponential, making a log transformation on the vertical axis will make the data straight. (Moore predicted that the number of transistors would increase every year by the same *percentage.* Since a ratio of numbers turns into a difference of their logs, an exponential—constant ratios—turns into a straight line—constant differences—under a log transformation.)

3. Make a new attribute, **logKT,** and give it a formula, **log(KTransistors).**

4. Make a new graph. Put **since1970** on the horizontal axis and **logKT** on the vertical axis. It should look like a straight line. Sketch the graph.

For a completely different, log-free strategy—drawing the curve directly—see *Moore's Law Redux* on page 110.

5. Choose **Movable Line** from the **Graph** menu. Move it to match the points.

6. Zoom in and read the graph to estimate the log of the number of transistors in 2005. Write that number and the equation of the line here.

7. Change the log back to a "regular" number. What does this strategy predict for the actual number (not the log of the number) of transistors in 2005?

Moore's Law Redux

Name(s): _____

Several "Moore's laws" are attributed to Gordon Moore, who was the first CEO of Intel, a company known for making computer CPUs (central processing units). The gist of these laws is that computers keep getting more powerful *exponentially*.

You need to know how to
plot a function

You'll learn how to
fit curves
make predictions

In this activity, *you'll predict the number of transistors in a CPU chip in the year 2005*. Our strategy is to fit a curve to the data.

1. Open **Moore.** There is one case for each major Intel CPU since 1970. The attributes are the name of the chip; **year,** the year it was released; **KTransistors,** the number of transistors in thousands (kilotransistors); and **since1970,** which is like **year,** except that it's years since 1970 instead of since the beginning of the Common era.

2. If it is not already made, make a graph with **since1970** on the horizontal axis and **KTransistors** on the vertical.

3. Try to make a function that fits the data as you see them. Since it's exponential, the formula can be of the form $A * 2^{(k\,*since1970)}$; the problem is figuring out **k** and **A.** Try different values until the curve fits the data well.

One way to make a function is to select the graph and choose **Plot Function** from the **Graph** menu. If you know about sliders, you can make sliders for **k** and **A.**

4. Sketch your graph, with labeled and scaled axes:

5. Use the graph or the function you find to predict the number of transistors in 2005. (There **since1970** will be equal to 35.) Write the function and your prediction here:

6. Extension: Moore's original law was stated in terms of doubling time, that is, the time you need for the quantity to increase by a factor of 2. Rewrite your equation in the form **KTransistors** $= A * 2^{(since1970\,/\,T)}$. Verify that it works by plotting it.

7. The constant **T** is the doubling time. Why?

8. The original statement Moore made in 1965 was that the number of transistors in a chip would double every two years. Did that turn out to be true?

Area and Perimeter: A Study in Limits

- Structured computer activity
- Data generated in simulation
- Student pages 112–113
- Intermediate, medium features

As described, students simulate creating random rectangles. You may also do this very effectively (especially with less experienced students) if you have them create genuine rectangles, cut them out, and measure them. Make sure, though, that students have experience with parabolas if you do the second page. If not, simply exploring the plot is worthwhile.

Topics
area and perimeter
parabolas
visualization
fitting nonlinear functions using
  variable parameters

What's Important Here

- Using random numbers for simulation.
- Using a scatter plot of geometrical data to illuminate geometrical restrictions.

Discussion Questions

➲ What do rectangles in the lower left look like? (Small.)

➲ How about rectangles in the lower right? (Long and skinny.)

➲ What are the shapes of the rectangles along the curved border? (They're squares.)

➲ Why do you suppose so many of the points seem to line up close to the boundary? (Large-area rectangles must be close to being squares or they'd have a dimension larger than 10. For smaller rectangles, you can have a surprisingly large **length / width** before the rectangle moves a long way from the border. But most important (and subtlest), the distribution of the quotient of two uniform random variables, **larger / smaller**, is greatly skewed toward 1. So you *do* get more squarish figures.)

What's the Formula?

Here's an elegant answer to *Going Further 1*, supplied by a teacher: The curved boundary is made of the rectangles with the maximum area for a given perimeter. Those are squares. So what's the area of a square with perimeter **P**? Each side is **P/4**, so the area is **P²/16**. Therefore, the equation is **A = (1/16) P²**.

There are other perfectly good approaches.

What about the *other* boundary? That's created because we're limited to 10 in **length** and **width**. So for some perimeters there is a *minimum* area. For example, with a **perimeter** of 30, what is the skinniest (minimum area) rectangle we can make? You can only spend a maximum of 20 on two **length**s, and you'll have 10 left over for the **width**s. You wind up with a rectangle of area 50. The width of such a rectangle (taking **length = 10** as the long side) is

$$width = \frac{(perimeter - 20)}{2}, \text{ so}$$

$$area_{min} = 10 \times \frac{(perimeter - 20)}{2} = 5(perimeter) - 100$$

which is the line we seek for **perimeter > 20**.

Area and Perimeter: A Study in Limits

Name(s): _____

How are areas and perimeters of rectangles related? We all know the formulas—*area = length · width, perimeter = 2(length + width)*—but if you look at them from a data perspective, what do you get?

In this activity, we'll use Fathom to generate the measurements for rectangles randomly and explore the relationships. You can also generate rectangles haphazardly using any other technique you like (asking people to make them, using *The Geometer's Sketchpad®*, etc.) and use those data.

1. Open a new Fathom document and create a new case table.

2. Make two attributes—**length** and **width**.

3. With the case table selected, choose **New Cases...** from the **Data** menu. Tell Fathom to make 200 cases. They appear, though their attributes have no values.

Making Random Rectangles

We won't actually make the rectangles here; we'll just make the measurements.

4. Select **length**, and choose **Edit Formula** from the **Edit** menu to bring up the formula editor.

5. In that box, enter the formula **random(10)**. Close the box by clicking **OK.** Now **length** is filled with random numbers ranging from 0 to 10.

6. Use that same formula to define values for **width**. Now you have random numbers for both attributes.

7. Make a scatter plot of these two attributes; it ought to look random.

Calculating Area and Perimeter

If you got your rectangles honestly (for example, by cutting them out of paper), join us here. Enter your data in the table and proceed.

8. Make two new attributes, **area** and **perimeter**. Make formulas to determine these; the formulas should depend only on **length** and **width**. Copy the first two or three cases from your table here:

9. Make a scatter plot with **perimeter** on the horizontal axis and **area** on the vertical axis. Sketch the graph at right; label and scale the axes.

10. If everything went well, there should be no points in the upper-left part of the graph—a region bounded by a curve. Explain why there are no points in that region.

You need to know how to
make new attributes
write formulas for attributes

You'll learn
how to plot functions
how to make sliders
one way to use random numbers

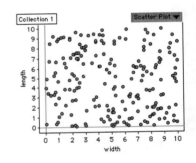

Data in Depth
© 2001 Key Curriculum Press

Area and Perimeter:
A Study in Limits (continued)

Name(s): _____

The Boundary

Now your goal is to figure out the equation for that curved upper boundary of the cloud of points. There are two strategies: the theoretical one and the empirical one. In the theoretical strategy, you figure it out from the equations and just plot it. These directions will concentrate on the empirical.

The boundary curves upward. It might be exponential, or it might be some polynomial (such as a quadratic). Since finding areas can involve squaring, we'll try a quadratic first, **area = perimeter²**.

11. Select the graph and choose **Plot Function** from the **Graph** menu. The formula box appears.

12. Enter **perimeter^2** into the box and close it. The curve will appear, as in the illustration. (Remember that you *don't* enter the left-hand side of a function in Fathom.) Unfortunately, the curve is too steep.

You can alter the formula on your own, but the following is fun . . .

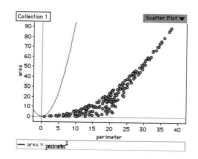

13. We'll make a slider. Choose **Slider** from the **Insert** menu. A slider appears; it looks like a number line with a pointer on it. There's also some text that gives the name of the variable and its value, for example **V1 = 5**. Change the name **V1** to **denom**.

14. Edit the plotted function (double-click the equation at the bottom of the graph). Change it to **perimeter² / denom**. Now you can control the value of **denom** by dragging the slider's thumb. As you do so, the function changes. You will have to change the scale of the slider. Do it the way you change an axis—by dragging in the numbers with the hand, or **CTRL-SHIFT**-clicking (Windows) or **OPTION-SHIFT**-clicking (Mac) to zoom out.

15. Change the value of **denom** until the curve accurately forms the boundary. What value of **denom** did you get? (It should be greater than 10.)

16. Study the points near the boundary. What is the shape of the rectangles near the boundary curve? That is, what do they have in common?

17. Explain why your answer to the preceding question makes sense. That is, why do all those rectangles have that property?

Going Further

1. Show, algebraically, what the curve's equation must be, and show that it's the same as the one you got by looking at the data.

2. Depending on how you made the rectangles, there may be another empty zone in the lower-right corner of the scatter plot. Why are there no rectangles there? What is the equation of *that* border? Why?

How Much Tape Is Left?

- Structured computer activity
- Data from measurement
- Student pages 116–117
- Independent, medium features

Here's the task: Figure out how to use the diameter of a roll of adding-machine tape to tell how much is left on the roll.

The function is nonlinear because you eat up more diameter per meter of paper as you get closer to the core—you go around more times. If you're careful measuring the paper tape, this activity works well. By using algebra and a little geometry, you can actually figure something out that you could imagine needing in various contexts: using wrapping paper or tape, filming a movie, or using a big printing press.

What's Important Here

- Prediction. Students agree that the function will be nonlinear and why. But they disagree as to which way it will curve. It's worth it to insist that we all sketch the curve before we start measuring. *It is not important, however, that we all get it right or that we agree.* The data will correct us soon enough!

- Careful measurement really helps.

- More advanced students can do more of the algebra, but you don't need it to use the data to make a plausible prediction about the total length.

- Straightening by squaring the diameter can be mysterious. The key points are (a) recognizing (from the sizes of the residuals) that the fit is better, and (b) being able to convert the squared value to a linear one—and understanding why you have to.

Discussion Questions

↪ When you make your plot of **D** and **L** on the first page, which attribute goes on which axis? (We're studying **L** as a function of **D**, so traditionally, **D** is horizontal.)

↪ Why is the function curved?

↪ How can it be that the data looked so straight?

Extensions

- The most obvious and fun one is to have each group unroll and measure their paper tape and compare it to their predictions.

- Have students do the (simple) algebra to turn their least-squares fit for **L** (the length remaining) as a function of **DD** (the square of the diameter) into an equation for **L** as a function of **D**. Then they can plot the curved function on the unsquared plot. They should use sliders for the coefficient and intercept, and make a residual plot. Then they can see how varying the parameters changes the fit.

- Advanced algebra students can do the algebra to derive the expected relationship between diameter and length. The derivation appears on page 115.

Topics
> nonlinear functions (parabolas)
> straightening
> residual plots

Materials
> one roll of adding-machine tape per group
> millimeter rulers
> space to measure

Students need to be able to
> input data
> define new attributes with formulas
> make scatter plots and least-squares lines

This activity is algebraically related to *The Great Toilet Paper Mystery* (page 119). Toilet paper is squishier than paper tape and therefore has more variability, so more experience and care are needed to get the activity to work. But it's really fun, too.

Note: The straightening (we square the diameter) requires a little algebraic sleight-of-hand. It works because the vertex of the parabola is on the axis (see the algebra below). That is, if the quadratic had an x-term, plotting x^2 against y would not yield a straight line.

How Much Tape Is Left?

- Combine this activity with *The Great Toilet Paper Mystery* (page 119). Discuss the differences between the materials and the setups, and how they affect what you do.

The Algebra

How does the amount left on a roll of adding-machine tape depend on its diameter?

We will make a fundamental (and good) assumption: that the length of tape is proportional to the cross-sectional area of the tape. That shape is an annulus because of the core in the middle of the roll. The area of an annulus is the area of the outside circle minus the area of the inside circle, so we have

$$L = KA_{annulus} \text{ or } L = \frac{K\pi}{4}(d^2 - c^2)$$

where L is the length of tape remaining, d is the diameter of the roll, c is the diameter of the core, and K is the constant of proportionality relating the area of the annulus to the length of the tape. If we invent a couple more "constants of convenience,"

$$B = \frac{K\pi}{4} \text{ and } V = \frac{K\pi}{4}c^2 = Bc^2,$$

we get $L = Bd^2 - V$.

Thus, $L(d)$ is a parabola that opens up with a vertex at $(0, -V)$. It crosses the *x*-axis (actually the *d*-axis) where $d = c$.

In our situation, however, we don't know L, the length of tape still on the roll. We know only P, the amount we have pulled off. And $L + P = T$, the total length of the tape. Substituting and solving for P,

$$P = (V + T) - Bd^2.$$

If we plot P as a function of d^2 instead of as a function of d, you can see from the last equation that we'll get a straight line with $-B$ as the slope and $(T + V)$ as the intercept. So that's exactly what we do, using a least-squares fit. With a numerical value for B, we measure c (the core diameter) to get V. With that and the numerical value for $(T + V)$—the intercept—we get T. That is, without unrolling the whole tape, we can solve for the length of the entire roll. And with that constant T we have a complete numerical description of P—or L—as a function of d.

It's worth asking what these constants mean. See if you can come to terms with these:

- $1/K$ is the thickness of the paper. B is just $\pi/4$ times that.

- V is the amount of paper that could fill the core if the tape were wound down to zero radius. So the intercept $(T + V)$ would be the total length of paper tape if the manufacturer had filled the core and kept the original diameter.

You don't have to use this section in order to get good math out of the activity. But in case you want the whole picture, we have included this.

Do not expect students to get the answer this quickly. This write-up (like most math-book derivations) benefits from our having thought about it, analyzed the data, and erased all the wrong paths we took.

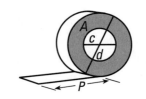

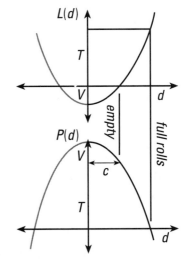

How Much Tape Is Left?

Name(s): _____

How do you use the diameter of a roll of adding-machine tape to tell how much tape is left on the roll?

That's the question for this activity. The trick is that we want to answer it *without unrolling the entire roll.* So first we'll explore a related question:

How is the amount of tape you've pulled off related to the diameter of the roll?

That we can work on. We'll get some data by measuring and unrolling part of the roll, measuring as we go. But first . . .

1. Measure the diameter of the full roll and the diameter of the core. Be really careful and precise. Make sure you and your group know how you'll do it exactly the same way every time. Record those values here:

2. Before you start unrolling, draw a graph of your prediction for length pulled off (**L**) as a function of diameter (**D**). Scale and label your axes as well as you can. For example, when **L = 0**, **D** is the diameter of the roll. As **L** increases, **D** gets smaller. The question is, *how?* Is it straight? Curved? If so, which way? Don't do any algebra—yet; just think about the situation. Sketch your "prediction" graph here:

3. Make your measurements and record them in the table shown here. Measure out a few meters and record the *total* length unrolled so far under **L**. Then measure the diameter *carefully* and record it under **D**. Stop when the roll is about half unrolled. For a typical roll of paper tape, you'll unroll about 25 meters of tape and have about 8 data points.

4. Enter the data into Fathom and make a scatter plot. If you're like us, the data look straight at first glance.

5. With the graph selected, choose **Least-Squares Line** from the **Graph** menu.

6. We need to see how good the fit is. Choose **Make Residual Plot** from the **Graph** menu. Our graph is shown here; yours should look similar.

Notice: Even though the least-squares fit has an r^2 close to 1.00, there is something systematically wrong with the line as a model. The residuals form an obvious and consistent bow, which you can barely make out on the top graph.

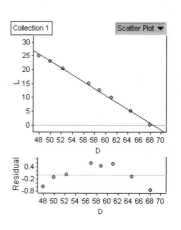

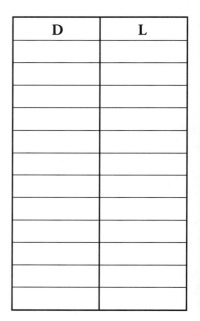

You need
roll of adding-machine tape
millimeter ruler

You need to know how to
input data
construct attributes with formulas
make scatter plots and least-squares lines

You'll learn about
using nonlinear functions to model data
predicting

D	L

Data in Depth
© 2001 Key Curriculum Press

7. Compare what you have in your graph so far to your prediction in Step 2. Which aspects of it are the same, and which are different?

Making the Fit

At this point, you could use some reasoning to figure out the best thing to do next, but we'll use guess-and-check here in the instructions. We'll return to reason in a moment.

8. You look at the residuals and say, "Looks like a parabola. I should try squaring something." But you don't know whether to square **D** or **L**. So you make two new attributes, **DD** and **LL**, which are the squares of those two attributes.

In the formula, don't forget to press * between the attributes, or to use the ^ to make an exponent. **DD** is just a name; by itself it doesn't mean "D times D."

9. Now plot all different combinations of **D**s and their squares (on the horizontal) against **L**s and their squares (vertical). One combination (**DD** versus **L**) will be close to a straight line, if everything has gone well. Verify that by trying them all with least-squares lines. Sketch your *four* residual plots here. Label *and scale* the vertical axes.

10. Write the equation for the least-squares line on the **DD** versus **L** plot here:

11. When you're out of tape, **D** will be the diameter of the core. What will **DD** be at that time? (Refer back to Step 1 for your measurement.)

12. Plug that into the formula you got in Step 10. That predicts the value of **L** when **D** is equal to the diameter of the core—in other words, how much tape you've pulled off when there is no more tape on the roll. It's the total length of the roll of tape. (a) What do you get for the total length? (b) How much is left?

13. We got lucky with that squaring trick—or maybe it wasn't luck. Work with your group—and anybody else you can get to help—to come up with at least one sound mathematical reason (preferably more) why the **D** should be squared. Write your reasons here.

Nonlinear Geometrical Sonatas

- Eight open-ended computer activities
- Data from measurement
- Student pages 119–126
- Intermediate, medium features

For the Sonatas, students should turn in the blackline master page that comes with each situation as the backbone of their solution. You can use the Sonata Summary Sheet (page xxii) with other problems.

Sonata 12: The Great Toilet Paper Mystery

This is a good follow-up to *How Much Tape Is Left?* Toilet paper is harder to measure because of the "squish factor," but its intrinsic interest may inspire your students to careful and creative measurement and data analysis.

Sonata 13: Printing Paragraphs

Even very experienced students, on seeing how height decreases with width, will say, "Oh, it must be exponential." But actually their product is roughly constant: **height · width = K**. They can even make that **K** a slider parameter to find its value.

   Then, since **(1 / height) = width / K**, you can straighten the data, by plotting **(1 / height)** as a function of **width**. Then ask, "What does **K** mean?" (It's the area.) We take this activity further, improving the model, in *Estimating Parameters Using Residuals,* page 183.

Sonata 14: Incredible Shrinking Text

The column length is roughly proportional to the square of the point size. This is because point size affects width as well as height, so it's proportional to the area of the character.

Sonata 15: Measuring the Bass

If you have access to an electric bass (or another large fretted instrument), you can discover—if you measure carefully—that the distance between the frets decreases exponentially as you go higher on the fingerboard. Thus, a semilog straightening works.

Sonata 16: Puff Puff Puff Puff Pop

With balloons, the volume is roughly proportional to the number of puffs. So circumference changes almost as the cube root of the number of puffs. Thus, **volume** is a useful attribute. A log-log plot will tell you the actual power relationship more accurately. But for pre-log-log students, comparing a cubic to a linear model is adequate.

More Ideas for Nonlinear Data

You can assign any of these four problems as Sonatas (give students the Summary Sheet from page xxii if they need it) or simply as problems or short projects.

Topics
   nonlinear functions and data measurement

Materials (Sonata 12)
   toilet paper (one roll per group)
   rulers

Materials (Sonata 13)
   copies of *Materials for Printing Paragraphs,* page 121
   rulers

Materials (Sonata 14)
   copies of *Materials for Incredible Shrinking Text,* page 123
   rulers

Materials (Sonata 15)
   electric bass
   rulers

Materials (Sonata 16)
   balloons
   rulers and string or measuring tapes

Students need to be able to
   enter data
   make scatter plots
   use formulas as functions in scatter plots

Sonata 12: The Great Toilet Paper Mystery

Name(s): _____

Your job is to come up with a way to determine the number of squares left on the toilet paper roll from measuring its diameter. There must be a *function* that will tell you the answer. You feed it the diameter; it spits out the number of squares.

You need
    roll of toilet paper
    millimeter ruler

Conjecture

Without measuring or unrolling, make your best guess as to the form of the function and sketch it in a labeled, scaled graph (making estimates of the measurements). Be sure to show how you figured out the form of the function and/or how you know the graph has the shape that it does. Be sure to write down your assumptions.

Measurement

You guessed it. Unroll the roll, measuring from time to time and, of course, counting the squares. It will go better if you have a plan for doing this in an organized fashion. Explain your plan below. Enter the data into Fathom.

Comparison

Compare your conjecture to reality. How close did you come? Explain any differences. If you have done the activity *How Much Tape Is Left?*, comment on how this one is different.

Sonata 13: Printing Paragraphs

Name(s): _____

You get a handout with some paragraphs on it. They're all exactly the same text, but they are set in columns of different widths. How does the height of the column depend on the width?

You need

> millimeter ruler
> copy of *Materials for Printing Paragraphs*

You'll show that you can

> measure accurately
> make decisions about measurements
> figure out how the two attributes are related

Conjectures

Look at the page (but don't measure). Your attributes are **height** and **width**. Think in advance about how they are related? What would a graph of them look like? How do you write that in algebra? If you don't know exactly, what can you say *about* the relationship? Extension: These paragraphs are set "ragged right"; that is, the right margin isn't straight. Can you take that into account in your algebra?

Measurement

Use centimeters and tenths of centimeters. You and your partner will have to decide how to measure height and width. Be as precise and consistent as you can. Describe what you decide.

Comparison

What did you discover? Do your measurements support your conjectures?

Data in Depth
© 2001 Key Curriculum Press

Materials for Printing Paragraphs

The subjects (or objects) of statistical examination are often called cases. Here, in the rows, the cases are individual Westvaco employees. Their characteristics, in the columns, are variables. If you pick a row, and read across, you get information about a single case. (For example, Robert Martin, in Row 44, was salaried, was born in September, 1937, was hired in October, 1967, was chosen for layoff in Round 2, and was 54 on 1/1/91.) Although reading across may seem the natural way to read the table, in statistics you will often find it useful to pick a column, and read down.

The subjects (or objects) of statistical examination are often called cases. Here, in the rows, the cases are individual Westvaco employees. Their characteristics, in the columns, are variables. If you pick a row, and read across, you get information about a single case. (For example, Robert Martin, in Row 44, was salaried, was born in September, 1937, was hired in October, 1967, was chosen for layoff in Round 2, and was 54 on 1/1/91.) Although reading across may seem the natural way to read the table, in statistics you will often find it useful to pick a column, and read down.

The subjects (or objects) of statistical examination are often called cases. Here, in the rows, the cases are individual Westvaco employees. Their characteristics, in the columns, are variables. If you pick a row, and read across, you get information about a single case. (For example, Robert Martin, in Row 44, was salaried, was born in September, 1937, was hired in October, 1967, was chosen for layoff in Round 2, and was 54 on 1/1/91.) Although reading across may seem the natural way to read the table, in statistics you will often find it useful to pick a column, and read down.

The subjects (or objects) of statistical examination are often called cases. Here, in the rows, the cases are individual Westvaco employees. Their characteristics, in the columns, are variables. If you pick a row, and read across, you get information about a single case. (For example, Robert Martin, in Row 44, was salaried, was born in September, 1937, was hired in October, 1967, was chosen for layoff in Round 2, and was 54 on 1/1/91.) Although reading across may seem the natural way to read the table, in statistics you will often find it useful to pick a column, and read down.

The subjects (or objects) of statistical examination are often called cases. Here, in the rows, the cases are individual Westvaco employees. Their characteristics, in the columns, are variables. If you pick a row, and read across, you get information about a single case. (For example, Robert Martin, in Row 44, was salaried, was born in September, 1937, was hired in October, 1967, was chosen for layoff in Round 2, and was 54 on 1/1/91.) Although reading across may seem the natural way to read the table, in statistics you will often find it useful to pick a column, and read down.

The subjects (or objects) of statistical examination are often called cases. Here, in the rows, the cases are individual Westvaco employees. Their characteristics, in the columns, are variables. If you pick a row, and read across, you get information about a single case. (For example, Robert Martin, in Row 44, was salaried, was born in September, 1937, was hired in October, 1967, was chosen for layoff in Round 2, and was 54 on 1/1/91.) Although reading across may seem the natural way to read the table, in statistics you will often find it useful to pick a column, and read down.

The subjects (or objects) of statistical examination are often called cases. Here, in the rows, the cases are individual Westvaco employees. Their characteristics, in the columns, are variables. If you pick a row, and read across, you get information about a single case. (For example, Robert Martin, in Row 44, was salaried, was born in September, 1937, was hired in October, 1967, was chosen for layoff in Round 2, and was 54 on 1/1/91.) Although reading across may seem the natural way to read the table, in statistics you will often find it useful to pick a column, and read down.

from *Statistics in Action: Practical Principles for a World of Uncertainty* by Scheaffer/Watkins.

Sonata 14: Incredible Shrinking Text

Name(s): _____

You need the page of text that has the same paragraph printed in different point sizes. All the columns are the same width. The question is how the **length** of the column depends on the **size** of the type.

You need
millimeter ruler
copy of *Materials for Incredible Shrinking Text*

Conjectures

Predict the *symbolic form* of the way **length** depends on **size**. The form is what matters, even if you have some constants wrong (estimate them anyway). That is, is it linear? Exponential? Quadratic? Sinusoidal? What would the equation look like? Write what you think and sketch a graph of **length** as a function of **size**.

You'll show that you can
measure accurately
make decisions about measurements
figure out how the two attributes are related

Measurement

Notice that the 14-point column is in two parts. Be sure you are consistent in how you measure length and width. Use centimeters and tenths of centimeters. Describe decisions or assumptions you made.

Comparison

Again, what did you discover? How did your conjectures do? How long do you predict an 18-point column would be? How about a 12-point column twice as wide? (Extension: How do you suppose the number of lines of text—as opposed to the length in centimeters—depends on the point size?)

Materials for Incredible Shrinking Text

(14) The subjects (or objects) of statistical examination are often called cases. Here, in the rows, the cases are individual Westvaco employees. Their characteristics, in the columns, are variables. If you pick a row, and read across, you get information about a single case. (For example, Robert Martin, in Row 44, was salaried, was born in September, 1937, was hired in October, 1967, was chosen for layoff in Round 2, and was 54 on 1/1/91.) Although reading across may seem the natural way to read the table, in statistics you will often find it useful to pick a column, and read down.

(5) The subjects (or objects) of statistical examination are often called cases. Here, in the rows, the cases are individual Westvaco employees. Their characteristics, in the columns, are variables. If you pick a row, and read across, you get information about a single case. (For example, Robert Martin, in Row 44, was salaried, was born in September, 1937, was hired in October, 1967, was chosen for layoff in Round 2, and was 54 on 1/1/91.) Although reading across may seem the natural way to read the table, in statistics you will often find it useful to pick a column, and read down.

(12) The subjects (or objects) of statistical examination are often called cases. Here, in the rows, the cases are individual Westvaco employees. Their characteristics, in the columns, are variables. If you pick a row, and read across, you get information about a single case. (For example, Robert Martin, in Row 44, was salaried, was born in September, 1937, was hired in October, 1967, was chosen for layoff in Round 2, and was 54 on 1/1/91.) Although reading across may seem the natural way to read the table, in statistics you will often find it useful to pick a column, and read down.

(11) The subjects (or objects) of statistical examination are often called cases. Here, in the rows, the cases are individual Westvaco employees. Their characteristics, in the columns, are variables. If you pick a row, and read across, you get information about a single case. (For example, Robert Martin, in Row 44, was salaried, was born in September, 1937, was hired in October, 1967, was chosen for layoff in Round 2, and was 54 on 1/1/91.) Although reading across may seem the natural way to read the table, in statistics you will often find it useful to pick a column, and read down.

(6) The subjects (or objects) of statistical examination are often called cases. Here, in the rows, the cases are individual Westvaco employees. Their characteristics, in the columns, are variables. If you pick a row, and read across, you get information about a single case. (For example, Robert Martin, in Row 44, was salaried, was born in September, 1937, was hired in October, 1967, was chosen for layoff in Round 2, and was 54 on 1/1/91.) Although reading across may seem the natural way to read the table, in statistics you will often find it useful to pick a column, and read down.

(10) The subjects (or objects) of statistical examination are often called cases. Here, in the rows, the cases are individual Westvaco employees. Their characteristics, in the columns, are variables. If you pick a row, and read across, you get information about a single case. (For example, Robert Martin, in Row 44, was salaried, was born in September, 1937, was hired in October, 1967, was chosen for layoff in Round 2, and was 54 on 1/1/91.) Although reading across may seem the natural way to read the table, in statistics you will often find it useful to pick a column, and read down.

(7) The subjects (or objects) of statistical examination are often called cases. Here, in the rows, the cases are individual Westvaco employees. Their characteristics, in the columns, are variables. If you pick a row, and read across, you get information about a single case. (For example, Robert Martin, in Row 44, was salaried, was born in September, 1937, was hired in October, 1967, was chosen for layoff in Round 2, and was 54 on 1/1/91.) Although reading across may seem the natural way to read the table, in statistics you will often find it useful to pick a column, and read down.

(9) The subjects (or objects) of statistical examination are often called cases. Here, in the rows, the cases are individual Westvaco employees. Their characteristics, in the columns, are variables. If you pick a row, and read across, you get information about a single case. (For example, Robert Martin, in Row 44, was salaried, was born in September, 1937, was hired in October, 1967, was chosen for layoff in Round 2, and was 54 on 1/1/91.) Although reading across may seem the natural way to read the table, in statistics you will often find it useful to pick a column, and read down.

(8) The subjects (or objects) of statistical examination are often called cases. Here, in the rows, the cases are individual Westvaco employees. Their characteristics, in the columns, are variables. If you pick a row, and read across, you get information about a single case. (For example, Robert Martin, in Row 44, was salaried, was born in September, 1937, was hired in October, 1967, was chosen for layoff in Round 2, and was 54 on 1/1/91.) Although reading across may seem the natural way to read the table, in statistics you will often find it useful to pick a column, and read down.

from *Statistics in Action: Practical Principles for a World of Uncertainty* by Scheaffer/Watkins.

Sonata 15: Measuring the Bass

Name(s): _____

You need
 a ruler
 an electric bass—or other large
  fretted instrument

You'll show that you can
 measure accurately
 make decisions about
  measurements
 predict the relationship between
  two attributes
 use data to check your
  prediction

You need a large fretted instrument, for example an electric bass. The question is how the size of the gap between the frets depends on which frets they are.

Conjectures

Without measuring, study the bass. See how the frets get closer together as they get farther from the tuning pegs? In your mind, number those gaps: gap #1 is the biggest, #2 is slightly smaller, and so forth. Sketch a graph showing how you think **gapSize** depends on **gapNumber**. If you can, make a conjecture about the symbolic form of that function.

Measurement

Measure the distances as accurately as you can. Describe how you did it. Plot the data and compare them to your conjecture. Also, try to find the function that fits the points as well as possible. Sketch the graph and report the function.

Comparison

What did you discover? How did your conjectures do? Will the gap between the frets ever get to zero? If so, where? Where does the function fit the data best? Is there any systematic way the function differs from the data? Explain how and why if you can.

Data in Depth
© 2001 Key Curriculum Press

Sonata 16: Puff Puff Puff Puff Pop

Name(s): _____

The idea is to puff consistently into a balloon—the same amount of air at every puff. Don't make them giant puffs or tiny ones. Just comfortable puffs. Small enough that you can do about seven and the balloon won't look dangerously close to popping.

After each puff, your partner measures the **circumference** of the balloon with a measuring tape as you hold it. Then you put in another puff, and so forth. Despite the title, don't pop the balloon.

Your job is to figure out as much as you can about the relationship between the number of **puffs** and the **circumference** of the balloon.

You need
- measuring tape (or a string and a ruler)
- a balloon

You'll show that you can
- measure accurately
- make decisions about measurements
- figure out how the two attributes are related

Conjectures

What do you think the graph of **circumference** will look like as a function of **puffs**? A straight line? A curve? See if you can predict the shape of the graph, and, if possible, the *form* of the function.

Measurement

Practicing is encouraged, both in puffing and in measuring. In fact, be sure the balloon you use has been blown up before.

Comparison

In addition to comparing your conjecture to the data, try to use your data to figure out the volume of each puff.

More Ideas for Nonlinear Data

Name(s): _____

Pick one of these to work on. In your write-up, be sure to describe the problem clearly and explain your assumptions. You could use the Sonata form—Conjecture, Measure, Compare—for your write-up. Try to go "above and beyond" in your investigation, possibly following up with some of the questions we have listed.

Bigfoot

How does the area of your foot depend on its length? Predict, measure, and compare. In the measurement, trace your shoeless foot on a piece of graph paper to measure the area; use the same tracing to get the length. Use many people; each person will be a new case.

- If you plot **length** as a function of **area**, what function would model the data?
- What other body measurements do you think will follow foot size? Make a prediction, take measurements from at least ten people, and comment on your results.

You need
feet
large graph paper
ruler

Good Vibes

Go to the band room and measure a vibraphone's keys. How are the dimensions of a key related to the number of half-steps between that key and the largest (lowest) key? Be sure you study the keys to determine what dimensions are relevant.

- You could do the same for the tubes that hang under the vibes—or for other instruments. How do their dimensions relate to the pitch of the note?
- Look up the frequencies of the pitches themselves. How are they related to the number of half-steps between the corresponding keys and the lowest one?

You need
a ruler or measuring tape
the band room—or wherever you can find a vibraphone, marimba, xylophone, or glockenspiel

Up Against the Wall

Draw a square on the overhead projector and move it close to the wall. Measure the **height** and **width** of the image and the **distance** to the floor. Now tilt the projector up so that it's higher on the wall. Again, measure **height** and **width** and **distance** to the floor. Repeat at different angles. What is the relationship among those three attributes?

You need
overhead projector
overhead pens and a transparency
ruler
wall space

Lines and Leverage

5

When we first started this book, we had no idea that this chapter would even exist. We didn't even know it was a topic in data analysis.

But as we worked through various data sets, trying out activities, we noticed certain problems kept recurring. We dealt with some of these problems by improving the software, but others kept requiring us to use our experience with data and other aspects of our mathematical intuition to deal with them.

Finally we had two choices: We could design the activities so that students would not come across these problems, or we could admit that these problems were part of dealing with real, unsanitized data—in which case, students deserved to be exposed to them.

We chose the latter. This chapter is the result.

What *are* the issues that gave rise to this chapter, then? They have to do with what we call *leverage*. Here's the idea: Suppose you're dealing with more-or-less linear data and you fit a line to it. The farther you get outside the range in the "horizontal" variable—the domain—the worse your ability to predict. This is because any tiny errors in the slope are magnified as you get farther out. (Notice that this is not true for errors in the intercept. It's errors in slope that cause the problem.)

If you then get new data far outside the original domain, and they adhere to the original linear model, you know the slope much more precisely than you did before. That point has a lot of *leverage*.

Leverage can bite you in strange ways, as some activities will demonstrate. Suppose you're predicting something as a function of time and you've been measuring time in years. So you have data from 1990, 1991, 1992, and so forth. You get a slope and an intercept. Your data are good to two significant figures, so you record just two figures in the slope. But when you try to predict, everything goes haywire. Why? Because your slope is multiplied by the year (about 2000), so any round-off error in the slope is magnified by that much—dwarfing your two significant figures. If, on the other hand, you had counted years from 1990, and had time values of 0, 1, 2, and so on, everything would have been fine.

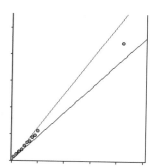

A small error in the slope makes a big difference in points farther out. Similarly, a point farther out "pins down" the slope.

Level

The activities in this chapter do not require math more sophisticated than linear functions in slope-intercept form. *Jupiter's Moons* is the subtlest, in that students need to truncate a number to an integer.

The Activities

The first three activities in this chapter all go together, though you do not have to do all three. They all use data you collect from the World Wide Web—data from the World Population Clock at the U.S. Census Web site.

- **Introducing the World Population Clock** does just that. Students collect a small amount of data and calculate (by hand or with a calculator) the rate at which the world population is increasing. They also compare their data to that of the class.

- **Predict-a-Pop** has students use Fathom to make a collection that will calculate predicted populations for the various models (slopes and intercepts) that different groups have determined.

- **World Population: A Little Leverage** uses the predictive collection from the preceding activity (or one you supply) as students return to the Web to get another data point on a later day—and improve their models.

- **Jupiter's Moons,** with background on page 139 and a student activity on pages 141–142, helps students deal with leverage and periodic functions. They determine the periods of the four Galilean satellites more precisely as their baseline of data becomes longer. We use Jovian data again in *Out on a Limb with Jupiter,* on page 195.

Objectives

- Students use the Web to collect data.
- Students come to understand that a longer baseline in time permits tighter predictions.

Introducing the World Population Clock

- Structured computer activity
- Data from the Web
- Student pages 131–132
- Intermediate, basic features

Students use the Web to access the World Population Clock at the U.S. Census site. At first *without* using Fathom, they find the population at different times and calculate the rate at which world population is increasing. Then, using Fathom, students get more data points and graph them, and see the slope of the data (population as a function of time) as that rate.

In addition, students look at the distribution of rates from the class, recognizing that people can get different answers (because they got data at slightly different times).

Topics
world population
proportion and rates

Materials
Internet connection

Students need to be able to make
a new collection and case table
new attributes
a formula to define an attribute

What's Important Here

- For some students, simply having a chance to use the Web will be the most important part of the activity. For others, Web access might be a discipline problem . . .

- The population of the world is a large number; dealing with large numbers is a challenge.

Discussion Questions

➲ (On the first page, using the Web.) Which numbers do you think are a better estimate of the population growth rate—the ones from Step 5 or the ones from Step 7? Or are they just about equally good? Why?

➲ In Step 9, why did different people get different rates?

➲ (On the second page, with Fathom.) In the graph of population as a function of time, the slope was the rate of increase in people per second (or per day). What if we had switched the axes? What would the slope be? And what would its *units* be?

Tech Notes

- In some lab setups, your Internet connection will grind to a halt if everyone in the class accesses the same site at the same time. You may need to figure out a way for students to start at slightly different times.

- But do not let them share data to save access! It is crucial that each group get its own data from the World Population Clock. If the whole class has the same data, parts of the activity will not work. There needs to be some variation in the results.

- During this activity, students will save their data so they can use them in the future. You will have to tell them where to save the data. Use whatever scheme adheres to your computers' rules and will help students actually retrieve the data next time they get to use the computers. For example, in a lab, you might give each workstation a floppy disk and collect the labeled disks as students leave the lab.

Introducing the World Population Clock

- Record the times you get from the Web as Greenwich (UTC) times, for consistency.

Where This Leads

This activity and the two that follow—*Predict-a-Pop* and *World Population: A Little Leverage*—are a sequence. We have made them separate here to give you, the teacher, maximum flexibility. While the handouts assume that you do all three, you can adapt the instructions to your needs and resources. For example, you might do part of the work for the class yourself if you don't have a lot of Web access.

Inference Connection

In these activities, the students collect values—usually estimates for a parameter such as a rate—from the class and look at the distribution of those estimates. While these are not strictly random samples, they do act as independent measurements. We create informal confidence intervals from these distributions and decide—as individuals or as a class, based on the class distribution—what range of values of that parameter we would consider reasonable. Values outside that range are implausible and call for another explanation.

   You could simply treat these as preparation for later exposure to formal confidence intervals. Or, if your students already know about confidence intervals, do something more elaborate, for example, assessing whether it's reasonable to treat the distributions you get as samples or as independent measurements.

Introducing the World Population Clock

Name(s): _____

The U.S. Census Bureau maintains a Web site with all kinds of interesting data.

1. Go there. It's **http://www.census.gov.**

2. If you don't see the World Population Clock on that Web page, there's probably a place to click that will take you to a population clock (this link was labeled *More Population Clocks* in March 1999). Click the link to go there.

3. Find the current population of the world. It should have a date and time associated with it. Record them here.

4. Wait a few seconds. If the numbers do not change on their own, click the **Reload** button. Record a new population and its time.

5. Based on those two points alone, by how many people does the world population increase per second? How many per day?

6. Be sure you've finished the calculation in the preceding step. Now **Reload** again and record the data a third time.

7. Compare these numbers with the first numbers you recorded (in Step 3). Now how many people per second do you get? How many per day?

8. If these numbers are not the same as they were the first time you calculated them (and generally they aren't), why do you think they're different?

9. Get estimates from the other class members. Make an estimate of the range of values that are reasonable for "increase per day." That will be two numbers, a minimum and a maximum. Choose the two numbers so that you would not be surprised if the true value were anywhere in the range, but would be surprised if it were outside. Write the range here.

You need
> a Web browser and a connection to the Internet
> calculator

You need to know how to
> surf the Web
> make a new collection and case table in Fathom
> make new attributes and cases
> make a formula to determine values for an attribute
> make a scatter plot

You'll learn about
> dealing with large numbers
> prediction and uncertainty in predictions

Name(s): _____

10. Keeping your browser running, start up Fathom.

11. Make a new case table with the attributes **hours**, **minutes**, **seconds**, and **pop**. The collection should appear as well.

12. Enter your data in the four columns, one case per observation. The World Population Clock lists its time in GMT, or Greenwich Mean Time in a 24-hour format. Use that format so that **hour** will range from 0 to 23 (not 1 to 12).

> GMT is the time zone at the Prime Meridian. It is also known as UTC, which is the agreed upon abbreviation designated for use in all languages to minimize confusion.

13. Create a new attribute, **totalSeconds**.

14. Give **totalSeconds** a formula so that its value is the total number of seconds *since midnight* (00:00 hours) *of the current day*. You'll need to use **hours**, **minutes**, and **seconds** to compute it. Write your formula here.

15. Save your work. (Choose **Save** in the **File** menu.)

> Save from time to time now; these data will be important in future assignments.

16. Switch back to the Web and click **Reload** to get a new data point. Enter it into Fathom.

17. Make a scatter plot with **totalSeconds** on the horizontal axis and **pop** on the vertical.

18. Put a least-squares line on the scatter plot.

19. Sketch the plot, with the line and the labeled axes. Include the line's equation.

> The points should line up very well. If they don't, check with other students around you. You may have a bogus point you need to replace.

20. What does the slope mean? What are its units?

21. Add a few more points—new points from the population clock. You should have at least 8 points altogether, spread over at least 20 minutes.

22. Extension: Make a residual plot of the data from the least-squares line. There are still residuals. Why don't the points line up perfectly?

> To make a residual plot, select the equation for the line and choose **Plot Residuals** from the **Graph** menu.

Data in Depth
© 2001 Key Curriculum Press

Predict-a-Pop

- Structured computer activity
- Data from previous activity
- Student pages 134–135
- Intermediate, medium features

In anticipation of another chance to use the Web (in the next activity), students use their data from the preceding activity to predict the population they'll find on the World Population Clock. *This activity is designed not to use the Web.*

You may have to organize the students' collecting the slopes from everyone in the class (Step 7).

What's Important Here

- Seeing that different groups get slightly different slopes for their lines
- Using those slopes to generate a distribution of predictions

Discussion Questions

➲ Why do you suppose the instructions use day zero? What would have been different if they had just used the date—the number of the day in the month? (One reason is that we will collect data on a different day; if that day were in the next month, there would be a problem.)

➲ What are all the different formulas students found for **totalDays** in Step 4? Discuss why they all work.

➲ How is the shape of the distribution of slopes related to the shape of the distribution of predicted populations? (They should be the same, but scaled differently.)

Tech Notes

- Students may never have used two collections at once before. It saves screen space if the students create the "rates" collection in a new document. To do that, choose **New** from the **File** menu. You get a blank document and can proceed with creating your case table and so on. *But do not close the original document!* You want them both open at once. To switch back and forth between them, use the **Window** menu.

- World Population Clock times are in Greenwich time, or UTC. Add 8 hours to Pacific Standard Time to get Greenwich, 7 to Mountain, 6 to Central, 5 to Eastern, and 4 to Atlantic. If you're in Hawaii, add 10. If you're on daylight savings time, subtract 1 from your correction. And all times entered in these activities should use a 24-hour clock.

- In Step 22, some students may need help finding their own predictions. One way they can do that is to make a case table and select their own names; Fathom will highlight the case in the graph.

Prerequisite
Introducing the World Population Clock, page 131 (or equivalent)

Topics
extrapolation
variability

Materials
file from *Introducing the World Population Clock* with three or more population clock measurements

Students need to be able to
open files
make new attributes
edit attribute formulas
make case tables

UTC stands for *Coordinated Universal Time* in English and *Temps universel coordonné* in French, for example. In trying to remain universal, the abbreviation UTC does not follow any language's word order.

Predict-a-Pop

Name(s): _____

You should already have data from the Internet's World Population Clock and a way to convert **hours, minutes,** and **seconds** into a single **time** attribute (the total number of seconds).

Soon we will add new data. It will be better if we change the **time** formula to give us total *days* instead of total *seconds.* This will make some of the times look strange (they'll be decimals), and it will change the slope of our best line—it will be people gained *per day* instead of people gained per second. We also need to add a new attribute to take the change of day into account.

1. Open the file in which you saved the data.
2. Add a new attribute, **day.** Enter zero (0) into each case from the first day; that is, they were on day zero. Figure out which day today is.
3. Double-click the formula box for the **totalSeconds** attribute. The formula editor appears.
4. Change the formula so that it gives time in days instead of in seconds. Also, be sure to include the new attribute, **day.** There are a number of (equally good) ways to do this. Write your new formula here:

5. Change the name of the attribute to **totalDays.** (Double-click its name.)
6. Write the new equation of the least-squares line and tell what units the slope is in:

7. Collect all the slopes and intercepts from the class's least-squares lines. We'll use Fathom to analyze them . . .
8. Make a new document and a new, empty case table.
9. Give it three attributes: **names, slope,** and **intercept.** Enter each **slope** and **intercept** from the class in a new case. Put the names in the group under **names** so that later you can tell who provided which data. (Save your work; call this document **Predictions.**)
10. Looking at the distribution of **slope**s from your class, what do you think is a reasonable *range* for possible values for the rate of increase in world population? Sketch the distribution as part of your answer.

Prerequisite
Introducing the World Population Clock, page 131

You need
the data you saved from *Introducing the World Population Clock*
calculator

You need to know how to
open files
edit an attribute formula

You'll learn about
measures
making predictions

When you zoom in to one of the later points, Fathom gives you more decimal points for the coefficients in fitted lines.

This will make a second collection. You're using two data sets at once—your population data is one; a separate data set containing rates from the class is the other. You can switch back and forth using the **Window** menu.

Making Predictions

Now we'll use these slopes and intercepts to make predictions. Eventually, we'll compare the predictions with what appears on the Web. We don't know the exact time we'll get to the World Population Clock, so we'll use Fathom to

Predict-a-Pop (continued)

Name(s): _____

make a tool that will let us just enter the time and automatically get predictions from each group's **slope** and **intercept**.

To do that, we'll use *measures*. These are numbers that apply to the whole collection, not just to individual cases.

11. Double-click the collection. The *inspector* appears.

12. Click on the **Measures** tab.

13. Add a new attribute by clicking **<new>**. Call it **hourP**. This will hold the hour part of the time we'll predict for (the *P* is for *Predict*).

14. Do the same for **minuteP, secondP**, and **dayP**. Put current values for these four time attributes in the middle **Value** column. Your inspector will look something like the one in the illustration. (2230 GMT is 2:30 p.m. Pacific time.)

15. Make another measure, **time**. It will hold the predicted time *calculated the same way as you calculated total time in the other collection.* That is, it will hold the number of decimal days since midnight of whatever day you started. But instead of using the old **hour, minute**, and so forth, we'll use these "prediction" attributes. Enter your formula into the **Formula** column and write it here:

The inspector has several panels—including one for measures and one that acts as a case template. **Note:** To make graphs, you can drag from the attribute labels in the case template—not just from the big case table.

Measure	Value	Formula
hourP	22	
minuteP	30	
secondP	45	
dayP	7	
<new>		

16. The number of decimal days should appear in the **Value** column of the **time** attribute. Write it here. Also, explain why the value you get is reasonable. If it isn't, adjust the formula until it is.

17. Now choose the **Cases** tab of your inspector. Here, you can create new attributes and their formulas just as you do on the case table.

18. Make a new attribute, **predictedPop**, for Predicted Population.

19. Set its formula to be **slope * time + intercept**. Now the values (as seen in a case table) should be the populations that each group's model would predict—for the time you specified in your measures. Explain why that formula works:

20. Now we'll look at the predictions. Choose **Graph** from the **Insert** menu to get a blank graph.

21. Drag the attribute label **predictedPop** from the inspector to an axis of the graph. (You could also have dragged from a case table.)

22. In the margin at right, sketch (be sure to scale the axis) the distribution of populations the class predicts for the current time, according to your graph. Figure out where *your* prediction is in that distribution and label it.

23. What is the range of world populations you think is reasonable for right now?

Teacher Notes

World Population: A Little Leverage

- Structured computer activity
- Data from previous activity and the Web
- Student pages 137–138
- Intermediate, medium features

Students look at the distribution of predictions from the whole class's models and see whether the real value falls within it. Then they get new data and see how the distribution of model parameters gets tighter—because they have the leverage of additional days on the time axis.

If students don't have the two files, you'll need to make them. Remember that for the original files (see *Introducing the World Population Clock*, page 131), each group's file should be slightly different, each with three or more population clock readings. You yourself can take about a dozen readings and get enough combinations of three to satisfy most classes' needs. The *second* file, **Predictions** will be the same for all groups, since it contains the collected slopes and intercepts of all the groups.

What's Important Here

- The extra leverage of perhaps several days' population growth greatly increases the precision of the slope we calculate.

- Attention to number of decimal places. If you want to predict the population of Earth to within one person, you have to keep more significant figures than you're used to.

Discussion Questions

- Make a residual plot of the original data. What is the range of residuals? Can you explain that? (Round-off error.)

- (Precalculus and above.) The data look pretty linear. What if the world population is curving? Even if it is, we're so "zoomed in" that it may look straight. How much data would we need to be able to detect the curvature? (Right now, in 1999, we're just about at an inflection point; the curve is expected to start curving downward—to have a negative second derivative. You can get more data from the same site. In fact, the author thinks they use a piecewise linear model.)

Tech Note

In Step 11, how many significant figures do you need? The pragmatic answer is "Enough to distinguish your value from everybody else's." By default, Fathom displays just a few figures—enough to define the line on the screen. Ordinarily, that's fine, but in this case—with ten significant figures in the population—we need more digits. A particularly revealing way to get them is to zoom in. As you zoom in, Fathom computes the number of decimals you need in order to define the line you're seeing. Thus, as you get closer, the number of digits increases.

Prerequisite
Predict-a-Pop, page 134 (or equivalent)

Topics
extrapolation
variability

Materials
Internet connection
Predictions file from *Predict-a-Pop* with slopes, intercepts, and population predictions from each group
original data file from *Introducing the World Population Clock*

Students need to be able to
open files
make new attributes
edit formulas for attributes
define measures

World Population: A Little Leverage

Name(s): _____

Now we're going to check our prediction.

Prerequisite
Predict-a-Pop, page 134

You need
Internet connection
the data you saved from
Predict-a-Pop
the data you saved from
*Introducing the World
Population Clock*
calculator

1. Start up your Web browser. Go to **www.census.gov** and find the world pop clock. Write down the time and the population:

2. Start Fathom. Open your **Predictions** file from last time.

3. Double-click the collection to open the inspector.

4. Enter the time from the World Population Clock into the time values (**hourP, minuteP, dayP**) in the measures pane. Don't forget to figure out **dayP** correctly. Remember, the first day you did this was day zero. Your **PredictedPop** attribute should now contain predictions—by each group's model—of what the population should be.

5. Sketch (with labels and scales) the distribution of these predictions. Indicate the actual current World Population Clock value on the distribution.

6. Find your own prediction. By how many people was it off? Show your calculation.

All these predictions were based on data you collected back on day zero. Now we'll add some new data and see how that affects our predictions.

7. Open your original World Population Clock file. (Do not close the **Predictions** file. You'll need it.)

8. Enter a new data point in your original collection. Be sure to put in the correct value for **day**.

9. Rescale your scatter plot of **pop** as a function of **totalDays** so that it includes all points. Be sure the least-squares line is showing.

10. Zoom in to the most recent point (the one in the upper right) in order to get as many significant figures as you can in the slope and intercept. Record the new equation for the least-squares line:

To automatically include all points again, choose **Scatter Plot** from the popup menu in the graph itself.

11. As in the preceding activity, collect the slopes and intercepts of the lines from the class and record them in the newer (**Predictions**) collection. This time, use new attributes called **slope2** and **intercept2**.

12. Sketch (with labeled and scaled axes) distributions for **slope** and **slope2** below. Adjust your scales before you sketch so that the horizontal axes have the same scale.

13. Chances are that the more recent distribution (**slope2**) is tighter. Explain why.

14. In your **Predictions** collection, make a new attribute, **PredictedPop2**, which is just like **PredictedPop** but uses the new slope and intercept instead of the old ones.

15. Change the value of **dayP** in your **Predictions** collection inspector to indicate *tomorrow* instead of today. Now your **Predictions** collection will show predictions for one day from now.

16. Below, sketch the distributions (labeled and scaled, of course) for **PredictedPop** and **PredictedPop2**.

17. Do two more predictions, both using **PredictedPop2**. Do one for one week from today and one for one year from today. Sketch these below and point out how the distributions are different—and why.

Going Further

1. Dwayne says that the distribution for **PredictedPop2** is tighter because there are more data points. "Everybody knows that you get a better result with a larger sample size," he says. Design and carry out a simple experiment that proves Dwayne wrong. Describe the experiment and the results.

2. Make a new attribute in your **Predictions** collection called **EightBillion**. Devise a formula that calculates how many days it will be—according to each of the models you have defined by **slope2** and **intercept2**—until the population of the world is 8,000,000,000. Write the formula, explain it, show its distribution, identify your own point, and list the assumptions behind the prediction it makes. Finally, what year will that be?

Jupiter's Moons

- Structured computer activity
- Data from file
- Student pages 141–142
- Intermediate, medium features

This activity is about accuracy. How accurately can you determine how long it takes one of the moons of Jupiter to go around that planet?

Background

If you look at one of Jupiter's moons from night to night, it seems to be swinging back and forth. It's really going around the planet, of course, but we're seeing the moon's orbit edge-on. If you record the distance of the moon from Jupiter—positive to the west, negative to the east—as a function of time, you get a wavy curve. We want to know the **period**. Students will propose one and overlay the waves to see whether they line up.

one period

Above is a diagram of the path of a moon, with a proposed period—but the period is too short. If we overlay the periods, it looks like the third diagram below right.

As students get the period closer and closer to being correct, the segments line up better and better. *The nearer periods will line up first; the far-away ones need a very accurate period to line up* because even a tiny error is multiplied by the total number of periods.

Some Students May Need Help . . .

The hard part is in Step 6. Students need to divide time up by their proposed **period** and plot the position of the moon against the *remainder* of the time—the **phase**. If **mjd** were 123.4 and **period** were 5.00, **phase** would be 3.4 because 120.0 is a whole number of cycles.

For the formula, take the time and subtract out the cycles. How many? Well, 123.4/5 = 24.68. So we subtract 5 · 24 (= 120), since 24 is the number of whole cycles. Fathom's function for the next-lowest whole number is **floor( )**. So the **phase** is

    mjd – period * floor(mjd / period).

What's Important Here

- The concept of overlaying the cycles, once grasped, is powerful. And while the arithmetic is easy—and common in data processing—many advanced students have never come across a calculation like it.

- Students see that the informal margin of error decreases with good use of available technology and leverage from a long time baseline.

Discussion Question

Besides going over the questions on the student sheet, ask students why the formula for **phase** (described above) works—and why it is needed.

Topics

extrapolation
phase
periodic motion
variability
trigonometry

Materials

JupiterMoons

Students need to be able to

use a slider
make new attributes
edit formulas for attributes
make scatter plots
make a formula to calculate phase

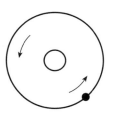

Seen from the top

Seen from Earth

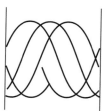

The Power of Translation

You get hurt by leverage when your data cover a small range in *x* but their absolute values are large. Then the differences in slope (in a linear fit) create errors in the model that can overwhelm you because tiny errors are magnified over that long distance from the *y*-axis. Let's see how that happens in detail and see what we can do about it besides getting lots of significant figures.

In the table, you can see some world population figures in "GigaPeeps." The data are plotted in the graph, with a least-squares line. That line has this equation:

GPeeps = 0.0725 · **year** − 139,

with the coefficients reported to three significant figures. It's obviously a good fit. But let's see what the regression line predicts for, say, 1978:

GPeeps = 0.0725 · 1978 − 139
= 4.405,

which you can see is off, just from the graph. What's going on?

The actual slope of the line, given by Fathom, is 0.072457. But that number of significant figures is utterly inappropriate to the two-place population figures. Yet when we rounded to 0.0725, the tiny difference in the slope was multiplied by almost 2000.

One solution is to translate the data. To translate to the vertical axis, we subtract from the horizontal coordinate. We'll translate **year** so that 1974 is at zero. We'll make a new attribute, **since74**, with a formula of **year − 1974**. That's plotted with population in the graph. Now Fathom reports only what's relevant:

GPeeps = 0.0725 · **since74** + 4.01.

What does that predict for 1978? In that year, **since74** is equal to 4, so

GPeeps = 0.0725 · 4 + 4.01
= 4.30,

which is clearly much better.

How could this be? Why does one way require more significant figures than another? Aren't all line calculations the same?

In a sense, they are. But we're so used to the slope-intercept form that we forget the alternatives. If we had written the second fit as a line in point-slope form, we'd see

(*GPeeps* − 4.01) = 0.0725 · (*year* − 1974),

which essentially says, "Imagine that the origin is at (1974, 4.01)." Now the line goes through that origin with slope 0.0725. No muss, no fuss, no pesky intercept.

World Population

Year	GPeeps
1974	4.01
1975	4.09
1976	4.16
1977	4.23
1978	4.30

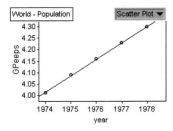

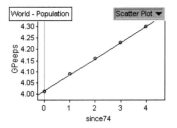

This technique of translating is a powerful tool for designing functions that do what you want them to do. Sometimes, though, it's nice to have values on the axis that make sense. We know what 1978 is without reading the documentation; if we see "year 4," we have to check. Fortunately, Fathom gives us enough figures to get the answer right in either case.

Jupiter's Moons

Name(s): _____

Working with a partner, you use the data in **JupiterMoons.** You will choose one of the moons—Ganymede, Io, Europa, or Callisto—and try to determine its period as accurately as possible. You'll see how useful it is to have data that span a wide interval of time.

The data in the file extend from December 31, 1999 to January 30, 2000. The data are more dense early on in that period.

1. Open the data and make a case table. Look over the attributes.

The attribute **mjd** is the date in decimal days. (*Modified Julian Date* means days since November 17, 1858.) The **year, mo, day, hour,** and **minute** are informational here; you don't need to calculate with them. Each moon has its own attribute, which is its distance—the angle in arc seconds—from the planet. The other attribute is **limb,** which is the angle from the center of Jupiter to its edge.

2. Pick a moon. Plot its distance against **mjd.** The data are closer together at the beginning. We've plotted an example (**Ganymede**) in the illustration.

3. Estimate the period from the graph. Write your first estimate here, with a "plus-or-minus" to show how well you think you know that value:

4. Make a slider for the period. Call it **period** and set it to your estimate.

5. Create a new attribute, **phase.**

6. Give **phase** a formula that calculates the phase of the current time (the attribute **mjd**), assuming the proposed **period** from the slider. The **phase** is how far that case is into its current cycle. (Try to figure this formula out yourself; if you need help, it's in the Teacher Notes. **Hint:** you do not need trig functions.)

7. Make a new graph (leave the old one intact) that plots your moon's distance as a function of **phase** instead of **mjd.** You'll see something like the graph in the illustration. (**period** for Ganymede is about 7.)

8. Try to adjust the slider. You should get squirrely behavior—the whole graph will jump around. Describe what you see as you adjust the **phase** slider:

The problem is that the **phase** calculation uses the whole magnitude of **mjd,** which is over 50,000. That makes *thousands* of cycles, and any tiny change will be amplified, moving even the first cycle arbitrarily around the graph.

9. So make a new attribute, **newjd,** which will be **mjd − 51544** (= 1 Jan 2000).

10. Edit the **phase** formula to use **newjd** instead of **mjd.** Now the first cycle will stay in the same place in the **phase** graph.

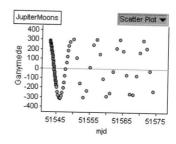

Ganymede as it is in the data file. You can see the periods.

An arc second is 1/60 of an arc minute—which is 1/60 of a degree. An arc second is roughly the apparent size of a quarter at a distance of three miles.

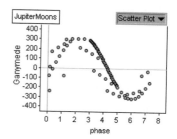

You can see that first cycle, but then the rest is fragmented. We need a better value for **period.**

Data in Depth
© 2001 Key Curriculum Press

Chapter 5—Lines and Leverage   **141**

11. Adjust the slider for **period** until the points line up. If you have trouble, select just the first period in the first (**mjd**) graph (so you can see which points are relevant) and line those up in the second (**phase**) graph; then select an additional period in the first, and so on. You may need to zoom in on the slider.

12. Write your next estimate for **period** here, with a "plus-or-minus" to show how accurate you think it is.

13. What did you do to make that estimate of accuracy?

14. Now add more data from July 2000. Here they are; type them in by hand.

Date	Julian Date	hh:mm	Io	Europa	Ganymede	Callisto
July 1	51726.0	00:00	27.28	−26.23	−239.64	−196.76
July 2	51727.0	00:00	14.45	−152.89	−83.11	−34.57

15. Rescale the nonphase (**newjd** vs. **Ganymede**, or whatever) scatter plot so you can see the July points. (Choose **Scatter Plot** again from the popup menu in the graph.)

16. Now adjust **period**, watching the **phase** plot, to get a new estimate of period. Again, you may need to zoom in on the **period** axis.

17. Once again, give your estimate of **period**, with a plus-or-minus quantity to indicate how accurate it is.

18. Explain, in words, why you think this estimate is so much more accurate than the first and second estimates you made in Steps 3 and 12.

Going Further

1. How do you know the distant "July" points are in the correct cycle? Could you be off by 1? Test your answer by changing the period. What do you find?

2. Predict the position of your moon at 00:00 Greenwich time on your birthday in 2001. Go to the Web and visit **http://ringside.arc.nasa.gov/www/tools/tracker_jup.html** to get the "official" predicted position. Compare. Redetermine your value for **period** if necessary.

3. Try to fit a sinusoid to the data. You will need sliders for amplitude and phase as well as for period. Residual plots will help.

4. Use values for **period** for all four moons (use results from other groups) and estimate the radii of the orbits (in arc seconds). The radius is how far from the planet these moons get at most. What is the relationship between radius and period for these moons?

Zoom in on a slider by holding down CTRL (Windows) or OPTION (Mac) and clicking on the axis. CTRL-clicking (or OPTION-clicking) or CTRL-dragging (or OPTION-dragging) in a scatter plot zooms in as well. Use CTRL-SHIFT-click or OPTION-SHIFT-click to zoom out.

If that URL is not current when you read this, two good search words to try together are *Ganymede* and *ephemeris*. An ephemeris is a table or program that gives you the positions of astronomical bodies.

Describing and Modeling Change

6

Time is the canvas of change. Whether you look at change with dread or excitement, change is interesting.

In this chapter, we will look at data that include time. While in many ways time behaves like any other continuous attribute, it's special. There's a betweenness about time—you can always interpolate—that lets you connect the dots if you want. And it's universal: Everybody experiences time. And anything you measure with respect to time is a function, because (so far, at least) there's no going back. It always appears on the horizontal axis.

As its title suggests, this chapter has two main parts: describing and modeling.

The first half of the chapter is an introduction to time-series data—data sets with repeated measurements. We'll look at trends or other patterns. While there are "official" techniques and representations commonly used in time-series data analysis, such as Fourier series and control charts, we will concentrate on exploration. What trends do you see? How well can you predict? What might have caused this effect?

The second half is about modeling. A mathematical model can be a function that predicts values for the *dependent variable* (or *response*) given values for the *independent variable*. We made such a model in an exponential situation when we looked at Moore's law, page 108.

But models can also be *recursive* so that each time-step depends on the results of the previous time-step instead of on the time itself. For example, suppose we want to make a simulation of population growth. We relate each case to the preceding case: The population at time t is the population at $(t - 1)$ plus the number of births, and at each step, the number of births is proportional to the population. This produces exponential growth—without using exponents.

We believe that this way of making models (as opposed to the closed-form, analytic approach) is important for two reasons: First, it may be easier for some students to understand the "why" behind such a model; second, people who do this kind of thing for a living frequently do it this way.

You can read more about recursive definitions on page 153.

Level

Students need only know about proportion until *Generation by Generation* (page 162), for which they need exponents. Precalculus students may recognize the definition of the derivative lurking in the *Radiosonde* activity (page 182).

The Activities

Many of these activities are "open at the top"; that is, they allow students with more experience to use it to their advantage.

The first half of the chapter involves relatively informal exploration of how things change with time. In the second half of this chapter, we get more involved with mathematical models.

- **Mauna Loa.** We look at atmospheric CO_2 measurements from the top of Mauna Loa and characterize the way the concentration of carbon dioxide has increased over time. We revisit these data in *Modeling Mauna Loa,* on page 190.

- **Carbon Dioxide: The Whole World.** We look at global CO_2 emissions records and use them to reflect on events in the second half of the twentieth century.

- **Carbon Dioxide by Region.** We look at the same data, broken down by region. We reflect on debates about restricting greenhouse-gas production.

The model-oriented second half includes the following:

- **Change Playground.** This is a short, simple page to introduce the use of the **prev( )** function.

- **Consumer Price Index.** We look at the CPI since its inception and compute inflation rates. This also highlights the difference between proportion and absolute difference. This activity echoes some of the concerns in *Moore's Law* (pages 108–110).

- **Radiosonde.** We look at a weather balloon ascent and study the speed at which the balloon is rising. This is good preparation for studying the derivative in calculus. We look at these data from a different perspective in *Radiosonde Residuals,* on page 182.

- **Generation by Generation.** These two activities develop a simulation of population growth that starts simple and exponential but becomes more interesting and complex with plagues and limits to growth.

- **Building the Weather Machine.** This is a finite-state, simplistic simulation of the weather. It also leads naturally to ideas of expected value and variability.

- **Change Sonatas and Investigations.** These activities include several more open-ended and challenging tasks.

Objectives

- Students learn about the situation—the data or the simulation—that Fathom helps them investigate. They also use their own knowledge of history and of the world to inform their explorations.

- Students see how to use Fathom to model and calculate change; in particular, they learn about the **prev( )** function and how to use it. While we do some continuous modeling here, you'll find more in Chapter 2, *Lines and Data* and more on nonlinear functions in Chapter 4, *Straighten Up!*

- Students see one simulation technique in Fathom; there are more in Chapter 9, *Probability Through Simulations.*

Mauna Loa

- Structured computer activity
- Data from file
- No student page
- Independent, basic features

Teacher Notes

These are the justly famous carbon dioxide measurements taken near the summit of Mauna Loa, a volcano on the island of Hawaii. They constitute the longest and best series of such data anywhere in the world, extending from 1958 to the present. The idea is that the air is so clean there, and the mountain is so far from industry, that any changes in CO_2 concentration measured there corresponds to a global (or at least hemispheric) change rather than the influence of some nearby factory.

Introduction

Begin with a brief discussion about global warming. Have students explain the basics: that "greenhouse gases" such as carbon dioxide (CO_2) and methane (CH_4) occur naturally in the atmosphere, but their concentrations may be increasing as a result of human activity. This increase may cause global climate change as these gases trap infrared (heat) radiation inside the atmosphere.

But (you may ask aloud) if we were being skeptical, what would we have to know to be convinced that this is true? Briefly make a list of things you need to know. There are difficult-to-prove connections, of course, but also very simple questions: Do we really emit a lot of CO_2? And are the concentrations of these gases really increasing?

We'll deal with this last question first. Explain that the data file contains readings, from the top of Mauna Loa, of the amount of CO_2 in the atmosphere (in parts per million) every month for about the last 40 years.

The Tasks

The students, working in pairs, will have up to four tasks. Write these (or the ones you think are appropriate for your students) where students can refer to them:

- Develop an accurate description of the data's behavior.
- Estimate the rate at which CO_2 is increasing overall.
- Extrapolate from the data to decide what the CO_2 concentration must be this month.
- Extrapolate from the data to decide what the CO_2 concentration will be on your 21st birthday.

What's Important Here

- Grasping the nature of the data—the long-term trend with seasonal variation.
- Using slope as a rate of increase in the CO_2 concentration.
- Figuring out a sensible way of extrapolating from these data (e.g., by taking the corresponding month in the preceding year, and using the slope between the corresponding months).
- Feeling comfortable using a formula to construct the "time" attribute.

Topics
exploring time-series data
rates
interpreting slope

Students need to be able to
make scatter plots
place movable lines
make a simple formula for a new attribute

Materials
Mauna

Mauna Loa

How the Graph Will Look

Students need to solve the problem of what to plot on the horizontal axis. In the file, time is expressed in two attributes—**year** and **month**. One way is to make a new attribute—and a formula to compute its values—that connects the **year** and **month** attributes to give a single time for each reading. (The simplest is **year + month / 12**, though there are others.)

As much as possible, let students figure out how to deal with this.

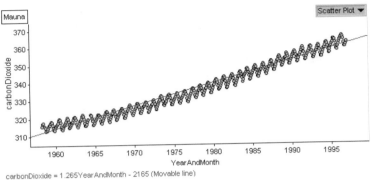

carbonDioxide = 1.265YearAndMonth − 2165 (Movable line)

The illustration shows what the data will look like when students make a new attribute (here, **YearAndMonth**) to incorporate both "time" attributes. The slope, 1.2 on the movable line, represents the overall increase in parts per million per year.

Discussion Questions

Once students have looked at the data, you can do any or all of the following:

- ➲ Discuss the shape of the data. Students should see the upward trend, possibly with an increasing slope. If they successfully make the "time" attribute, they should also see the seasonal variation. You might discuss their different "time" formulas if there is some variation among them.

- ➲ This might also be a good time to reinforce (or introduce) some terminology: Ask students to estimate the *amplitude* of the seasonal variation (about eight units) and its *period* (one year). There are many ways to estimate either quantity.

- ➲ Collect and plot the birthday concentrations on the overhead. See if you can see the seasonal variation. Discuss why they may not line up as well as the data points (because different groups may have extrapolated in different ways).

- ➲ Collect groups' estimates for the slope—the rate at which CO_2 concentration seems to be increasing overall. The movable line on the graph in the illustration suggests that 1.2 units per year is a plausible slope. Let groups explain how they determined their rates. Discuss, if necessary, different slopes in the overall graph and why the short-term slopes from the seasonal variation are not important to that estimate.

You can follow this activity directly with *Modeling Mauna Loa,* page 191, in which students make a quantitative model and look at residuals.

Carbon Dioxide: The Whole World

- Structured computer activity
- Data from file
- Student page 149
- Intermediate, basic features

In the previous activity, you may have asked whether we humans really are emitting a lot of carbon dioxide. We'll look at data collected by a group called the Carbon Dioxide Information Analysis Center (CDIAC) at Oak Ridge National Laboratory in Tennessee.

These data report carbon dioxide *emissions* (the amount we put into the atmosphere, as opposed to the amount we find there) from various sources around the world, every year from 1950 to 1994. We use the file **GlobalCarbon,** which lumps the whole world together.

The file reports the total emissions in metric tons of carbon and breaks the total down into component parts: **solid** (e.g., coal), **liquid** (e.g., petroleum), **gas** (e.g., natural gas), **cement** (I didn't know cement production made carbon dioxide, did you?), and **flaring** (the burning of gas at refineries and drilling sites). The file also lists per capita carbon dioxide production in metric tons per person per year.

Topics

exploring time-series data
application to social studies

Students need to be able to

make scatter plots
make new attributes
make a simple formula for a
new attribute

Materials
GlobalCarbon

What's Important Here

- These are time-series data. Therefore we traditionally put *time* attributes (**year** in this case) on the horizontal axis. This is because we generally consider the *other* attributes to be functions of time.

- Question 5—the one about the percentage of the total from burning solids—illuminates using statistics to say what you want by choosing whether to use the absolute quantity or the proportion.

- Data connects to the real world. The graphs in this activity tell an important part of the story of twentieth-century history. In class, watch and listen: This may excite some students for whom mathematics has not been appealing.

Discussion Questions

➲ What was happening when the graph of **total** was declining?

➲ In question 5—the one about burning solids, with the two graphs—what kind of person would use the graph of the percentage? Who would use the one with the absolute amount? Which do you think tells the more accurate story?

Extension

Have students make a scatter plot of **flaring** versus **total**. It looks strange. Sketch it and label two or three important features of the graph with the years they represent. Explain what it means for the "path" to go up, or come down, or make a loop.

Carbon Dioxide: The Whole World

Tech Note

Students should not forget that to figure out what year a particular point corresponds to, they can point at the point in the graph and look in the status bar at the bottom of the window. The point's coordinates appear.

Answers to Questions on the Student Page

In the first question, students should notice that the scatter plot doesn't go up continuously (*monotonically*, a good mathematical term to introduce). In the early eighties, global CO_2 emissions actually declined.

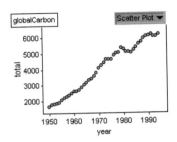

In the second question, students have to make a new attribute (maybe **solidFrac**) and define its values with a formula (e.g., **solid / total**). When they plot it, they'll see that unlike the other graphs they've seen, this one declines *even though the "straight" solid graph goes up*. That is, even though CO_2 emissions due to burning solid fuels continue to increase, their importance relative to other CO_2 sources is declining—from 65% of world emissions in 1950 to under 40% today.

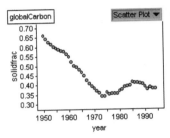

The third question is really about proportion and units: If we have per capita data, we can get something like population by taking **total / percapita**. To get the population in units or in billions, students have to multiply or divide by some large number; reasoning or experimentation will help them see which.

The extension on the preceding page produces a graph like the third one shown here. Because the quantities do not change radically from year to year, we can actually see the path taken by CO_2 resulting from **flaring** worldwide compared with **total** CO_2. Unlike the other graphs, this is not a function; for a given value of **total** CO_2, there may be multiple values of **flaring** from different years. This kind of graph might be better with the points connected by lines (a **Line Scatter Plot** in Fathom). This graph is related to parametric equations and to *phase space* graphs, which are important in analyzing dynamical systems.

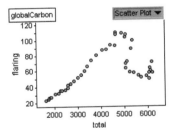

Carbon Dioxide: The Whole World

Name(s): _____

We're going to investigate the amount of carbon dioxide (CO_2) we humans dump into the atmosphere as a result of our peculiarly human activities—activities such as driving cars, generating electricity, and producing cement. Breathing doesn't count (though it produces CO_2)—just those things that *only* humans do.

1. Open the file **GlobalCarbon.** It has several attributes that are described in the file itself.

2. Make a scatter plot of **total** as a function of **year.** The graph shows how the total global emission of carbon (the "C" part of CO_2) into the atmosphere has increased since 1950. The units are millions of metric tons per year. Look at the graph carefully to see its features.

If you don't remember how to make a scatter plot, look it up in **Help.**

3. The other attributes (except **percapita**) are parts of that total—the part due to burning solid fuel, liquid, gas, and so on. Make scatter plots of them as well, and look at these new graphs to see what features they exhibit.

4. What are the features you see in the **total** graph? Describe them below. Do the same for *one* of the other graphs, concentrating on its differences from the **total** graph.

A *feature* of a scatter plot is an observation you could make about the graph. Here are some examples that may or may not be true: "It always increases." "There's a peak in 1964." "It's flat throughout the eighties." "The graph of **gas** goes up faster than the graph of **solid.**"

5. Has the *percentage* of CO_2 from burning solid fuel increased, decreased, or stayed the same? On your paper, sketch this new graph and discuss its features. Compare it to the regular graph of **solid** as a function of **year.** (They look really different. Why?) Write a clear explanation of what it all means.

Make a new attribute (you need a formula) for the *proportion* of global CO_2 emissions that are due to burning solids (e.g., coal). Graph it as a function of **year.**

6. About how long does it take Earth's population to double? Sketch the graph of the population from 1950 to the present. Answer the question about doubling. Then explain your formula for **population** and why it works. Also, explain why it makes sense (i.e., is the number right?).

Make a new attribute, **population.** Use **total** and **percapita** to compute the population of the world as a function of time. Adjust your formula so that the answer you get is in billions.

Carbon Dioxide by Region

- Open-ended computer activity
- Data from file
- Student page 151
- Intermediate, basic features

This file—**RegionalCarbon**—separates the globe into different regions, so you can see how trends in CO_2 production are different in different parts of the world.

Students study these regional differences, reflecting on international agreements and protocols such as the Kyoto summit. One resource (as of January 1999) is **http://www.cop3.org**.

The Comments pane in the file tells you a lot about which region is which, but students still have to decide what parts of the world are (industrially) developing and which are already developed. The author thinks that NAM (U.S. and Canada), WEU (Western Europe), OCE (Oceania and Japan), and possibly CPE (the former Soviet Bloc) qualify as developed for the purposes of this activity.

Discussion Questions

This activity, as written, is open-ended. Each response could be quite elaborate. Here are some more specific questions you can use to help focus the students' thinking:

➲ **Related to Conflict 1**: If things go on as they are, when will the industrially developing world catch up with the developed world in its total CO_2 emissions? What will the per capita emissions of the two be at that time?

➲ **Related to Conflict 2**: The agreement that was finally reached in Kyoto asks the developed countries to restrict CO_2 emissions to about 5% below 1990 levels starting in 2012. How much does each of the regions need to reduce in order to meet this goal? Give answers in percentages, absolute tons of carbon, and per capita reductions.

Another Idea for a Task

Post the following list of events. The task is to figure out when they occurred and then to look in the data to see if the events are reflected by features in the graph. Students should sketch the relevant parts of the graph and describe, for one event, how and why the graph is related to the event.

- The Gulf war
- The OPEC oil embargo and the "gas crisis"
- The recession in the 1980s
- Increased public environmental awareness
- Automobile emissions controls are in one place
- Postwar economic boom in the U.S. (the war referred to here is World War II)
- Britain discovers natural gas under the North Sea

Topics

exploring time-series data
application to social studies

Students need to be able to

make graphs
make a simple formula for a
new attribute

Materials

RegionalCarbon

Where's the Comments pane?
Double-click the collection (the icon of the box) to bring up its *inspector*. Then, click on the **Comments** tab (which may just read **Com...**) to see the Comments pane.

Carbon Dioxide by Region

Name(s): _____

There were conflicts at the summit meeting in Kyoto in December 1997. Two of them went something like this:

Conflict 1—Industrialized Versus Developing World: Developing countries said that they use less CO_2 per person than industrialized countries, and that industrialized countries are the sources of almost all the CO_2 dumped into the atmosphere so far. Since the developing countries still need to develop, and industrialization takes fuel, it's not fair to restrict the developing countries. Some Americans countered that there are many more people in developing countries than in the industrialized world, and that they're starting to emit CO_2 at prodigious rates. Therefore, not restricting the developing countries as well would be courting ecological disaster.

Conflict 2—U.S. Versus Europe: Europe said that we should stabilize emissions at some percentage (say, 15%) below 1990 levels. The U.S. said that this would be too hard, because it amounts to a 30% reduction below 1996 levels. Europe countered that the U.S. said this because it had increased emissions so much during the period 1990–96, while the Europeans had not increased emissions so much. The U.S. countered right back, saying, "You didn't limit emissions because you were ecologically minded; it was because you were economically stagnant."

We'll use the file **RegionalCarbon** to study these two conflicts. The file has a lot of the same information as the global file we looked at before, but broken down by region.

1. Open the file **RegionalCarbon.**

2. Make a scatter plot of **total** as a function of **year**. We can see the graphs of the different regions all together.

3. Drag the **region** variable into the *interior* of the scatter plot and drop it. A legend will appear so you can tell which region belongs to which line. Click on a category in the legend to select those cases.

Turn these in on a separate sheet:

4. Pick one of the conflicts and use the data to explain it as clearly as possible in terms of the data. That is, how do each side's arguments make sense? Be quantitative. Don't just say, "The U.S. makes more carbon"; tell us how much more, and over what period of time, and in what direction it is going. Focus on the facts—what the data tell you. Avoid opinion.

5. For the same conflict, give your opinion. Again, be quantitative. Who is right? What would a reasonable compromise be?

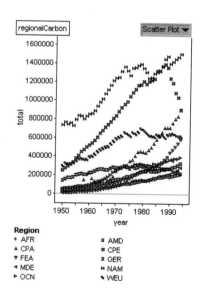

Change Playground

- Structured computer activity
- Data simulated in the activity
- Student pages 154–155
- Intermediate, basic features

This is a gentle introduction to the **prev( )** function, and it's "structured" only in that there is a sequence of steps to go though and problems to solve. One goal here is familiarity with the function, but students will also get to manipulate the numbers of a sequence to see how their differences behave. This is also a terrific preparation for learning the derivative in calculus.

What's Important Here

- Students become familiar with how recursive data sets behave.
- Students learn more about dragging points in Fathom.

Discussion Questions

➲ What is **prev( )** of something when it's the first case in a data set? (Zero.)

➲ When you dragged a point in an **A** graph, how many points moved in the **B** graph? (Two.) Why? (Two of the **B** formulas refer to the single **A** attribute: the one in its case and the one in the next case, for which this one is the **prev(A)**.)

➲ Suppose you wanted to make a new attribute, **C**, that was the cumulative total of what was in **A** so far. What formula would you give it? **(A + prev(C))**. Note that it's not **A + prev(A)** because that gives you only the sum of two terms. (Note also the calculus connection: **B** is the derivative; **C** is the integral.)

Topics
change
recursive definitions

Students need to be able to
make a graph

Materials
none

Connections
discrete mathematics
calculus (the derivative)

Recursive Definitions and Recurrence Relations

Let's back away from Fathom for a moment and discuss the difference between recursive and closed-form sequences.

A sequence is a list of numbers. If we look at the sums of the integers, we get the sequence of *triangular numbers,* namely, 1, 3, 6, 10, 15, 21, . . .

If we want to know the nth triangular number, we use the familiar formula

$$T_n = \frac{n(n + 1)}{2}.$$

This is called an expression *in closed form.* But there's another way to specify the sequence. You could define it recursively, using what mathematicians call a recurrence relation.

$$T_n = T_{n-1} + n, \text{ where } T_0 = 0.$$

That is, in order to know the *n*th number in the sequence, take the *previous* number and add *n* to it. So the sixth triangular number is the fifth triangular number plus 6. The fifth one is 15, so the sixth is 21, which is correct. To find the fifth, you need the fourth, and the third, and so on.

This process comes to a halt when you get to zero because of the second clause in the definition above. It states that the zeroth number in the sequence is zero. Without that, you cannot find the value for the fifth, the sixth, or any other number.

Thus, a recursive definition has two parts: the *initial conditions* and the *recursive step.* Another example, the Fibonacci sequence, is usually defined recursively:

$$F_1 = 1 \text{ and } F_2 = 1 \qquad \text{(the initial conditions)}$$

$$F_n = F_{n-1} + F_{n-2} \qquad \text{(the recursive step)}$$

Sometimes it's easier or more useful to find an equation in closed form for a sequence; other times, recurrence relations are best.

In Fathom, we can write formulas to give us sequences either way. The closed form is easy; you just write a formula for an attribute. For recursion, you also write a formula, but when you do, you have to take care of the initial conditions. A formula for triangular numbers in Fathom might look like this:

□ triangulars
prev (triangulars, 0) + caseIndex

- The special constant **caseIndex** is the number of the case (so it's 1 for the first case, equivalent to the *n* subscript).

- You deal with the initial condition in the optional argument for the **prev( )** function (in this case, setting case number zero to 0).

This idea is similar to the structure of proof by mathematical induction. That's no accident—it's the same principle. In fact, a good way to prove that many of the closed-form expressions are correct is to use induction.

Triangles	triangulars
1	1
2	3
3	6
4	10
5	15
6	21
7	28

The case table for the triangular numbers.

Change Playground

Name(s): _____

In this activity, we'll experiment with change and how you can calculate change in Fathom using the **prev( )** function.

We'll make a "playground" to experiment in.

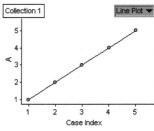

1. In a new Fathom document, make a new case table (by dragging it from the shelf or choosing **Case Table** from the **Insert** menu).

2. Make a new attribute, **A**, and give it five cases with the values {1, 2, 3, 4, 5}.

3. Make a new attribute, **B**. Now your case table should look like the one in the illustration.

4. Give **B** a formula. (Select the **B** label and choose **Edit Formula** from the **Edit** menu.) Enter the formula **A – prev(A)**. Click the **OK** button to close the formula editor. **B** now has values. (They should all be 1. If they're not, check your formula and the values in **A**.)

5. Make two graphs. In one, put **A** on the vertical axis; in the other, put **B** on the vertical. Make both graphs line plots by choosing **Line Plot** from the popup menu in the graph itself. The two graphs should look like the ones shown here.

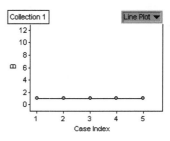

Exploring

6. Now the fun begins. In the **A** graph, grab point #3 and drag it. You will see the value changing in the case table. You can only drag it up and down. Describe the effect this has on the two graphs.

7. Change the data in **A** to {10, 8, 6, 4, 2}. Rescale the plots so you can see all the points by choosing **Line Plot** again from the popup menu (or by dragging on the axes). Sketch the graphs here.

8. Drag points around some more, rescaling as necessary. What is the relationship between attributes **A** and **B**? What is special about the first point in **B**?

Exercises

In these exercises, we show you some **B** graphs and a **B** case table. Your job is to draw an **A** graph or case table that produces each **B**. Be sure to label and scale your axes!

1.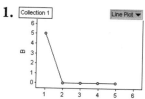

2.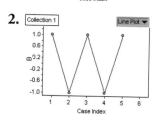

3.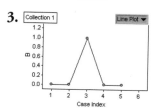

4. Careful—look at the scale.

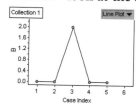

5.

6.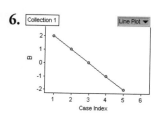

Going Further

1. Why do you suppose you can't drag the points in the **B** graphs?
2. If the **B** graph is flat, what does that imply for the **A** graph?

Consumer Price Index

- Structured computer activity
- Data from file
- Student page 157
- Intermediate, basic features

The next two activities, *Consumer Price Index* and *Radiosonde*, are both about computing rates. In one, students compute a rate simply by taking the difference between one case and its predecessor. In the other, students must also divide by the difference in time, just as when they take derivatives in calculus.

What's Important Here

- Students learn how to use **prev( )** to make a formula look at the previous row.

- Subtracting the previous value from the current one in order to calculate change is a cornerstone of numerical analysis. Time spent checking for understanding will be a good investment.

- Students begin to see that the first case in a recursive or inductive definition may have to be treated specially.

- Students see the relationship between a graph of the data and a graph of the change in the data.

- Students see and calculate the difference between change as an absolute quantity and change as a relative (percentage) quantity.

Discussion Questions

⊃ In the graph of **deltaCPI**, why is the first point so strange?

⊃ Given the data we have up to 1998, what do you think the CPI is now?

⊃ Ask if anyone can remember the price of something in 1997 or earlier. Then ask students to use the CPI and extrapolate to the present to predict the price now. Does the price match? If the prediction is high or low, what does that mean?

⊃ Sometimes people use a CPI based on a different year. What formula would you use to convert the 1967 = 100 CPI to one in which 1990 = 100?

⊃ Why would you want to look at the percentage increase in the CPI rather than the absolute increase?

⊃ What historical features can you see on the graphs? Can you explain them? (The Great Depression, World War II, the 1980s recession.)

⊃ If there's a peak in the "delta" graph, what does that mean on the "straight" graph? (It's at a high slope.) If there's a peak in the "straight" graph, what does that mean in the "delta" one? (It's descending through zero.)

Tech Note

In this activity, we ask students to identify points on a scatter plot; for example, "In which year did the CPI increase the most?" Students can read the numbers off the axis or find them in the table, but they can also simply point at the point. The cursor changes to a left arrow and the coordinates of the point appear in the status bar.

Topics
 rates
 proportional rates

Students need to be able to
 open a file
 make a scatter plot

Materials
 CPI

Consumer Price Index data are from **http://stats.bls.gov/cpihome.htm.**

Notes about *Radiosonde* appear on page 158.

We have intentionally chosen this set of data to minimize the issue of initial conditions; see *Recursive Definitions and Recurrence Relations* on page 153.

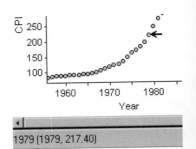

1979 (1979, 217.40)

Consumer Price Index

Name(s): _____

In general, things get more expensive over time. How much more expensive? One way to tell is to look at a statistic called the Consumer Price Index (CPI). The CPI in these data is set so that 1967 = 100. This means that when the CPI is 200, things generally cost twice as much as they did in 1967.

1. The file **CPI** contains annual data from 1913 to 1997. Open it.

2. Make a scatter plot showing **CPI** as a function of **year**. Your graph should look like the one in the illustration. As you can see, things just keep getting more expensive.

3. People worry a lot about inflation. One way to define inflation is that it's the amount by which the CPI is increasing. Look at the graph: In what year does it look as if the CPI was increasing most steeply?

4. Let's figure out just how steep, using Fathom. Make a new attribute by clicking in the column header marked **<new>**. Call it **deltaCPI**.

5. Now we make a formula that computes the change of **CPI** from the preceding year to this one. Open the formula editor by selecting your new attribute name and choosing **Edit Formula** from the **Edit** menu.

6. Enter **CPI – prev(CPI)** (**prev** stands for "previous"). Click **OK** to close the formula editor. The differences should appear in your **deltaCPI** column.

7. Make a new graph that shows **deltaCPI** as a function of **year**. It should look like the graph shown here. Now, in what year did the CPI increase most steeply? Explain how you used the graph to tell.

Some people would say that a big increase doesn't matter—only a big *percentage* increase does. After all, a CPI increase of 20 when the CPI is 300 is not as important as when the CPI is 50. We'll investigate this.

8. Make a new attribute, **percentChange**, that calculates the percent change of the **CPI** from the preceding year. Graph **percentChange** as a function of **year**. Sketch and label that graph at right, and write the formula you used for **percentChange**.

9. What's a typical **percentChange** in the last decade of data? In what year, since the beginning, was the percent change the greatest?

You'll learn how to
make new attributes
use the formula editor
compute differences in Fathom

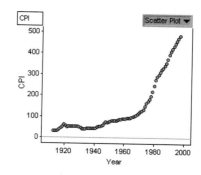

Scientists often use the Greek letter *delta* to mean "change of."

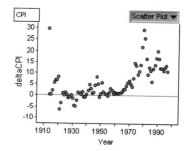

Notice you get a bogus result in the first year because there's no previous year. Remember to ignore that first point (we'll deal with it more explicitly in a future activity).

Radiosonde

- Structured computer activity
- Data from file
- Student pages 159–160
- Intermediate, basic features

This activity includes mathematics about rates and physics about the atmosphere. We get data from a radiosonde (an instrument sent aloft in a weather balloon) that include **height** and **time**. With these two, we can compute speed.

What's Important Here

- Students should not let calculations get in the way of making sense. When they look at the slope in the very first graph, students see that the speed is roughly constant. The detailed calculation shows structure in the speed that's invisible at that scale, but they can rule out the first "bad" graph (shown) without calculation.

- The instructions deliberately lead the students to make a common mistake so they can see its consequences—and how to fix it.

- Students may also wonder why we're not using **speed = height / time**. That formula is good for *average* speed, but not for *instantaneous* speed. (See the second sample graph shown here.)

- This development of speed is similar to the derivative in calculus.

Discussion Questions

- ⮌ In the *Consumer Price Index* activity, we didn't have to divide by a difference in time. Why not? (There was one data point per year, so the difference was one year. We'd always be dividing by 1.)

- ⮌ About how fast is 4 m per second? Can you run that fast? Can you go that fast vertically up a ladder, staircase, or elevator? If you saw a balloon being launched, would it shoot up out of sight, rise gradually, or what?

- ⮌ In the third graph, **speed** versus **time**, the balloon starts out fast, slows down a little, then gradually speeds up. Can you see those changes as changes in slope in the original (**height** versus **time**) graph? (Probably not; that's why these "derivative" graphs are useful.)

- ⮌ A residual plot of the height (you could make one for the students and project it) looks a lot like the **speed** plot. What's the difference? Where would you use one and not the other? (Despite superficial similarities—they both have much smaller amplitude than the original graph—they measure completely different things.)

- ⮌ (Precalculus.) How could you tell just by looking at the graph of "bad" speed versus time that something was wrong? (The original graph looked linear, so the speed—the slope—should be nearly constant. But this one curves up.)

The activity *Introduction to Residuals III: Radiosonde Residuals,* page 182, uses these same data.

Topics
   slope
   calculating speed

Students need to be able to
   open files
   make graphs

Materials
   Radiosonde

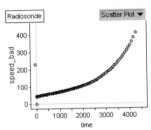

A graph of "bad" speed against time. The first two points are strange because they are at the beginning of the series. The data curve upward erroneously.

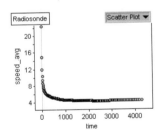

If we plot **height / time** against **time**, we get the plot above. It's wrong because **height** includes the altitude of the site (the intercept of the **height-time** graph).

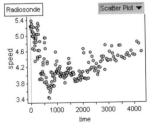

A "good" graph of instantaneous speed as a function of time. Note the small range.

Data in Depth
© 2001 Key Curriculum Press

Radiosonde

Name(s): _____

In this activity, you will study data from a balloon ascent from Kansas in 1991 (Dorothy was not aboard). This balloon carried a *radiosonde,* a device that sent weather data back to Earth by radio: altitude, temperature, pressure, humidity, winds, and so forth. Here we will focus on some *rates,* for example the speed of the ascent. Here are two of the several attributes in the file:

time   time in seconds since launch

height   height in meters above sea level

1. Open the file **Radiosonde.**

2. Make a graph of **height** (vertical axis) as a function of **time** (horizontal). The graph should look seriously linear, as in the illustration. Estimate the slope of the data by fitting a movable line to the points. What is the equation of the line?

3. Based on the equation, about how fast do you think the balloon is ascending? (Give units to your answer as well. If you're not sure about the units, look in the comments of the collection: double-click the collection to get the collection inspector, then look in the **Comments** pane.)

You'll learn how to
   make new attributes
   use the formula editor
   compute differences in Fathom

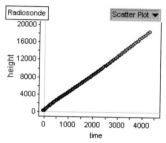

A typical, seriously linear plot.

Calculating the Speed—the Wrong Way

Now we'll have Fathom calculate speeds. (At first, we're going to do it wrong. Bear with us. We'll also show you how to fix it.)

4. Click the column heading labeled **<new>** to make a new attribute called **speed.** (You can move the attribute to a better place in the table by dragging its title.)

5. Select **Show Formula** from the **Display** menu, and double-click the formula cell for speed. Now we'll enter the formula for the speed.

6. Enter **height – prev(height).** That will give us the difference in heights since the previous reading. Close the formula editor. Values appear in the **speed** column.

7. Make a graph of **speed** as a function of **time.** Sketch and scale your graph at right.

8. The first two speeds don't fit with the rest. Why not? (By the way, this is *not* what's wrong.)

9. Select the graph and choose **Add Filter** from the **Data** menu. The formula editor appears.

Rate calculations are often strange right at the beginning of a series of data, for a variety of reasons. Filtering is a good technique for setting those points aside.

10. Enter **caseIndex > 2** and close the editor. This will "filter out" those first two cases so that they won't appear in the graph.

11. The first (originally third) value for **speed** should be about 43. What are its units?

12. Why is it so different from the speed you found in Step 3?

The Right Way

We have to fix our formula for **speed**. We found only difference in **height**. To find **speed**, we have to divide difference in **height** by difference in **time**.

13. Double-click the formula cell to bring up the formula editor again.

14. Edit the formula to take the difference in time into account. The diagrams show a fast way to do that.

15. When you're finished, close the formula editor. The numbers *and the graph* should change. Rescale the graph if necessary by choosing **Scatter Plot** or **Line Scatter Plot** from the popup menu in the graph. Sketch the graph here and scale it.

First, select the existing formula.

Then press the division key.

height – prev (height)

Finally, type the denominator.

$$\frac{\text{height} - \text{prev (height)}}{\text{time} - \text{prev (time)}}$$

16. What's a typical value for **speed**? How does that match with the slope of the line in Step 2?

Going Further

1. In Step 2, in the equation for the line, what does the intercept mean?

2. Why don't we just use **height / time** as a formula for **speed**?

3. How do you calculate the average of the values in **speed**? Why is that average different from the slope of the least-squares line of **height** as a function of **time**?

4. Make a new attribute, **tempRate**, which is the rate of change of *temperature* in degrees per second. Is it usually positive or negative? What's happening when it changes sign?

5. Make another attribute, **tempLapse**, which is the rate of change of temperature in *degrees per kilometer*. This is called the lapse rate. Graph it. What are typical values? Why would you ever want to know this quantity?

Sometimes you get a great-looking graph that looks like a real scientific result—and it's completely wrong. Don't let nicely formatted graphics or tables shut down your common sense. Look at the numbers and ask, "Is this reasonable?"

If you're really ambitious, do this in degrees Fahrenheit per thousand feet.

Generation by Generation

These activities lead students through the process of creating a simulation of a changing population and studying some of its mathematical properties.

- Two structured computer activities
- Data generated in simulation
- Student pages 162–166
- Guided, medium features

Generation II: Limits to Growth

This activity begins on page 165. It requires a file to start with—either the one produced in the first activity or the one on the CD called **GenerationII**. The model of population limit that we use produces a *logistic* population growth function rather than an exponential one.

Topics

simulation of change
exponential growth

Students need no Fathom experience, but some exposure would be helpful.

No materials needed for
Generation by Generation.
The second activity requires either the file made in the first or **GenerationII**.

What's Important Here

- Students will see that population growth is exponential under simple assumptions.

- After the "easy part," however, things get more complex, realistic, and interesting. The most important thing is that students explore the consequences of changing the assumptions and use mathematics to predict and explain the effects of those changes.

Discussion Questions

In addition to discussing the questions on the student pages, consider:

- ➲ Which do you think is a better way to represent the way population growth works—doing each year as a separate step the way we did, or writing an exponential formula? (Students can make a good argument for either technique.)

- ➲ How could you imagine changing the simulation to make the population model more realistic? (There are many possibilities, including the ones described in *Generation II*.)

Tech Notes

- You can type numerical values right into a slider if you want. Just select the number and edit it.

- In the formula editor, you open up lists by clicking the little plus-boxes. Close them by clicking the minus-boxes that appear. To enter a function in the formula pane, type it or double-click it in the list.

- If your students have experience with exponential growth, they can skip the second page and just put in the function. They'll need to remember not to put in the $y =$ part because the formula editor specifies just the right-hand side of a function when you choose **Plot Function** from the **Graph** menu.

If students do not have experience, this is a great chance for discovery. Fitting this function can be tricky, though, because it's hard to tell which way to move the parameters.

Generation by Generation

Name(s): _____

In this activity, you'll simulate the way a population changes under certain simple assumptions. There are two things to pay attention to:

- The mathematics. You'll see that population increases exponentially. If you already know about that, you'll refine your understanding (and we'll go beyond it in the next activity).

- The technology. You'll see how Fathom (and practically any other system) handles this kind of simulation.

At first, we'll make our population start at 100 and increase by 5% per year.

1. Open Fathom and make a new document.

2. Choose **Case Table** from the **Insert** menu. An empty case table appears.

3. Click on **<new>** to make a new attribute. Call it **pop** (for population).

4. Make two more new attributes. Call them **births** and **year**.

5. With the case table active, choose **New Cases...** from the **Data** menu. Give it 10 new cases.

6. We have cases, but no data. Give your attributes formulas. Copy the ones in the table.

Formula for **year**	Formula for **births**	Formula for **pop**
caseIndex − 1	**pop · 0.05**	if (caseIndex = 1) $\begin{cases} 100 \\ \text{prev (pop) + prev (births)} \end{cases}$ **Note:** This will "wrap" and look strange unless you make your formula editor wider.

7. Graph **pop** as a function of **year**. It should increase, as in the graph shown here.

8. Select the table and make 40 new cases (for a total of 50). Rescale the plot by again choosing **Scatter Plot** from the popup menu in the graph. Besides the difference in scale and the larger number of points, what's different about the graph? Describe the differences below and sketch the graph.

Enter the formula, then press **OK** to close the editor.

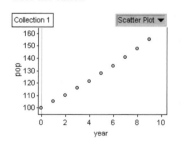

Now we'll make a function to fit our data. **Note:** If you want to do this without hints and detailed instructions, skip the next page and try to fit a function to your graph. You'll choose **Plot Function** from the **Graph** menu. Good luck!

Making a Function to Fit

We're going to make an *exponential* function to fit this population growth. To do that, we'll need two parameters. We'll use sliders for those parameters.

9. Make two sliders. (Choose **New Slider** from the **Insert** menu.) Name them **A** and **B**.

10. Select the graph and choose **Plot Function** from the **Graph** menu. The formula editor opens.

11. Make the formula shown here. Then close the formula editor. A curve appears on the graph.

12. Move the **A** slider. (If you want to change it a lot, you'll have to change the bounds on the slider axis by dragging on the numbers. That is, pull larger numbers into view.) Describe the way the curve changes when you change the value of **A**.

13. Move the **B** slider. (The curve is very sensitive; you may want to restrict the values of **B** that you see. You can push the unwanted numbers off the axis.) Describe the way the curve changes.

14. Move both sliders until you can fit the data as well as possible. Report the values of **A** and **B**, and describe the way you made the curve fit (e.g., which slider you moved first, what problems there were, etc.).

15. Look at your results and at the function, and at other students' work. Explain as clearly as you can what **A** and **B** mean.

16. Suggest new names for **A** and **B** that would reflect their meanings.

17. Save your work for future use. Give the file a good name, such as **PopulationSim.**

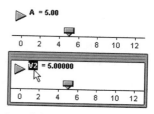

Two sliders named **A** and **V2** (we're changing **V2** to **B**). Their current values are 5.0, since we've just made them.

That's **A** times **B** to the **year** power.

Here are the keystrokes to make the formula:

A * B ^ year

Note 1: You need the * for multiplication or Fathom will treat **AB** as a single attribute.

Note 2: You won't see the ^; it just moves you up into the exponent position.

Note 3: ^ is SHIFT-6.

Making the Simulation More Realistic

18. One really unrealistic part of our simulation so far is that it gives us decimal people. Change the formula for **births** so that it gives only integer results. Write your new formula here.

You can find functions to make your decimals into integers by looking in the formula editor. In the browser pane, look under **Functions/Arithmetic,** shown here.

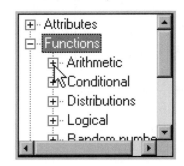

19. Another problem is that we have **births** but not **deaths**. Make a new attribute, **deaths**, with a formula of **pop*0.02**; that is, 2% of the people die every year. Alter the formula to make sure it's an integer, not a decimal. **Note:** Just making a formula for **deaths** doesn't incorporate it into our model. That's OK. We will in Step 21 below.

20. Predict: When you incorporate deaths into your model, what will happen to the way **pop** changes?

21. Now change the formula for **pop** to take **deaths** into account. What's the new formula?

22. How did including **deaths** change the pattern of **pop**? That is, how good was your prediction in Step 20?

23. Make two sliders; name them **birthRate** and **deathRate**. Give them the values 0.05 and 0.02, respectively. (You can type the values right into the slider.)

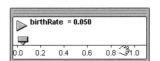

You may also want to change the scale of the slider axis, as shown.

24. Edit the formulas for **births** and **deaths** to substitute the sliders for the numerical constants.

25. Play with the values of **birthRate** and **deathRate**. If your **pop** values don't change, something's wrong. Change your formulas until it's right.

26. What happens to **pop** when you change **deathRate**?

27. What happens when **deathRate > birthRate**?

Going Further

Explore the way making the population integer-only affects the best-fit function. Change the formula for **births** back and forth between integer and real number. What do you notice about the function that fits each condition best? Can you explain what you see?

Generation II: Limits to Growth

Name(s): _____

Real populations do not grow boundlessly. In this section, we'll add two phenomena to rein in our population growth: a "crowding" effect and a plague.

The idea behind a crowding effect is that you can't go on growing forever. Maybe there's a limit to the amount of food you can produce, or maybe people don't have as many children when they're all packed together. In our simulation, we'll have the death rate go up when there are more people.

You need

your saved file from the preceding activity, or, alternatively, ours: **GenerationII.**

1. On the sliders, set **birthRate** to 0.10 and **deathRate** to 0.02. Your population should increase rapidly, passing 1000 in about year 30.

The population will keep growing without limit because, with the formulas we have, the number of births will always be greater than the number of deaths. We need a way to increase the number of deaths beyond the number of births, but only when the population gets large.

There are several ways to do this. One of the most interesting ways is to change the formula so the death rate gradually increases with the population. That's what we'll do.

2. Edit your formula for **deaths**. Where you now have **pop * deathRate**, multiply that quantity by **(pop / 200)**. That way, there will be *fewer* deaths when **pop** is less than 200 (that is, when **pop / 200 < 1**) and *more* deaths when **pop > 200**.

floor (pop•deathRate ($\frac{pop}{200}$))

The **floor ( )** function makes the result the next lower integer.

3. Plot **pop** as a function of **year**. Sketch the graph and describe what is happening.

4. Plot **deaths** as a function of **pop**. Sketch the graph and describe what is happening.

5. At what number does the population stabilize? (You may have to add more cases.) Explain why that's the value.

6. Predict: If you increase **birthRate** to 0.2, what will the stable population be?

7. Do it. What do you find?

A Plague

$$\text{if (random ( ) < 0.05)} \begin{cases} \dfrac{pop}{2} \\ 0 \end{cases}$$

8. Now let's add a plague. Make a new attribute, **plague**. Give it the formula shown here.

9. Now change the **deaths** formula. Simply add **plague** to what you already have. That is, the number of people who die is the number who normally die plus the number who die of the plague.

10. Plot **pop** again. Press **CTRL-Y** (Windows) or ⌘**-Y** (Mac) repeatedly to rerandomize. Describe what you see and sketch an example here.

11. Explain how the **plague** formula works.

Going Further

1. When we made a limit, we put **pop / 200** in the **deaths** formula. Explain clearly how that term works.

2. What if we used a number different from 200 in the **deaths** formula—what would the stable population be then? See if you can find a formula that gives you the stable population as a function of the number in the formula. Then explain it.

3. Once you have a plague, plot **deaths** against **births** and make a **Line Scatter Plot.** Sketch it and explain what you see.

4. Maybe we don't need the **(pop / 200)** term to control population—maybe we can do it entirely with plagues, especially if the chance of a plague increases with population. Experiment with that idea and report what you find.

Building the Weather Machine

In *Building the Weather Machine,* students construct an extremely simple model of the weather. Then, they use the model—a simulation—to answer a question. They may also alter the simulation in order to answer additional questions.

You can read the setup of the problem at the top of the first student page (page 168).

What's Important Here

- Simulations and models are not all about functions that we represent on the Cartesian plane. This is discrete mathematics through and through.

- Students actually construct a graph. They build it from scratch out of the open collection—the little gold balls.

The Question

When the students have built the simulation, but they're still at the computers, ask, "In a month of 30 days, how many will be sunny?" A response should include some estimate of the variability.

The Answer

Five-eighths of the days, or about 19. You can do it theoretically by using Markov chains or common-sense difference equation thinking. This answer does not take into account that we know the first day is sunny. But how much does that skew the data toward sunniness? (Statistics teachers: Imagine taking 10 simulations starting with a sunny day and 10 starting with a rainy one. Do you think you can detect the difference in the number of sunny days out of 30?)

Suggestions to Students

- Increase the number of cases (days) to get a better handle on the expected value.

- Keep the number of days equal to 30, but do lots of runs, to get a better variability.

- If students know about measures collections (introduced in *Random Walks: Inventing Spread,* on page 200), they can use them to collect measurements over many months.

Discussion Questions

➲ What if the probability of a sunny day following a sunny day increased to 90% from 70%? What difference would that make in the answer?

➲ How would you figure out the theoretical answer to this question? What is it?

➲ What difference does it make that the first day is sunny?

➲ This is a simplistic weather model. Suppose you were going to try to model the weather where you live. What would you add first?

- Structured computer activity
- Data generated in simulation
- Student pages 168–169
- Intermediate, medium features

Topics

discrete modeling
probability

No Fathom skills needed

all instructions are given, but this is complicated, so comfort is a plus

No materials needed

If you want to avoid building the simulation, start with the question and a prebuilt simulation (**WeatherMachine**). This is more black-boxish, of course, but it may get more quickly to what you're after.

The 10-second introduction to measures collections:

They collect values of *measures* as *cases.* First define a measure, for example **sunnyDays**, which might be **count(weather = "sun")**. Then choose **Collect Measures** from the **Analyze** menu. This gives you a *measures* collection of *months*—in which each case has just the number of sunny days in it. Open that collection's inspector and click the **Collect Measures** tab to control how many months you collect.

Building the Weather Machine

Name(s): _____

In this activity, you'll use Fathom to create a simulation. This one is a simple model of the weather—far too simple. In fact, it will be terrible for predicting the weather, but great for learning how to build such a simulation.

Suppose weather works like this:

- If it's a sunny day, there's a 70% chance that it will be sunny tomorrow, and a 30% chance that it will rain.

- If it's a rainy day, there's a 50% chance that it will rain tomorrow. Otherwise, it will be sunny.

The main question is "In a month of 30 days, how many sunny days should you expect to get?"

A secondary question is "How much will that quantity vary from month to month?"

1. Open a new Fathom document.

2. Make a new case table. (Choose **Case Table** from the **Insert** menu.)

3. Make a new attribute by clicking the **<new>** column header. Call it **weather**.

4. Select **weather** and choose **Edit Formula** from the **Edit** menu to open the formula editor.

5. Make the formula editor wide (this will be a long formula) and tall.

6. Start by entering this much:

$$\text{if (caseIndex = 1)} \begin{cases} \text{"sun"} \\ \text{?} \end{cases}$$

This tells Fathom that the first day will be sunny. Now we have to tell it what to do when it's not the first day.

7. That will depend on what the weather was yesterday. Continue entering the formula so that it looks like this:

$$\text{if (caseIndex = 1)} \begin{cases} \text{"sun"} \\ \text{if (prev (weather) = "sun")} \begin{cases} \blacksquare \\ \text{?} \end{cases} \end{cases}$$

So the top (highlighted) question mark will contain what we do if it was sunny; the bottom one will contain what we do if it was rainy.

8. Fill in the "sunny" phrase:

$$\text{if (caseIndex = 1)} \begin{cases} \text{"sun"} \\ \text{if (prev (weather) = "sun")} \begin{cases} \text{if (random ( ) < 0.7)} \begin{cases} \text{"sun"} \\ \text{"rain"} \end{cases} \\ \text{?} \end{cases} \end{cases}$$

random(1) gives a random number between 0 and 1. So 70% of the time, that new phrase will give "sun," just as we want.

You'll learn how to
make insanely complicated formulas
use a summary table
design a new kind of graph

If you've never entered an **if( )** function in Fathom before, fear not. Start by typing **if(** and see what happens.

By the way, pressing **TAB** always moves you to a question mark.

These instructions have you make **if( )**s inside **if( )**s. You could accomplish the same thing by using additional attributes.

9. Finish the formula:

$$\text{if (caseIndex = 1)} \begin{cases} \text{"sun"} \\ \text{if (prev (weather) = "sun")} \begin{cases} \text{if (random ( ) < 0.7)} \begin{cases} \text{"sun"} \\ \text{"rain"} \end{cases} \\ \text{if (random ( ) < 0.5)} \begin{cases} \text{"rain"} \\ \text{"sun"} \end{cases} \end{cases} \end{cases}$$

10. You're finished! Close the formula editor with **OK**.

11. Now you need the days. Select the table and choose **New Cases...** from the **Data** menu. Ask it for 30 cases (the month).

12. Let's summarize the data. Choose **Summary Table** from the **Insert** menu.

13. Drag the column header for **weather**—the name itself—from the case table to the right arrow on the summary table. You can now see frequencies (counts) for the different kinds of weather.

14. Choose **Rerandomize** from the **Analyze** menu. See how the numbers change in the summary table and how the values change among the cases themselves.

Additional Features

You have now made enough of the simulation to see it work. But if you have the time and the screen space, here are some additional things to try:

15. Make a graph of the data. What kind of graph did you make? Sketch it here.

16. Double-click the collection to open the inspector, and click the **Display Attributes** tab. Among the attributes that show up are **x**, **y**, and **caption**. They are the *x* and *y* positions of the gold balls and their labels.

17. Change the formula for **caption**. (It's currently "a case.") Make it simply **weather**. The weather appears beneath each gold ball.

18. Let's make the position mean something. Change the formula for **x** to **caseIndex * 16** and change the formula for **y** to look like this:

19. Close the editor and open the collection so you can see the whole month— 30 gold balls.

Your collection will look like this, only longer.

20. Choose **Rerandomize** repeatedly from the **Analyze** menu. **CTRL-Y** (Windows) or **⌘-Y** (Mac) is the shortcut. What do you notice about the patterns of sunny and rainy days?

Change Sonatas and Investigations

- Five open-ended computer investigations
- Data from simulation and files
- Student pages 171–173
- Independent, basic→medium

You may want to give students a copy of *Recursive Definitions and Recurrence Relations*, page 153, to aid them in some of these tasks.

Sonata 17: Sequences of Squares

This is perhaps the easiest Sonata in the book, accessible to quite young students. We expect them to see that the difference between adjacent squares is an odd number. If possible, we hope that they will predict—or at least notice—that the difference is twice the square root of the lower square, plus 1. That is, the difference between 4^2 and 5^2 is $(2*4 + 1)$, or 9.

The trick is making Fathom do the work; students need to remember to use **caseIndex** for the row number (so **caseIndex²** is a good formula to use for **square**), and use **next(square)** to get the next square in the sequence.

Sonata 18: Fibonacci

There is a universe of activities and problems about Fibonacci numbers. The student sheet can only touch the surface. Feel free to adapt this activity using any resources you have.

The tricky part is the formula for the sequence itself. The author can think of two main strategies: using "secondary" attributes that hold parts of the computation, and using nested **prev( )** functions. In addition, you have to account for the first two cases, which are special. A particularly nice way to do it looks like this:

The Web, especially the Math Forum (**http://forum.swarthmore.edu**), is a good place to look for Fibonacci resources if you have none on your shelf. At the Math Forum site, look for Ron Knott's page:

http://forum.swarthmore.edu/~ron/ FibProblemSheet/FibProblemSheet.html (August, 1999)

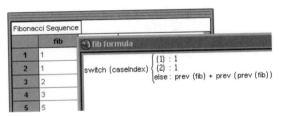

In this way, you could substitute sliders for the two 1s and have a very flexible (and noninteger!) Fibonacci machine.

Change Challenges

A Better Weather Machine. Speaking of machines, the *Building the Weather Machine* (page 168) is fun, but limited. Some enterprising students might want to take it further.

An Island of One's Own. Similarly, students can enliven the *Generations* activities (pages 162–166)—though they are already fairly complex—with additional complications. The proposed conflict, that of land for housing versus agriculture, is a real one in society.

Text Analysis. This activity has a chance of being much shorter than the previous two. It's fun, too, because the data are unusual. Students may want to know about the **concat( )** function: If you write **concat(prev(char), char)**, you get a digraph: two adjacent letters.

There's more text analysis in Chapter 10, *Inference with Fathom*, on page 298.

Sonata 17: Sequences of Squares

Name(s): _____

This Sonata is about square numbers: 1, 4, 9, 16, and so forth.

You'll show that you can

- recognize relationships in a sequence
- use Fathom to show those relationships
- make a convincing explanation telling why the relationship is true

Conjecture

Without using Fathom or a calculator, explain the relationship between each square number and the one that follows it. Make your conjecture before you use any technology. Also, make your conjecture as encompassing as possible: What *exactly* will the relationship be? Write it here.

Calculation

Use Fathom to test your conjecture. Make a collection in which one attribute is the squares and another computes the relationship you were trying to predict. Describe what happened below, and list the formulas you used.

Comparison

Did you notice anything in the pattern you found that was not part of your conjecture? If so, what?

Did your calculations match your conjecture? If not, explain why and come up with a new conjecture.

If you can, make a convincing explanation (algebraically, geometrically, or in words) telling why your conjecture is true for all squares.

Sonata 18: Fibonacci

Name(s): _____

This Sonata is about the Fibonacci sequence: 1, 1, 2, 3, 5, 8, 13, and so forth. After the first two, which are both 1, each number is the sum of the previous two.

Conjecture

Figure out how to use Fathom to get the Fibonacci sequence. Then, before you use the computer, make a conjecture about one or more of the following:

- What would happen if you changed the first two elements?
- What does the sequence of ratios of Fibonacci numbers to their successors look like?
- What function would approximate the Fibonacci sequence?
- What happens if you add a Fibonacci number to the one *two earlier* in the sequence? What sequence does that make?

To figure these out, don't forget:

caseIndex is a special variable equal to the number of the row you're in.

prev(A) gives the value of **A** in the previous case.

next(A) gives the value of **A** in the next case.

Calculation

Use Fathom to test your conjecture. Make a collection in which one attribute is the Fibonacci numbers and another computes the relationship you were trying to predict. Describe what happened below, and list the formulas you used.

Comparison

Did you notice anything in the pattern you found that was not part of your conjecture? If so, what?

Did your calculations match your conjecture? If not, explain why and come up with a new conjecture.

If you can, make a convincing explanation (algebraically, geometrically, or in words) telling why your conjecture is true.

Change Challenges

Name(s): _____

Here are a few suggestions for Sonatas or projects you could do using some of the ideas in this chapter, such as the **prev( )** function.

A Better Weather Machine

The weather machine that we built (pages 168–169) was all right, but too simplistic. Make a weather modeler that is more complex and makes weather that seems more like a sequence of real weather—for example, from your area. A suggestion: Add only a little bit at a time. These things have a way of getting out of hand in their complexity.

An Island of One's Own

Simulate an isolated island over the years. It's small, with only 1000 acres of land that you can farm. Each acre can grow enough to feed 10 people. Or they can use the acre to build enough houses for 50. It all starts with only 500 people, so there's plenty of room—at first. Each year is a case. Everybody has to eat. Everybody has to have a house. You decide whether they can store food. What happens?

    An extension question: What is the "steady state" for this society?

Text Analysis

We have included several Fathom files with famous text: the beginning of the Declaration of Independence (**Declaration**), the Gettysburg Address (**Gettysburg**), the opening of *The Old Man and the Sea* (**OldManAndTheSea**), and George Bush's inaugural address (**BushInaugural**). In these files, each letter is a case. Pick whichever file interests you and analyze it. Here is one question you might investigate:

    In this text, for a given letter, what letters are most likely to follow it? For example, *q* is most often followed by *u*. Predict first, especially for the most common letters. (What *are* the most common letters? You can find out using these data.)

What to Do with Leftovers

7

This chapter is all about residuals and using residual plots. Residual plots show how far the data points in a scatter plot are from some function—often, but not necessarily, a line. We'll be calling that function a *model* throughout this chapter.

Looking at residuals can tell you several different things. We'll focus on these two:

- The pattern of residuals can tell you whether your model is missing something.

- The size of the residuals can tell you how good your model is at predicting the data.

In addition, just playing with Fathom's dynamic residual plots will give students more intuition about functions and how they're put together.

Level

The activities in this chapter are probably best suited to students who are at least taking an algebra course, because of the formulas involved. Mature middle-schoolers are welcome, of course.

The Activities

- **Residuals Playground.** A simple activity that introduces residuals, which students compute themselves.

- **Heating Water.** Lets students fit a line to rising water temperature. It looks linear, but making a residual plot shows previously unseen structure. This is the introduction to residual plots. It works especially well with chemistry, physics, and statistics.

- **Radiosonde Residuals.** Gives students additional practice with residuals in a mathematically similar situation.

- **Estimating Parameters Using Residuals.** Students look at data from *Printing Paragraphs,* the Sonata on page 120. The length of a paragraph decreases as its width increases, but how? Students use sliders to represent the parameter and the residual plot to assess how good the parameter is. Then they refine the model, adding another parameter.

- **Inverting Residual Plots.** A collection of exercises you can assign at your discretion. Only the most experienced students should attempt them all.

- **British Couples.** Uses residuals to draw conclusions about the *data*, not just about the *model*. Like *Heating Water*, it explores the basic meaning of residuals. However, it also introduces a goodness-of-fit measure that foreshadows least squares.

- **Modeling Mauna Loa.** Students use residuals to help model data that are increasing but with seasonal variation superimposed. That is, we fit a sine to the residuals of a linear fit to derive the more complex function.

- **Cooling Off.** This Sonata gives students a chance to analyze data from the author's kitchen. The data came from doing the extension of *In Hot Water*, on page 66.

- **Out on a Limb with Jupiter.** A Sonata that is good for experienced students. Trigonometry and a good visual sense are prerequisites.

Objectives

In activities from this chapter, students will show that they can

- Use residual plots to find patterns in data that are not evident when they just look at the plot itself

- Use residual plots as an aid in improving the model—through recognizing when a model is of the wrong form, and also to help in estimating a parameter when the model is of the right form

- Use a "goodness of fit" measure—a function of the residuals—to optimize fitted functions

- Learn about the situations from which the data arise by interpreting features in residual plots

Where Else Can We Use Residual Plots?

Residual plots are useful throughout this book. The most relevant activities include:

- *How Much Tape Is Left?*, page 116, a measurement and prediction activity that benefits from using residual plots

- *Straight or Curved?*, page 218

Errors and Mistakes

There are two fundamental sources for residuals: *errors* and *mistakes*. The difference is that errors are unavoidable. In our data analysis, we want to minimize and measure error, and to avoid mistakes. Sometimes it is hard (or even pointless) to tell the difference. But more often, distinguishing between these categories and their causes will help you make better sense of your data—and more valid conclusions.

Mistakes

Mistakes come in two varieties: *bias* and *wrong models*.

Bias is something systematically wrong with your measurements. If you're taking a survey about favorite foods and you stand in the produce section to do it, you'll have *sampling bias*, because you'll poll only people who come to the produce section.

If you're measuring the speed of runners and your stopwatch is running slow, your speeds will all be too fast. You can correct for this kind of bias by comparing the stopwatch to one that runs properly and compensating accordingly. This process is called *calibration*, and is a vital concept in experimental science.

Bias is especially cruel because you can't always detect it by exploring the data. The data look fine on their own. They may even tell you what you want to hear: You think the groat clusters are making the track team stronger; actually, the stopwatch battery is getting weak.

One form of a wrong model is modeling something curvy with a line or vice versa. We can never model everything, so we like to err on the side of simpler (usually linear) models. On the other hand, sometimes everything interesting is in the curve.

Errors

There are two kinds of error as well: what I'll call *quantity error* and *process error*.

Quantity error includes all forms of measurement error—we are unable to come up with perfectly precise numbers. When you measure something to the nearest millimeter, that 0.5 mm slop is inevitable. In that sense, this is the same as round-off error, which can occur without any physical measurement. This kind of error includes natural variability. Scoops of ice cream will not all weigh the same because the quantities are slightly different. It's not the scoop's fault, or the scale's. It's naturally inexact.

Process error includes sampling error. If you are trying to figure out the total income of everyone in the town, you may decide to sample from the population. Your answer will be wrong, but it won't be your fault. You can, however, figure out how far off you're likely to be: that's the reason we have confidence intervals.

When It's Hard To Tell

Sometimes we find ourselves in the cracks between errors and mistakes. I think it depends on our purpose (which can change during the course of an investigation). When we switch from scooping ice cream to scooping caviar, we may start to care whether we're scooping too much; what we earlier accepted as allowable error may become unwanted bias.

Introduction to Residuals

- Three structured computer activities
- Data from files
- Student pages 179–182
- Intermediate, basic features

The goal of these activities is to help students understand residuals and residual plots. Our approach in *Residuals Playground* and *Heating Water* is to have students calculate residuals directly—by having Fathom calculate from the given function—before introducing the **Make Residual Plot** command.

The third activity, *Radiosonde Residuals*, is suitable either as practice to follow the second or as a quick introduction for more experienced students. It's also suitable for homework or open lab time.

Topics
residuals

Students need to be able to
make scatter plots
make new attributes
use formulas to define attributes

What's Important Here

We use residuals for many purposes in data analysis. These activities focus on using residuals to see patterns that are invisible in a "regular" graph.

- You can see deviations (from the curve) or a pattern (e.g., nonlinearity) better because the vertical scale of the residual plot is so different from the one in the main plot. Making the residual plot magnifies the data with respect to the model (the line).

- If residuals don't look random, we should question the model. In *Heating Water*, for example, the linear model is OK for some purposes (interpolating temperatures to within a degree, say), but we can see that the phenomenon is really not linear.

One way to think of residual plots is that we turn the model—the line or curve—into a new axis.

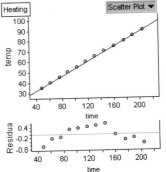

A graph from *Heating Water* (page 180) with a residual plot.

Discussion Questions

➲ What are the units on the vertical scale of the residual plot? (degrees Celsius; meters)

➲ Compare the main plot to the residual plot. Why are the scales so different?

➲ (Especially in *Residuals Playground*.) What would happen if we defined a residual as (*predicted – observed*) instead of the other way around? (For one thing, when we moved the data one way, residuals would go the other. It would be confusing.)

Tech Notes

- Students need to zoom in for *Heating Water*. To do so, hold down the **CTRL** key (Windows) or **OPTION** key (Mac) so that the cursor changes to a magnifying glass, and drag a rectangle around the region you want to investigate. The rectangle expands to fill the whole graph. Rechoosing **Scatter Plot** from the popup menu in the graph rescales the plot.

- You can do *Heating Water* with your own data (especially if you're teaching chemistry, for example). If the burner is hot, you get a good, linear-looking regime in the middle. At the beginning, it flattens out as the container heats; at the end, it flattens as the water gets closer to boiling. If you include these "flat" areas, (a) students should definitely use the movable line—not least squares—and fit it to the linear part of the data, and (b) students will need to expand the vertical scale of the residual plot in order to see the curve in the linear part of the temperature graph.

Note: The student pages do not tell students how to zoom in. We describe one way here; you can also encourage students to look in **Help**.

Data in Depth
© 2001 Key Curriculum Press

Introduction to Residuals I: Residuals Playground

Name(s): _____

In this activity, we'll explore *residuals,* which are the amounts "left over" when you model data with a function.

1. Open **Circles.** It contains made-up data about a project in which you might measure the radius and area of circles, in order to learn about the area formula, $A = \pi r^2$. The file also has a graph of area as a function of radius, with the "correct" function plotted. It looks like the picture shown here. You can see that the points don't all lie on the curve.

2. Move some points on the graph. Notice that they move only vertically.

3. A *residual* is the vertical distance from the point to its *predicted* value—the curve. First, let's calculate that predicted value. Make a new attribute called **areaP** (P for Predicted). Give it the formula **pi * radius²**.

4. Replace **area** on the graph with **areaP**. What do you notice? Explain why that happens.

5. Put **area** back on the vertical axis. Now make a new attribute, **residual.** Give it the formula **area – areaP**. This is the vertical distance from the point to the line. Explain why.

6. Make a separate new graph, with **residual** on the vertical axis and **radius** on the horizontal. This is a *residual plot.*

7. Move points in the original graph. Describe what happens on the residual plot.

8. In the original graph, move all the points so they lie on the "predicted" curve as well as possible.

9. In the residual plot, again choose **Scatter Plot** from the popup menu on the graph. This rescales the residual plot. Sketch the residual plot below. Be sure to label the scale of the vertical axis.

10. Explain what happened. If the points are on the curve, why aren't the residuals zero?

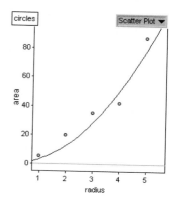

In this plot, the residuals are imaginary vertical segments from the points to the curve. The point where radius = 4 has a negative residual.

Especially, when is a residual positive? When is it zero? In what direction do residuals move as you move the original points?

Introduction to Residuals II: Heating Water

Name(s): _____

In this activity, we'll explore *residuals,* which are the amounts "left over" when you model data with a function.

The author heated a pan of water, recording how many minutes and seconds had passed each time the temperature increased by 5 degrees Celsius. **HeatingWater** has the data for temperatures between 35 and 90 degrees Celsius, which span the times between 40 seconds and 205 seconds after the heat was turned on.

1. Before you open the file, sketch what you think the graph will look like. That is, how does temperature increase with time for a pan of water on the stove? Is it linear? If not, how does it curve? Make a labeled and scaled sketch at right.

   Sketch your prediction here:

2. Now open the file. Make a new graph. Put **time** on the horizontal axis and **temp** on the vertical. Describe how the actual graph differs from your prediction.

3. Choose **Least-Squares Line** from the **Graph** menu. A least-squares fit to the data appears. Write the equation for the least-squares line below and tell what the slope means (e.g., what are its units?).

The line should look as if it goes through all the points, and r^2 should be very close to 1.00. We might make a mistake here and say, "Wow—temperature increases linearly. The fit is nearly perfect." That is, we might think we're finished. It's true that the line explains a lot of the temperature change, but two things should bother you:

- It's hard to believe that it really is linear, that is, that the stove can heat hot water as fast as it can heat cold water.

- It's hard to believe that our measurements of times and temperatures are so accurate that the points fall on the line *exactly.*

So we'll look at the graph more closely.

Temp.	How Far Off
35	
40	
45	
50	
55	
60	
65	
70	
75	
80	
85	
90	

(You don't have to do all the points—just enough to see a pattern.)

4. For several of the points, zoom in to the point and record, in the table we've provided, approximately how far it is from the line (in degrees Celsius). Use positive numbers for above the line, negative for below. These numbers are called the residuals.

5. Describe any pattern you see in the residuals.

6. Let's make this process easier. Make a new attribute called **predictedTemp**.

7. Give **predictedTemp** a formula—the formula of the least-squares line. Now the values of **predictedTemp** are the temperatures *on the line* for each of the times in the collection.

8. Make another new attribute, **residuals**. Give it the formula **temp – predictedTemp**. Explain why these **residuals** are the same as the "distance in degrees Celsius" you reported in Step 4 (especially, is the sign right?).

9. Make a new separate graph and plot **residuals** as a function of **time**. Sketch that graph (labeled and scaled) at right. The pattern you see in the graph should be the same as the one you saw in the numbers in Step 5. Now, what does that pattern (the curve) *mean* in terms of the situation of heating water? That is, it's *not* linear. In what way is it not linear, and why do you suppose that's true?

A Great Shortcut

10. Click on the original graph (**temp** as a function of **time**) to select it. Choose **Make Residual Plot** from the **Graph** menu. Describe what appears.

11. Drag a point on the graph. Describe what happens to the line and to the residual plot (undo the drag afterwards so that your data are safe).

Going Further

1. You can also use the residual plot to assess the accuracy of the measurements. The thermometer was scaled with lines every degree (about 1.5 mm apart). One possibility is that the line really is a good model and the residuals are just due to errors in measuring temperature. Is that very likely? Base your response on the *size* of the residuals and on the *pattern* of the residuals.

2. The author claims that he watched the thermometer and wrote down the time when the temperature passed 30, 35, 40, . . . degrees. Do you think he had enough time to do this (or did he invent the data)? If he was honest, how accurate do you think his **time** measurements were?

3. Suppose the temperature measurements were completely correct and accurate. What measurement blunders (in size and pattern) would the author have had to make in the **time** measurements to produce the pattern in the residuals?

4. Suppose the author, seeing the thermometer pass a temperature where he needed to take a reading, did the same thing for every measurement: He turned from the stove, wrote down the temperature, looked at his watch, and wrote down the time. There is a delay between the time when the temperature was correct and the time when he looked at his watch. Describe the effect this might have on the fitted line and on the pattern of residuals.

Introduction to Residuals III: Radiosonde Residuals

Name(s): _____

In this activity, you make a residual plot that shows an underlying pattern and interpret it.

1. Open the file **Radiosonde.** These are data from a weather balloon ascent in December 1991, at Coffeyville, Kansas.

2. Make a scatter plot of **height** as a function of **time**. It should look extremely linear, like the top part of the picture.

3. With the graph selected, choose **Least-Squares Line** from the **Graph** menu. The least-squares line appears; this is pretty much coincident with the data. Describe any features you can see in the graph (e.g., can you see where the data leave the line?).

4. Choose **Make Residual Plot** from the **Graph** menu. A residual plot appears. Stretch the graph vertically so you can see it better. It should look like the picture.

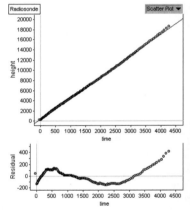

The trick with residual plots is learning to see that the data in the residual plot are exactly the same data as in the main plot, just transformed so that you can see features more clearly. Use Fathom and the residual plot to answer the next few questions.

5. Describe features you see in the graph. If it helps, identify regions on the graph where different things seem to be happening.

6. In the middle, where the residual plot is decreasing, some students might say that that's where the balloon is going down. Explain why that's wrong and what's really happening there.

7. Pick a point at the first hump of the residual plot. Use Fathom to find its coordinates in the residual plot and its coordinates in the main plot. Write those here.

8. Their *x*-coordinates (**time**) should be the same, but the *y*-coordinates are different. Subtract to find the difference, tell what its units are, and explain what that quantity means.

Estimating Parameters Using Residuals

- Structured computer activity
- Data from file (or previous work)
- Student pages 184–186
- Intermediate, medium features

This activity is about how to use residuals to estimate parameters. The work of coming up with a model to explain the phenomenon is done for the students here, using just one of many possible approaches. If you want students to come up with the model themselves, here are two suggestions:

- Have them do *Printing Paragraphs* (page 120) as a Sonata first. Thoroughly discuss the activity so you can assess whether the students understand the model. Even if you don't do the activity, students should see the paragraphs (page 121).

- Lead students through figuring out a model as a whole class; pass out the first page after they have figured out the area model. Then, when we try to improve the model, work as a whole class again before passing out the second page. ("We came up with a solution; the author's solution is different. On this page, you can implement our solution or the one that's written.")

What's Important Here

- The difference between a *parameter* and an *attribute* (or variable). A parameter is a constant of the situation that may be unknown. In this case, it's the area of the text. An attribute takes on different values depending on which case you're looking at. Sliders let you change parameters and see the effect of a change immediately.

- The model (a function) comes from the parameters. The residuals tell you whether the model is good. The smaller they get, the better the parameters are.

- Often you can interpret the parameters as something meaningful in the situation. On the second page, the **dw** parameter is about half the width of the "ragged-edge zone" of the paragraphs.

- As we use better tools, we get better estimates for parameters. Most students will have a smaller range of "reasonable" **area**s when they use the residual plot (Step 10) than they had without it (Step 7).

Discussion Questions

➣ Why would anyone ever need to predict the length of a block of text?

➣ When you decide that a parameter for a curve is unreasonable (e.g., in Step 6), how do you know it's unreasonable? (Answers will vary, but students may say that if all the points are on one side of the curve, it can't be right. Observations like these are great and help students make sense of whether residual plots are reasonable as well.)

➣ When you look at the residual plot, how do you decide what's a good fit? (One reasonable answer is that the two narrowest paragraphs look funny anyway, so if you ignore them, make the curve fit the other five.)

➣ Compare your ranges for using just the graph and using the residuals. Which method had a smaller range?

Topics

nonlinear functions
parameters
residuals

Students need to know how to

use sliders
change scales of axes

Materials

PrintingParagraphs
Materials for Printing Paragraphs (page 121)
or data from the *Printing Paragraphs* activity (page 120)

Connections

This activity is closely related to some in Chapter 4, such as *Fitting a Curve to the Planets* (page 104); also to *Modeling Mauna Loa,* (pages 191–192).

Estimating Parameters Using Residuals

Name(s): _____

In this activity, you'll use sliders and residuals to estimate parameters. We'll use data generated in another activity in this book, *Printing Paragraphs*. Our goal is to predict the vertical length of a paragraph of text if we know the width.

You need

a page of printed paragraphs
PrintingParagraphs

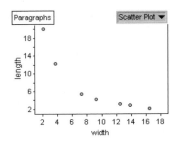

We took a paragraph of text and printed it out seven times, with different margins each time. Then we measured the lengths and the widths of the seven paragraphs. Each one is a case. As you might expect, when we made the paragraphs wide, they were short. Narrow paragraphs were really long. If you plot **length** as a function of **width**, you get the graph shown here.

In fact (and if you've done *Printing Paragraphs,* this is the Big Insight), we might suspect that the *area* of the paragraphs is a constant (after all, it's the same number of characters over and over). In that case, since **area = length * width**, we could predict length with the formula **length = area / width**.

1. Open **PrintingParagraphs** and graph **length** as a function of **width**.

2. Make a new slider (either choose **Slider** from the **Insert** menu or drag one off the shelf). Give it a new name, **area**, instead of **V1**.

3. With the graph selected, choose **Plot Function** from the **Graph** menu. The formula editor appears.

4. Enter **area / width** and click **OK** to close the editor. A curve appears.

5. Use the slider to make the curve fit the points as well as possible. What value do you get for **area**?

6. Why is that value a reasonable value for **area**? (If it is not, explain why not.) What are its units?

To extend the range of the slider, just drag on the numbers as you would on any axis. Think of it as pulling new numbers into the range.

7. Tweak the slider value up and down to find the largest and smallest values for **area** that you think are reasonable. (You may need to zoom in to the **area** slider to get finer control.) What are those values?

8. With the graph selected, choose **Make Residual Plot** from the **Graph** menu. A residual plot appears; stretch the graph vertically to give it more space. Sketch it at right.

9. Now tweak the slider value again. Looking at the points in the residual plot, find the best value you can for **area**. What value did you get? How did you decide what value was best?

10. Again, find the minimum and maximum "acceptable" values based on your criteria in the previous step. What are those values?

Estimating Parameters
Using Residuals (continued)

Improving the Model

If we do our best to fit the last five points, we can do pretty well, but the first two leap out of the graph. Some people say that's reasonable because the narrow paragraphs have more extra space at the ends of lines, so their lengths will be bigger than you would expect. You can see that in the residual plot.

    Let's take that into account. Here is one way to think about it:

    The lines have many different lengths. A line may or may not have extra white space at the end because of words moving to the next line. Let's assume that the average amount of white space is the same amount for every line. Call it **dw**. Then the area of the type is **area = length * (width − dw)**. (Discuss this in your group; make sure you understand that equation, especially the sign of **dw**.)

This is only one of many approaches.

11. Make a new slider and name it **dw**. Give it a value of 1.00.

12. Double-click the formula at the bottom of the graph (**area / width**) to bring up the formula editor.

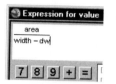

13. Change the formula to match the picture. Click **OK** to close the editor.

14. Rescale the residual plot to give you about plus or minus 4 cm.

15. Look at the residual plot and change the value for **area**. Describe what happens to the points.

16. Now change the value of **dw** with the slider. How does the curve change?

17. Now find the best values you can for **area** and **dw**. You will have to change the scale on the residual plot. You should be able to get all the residuals under 0.5 cm. What values did you get for **area** and **dw**?

18. Was your value for **area** bigger or smaller than it was before you added **dw** to the model? Tell which and explain why.

19. Why does **dw** have a bigger effect on the "left-hand" points than on the rest?

Going Further

1. There are two ways to answer Step 19. One has to do with the algebra of the formula, the other with the paragraphs themselves, on the paper. Whichever way you answered it, answer it the other way.

2. Make a new graph, but reverse the axes. Try to predict **width** as a function of **length**. Begin with a simple area model. Find the best value for **area** you can, illustrating your work with (among other things) residual plots. Then include **dw** to improve the model. Be careful where you put it!

Exercises: Inverting Residual Plots

Name(s): _____

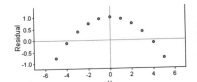

The first picture shown here is a residual plot. Your job is to make a collection of data and choose a function that produces that residual plot as accurately as possible. By accurately, we mean

- There are 11 points whose horizontal values (**H**) range from –5 to +5.
- The residuals form a curve opening downward.
- The values of the residuals range from about –1 (at both ends) to +1 (in the middle).

Each exercise tells you additional constraints. We have solved the first one as an example. For each exercise, produce the graph (and the residual plot) in Fathom, sketch it (label the axes, etc.), and write the function whose residuals constitute the plot.

1. The data points all have a (vertical) value of zero.
   Example solution: The function could be $y = 0.07x^2 – 1$.
2. The function is linear, sloping upward from –10 to +10. (What are the data points?)
3. The data points are linear, sloping upward from –10 to +10. (What is the function?)
4. The function is a parabola opening *downward*.
5. The data points are not linear, but their values decrease over the whole domain.

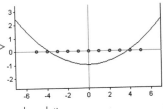

Example solution

Now we're finished with the residual plot. The next few questions involve a new situation: You have a set of data—again, 11 points—that extends from (**H**, **V**) = (–5,–100) to (+5, +100). When you plot them, they look linear. When you fit a least-squares line, all the points line up with an r^2 close to 1.00 (as at right). But when you make a residual plot, the points make the plots pictured below.

For each plot, make a set of data that produces the plot. You can do this by

- Finding individual values for the attributes that make the plot
- Finding a formula for the attribute **V** that produces the plot

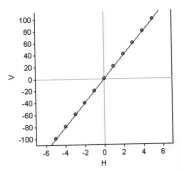

This is what the top part of the plot looks like for all of the problems at left. Only the residual plots look different.

6.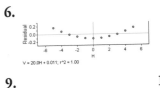
V = 20.0H + 0.011; r^2 = 1.00

7.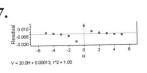
V = 20.0H + 0.00013; r^2 = 1.00

8.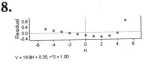
V = 19.9H + 0.35; r^2 = 1.00

9.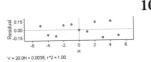
V = 20.0H + 0.0035; r^2 = 1.00

10.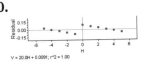
V = 20.0H + 0.0091; r^2 = 1.00

11.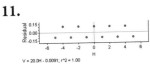
V = 20.0H - 0.0091; r^2 = 1.00

Data in Depth
© 2001 Key Curriculum Press

British Couples

This activity uses data about the heights of husbands and wives. We will try to make the best line to predict the height of a husband, given that of his wife.

> • Structured computer activity
> • Data from file
> • Student pages 188–189
> • Intermediate, basic features

What's Important Here

- The goodness-of-fit measure. Students need to understand that this quantity is a single number—a statistic—that tells how well the model (in this case, a line) fits the data. Generally, the smaller this number is, the better.

- Some students will probably make their first line—before the residual plot, in Step 7—with a slope of about 1. This line works visually because it's along the major axis of the "ellipse" of points. But when you look at residuals, you see that a shallower line works better, in the sense that your prediction will not be biased: The steep line predicts taller spouses for tall people, and shorter spouses for short people, than we see in the data.

- The predicted value for the dependent (*y*-axis) variable for a fitted function is simply the independent (*x*-axis) value plugged into the function. That's what the cut-paste maneuver accomplishes in Step 10. *Those* are the values that get subtracted from the data values in order to make the residuals.

Topics
    residuals
    goodness of fit

Students need to know how to
    make scatter plots
    make new attributes
    use the formula editor

Materials
    Couples

Discussion Questions

➲ Point to a point on the graph; ask what the couple might look like.

➲ What does the slope mean in the graph? What are its units?

➲ Why do you think some of the lines we found in Step 7 had steeper slopes than we eventually found with the residual plots?

➲ Why did the mean of the residuals come out so close to zero? ("The mean of the residuals is always zero" is *incorrect*. It's true here because we forced the line to go through the means—and it's true for least-squares linear regression lines, which share that property.)

➲ Why was the mean of the residuals not exactly zero? (Computer round-off error.)

Extension

These data show a phenomenon called *regression toward the mean*. Here's one way to illustrate it. Pick a tall, famous woman, such as a basketball player. Calculate her height in millimeters. Use a line from this activity to predict the height of her "British, statistical" husband.

    Then *reverse the axes on the plot* so that you're predicting wife height from husband height. Make a regression line and predict, based on that husband's height, the likely height of his wife. She's shorter than the original woman you started with. Why?

In case no one can find one, Sheryl Swoopes is 6'0", or 1829 mm. The author does not know how tall her husband, Eric Jackson, really is.

British Couples

Name(s): _____

In this activity, we'll use residuals to help decide on the best way to fit a line to some data. We'll look at data on height from a group of married couples from Great Britain. Specifically, we're going to try to get the best estimate of a woman's husband's height if we know her height. If you'd rather predict the wife's height given the husband's, *reverse the axes and attributes throughout this activity.*

You'll learn how to
  define measures
  calculate residuals
  use a summary table
  evaluate how well a line fits data

1. Open **Couples.** Make a scatter plot of **H_height** (husband's height) as a function of **W_height** (wife's height). You should see a graph like the one shown here.
2. What does the generally positive slope of the graph mean?

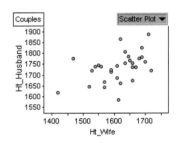

Let's make a line to fit these data. We *could* use a least-squares line, but instead we'll make our own, using a formula.

    To prepare, we will make one simplifying assumption right up front. We will assume that the best line goes through the overall average point, that is, (*mean of the wives' height, mean of the husbands' height*). Let's call that point **(wbar, hbar)**—bar usually means an average. If that's the case, the equation for a line through that point with slope **m** is

      H_height = m(W_height − wbar) + hbar

3. Explain why that equation makes the line go through the means.

4. Make two new measures, **hbar** and **wbar**. Write equations to make them the mean heights of the husbands and wives, respectively.
5. Make a new slider for the slope. Change its name from **V1** to **m**. Set its value to 1.
6. Select the graph and choose **Plot Function** from the **Graph** menu. Enter **m(W_height − wbar) + hbar**. That's the formula we saw a little earlier. Click the **OK** button to close the editor and make the line show.
7. Drag the **m** slider. Describe what happens. What value of **m** looks best?

A *measure* is an attribute that applies to the whole collection. To make a measure, double-click the collection to open its inspector. Click on the **Measures** tab. Define the measure in that pane.

8. With the graph selected, choose **Make Residual Plot** from the **Graph** menu. Sketch your plot at right. Adjust the value of **m** as needed to make it better. What is the slope now?

Goodness of Fit

You found **m** by moving the slider and eyeballing the fit. Human eyes generally do well at this, but how do we know we have the best **slope**?

Let's devise a *statistic*—a single number—that will tell us how well the line models the data. For our statistic, we'll do computations using residuals.

9. For residuals, we need *predicted values*. Make a new case attribute **HHpred**.

10. Give **HHpred** the same formula as the line. Click the equation at the bottom of the graph. Choose **Copy Formula.** Then click the new attribute name. Choose **Paste Formula.** The attribute should fill with values.

11. Make a new attribute, **residual**. Give it the formula **H_height – HHpred.** That's the vertical distance between each husband's height and the line. Explain why.

> If you're not sure you've done this right, plot **residual** as a function of **W_height**. It should be identical to the residual plot at the bottom of your first scatter plot except for scale. If it isn't, fix it.

12. Now we need to do computations on the residuals. We'll do that in a summary table. Choose **Summary Table** from the **Insert** menu.

13. Drag the attribute label for **residual** onto the right arrow at the top of the summary table. The summary table will compute the mean of **residual.**

14. Play with the slider for **slope**. How does the mean residual change as you change the slope? Why is it not a good measure for telling us how accurate the fit is?

> Do not spend too much time counting zeros in this step.

15. Instead, let's find the mean of the *absolute value* of the residual. Make another new attribute, **abs_residual**, and give it the formula **I residual I.** Put its name in the summary table too. Draw what you see at right.

16. Now play with the slider. What value of the statistic—**mean(abs_residual)**— indicates a good fit? Why?

17. Set the slope **m** to get the best value you can. What slope did you get?

18. What are the advantages and disadvantages of using a computational scheme like this one compared to your eyeballed slope?

Going Further

1. Compute the squares of the residuals. Use them instead of the absolute values to find the slope. Is the slope any different?

2. Compare your various equations to the least-squares line and the median-median line. What are the similarities and differences?

3. Use algebra to explain why the mean of the residuals was so close to zero no matter what the slope.

Modeling Mauna Loa

- Structured computer activity
- Data from file
- Student pages 191–192
- Guided, medium features

What's Important Here

- If you can't immediately figure out a function to fit some data, sometimes you can subtract out what you do understand (in this case, a general linear trend) and operate on the residuals (in this case, fit them with a sinusoid).

- Then in the last step, 16, you can simply add the sine to the line to get a function that fits the original data pretty well.

- A good model "explains" data. Statistical packages often report this in r^2, which we call "the percent of the variance explained by the model." But less experienced students can get the point without "variance" by looking at the *range* of the residuals which decreases from 23.5 to 7 to 3 as we add linear and sinusoidal components to the model. Each part of the model contributes substantially (though imperfectly) to explaining the data.

- This explanation has nothing to do with causation! *Explain,* in this context, refers only to how well the model—the function—fits the data.

Discussion Questions

- Extrapolating these data to the present, what do you think the value of CO_2 is? (Students can find current data on the Web.)

- Suppose you lose three years of data from the middle of the data set. You have to fill them in by suggesting values for CO_2 plus or minus something. Plus or minus what?

Special Trigonometric Function Issues

What is appropriate will depend a lot on the experience of your students.

- Students may notice that many of their biggest residuals from the sine probably occur where the sine curve is *steep,* not where it is at an extreme.

- A sinusoid actually needs three parameters—an amplitude, a frequency, and a phase (and maybe even a fourth—a constant term). Yet we used only two. Why? The fact is, we didn't need the frequency or the constant. If the variation is truly seasonal, it repeats every year, so the fundamental frequency is one year. That's why the 2π takes care of it. As for the constant term, we're looking at residuals from a least-squares fit, so they cluster around zero very well.

- You can learn a lot about sinusoids from watching how the residual plot from the sine changes as you change the parameters with the sliders. The faster your computer, the more dynamic this is.

- When students make residual plots from the sine, they will often see residuals that have a frequency of *two* complete cycles per year. This is because the data do not have a perfectly sinusoidal shape. This can lead to understanding how Fourier series work.

Topics
subtracting out the trend
modeling periodic behavior in the residuals
addition of functions

Students need to be able to
make a graph
make a new attribute
write an equation for an attribute
zoom in to a graph

Materials
MaunaShort

Note: These data are a subset of the data in **Mauna** that we used in *Mauna Loa* (page 145).

Modeling Mauna Loa

Name(s): _____

Data on carbon dioxide from the summit of Mauna Loa show an overall increase from 1950 to the present, with seasonal variation. In this activity, we'll see how to use residual plots to make a model (a function) that describes the data. We can use a good model to test theories about the data and to predict the future.

One way to evaluate a model is to figure out how much variation it explains. In this case, we're interested in modeling the carbon dioxide concentration. We'll look informally at the range of values we see as we refine the model. Here we go!

1. Open **MaunaShort**. Look at the data; they extend from 1975 to 1987. You'll see the attributes **year**, **month**, **CO2**, and **time**.

2. The attribute **time** is computed from **year** and **month** to give decimal years. Write its formula here and explain the "minus one."

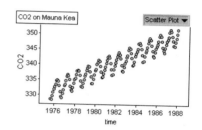

3. Make a graph of **CO2** as a function of **time**. You can see how it increases. What is the total *range* (the difference between maximum and minimum) of **carbonDioxide** readings? (This is a measure of how well we'd be able to determine the reading if we didn't know when it was taken.)

4. Zoom in to your scatter plot so that you're just looking at a few years. Sketch the graph at right (label and scale as usual). Describe in words how the carbon dioxide concentration changes with time.

5. Zoom back out (rechoose **Scatter Plot** in the popup menu in the graph). With the graph selected (it has a border), choose **Least-Squares Line** from the **Graph** menu. Then choose **Make Residual Plot**. A residual plot appears.

6. What is the range of carbon dioxide readings *in the residual plot?*

The amount by which we have reduced the range shows how much better we can determine the reading if we use a straight line to model the data. The new range is less than the one we saw in Step 3. That's because the line takes care of the gross, overall increase. Seasonal variation and any other errors remain.

Seasonal Variation

We will model the seasonal variation with a sine wave. Our first step will be to make an attribute of the residuals; basically, we subtract out the line.

7. Make a new attribute, **afterLine**. Open up the formula editor for its formula.

8. Enter **CO2 – (the equation for the line)**. Substitute the actual equation of the least-squares line. Just read it off the graph. So it will look like **CO2 – (1.5 * time – 2600)**, except your numbers will be slightly different.

9. Make a graph of **afterLine** as a function of **time**. It should look exactly like the residual plot. If it doesn't, change it until it does.

   We'll model these data with the sinusoid. That function will have the form

   $$y = A \sin (2\pi(t - P)),$$

   where A is the amplitude, t is the time in years, and P is a phase. Why 2π? Because sin's argument is in radians, and one year is a complete cycle of 2π. We don't know the values of A and P, so we'll make sliders for these parameters.

10. Make two new sliders (choose **Slider** from the **Insert** menu, or drag them off the shelf) and name them **amp** and **phase**.

Never enter the "y =" part of a function into a Fathom formula. And just type "pi" to get "π."

11. With the graph of **afterLine** selected, choose **Plot Function** from the **Graph** menu. The formula editor appears.

12. Enter **amp * sin(2 * pi * (time – phase))**. Your formula should look like the one in the picture. Close the formula editor by pressing **OK**.

13. Play with the sliders for **amp** and **phase**. Describe how each one changes the function.

14. Zoom in to part of the curve and tweak the sliders to make the function fit the data as well as you can. What values do you get for **amp** and **phase**?

You get better control over slider values if you zoom in to the slider axes. Also, you may simply edit the values in the slider and press **ENTER** if you prefer.

15. Make a residual plot in the new graph. Sketch it, labeled and scaled, at right. *Now* what is the range of residuals you have left? (The change from Step 6, above, shows how much the sine improved our model of the data.)

16. Plot a function on the *original* graph (the **CO2** graph) that models the data, combining overall change and seasonal variation. Write the function here.

Going Further

1. During what part of the year does your sinusoidal model fit best? Worst?

2. The last residual plot you made (the residuals from the sine curve) probably looks periodic (though pretty ragged). Explain how you can still see a periodic residual plot even though you've just accounted for periodic change.

3. If you have already learned about goodness-of-fit measures (e.g., in the activity *British Couples*), use a goodness-of-fit measure on your sine fit. Try to improve your choices of **amp** and **phase**. How much difference does it make?

4. The file **Mauna** includes more data. Analyze this larger data set instead of the short one here. Try to make a function that models the data as well as possible. What additional effects do you see? How did you model them?

Residual Investigations

- Four open-ended computer activities
- Data from files
- Student pages 194–196
- Intermediate, medium features

Here are four problems—two Sonatas and two in any format you like—that you can assign to give students additional practice using residuals.

Sonata 19: Cooling Off

This activity asks students to predict the functional form they will see when they plot the temperature of a cooling pot of water as a function of time. Students then use residual plots to assess their models and get the best parameter values they can.

Materials
HeatingAndCooling

Sonata 20: Out on a Limb with Jupiter

This activity is most appropriate for students with trigonometry experience, or for really good geometers. The main problem is to figure out how the distance from Earth to Jupiter changes with time, given that they're circling the sun at different rates.

Materials
JupiterRadius
Planets

Other Residual Investigations

Which State Is Smartest? These fascinating data show that the greater the proportion of students in a state who take the SAT, in general, the lower the average SAT score is. Students are challenged to model these data, perhaps with a piecewise linear function.

Materials
States - SAT

Another question is why this effect takes place and why there are two distinct regions in the data. One factor to bear in mind is that in many states more students take the ACT because the SAT is not required for admission to the land-grant universities in their states.

Residual Plots with Two Predictors. In this problem, students use data related to the *Printing Paragraphs* activity (page 120). The question is how you can predict the column length of a printed paragraph given the number of words and the typeface. We'll find that Times Roman is more compact than Arial; students actually determine the "fudge factor" relating the two.

Materials
TwoFonts

Sonata 19: Cooling Off

Name(s): _____

The data file **HeatingAndCooling** has your data, unless you want to make some data yourself. These data are temperature data as a function of time as the author heated 500 ml of water to boiling. Then the author turned the heat off and let the pan sit there. If you want to do the experiment yourselves, by all means do so . . .

You'll show that you can

make a prediction

fit a nonlinear function to data

use residuals to help you find parameter values

evaluate your fit

Conjecture

. . . but before you look at the data, predict! Sketch a scaled, labeled scatter plot showing what you think the data will show. Be as accurate as you can. In addition, see if you can predict the symbolic form of the function after the water starts to cool.

Analysis

Open the data file and see what you get. Try to fit a function to the decreasing part after the heat is turned off. You may need to use sliders for parameters. Explain what you did and any assumptions you made.

Comparison

How did the data compare to your original conjectures? Reflect, also, on the curve-fitting process: What worked and what didn't? How confident are you about your parameter values? Can you explain what the parameters mean?

Extension (turn in on a separate sheet)

From these data, you can determine various temperatures in the author's kitchen (besides the water on the stove). What are the temperatures, how did you find them, and what are they temperatures of?

Data in Depth
© 2001 Key Curriculum Press

Sonata 20: Out on a Limb with Jupiter

Name(s): _____

JupiterRadius has data on the apparent radius of Jupiter as seen from Earth over a two-year period. The data look like the graph shown here. What form do you suppose that function takes? A simple sine is *not* good enough.

Conjecture

Before you look at these data in detail, try to figure out what function will fit them. You will not know the values of some parameters. Represent them with sliders. You should still *estimate* the values of the parameters when you can. You will find basic data about Jupiter in **Planets.** You can assume that the orbits of Jupiter and Earth are circular.

You need to know
   simple trigonometry
   the Pythagorean theorem

You'll show that you can
   predict the form of a periodic function based on the geometry of the situation
   use residuals to help find parameter values
   interpret residual plots

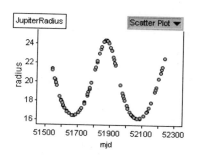

Measurement

Test your conjecture. Find the best possible values for your parameters. To see how well you're doing, construct a plot showing how far off your model is (a residual plot, though you might want to create it yourself rather than use Fathom's). Be sure to draw your graph carefully. The author's is shown here. See if you can beat it.

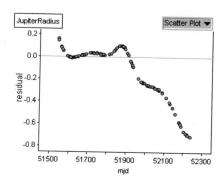

Comparison

Reflect on how well your model worked. Were the parameters roughly what you expected? Did you have to add any completely unforeseen terms? What sorts of patterns do you see in the residuals? What unmodeled effects could account for them?

Other Residual Investigations

Name(s): _____

Which State Is Smartest?

Use the file **States - SAT**. It gives average SAT scores by state. It also gives, for each state, the percentage of graduating high school students who take the test. Plotting score against this percentage, you see a negative correlation. Why?

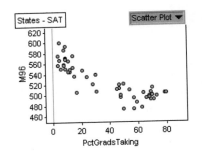

Make a mathematical model for this relationship so you can evaluate how "good" states are, *taking the proportion of test takers into account*. This is the idea of controlling for a continuous variable.

A straight line may not be the best model, but a *piecewise* linear model (a line that changes slope in the middle) looks pretty good. You can make a piecewise linear model using an **if( )** function.

As you think about possible causes for the appearance of the graph, consider: Is there any difference between the states to the left of the "gap" and the ones to the right? That is, why do so few students on the left take the SAT?

Residual Plots with Two Predictors

(This activity is mostly for students in AP or college statistics.)

The residual plots we've seen have shown the residual as a function of the "predictor" variable—the *x* variable, if you like. But what if your model has more than one predictor? What do you plot against? The traditional way is to plot the residual against the *predicted value*.

The file **TwoFonts** has data from a text experiment related to the *Printing Paragraphs* Sonatas (pages 120–123). We set various paragraphs in the fonts Times Roman and Arial. The file has the number of words, the typeface, and the length of the story in column inches (as measured in the word processor's window).

Your goal is to predict **inches** given **font** and **words**. Make an attribute, **inchesP** (P is for Predicted), that's a function of **font** and **words**. Begin with the formula shown in the picture. The model is: Length in **inches** is proportional to **words**. There's a constant of proportionality **k**, which is governed by a slider. (What are its units? Don't forget that it's in the denominator.) The other part of the model is: If the font is **Times**, you're finished (multiply by 1.00). Otherwise (**Arial**), multiply by a **fudge** factor (another slider). The attribute **residual** is (as usual) **inches – inchesP**.

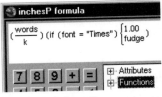

Multiplying by an if-function is not common, but it is extremely useful.

- Plot **residual** as a function of **inchesP**. Drag **font** into the body of the plot so you can see which points are **Times** and which are **Arial**.

- Adjust the sliders to get a good fit. If you like, invent a goodness-of-fit measure (or just use least squares) to make your fit as good as possible.

- Improve the model if it needs it.

- Report on all of this, including why anyone would ever need such a model, and ways in which you might extend the activity.

Under a Cloud

8

Here is a principle of real-life problem solving: You can seldom find the answer to a question. You can, however, find out as much as you can *about* the answer.

Sometimes you're lucky and the points on a graph line up. When they do, you can make a model (for example, a function) and predict new values with great accuracy. But if they don't line up, what then?

Then you need statistics—where things are neither predictable nor clean. This messiness can be frustrating and disillusioning to some students (and some teachers). But it also opens the door to finding out how useful mathematics and statistics can be.

Real life is seldom straight and narrow. There's scatter around the model line—a cloud of unpredictable error and inaccuracy. So since the model doesn't tell the story, we use mathematics to get to know the cloud.

A Reminder About Expectations

The activities in this chapter, used alone, could be an excellent review for someone who once learned these topics and wants a refresher and a deeper understanding. But do not rely solely on these few pages to develop these complex and important topics for the first time. Students will need more offline experiences, more calculator work, and so forth. Chances are that your textbook (for whatever course you are teaching, from algebra to physical chemistry) addresses these topics; you can consider this chapter a supplement.

In this chapter, we'll develop tools to "get to know the cloud"—to understand how variability works and how to describe it.

- In the one-dimensional case, we'll invent measures of spread, leading to standard deviation.

- In the two-dimensional case, we'll extend the idea of goodness of fit that we introduced in *British Couples* (pages 188–189) and develop the correlation coefficient.

In order to make this all work, we'll learn a new concept in Fathom: the idea of a *measure*. A measure has a *single* value that applies to the *entire* collection. For example, in a collection of students, each case—each student—would have a **height**. But the collection itself could have attributes for the sum of the heights, the mean of the heights, the standard deviation of the heights, and so forth. We could use predefined formulas to define these (e.g., **sum(height)**), but we can also define measures that are more complex and nontraditional, for example the sum of the absolute values of the differences of points from the mean.

Level

Getting the most out of these activities generally requires some algebra experience. Exposure to the standard deviation is a plus (though not essential at the beginning). The activity *Exploring Correlation* is aimed at statistics students, and they will benefit from previous exposure to—but need not have mastered—the idea of a *z*-score.

The Activities

- **Random Walk.** Students learn to simulate a random walk using Fathom, and develop a measure of spread to go with its results.

- **SATs and GPAs.** We look at gender differences in SAT scores and GPAs for 1000 first-year college students. We try to figure out how meaningful the differences we see are.

- **Exploring the Normal Distribution.** Students explore properties of normally distributed data.

- **Exploring Correlation.** Students explore correlation and the correlation coefficient, *r*.

- **Building a Cloud from Scratch.** Students construct a data set that is a cloud of points—a linear relationship with error superimposed. They explore the effects of that error on the fitted slope and on the correlation.

- **Straight or Curved?** Here, students add error to a nonlinear relationship. The question is: How much error can you add and still see the curve?

Then in the *Cloud Sonatas,* there are several more open-ended activities:

- **Predicting Spread.** We study the way the spread of random-walk results depends on the number of steps in the walk.

- **Additional Random Walk Sonatas.** A collection of ideas for small projects using random walks.

- **The Proto-Yahtzee Sonatas.** Two activities about strategies in dice games. Students use Fathom to analyze their strategies and decide which is best.

- **The Error in the Sum.** Students simulate measurements with error and compare the spread of their sums with what theory predicts.

You can easily modify this activity to explore other error-analysis formulas, such as the error in a quotient.

- **Combined SAT Scores.** This problem is an adaptation of one from the 1996 College Board *Advanced Placement Course Description* "acorn" book having to do with the spread of the sum—but a different aspect of this common issue from that shown in *The Error in the Sum* (page 225).

Connections

Several activities in the book could just as easily have gone into this chapter, for example

- *Great Expectations,* page 239
- *British Couples,* page 187

Random Walk: Inventing Spread

- Structured computer activity
- Data generated in simulation
- Student pages 200–203
- Starter, complex features

Topics
random walks
spread

Materials
RandomWalk (optional)

The random walk is a basic situation for the theoretical study of spread. Under the hood, it's a binomial problem—the populations at the various positions after n steps follow the distribution in the nth row of Pascal's triangle. With enough steps, the distribution approaches normality, and (of vital importance) the size of the standard deviation *increases* proportional to the square root of n.

Here we ask a less sophisticated question: What's the average distance you've gone after a random walk of 10 steps?

What's Important Here

- This activity gives students some experience with which to underpin the random-walk situation.
- What we mean by *average* (e.g., whether we take the absolute value) varies with context.
- The activity develops experiences that will help students understand the theoretical results.

Discussion Questions

- What's the horizontal axis in a line plot?
- What does the histogram of the **final**s really mean? Explain the graph to someone who hasn't done the activity.
- In general, do you expect someone who has taken more random steps to be farther from the start? Why?
- In general, do you expect someone who has taken twice as many random steps to be twice as far from the start? Why?

A Big Fathom Idea

This activity introduces *derived collections*. We create what we call a *measures collection*—a collection whose job is to collect summary values from another collection. Those values are statistics—measures of that "source" collection. In the case of our random walk, they're the final position of the walk. Here's a table that compares them.

Random Walk (Source) Collection	Measures Collection
Each case is a step.	Each case represents one random walk.
The whole collection is one random walk: a collection of steps.	The collection summarizes many random walks (5 by default).
The final position is a single number (a statistic, a measure) that summarizes the whole walk.	Each case contains the final position of one walk, so the collection has many "final positions."
You can't calculate the mean distance from the origin here because this collection is only one example.	You can calculate the mean distance from the origin in this collection—by averaging the final positions.

Random Walk: Inventing Spread

Name(s): _____

A *random walk* is a process in which, for every step, you flip a coin. Heads, you step east. Tails, you step west. On the average, you'll wind up where you started—or will you? It depends on what you mean by *average*. This activity will help you explore the random-walk situation.

You'll learn how to

build a simulation
use the inspector
define measures
collect measures

Building the Simulation

We'll begin by building a simulation of a random walk in which we'll take 10 random steps from zero. Each step will be +1 or −1.

1. Open a new Fathom document.

2. Create a new case table, either by dragging one off the shelf or by choosing **Case Table** from the **Insert** menu.

3. Make a new attribute, **distance**. To do this, click in the table header marked **<new>**. Type **distance** in place of **<new>** and press **ENTER**. This attribute, **distance**, will record our distance from the start during our random walk.

4. Make 10 cases (these will be the steps in the walk). Choose **New Cases...** from the **Data** menu, enter **10**, and click on **OK** to close the box. Ten (empty) cases appear in the table.

We now have 10 cases for **distance**. We need a formula to compute the values for **distance**.

5. Select **distance**. Choose **Edit Formula** from the **Edit** menu. The formula editor appears.

6. Enter this formula: **prev(distance) + randomPick(−1, 1)**. That is, our distance from the beginning at every step is the preceding distance plus either +1 or −1. Click **OK** to close the formula editor. Numbers appear in the table, representing our distance from the beginning after each step.

7. Press **CTRL-Y** (Windows) or **⌘-Y** (Mac) to rerandomize. Do this a few times. Describe what happens.

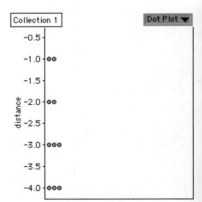

8. Let's make a graph. Make a new graph by dragging one off the shelf or by choosing **Graph** from the **Insert** menu.

9. Drag the attribute *label* for **distance** from the top of the column in the case table to the vertical axis of the graph. You'll see a graph like the upper one shown here.

10. The dots show us what values **distance** took during our walk. Choose **Line Plot** from the popup menu in the graph. You'll see a graph like the lower one shown here.

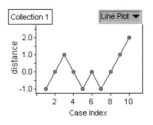

11. Press **CTRL-Y** (Windows) or **⌘-Y** (Mac) to rerandomize again; you'll see the graph wiggle. (**Note:** The graph may wiggle out of its original bounds. To change the bounds, drag the numbers on the vertical axis. The cursor-hand changes depending on where on the axis you drag. That tells you what happens to the numbers.)

12. Let's rename our collection. Double-click its name (**Collection 1**) and rename it **Steps.**

13. Save your work. Call the file **RandomWalk.**

Finding the Averages

Each random walk is different. We want to know, on the average, how far you are from the place where you started.

14. Rerandomize 20 times. Each time, record the position (positive or negative) after the tenth step.

If you start the activity here, use the pre-made file **RandomWalk** that comes with Fathom.

15. Calculate (by hand or with a calculator) the average of those numbers. What do you get?

16. What do you expect to get in the long run? Why?

17. This time, calculate the average of the *absolute values* of the positions. What do you get?

18. Explain the difference between the meanings of the two averages above. Why would you ever use one? Why the other?

Collecting Measures

It should not be obvious what to expect in the long run from the absolute values. But if we do more walks, we should get a better idea. Fathom will help us record the final positions and calculate the means.

To do that, we need to find the last value for **distance** in the simulation. We'll call that **final**. Then we need to collect a set of **final**s so we can average them. Here's how:

19. Double-click on the collection (box of balls) icon to bring up the *inspector.*

20. Click on the **Measures** tab (it may just say **Mea . . .**). We're heading for something like the picture shown here.

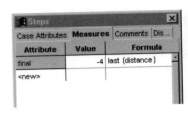

21. Make a new measure by clicking on the **<new>** label and typing **final**. Press **ENTER** when you're finished typing the name.

22. Double-click to the right of **final** in the **Formula** column to bring up the formula editor.

23. Enter this formula: **last(distance)**. The function **last( )** returns the last value in the list.

24. *Leaving the inspector open,* press **CTRL-Y** (Windows) or **⌘-Y** (Mac) to see the value of **final** change. Be sure that it does before closing the inspector.

25. Now we'll get Fathom to collect the **final**s. Select the collection (the box of balls). Choose **Collect Measures** from the **Analyze** menu. A new collection appears (called **Measures from Steps**; it may be under the inspector).

26. With the new (measures) collection selected (it should already be selected), choose **Case Table** from the **Insert** menu. Now you can see the various **final** positions. This list should resemble the one you made by hand.

27. Make a new graph and drag **final** to the horizontal axis. Change the graph to a histogram by choosing **Histogram** from the popup menu in the graph.

28. We need to see the mean. With the graph selected, choose **Plot Value** from the **Graph** menu. The formula editor appears.

29. Enter **mean( )** and close the editor with **OK.** The value and a line appear on the graph.

30. Sketch the graph at right. Explain below what the graph represents in terms of the walk. That is, where did those numbers come from? Be precise and concise.

31. We also want to see the mean of the absolute values. Plot another value with the formula **mean(|final|)**. Sketch its position on the graph you drew for Step 30. Explain why this number is greater than the previous one.

32. Now we want to do it again. Instead, double-click on the measures collection to bring up its inspector. It has a **Collect Measures** pane. Select it; you'll see something like the one shown here.

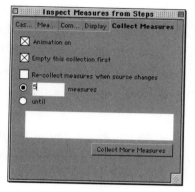

33. Click **Collect More Measures** to collect a new set of 5. If you position the inspector right, you can see both graphs update.

34. Increase the number of measures to 40. Collect measures again. What do you think are reasonable values for the "eventual" mean of **final** and the mean of the absolute value of **final**?

Going Further

1. If you've studied the binomial theorem and expected values, compute the theoretical mean of the absolute value and compare it to the result of your experiment.

2. How will the mean of the absolute value change if we collect 400 walks, say, instead of 40? Explain why.

3. How will the mean change if our walk is 40 steps instead of 10? Explain why and do the experiment. Compare your results to your prediction (see *Sonata 21: Predicting Spread*).

SATs and GPAs

- Structured computer activity
- Data from file
- Student pages 206–208
- Guided, basic features

Gender differences in academic performance are a deep social concern and therefore provide a rich context for data and discussion. Everyone should come away realizing that these data cannot definitively answer most of the social questions that arise or put to rest the biases that we bring to them.

As a teacher, you understand your need to be prepared to field what may be a provocative discussion, insisting on fairness and thoughtful listening while taking care not to alienate. We hope you find the suggestions offered in *Stereotypes, Sensitive Issues, and Data*, following on page 205, useful.

What's Important Here

These are some of the most basic lessons of statistics.

- A difference between means or medians is meaningless if you know nothing about the spread.

- You can assess the relevance of a between-groups difference by comparing it to the within-group variations.

These two lessons are the foundation of sophisticated statistical methods, such as *t*-tests and analysis of variance.

Discussion Questions

➲ What pattern do you see? Can you propose one or more causes for the pattern we see—that males generally outperform females on the SATs, but females outperform males in GPA?

➲ If someone says, "Males outperform females on the math SAT by 40 points," or, if someone says, "Females outperform males by 0.15 in their GPAs," in what way is that the truth, and in what way is it not the whole story?

Tech Notes

- On the first page, a sticky point arises when the students produce the histograms of GPAs. Fathom's binning algorithm makes the bins wide. Students should grab the edge of a bin and drag. As they make the bins narrower, the bins come to have fewer cases in them, so students need to adjust the vertical **(Count)** axis to make the graphs look right. *Do not* reselect **Histogram** from the popup menu in the graph. That will completely reset the graph, bin widths and all.

- The second page asks students to create a second summary table. It is vital that they not keep using the first one, because we have dropped the categorical attribute **sex** onto it. We're using the entire collection to calculate statistics that describe the difference between males and females. We don't want to calculate them separately. Therefore, take care that students create a new summary table when they get to Step 10.

Topics
comparing two groups
using spread to assess difference

Connections
This activity foreshadows *z*-scores; *Exploring Correlation* (pages 213–214) uses them.

Materials
SATGPA

Students need to be able to
make graphs

Stereotypes, Sensitive Issues, and Data

When we work with real data, sensitive issues sometimes emerge. *SATs and GPAs* (page 206) raises the issue of how boys and girls perform on standardized tests and in school.

If you agree with us that the positive value of investigating these data outweighs the potential for controversy, then here are two issues to prepare for.

- Real data contain report information that may be interpreted as revealing social inequity.

- The biases (conscious or unconscious) of the interpreter often lead to erroneous conclusions.

Both of these problems occur naturally in the classroom and you can use both to make the discussions more positive and make the learning more profound.

- If possible, try to include many types of data that bear on the possible conclusions. In this case, we include data on GPAs as well as on SATs because both have a bearing on future academic performance.

- Help students understand the source of the data, how it was collected, and whether the data themselves are a result of, or include some element of, bias. (Is the SAT test a valid test? Who takes it?)

- Help students be clear about what the data actually say. Challenge blanket statements. For example, "boys are better at math than girls," or even "boys do better on the math SAT" go further than the data. The *mean* SAT score is higher, but the distributions substantially overlap.

- Probe more deeply into the meaning of the data. What does it mean to get a high score on the math SAT? (Does getting a high score imply deep mathematical understanding? Good test-taking ability? Privilege? Luck?)

- Help students look for alternative hypotheses. What factors could explain the difference in scores? Ask students how they could define variables and collect data to test their hypotheses.

An interesting question is: What is the chance that a boy chosen at random will have a higher score than a girl chosen at random? (Only about 65% if you assume normal distributions for the scores.)

SATs and GPAs

Name(s): _____

This activity is about gender differences in SAT scores and grade point averages (GPAs) among first-year students at an unnamed college. Here are statistics from the data, displayed in a Fathom summary table:

SATGPA	Summary Table	math	FYGPA
sex	F	521.9	2.545
sex	M	564.6	2.396
Column Summary		543.9	2.468

S1 = mean ( )

You'll learn about
comparing two groups using summary tables

1. What do you notice based on these statistics alone?

In this collection,
math is math SAT score
verbal is verbal SAT score
HSGPA is high school GPA
FYGPA is first-year college GPA

2. Now let's look at the raw data and explore further. Open the file **SATGPA.**

3. Verify the table shown above by constructing it. To get the empty table, choose **Summary Table** from the **Insert** menu. Drag the attributes (**math, FYGPA,** and **sex**) to the appropriate arrows in the table.

Dropping an attribute on top of another attribute replaces the old attribute; dropping it on an arrow adds the new attribute.

4. Means are never the whole story. Look at a distribution. Make a new graph and put **math** on the horizontal axis. You get a dot plot. Change it to a histogram by choosing **Histogram** from the popup menu in the graph.

5. To get separate graphs for males and females, drag the attribute **sex** onto the vertical axis. You should see a graph like the first one shown here. You can see that the males' scores are centered higher, and the proportion of males' scores above about 600 is greater.

6. Make a second graph and do the same for **FYGPA.** The bin widths may be too great for you to compare the two graphs easily. Drag on the edge of a bin to adjust it. You'll have to adjust the vertical scale as well. You should see something like the second graph shown here.

It should look as if the females' scores are centered higher: More females get a GPA of 3.0 or better. Let's also look at verbal to add to our information.

7. Replace **FYGPA** with **verbal** on the second graph. Now the results for males and females are nearly identical (though the males' are slightly higher). But both the **math** and **FYGPA** sex differences are greater than the **verbal** one.

8. Change this graph to a box plot by choosing **Box Plot** from the popup menu in the graph. Do the same to the math graph. Sketch the two graphs. Label and scale the axes.

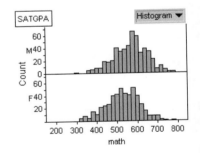

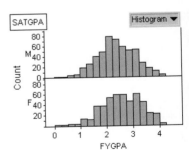

9. Describe in words how you know from the graph that the difference in math scores is more meaningful (not just greater) than the difference in verbal scores.

Making it Quantitative

One way to describe the difference between the **math** and **verbal** graphs is that the difference in medians (the middle line) is bigger *compared to the size of the boxes*. The size of the boxes is the *interquartile range* (IQR), which is the **iqr( )** function in Fathom. Armed with that function and **median( )**, we can make this difference quantitative.

10. Make a new summary table. Drag **math**, **verbal**, and **FYGPA** to the right arrow, but *do not drag* the attribute **sex**. The means of the attributes appear.

11. Instead of the means, we want to see interquartile ranges. So double-click on the place where it says **mean( )**. The formula editor appears.

12. Enter **iqr( )**. Do not enter anything inside the parentheses; empty parentheses mean "fill in the appropriate attribute name." Close the formula editor by clicking on **OK.** Fill in the second row of the table below with what you see.

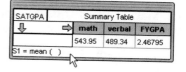

Quantity	math	verbal	FYGPA	totalSAT (later)
iqr( )				

13. With the summary table selected, choose **Add Formula** from the **Summary** menu. Enter a formula that computes the difference between the medians. It will look like the formula shown here.

Do not type the question marks; they appear automatically. Stretch the editor horizontally, as we have done.

14. When you click on **OK** to close the formula editor, the table includes your new calculation. Enter the values in the third row of the table above.

15. How do the differences in **math**, **verbal**, and **FYGPA** compare in size to their respective IQRs?

16. One way to make that comparison numerically is with a ratio. We'll look at the difference (in SATs, in GPAs, etc.) *divided by* the IQR. Make a new row in the summary table (using the **Add Formula** command in the **Summary** menu) that will calculate that ratio. (This formula will be just like the last one, except that you'll need to divide by **iqr( )**.) Write the results in the fourth row of the table on the previous page.

IQR is a measure of *spread* that goes with median (a measure of *center*). We also use **mean** as a measure of center; one measure of spread that goes with it is *standard deviation*, which is **stdDev( )** in Fathom's formulas.

17. Make another new row in the summary table. This one will compute the sex differences as differences in mean divided by the standard deviation. Enter the values in that same table. Write the formula here.

18. What do you conclude about sex differences in SAT scores and first-year college GPAs?

19. Make a new attribute, **totalSAT**, which is the sum of **math** and **verbal**. Perform this activity's analysis on that new attribute—that is, drop **totalSAT** onto the right arrow in the summary table. What does this add to our analysis of sex differences?

20. Someone could argue that the difference in SAT scores is over 40, but the difference in GPAs is only about 0.15, and therefore the difference in SATs is more significant. Explain why that isn't important *without* using the terms *interquartile range, standard deviation,* or *variance.*

Going Further

1. In this data set, which is a better predictor of college performance—high school GPA or SAT score? Is either of them very good? If you were a college admissions officer, what would you use?

2. Fit a least-squares line to a graph of **FYGPA** as a function of **HSGPA**. What does the slope mean?

Exploring the Normal Distribution

- Structured computer activity
- Data generated in simulation
- Student pages 210–211
- Intermediate, basic features

What's Important Here

- Students get to become familiar with normally distributed *data*, not just the normal distribution. That is, they will see variability in simulation that you don't see if you stick to the curve.

- Students see how when you add random variables, you do not add their standard deviations. (*The Error in the Sum*, page 225, explores this in greater detail.)

- Students see how multiplying normally distributed variables doesn't yield a normal distribution.

Topics
  normal distributions
  standard deviation
  operations on random variables

Students need to be able to
  make collections
  use the formula editor
  make new attributes
  make graphs
  use summary tables or plotted
    values

Students may need to
  use the inspector
  use measures collections

Discussion Questions

In these questions, **a** and **b** are normally distributed attributes that students make during the activity.

- ➲ When we multiplied **a** by 2, the standard deviation doubled. Why?

- ➲ When we added **a** to **b**, it did not double. Why not?

- ➲ We saw how the percentage of cases within one standard deviation varied around 68% but wasn't right on. What could we do to the simulation to reduce that variability? (Add more cases.)

- ➲ Suppose we looked at the distribution of **a**^{2}. Would that be normal? (No!) Why not? (For one thing, it would always be positive.) What would the distribution look like? (It's skewed to the right.)

- ➲ (Advanced students.) We saw that the distribution of a product was not normal. But look:

$$e^{-x^2} \cdot e^{-x^2} = e^{-2x^2}$$

It certainly looks normal—it will just have a different standard deviation. What's going on? (The problem is not that we used *x* twice, though that's pretty bad. You can't just multiply distributions together to get the distribution of the product of their random variables. Consider two disjoint distributions—their product would always be zero!)

Exploring the Normal Distribution

Name(s): _____

This activity has two parts: first, a little setup while you build a tool, and second, some problems to solve. The tool is based on the function **randomNormal(mean, sd)**, which gives you a random number from a normal distribution of the given mean and standard deviation.

1. Open Fathom and make a collection. Give it one attribute. Call it **a**. Make 100 cases.

2. Give **a** this formula: **randomNormal(0, 1)**. The cases should fill with random numbers taken from a normal distribution with a mean of zero and a standard deviation of 1.

3. Make a histogram of **a**. It should look something like the one shown here.

4. Save your document!

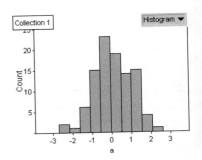

Now for the problems. You'll have to alter your setup to solve them. Here are some Fathom techniques to remember; use **Help** if you forget.

- Make sliders for variable parameters (such as the mean).

- Add extra cases or graphs or attributes if you need them.

- Rerandomize with **CTRL-Y** (Windows) or **⌘-Y** (Mac).

- Use formulas in plotted values and summary tables to compute useful quantities (e.g., **count(|a|< 1)**).

The Problems

For each problem, give the answer, but also explain briefly how you reached it.

1. About what proportion of the cases are within one standard deviation of the mean?

2. How many standard deviations do you have to go from the mean to enclose half of the cases?

3. You may know that 95% of all cases are said to fall within 1.96 standard deviations of the mean. Suppose you rounded that off to 2. How far off would you be?

Data in Depth
© 2001 Key Curriculum Press

4. Make a new attribute **twicea** with the formula **2 * a**. (It's just twice **a**.) What are its mean and standard deviation?

5. Make another attribute, **b**, with the formula **randomNormal(0, 1)**. (So it's *like* **a** but not *equal* to **a**.) What is the standard deviation of **(a + b)**? How many attributes like **a** do you have to add up to get a standard deviation of 2?

6. Change **b** to a normally distributed attribute with a mean *not equal* to zero, but still with a standard deviation of 1. Imagine these two attributes have a contest. Every time **b > a**, **b** wins. How big does **b**'s mean have to be for **b** to win two thirds of the time? (Use a slider for the mean of **b**.)

7. Now imagine that **b**'s mean is fixed at that 2/3-winning value. But **b**'s standard deviation begins to increase. What will happen to its winning percentage? Before you try it, predict: Increase? Decrease? Stay the same? Choose one and tell why you think it's true.

8. Now try it and describe what happens.

9. Make the distribution of the *product* of two attributes like **a** (e.g., set **b**'s mean to zero and make a new attribute in which you multiply **a * b**). Make its histogram. It does not look normally distributed. Describe in words the way in which it does not look normal.

10. Use Fathom to make a convincing argument that the product of two standard normal distributions is not normal.

Exploring Correlation

- Structured computer activity
- Data from file
- Student pages 213–214
- Intermediate, basic features

This activity is a demonstration that the correlation coefficient is the mean of the product of the *z*-scores. *Students should have seen z-scores before this activity.*

What's Important Here

Topics
  correlation coefficient
  application of *z*-scores

Students need to be able to
  make new attributes
  use the formula editor
  make graphs

- Correlation can be positive or negative, between –1 and +1, and it measures how well the points are arranged in a line.

- The product of your coordinates—relative to the means—is your contribution to the correlation. If you're in the first or third quadrant—relative to the means—your contribution is positive; if you're in the second or fourth, it's negative.

- *Z*-values are useful coordinates because they move the origin to the means of the two coordinates.

- When you move a point in the original graph, *the origin moves* in the *z*-graph—because you're changing the mean.

Discussion Questions

You should definitely discuss the questions posed on the student sheet. In addition, consider these:

- ➲ If we mapped the origin in the *z*-plot back into the original plot, where would it be? (At the coordinates of the means.)

- ➲ What's the relationship between the correlation and the slope? (Only the sign.)

- ➲ What would be a good name for this quantity, the mean of the **prod**s? (You could let students name it—but inasmuch as it is the square root of r^2, r is not a bad name.)

Extensions

- Have students try to explain clearly and convincingly, in writing, why the correlation coefficient works the way it does. That is, how is it that this product-of-*z*-scores thing gives us a number that tells us how well the points are lined up?

- Have students try to explain—possibly with algebra—why the average of the product of *z*-scores cannot leave the interval [–1, 1].

Exploring Correlation

Name(s): _____

You need

CorrelationPlay

In this activity, you'll discover things about the correlation coefficient.

1. Open the file **CorrelationPlay.** You'll see a table and a graph. The graph has a line in it (the least-squares line). Below the graph is the equation of the line and the square of the correlation coefficient, r^2, written **r^2** on the screen, and pronounced "r squared."

2. Drag the points with the mouse so that they line up in a straight line, slanted upward. What's the value of r^2?

3. Make the points line up slanted downward. Now what's the value of r^2?

4. Put the points in a circle. *Now* what's the value of r^2?

5. Make a new attribute, **zx**. This is the z-score in the x-direction. It's the number of standard deviations between the x-value and the mean of x. Its formula is the one shown here. Enter that formula for **zx**.

6. Do the analogous thing for another new attribute, **zy**.

7. Make a new graph with **zy** on the vertical axis and **zx** on the horizontal axis. Make sure you can see both the **x-y** graph and the **zx-zy** one.

8. Move a few points on the **x-y** graph. Describe what happens on the other graph.

9. One of the differences between the two graphs is that the one for the z-scores contains the origin. It has to. Why?

10. Make a new attribute, **prod**. Give it the formula **zx * zy**. That is, it's the product of the z-scores.

11. Make a graph—a simple dot plot—of **prod**. Now you have three graphs: two scatter plots and a dot plot. Make sure you can see them all.

Name(s): _____

12. What has to be true of a point for its **prod** to be positive? What has to be true for **prod** to be negative? Move points around in the original graph to explore this.

Remember, you can only adjust the points in the original graph. Why is that?

13. Now select the **prod** graph and choose **Plot Value** from the **Graph** menu. In the formula editor, enter **mean( )**. Close the editor. Now the mean of the **prod**s is displayed on the graph.

14. Once again, make all the points line up slanting upward. What is the mean of the **prod**s?

15. Fill in this table:

Point Slant	r^2	Mean of the **prod**s
Upward	1.00	
Upward	0.64	
Upward	0.25	
Upward		0.3
Downward	1.00	
Downward	0.49	
Downward		−0.5
	0.0625	−0.25

16. Generalize: What's the relationship between r^2 and the mean of the **prod**s?

17. Describe in words what the mean of the **prod**s tells you about the original graph of the points.

Building a Cloud from Scratch

- Structured computer activity
- Data generated in simulation
- Student page 216
- Intermediate, basic features

In this activity, students create a simple linear relationship that they then cloud up by introducing error.

What's Important Here

- The activity makes explicit a common construction in statistics: the observations consist of a signal plus an error term.

- Adding error reduces the correlation coefficient. If the errors are much larger than the scale of the function, r^2 can appear to go to zero.

- Horizontal errors reduce the slope of the least-squares line—but vertical errors do not change it. This is because the residuals we look at to make least-squares are vertical. You can think of the least-squares line as trying to go through the mean value in each vertical stripe. That mean will be the same no matter how much error is added in.

Topics

variability
slope and correlation
simulating error

Students need to be able to

make case tables
make graphs
use formulas to define attributes
add least-squares lines to scatter plots

Discussion Questions

➲ What does **randomNormal(0, SD)** mean in the formula for **error**?

➲ Why is the correlation coefficient the same no matter which attribute is on which axis? (It's fundamentally different from the slope of the least-squares line. It's a measure of association between the attributes, not an analysis of how one depends on the other. The formula for the correlation coefficient is completely symmetrical.)

➲ When you see the two graphs and the two least-squares lines, do the lines go through the same points? How do you know? Why or why not? (Here are two strategies for finding out: One is to select points in one graph and see that, for example, points on the line in one graph are off the line in the other; the second is to do the algebra on the two equations and show that when you solve for **effect** they are not the same.)

Building a Cloud from Scratch

Name(s): _____

This activity assumes you know how to drive Fathom, so we'll move quickly at the beginning. If you have trouble, don't hesitate to use **Help.**

    We will be looking at how errors affect the way we interpret linear fits to data.

1. In a new document, make a case table with two attributes: **cause** and **effect.**

2. Make 100 cases with these formulas: For **cause,** use **randomNormal(100,10).** For **effect,** use **cause.**

3. Make a scatter plot of **effect** as a function of **cause,** and show the least-squares linear regression line. It should have a slope of 1 and an r^2 of 1.00, as shown in the picture.

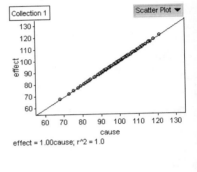

We have set up a very simple situation. Let's make it more complicated. So far, **effect** has been perfectly related to **cause.** Now we'll add error to **effect** and see what happens.

4. Make a slider and name it **SD.**

5. Make a new attribute, **error,** and give it the formula **randomNormal(0, SD).**

6. Now change the formula for **effect** to **cause + error.**

7. Move the slider. What happens when **SD** is near zero?

8. As **SD** gets larger, what happens to r^2, the square of the correlation coefficient?

9. As **SD** gets larger, what happens to the slope? Explain why this happens.

10. Sometimes we get cause and effect mixed up. Make a second scatter plot. Put **effect** on the horizontal axis and **cause** on the vertical axis. Add a least-squares line.

This will have the effect of making the errors horizontal instead of vertical.

11. Move the slider some more. Tell what happens to the slope and the correlation coefficient in the new graph.

12. Explain why the slope and the correlation coefficient behave differently in the other scatter plot.

Data in Depth

Straight or Curved?

This activity explores two issues: using residual plots to identify underlying shape in a distribution, and the way measurement error can obscure a model. We do this by simulating data that lie along a parabola, then adding variable amounts of error.

- Structured computer activity
- Data from simulation
- Student pages 218–219
- Intermediate, medium features

What's Important Here

- Random error can make it impossible to see an effect.
- You can test the effect of error by simulating it. That is, after the activity, we know that to detect the curvature in the data, we'll need to measure to within about 0.1.

Topics
residuals
random error

Discussion Questions

➲ Before you started this activity, how much randomness would you have said you could add and still see the curvature?

➲ Were the residual plots helpful in looking for the effect? Were there times when you could see the curve in the residual plot but not in the main graph?

➲ How much did the "critical value" for the amount of randomness we add vary throughout the class? (One issue is: Are some people more eager to see what they know is there?)

➲ How would you design an experiment to test individuals' ability to detect curvature visually in noisy data?

Sample Graphs

Shown here are three graphs like the ones the students should produce. All three have the same data—the function $y = x^2$—but have different amounts of error added. The standard deviation of the first graph's error is 1.0, and the curvature is completely washed out. In the second, **SD** is only 0.15, and you can detect the curvature if you have a good imagination. Finally, at **SD = 0.04**—amazingly small—the curvature is obvious, especially in the residual plot. Notice the vertical scales on these plots.

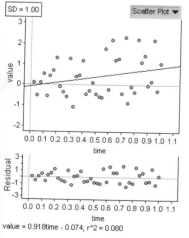

value = 0.918time - 0.074; r^2 = 0.080

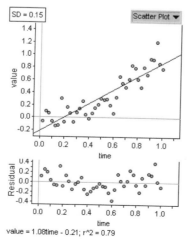

value = 1.08time - 0.21; r^2 = 0.79

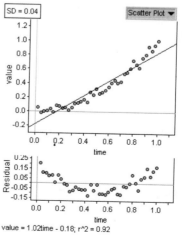

value = 1.02time - 0.18; r^2 = 0.92

Straight or Curved?

Name(s): _____

In this activity, we'll explore how measurement error can obscure the true shapes of functions. We'll also see why residual plots are so useful. To do this, we'll construct *simulated* data: We'll have Fathom make it all up.

1. Make a new case table (choose **Case Table** from the **Insert** menu).
2. First we'll make new attributes. Click at the top of a table column, where it says **<new>**. Type **time** and press **ENTER**.
3. Make another new attribute called **value**.
4. Make 40 (blank) cases: Choose **New Cases** from the **Data** menu. In the dialog box, enter **40** and click **OK**. Forty cases appear in the case table.
5. Now we'll give these attributes formulas. From the **Display** menu, choose **Show Formulas**. Double-click the formula cell for **time**. The formula editor appears.
6. Enter **caseIndex/40**. Close the formula editor by clicking **OK**. Now the 40 cases in the **time** attribute should have values ranging from 0.025 to 1.0.
7. Make a formula for the **value** attribute by bringing up the formula editor. Enter **time²**. (Type "time^2," without the quotes. The "^" will not appear—it just moves you up into exponent land.) Close the formula editor. The cases should have **values** from about 0 to 1.
8. Make a graph of **value** as a function of **time**. (Choose **Graph** from the **Insert** menu, then drag the attributes from the table's column headers to the axes of the graph.) Your graph should look like the first one shown here.

The graph is familiar: It's the $y = x^2$ parabola between 0 and 1. It looks curved, obviously curved—for the moment. Let's fit a line to it . . .

9. With the graph selected, choose **Least-Squares Line** from the **Graph** menu. A line appears.
10. Choose **Make Residual Plot** from the **Graph** menu. This shows how far vertically each of the points in the first graph is from the line. You may want to stretch the graph vertically to make more room for the residual plot. (To stretch a graph, select it and drag the bottom edge.)
11. Between **time = 0** and **time = 0.5**, the function is increasing, but the residual plot is decreasing. Explain why.

Adding Randomness

Right now, everything is nice and smooth. Let's add randomness. We'll start by making a slider that we will use to control the amount of randomness we add.

12. Choose **Slider** from the **Insert** menu. Change its name from **V1** to **SD** (for standard deviation), and set it to about **1.00**. Make its axis run from 0 to 1.

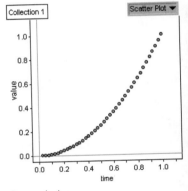

Original plot

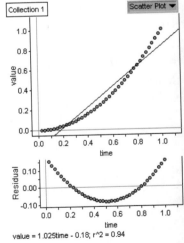

value = 1.025time - 0.18; r^2 = 0.94

Original with least-squares line and residual plot

Change the scale of an axis by dragging numbers on the axis. You can also double-click on an axis and edit the text that appears.

Data in Depth
© 2001 Key Curriculum Press

13. Now edit the formula for **value**. Make it **time² + randomNormal(0, SD)**. This adds a random, normally distributed amount to **value**. That amount has a mean of 0 and a standard deviation of **SD**, in this case 1.

14. The graph will change, and many points will be out of range. Reselect **Scatter Plot** from the popup menu on the graph. A sample result is shown here.

If everything has gone according to plan, you probably see that the graph seems to increase somewhat, but that *you can no longer tell that it's curved*. The randomness is so great that the curve is overwhelmed. You can confirm this by looking at the residual plot. It looks flat and random. That is the sign that the model—the straight line—is a good model for our data.

Yet we know that the "real" data are curved. The question is: How much randomness can that curved model take before it no longer looks curved?

15. Move the **SD** slider to near 0 and rescale the plot. (Reselect **Scatter Plot** from the popup menu.) Now the curve is obvious.

16. Gradually increase the slider (rescaling as necessary) until the residual plot first looks flat and random. What value of **SD** makes this happen for you?

17. Now repeatedly choose **Rerandomize** from the **Analyze** menu (or press **CTRL-Y** (Windows) or **⌘-Y** (Mac)). Fathom reassigns all the error terms. Chances are that you can see the curvature sometimes now.

18. Readjust the slider, repeatedly rerandomizing, to find the largest value for **SD** you can use and *still see the curvature in the residual plot most of the time*. What value do you get?

Going Further

1. Leaving **SD** at that critical value, change the formula for **time** by adding 10. That is, make it **(caseIndex/40) + 10**. Sketch the resulting graph and explain why it looks so different after you put in the 10.

2. Change the formula for **time** so that the positions of the points are random within the interval (0, 1) instead of evenly spaced. What formula did you use? Does that make any difference in the amount of error you can put in and still detect the curvature?

3. Change the number of cases (by adding and deleting them) without changing the range of **time** values. Does that make any difference in the amount of error you can put in and still detect the curvature?

4. If you're trying to detect an effect (e.g., curvature), you have a better chance if your measurements have less error. This activity helped quantify the amount of error you can have and still detect the effect. Give some suggestions as to how you can improve your chance of detecting an effect if you're looking for one that's right on the edge of detectability.

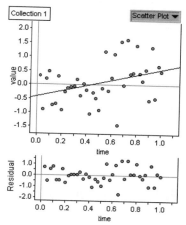

Residuals are flat and random with **SD** = 1.00.

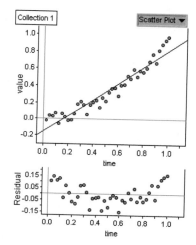

SD = 0.07. Still curved. Note the difference in the scale of the residual plot from the **SD** = 1.00 plot above.

Cloud Sonatas

- Nine open-ended computer activities
- Data from files and simulation
- Student pages 221–226
- Independent, basic features

Predicting Spread

Students who have done *Random Walk* (pages 200–203) can use this Sonata to explore further—in this case, how the spread depends on the number of steps.

Additional Random Walk Sonatas

This is a collection of four ideas, each of which could be expanded into a Sonata. Use the generic Sonata page (page xxii) if you like, or assign these in any format you like.

Pre-Proto-Yahtzee

The subtle relationship emerges when you plot **SecondScore** as a function of **FirstScore**. The slope is not 1. Why not? Because the higher **FirstScore** is, the less your expected improvement is (you are probably rerolling higher-numbered dice).

In this activity and in *Proto-Yahtzee,* students may need help deciding how to record their data. You might suggest a two-column table: one column for the score after the first roll and one for the score after the second. For *Proto-Yahtzee,* add a third column as a reminder of how many dice were rerolled each time. Some students might be tempted to record only the "improvement," which is not enough. However, it's fine if they want *more* information (e.g., the rolls of the individual dice).

Proto-Yahtzee

You can think of it this way: Rolling five dice is no better than choosing not to roll any. But rerolling any other number of dice improves the sum on the average. It's not as obvious (but it's still true) that, in the mean, rolling one die is the same as rolling four dice. The symmetry continues: rolling two dice is the same as rolling three dice, and they're the best.

Note to statistics teachers: this is a good paired-*t* situation. The distinctions among the different numbers of dice are more striking when you look at a difference measure than when you look at overall performance.

Everyone will get tired of rolling dice. Unfortunately, constructing the simulation is a little more complex than constructing some of the others we show in this book. If you would like some data to show students, you can find them in **ProtoYahtzeeData.** The file contains simulated data for the six possible conditions—rerolling zero to five dice, 100 trials each.

The Error in the Sum

Students create a Fathom document to demonstrate that the Pythagorean rule for adding up the errors of independent measurements works.

Combined SAT Scores

This is suitable primarily for students of statistics. It's based on multiple-choice question 6 from the 1996 "acorn" book—the *Advanced Placement Course Description,* published by The College Board to help us get ready for the AP statistics exam.

Topics
variation
correlation

Students need to be able to
make case tables
make graphs
define attributes by formula

Sonata 21: Predicting Spread

Name(s): _____

You can think of a random walk as occurring on a number line. You start at zero, and each step is either +1 or −1—a 50% chance either way. On the average, your position will be zero because sometimes you'll go positive, sometimes negative. Yet being at *exactly zero* is rare. In fact, your expected distance from the origin increases with the number of steps you take.

Conjecture

How do you suppose your expected distance from the origin increases with the number of steps you take? Be as specific as you can. If possible, give a rule (e.g., a function) that calculates expected distance given number of steps.

Measurement

Devise a simulation in Fathom to measure your distance from the origin on the average after a random walk of *n* steps. Describe the simulation below and write the most important formulas. Sketch a graph or two of your results. Choose your graphs carefully.

Comparison

Compare your conjecture to your simulation. Revise your conjecture in light of your experience.

Additional Random Walk Sonatas

Name(s): _____

The random walk is a rich field for learning about spread and error. Here are a few questions, each of which could turn into a small project worthy of attention.

To use these as Sonatas, consider using the Sonata Summary Sheet on page xxii.

Standardly Deviant Steps

Previously, in our discussions of random walks, we've explored the expected (or average) distance from the origin after *n* steps. What if, instead, we looked at the *standard deviation* of the positions of many walkers after *n* steps? How (if at all) are those two quantities (the average distance and the standard deviation) related to one another?

Random Walk on a Slope

Suppose you have a random walk in which the chance of moving +1 or −1 is not 50%. Now our position will depend both on the probabilities and on the number of steps we take. How does our position depend on these two parameters? (You may consider either average absolute distance or standard deviation, or both.)

Two-Dimensional Random Walk

What if our random walk were two-dimensional? On each step, we would change our *x*-position by +1 or −1 (with a 50-50 chance either way); we would also change our *y*-position in the same manner. How would that affect our position?

What Color Is the Bear?

Suppose that instead of a Cartesian random walk (doing the *x*- and *y*-coordinates separately) we do a polar random walk. On each step, choose a number between 0 and 2π. Turn that angle (in radians) from the positive *x*-axis, and take *one* step in that direction. Now what is our position?

Sonata 22: Pre-Proto-Yahtzee

Name(s): _____

This situation is a game. As a game, it's pretty limited at first, because there's no strategy. The next activity, *Sonata 23: Proto-Yahtzee,* puts your work here to use. Also, we expect you to roll the dice and not to simulate this game using Fathom.

You need
five dice
paper for record keeping

The Game

The goal is to get a high score. On your turn, roll five dice. Add them to get your first score. Then reroll the lowest die (once per turn), trying to improve your score. That gives you your second and final score.

    This is not a competition.

Conjectures

The relevant attributes are **FirstScore** and **SecondScore**. What will be their distributions? How will they be related? (For instance, will **SecondScore** be larger than **FirstScore**? Will the spread be the same?)

Measurement

Decide how you're going to roll, who will record, and so on. Write that here briefly.

Comparison

Use Fathom to study your conjectures. (**Hint:** A new attribute, **difference**, might be useful.) Write what you find out about how **FirstScore** and **SecondScore** are related.

Sonata 23: Proto-Yahtzee

Name(s): _____

You need
five dice
paper for record keeping

Now we'll make the game competitive.

On your turn, you roll five dice, trying to get the highest sum. Then you pick up some or all of the dice and roll them again, trying to improve your score. Your partner does the same.

Here's the catch: You each have to tell how many dice you will reroll *before* either of you rolls the first time! So how many dice should you reroll in order to get the best score?

Conjectures

Two of the relevant attributes are still **FirstScore** and **SecondScore**. Now there's also a number of dice to be rerolled. How many do you think are best? (**Hint:** Think about limits. Rerolling zero dice clearly makes no difference. What about always rerolling five dice?) What do you mean by *best*?

Measurement

Make a plan for figuring out how many dice to reroll. It should involve trying out the game under various decisions and comparing the results. You'll have to decide whether to have the new "number of dice" attribute in the same data set or to cover the different situations separately. You may need to get other groups to help collect data. Describe what you have decided to do.

Comparison

Use Fathom to study your conjectures. Were you right? What *is* the best strategy?

Sonata 24: The Error in the Sum

Name(s): _____

In this Sonata, you do not make a conjecture so much as you make a simulation to test an official formula. It says that if you add two independent quantities, and each has a measurement error, the error in the sum is the *Pythagorean sum* of the two individual errors. That is,

$$E^2_{sum} = E^2_1 + E^2_2$$

Design

Design a simulation in Fathom to study this equation. See if it holds up. Don't make real measurements. Instead, write formulas to determine the attribute values—formulas with random parts to simulate the errors. The formula for the sum is the simple addition of the two components. You have several design decisions to make:

- What kind of random numbers will you use?
- If you make a graph, what will you plot?
- How will you calculate the error in the measurements?

Before you go to the computer, explain here how you plan to set up your simulation.

Hint: See how the amount of error (variation) in the sum changes as you change the amount of error in *only one* of the addends. That way, you can plot it in two dimensions.

Construction

Execute your design. See if it works. If parts of it don't work, fix them. Describe the changes you had to make and explain why.

Comparison and Reflection

Sketch a labeled graph below that confirms or refutes the original formula. Did anything surprise you when you were doing this? What other observations do you have about simulating and adding measurements with errors?

Sonata 25: Combined SAT Scores

Name(s): _____

Dudley and Isabella saw this problem on their test:

The file **SATGPA** has information on 1000 first-year college students. Their mean verbal SAT score (**verbal**) is 489 with a standard deviation of about 82 and the mean SAT math score (**math**) is 544 with a standard deviation of about 84. If the two scores are added (to make **total**), what is the standard deviation of the combined verbal and math scores?

Dudley said, "The trick answer is $\sqrt{82^2 + 84^2}$. But that's wrong because the scores are not independent."

Isabella said, "You're right. And the standard deviation will be bigger than $\sqrt{82^2 + 84^2}$, because **total** is bigger than **math** or **verbal**."

Dudley replied, "No, Isabella, it will be smaller, because the numbers are correlated—they're tighter together."

You need
SATGPA

You'll show that you can
make sums of attributes
compute standard deviations
construct a simulation of the data
make a convincing argument

Conjecture

Do you agree with either of them? Say as much as you can about the standard deviation of **total** without calculating it.

Calculation

Use **SATGPA,** the data about the 1000 first-year college students. In addition, construct a data set that simulates what those math and verbal scores would look like if they were independent. Then find the standard deviations of the combined scores in both the real and the simulated data sets. Describe what you find. Copy any relevant tables and sketch relevant graphs.

Summary tables are useful here for summarizing data sets. And you'll need **randomNormal(mean, sd)** to produce simulated scores. Just substitute the real mean and standard deviation.

Comparison

If your conjecture was incorrect, correct it and explain what was really going on. Be clear about the reason the standard deviation is either larger or smaller than you would expect. If your conjecture was completely perfect, make a defensible observation about the difference between these college students and SAT-takers in general, whose means are lower but whose standard deviations are larger.

Data in Depth
© 2001 Key Curriculum Press

Probability Through Simulations

9

Making simulations is essential for understanding the probability that lives in inferential statistics. It's also a lot of fun.

Simulation itself is a wide-ranging endeavor, stretching into mathematical models of world economies, nascent star systems, and epidemics; games played by generals and teenagers; and engineering tests of cars, spacecraft, and baby buggies. We will not travel quite so far in this thin chapter, but instead we will explore our statistical neighborhood. Fathom has considerable depth when it comes to simulating data in the service of learning about probability.

We have already made simulations in earlier chapters. For example, in *Straight or Curved?* (page 218), we added random noise to artificial data. In *Area and Perimeter* (page 112), we generated measurements for rectangles. And in *Random Walk* (page 200), we not only simulated the walk but also used Fathom to collect the data. Here we turn explicitly to probability.

There are two main flavors of probability: theoretical and empirical. These activities focus on the empirical, or experimental, kind. We flip a coin 1000 times and get 476 heads. Based on experience, P(heads) = 0.476. Pedagogically, this sort of probability works hand-in-hand with the theoretical kind, giving learners another take on the problems—one that is a step more concrete. Wherever possible, students should reconcile their simulated results with what they expect theoretically.

We should say, however, that simply using empirical probability does not suddenly make probability easy. For everything that's hard in theoretical probability, we can find analogous pitfalls in the experimental world. The main problem in both is the setup—the process of understanding the problem so that you know what rules apply. Shall we sample with or without replacement? Are the events independent? These difficulties seem to be inherent in the field, so when we're learning, it's good to have as many approaches as we can get. Experienced teachers we speak with agree that they too get new insights, and build their understanding of probability, by using simulation.

Level

Probability is by nature somewhat slippery, but it doesn't require a lot of mathematical baggage, at least at first. So these activities are appropriate for mature middle-schoolers, though many will be challenging for adults as well.

The Activities

- **Rolling Dice.** Students use random numbers to simulate rolling dice. This is a prototypical probability situation and doesn't require collecting statistics.

- **Exploring Sampling.** These two activities introduce students to sampling including the difference between sampling with and without replacement. Students also have to collect statistics about the samples—in this case, whether two cards drawn from a deck constitute a pair. By repeating the sampling, we can calculate the empirical probability of drawing a pair from a standard deck.

- **Just You Wait!** Here we return to dice, this time in a sampling setting. Only here, instead of rolling (i.e., sampling) a fixed number of times, we roll until we get a particular event—in this case, until we roll a six. Then we collect the numbers of rolls we needed and find the average.

- **Great Expectations.** This activity uses simulation to solve a straightforward expected-value problem—and gives us additional information besides.

- **HIV Testing.** These two activities explore problems of false positives and trying to infer the actual incidence of a condition when the test is imperfect. Here, the simulation part is the test itself—we use random numbers to determine whether the test gives the correct result.

- **Simulation Problems and Sonatas.** This is a collection of more challenging simulation problems, some of which are follow-ups to activities in this chapter.

Objectives

- Students will become more comfortable devising simulations to answer probability questions.

- In making their simulations, students will appreciate the different layers of simulations in most of these problems—for example, constructing a single trial; deciding what numbers (statistics) are relevant to that trial; then repeating many trials, collecting those statistics for each trial.

Rolling Dice

- Structured computer activity
- Data from simulation
- Student pages 230–231
- Guided, basic features

This activity introduces students to one of the most efficient methods of simulation: using a random-number function to generate the randomness. After this, students are ready for *Dice Probability Problems,* on page 252.

What's Important Here

Topics
probability
simulation

- You can simulate many simple random events very quickly, and treat them as you do any data. In particular, you can use any exploratory tools on them, such as histograms.

- You can combine random events arithmetically and use the same tools. Here, we add two dice.

Discussion Questions

➲ Explain in words why seven is the most likely sum of two dice.

➲ Suppose you had a loaded die. How would you be able to tell? (This question foreshadows *Constructivist Dice,* page 260.)

➲ What would be a formula that would give you the sum of two dice in a single formula instead of using three attributes and three formulas, as we did? (One might be **randomPick(1,2,3,4,5,6)** + **randomPick(1,2,3,4,5,6)**.)

➲ What are the advantages and disadvantages of putting the machinery into a single formula?

Tech Note: Random-Number Functions

Fathom supports an interesting set of random-number functions. You can read about all of them in **Help,** but let's discuss a few right here.

random( ) returns a random real number between 0.00 and 1.00. You can also give this function arguments, so **random(37)** gives a number between 0 and 37.00; and **random(–1, 1)** gives a random number between –1.00 and +1.00.

randomNormal(mean,sd) returns a random number from a normal distribution with the given mean and standard deviation. So the standard normal distribution is **randomNormal(0,1)**. In simulations, we use this function to generate some random error, as we did in *Straight or Curved?* (page 218) and *Building a Cloud from Scratch* (page 216).

randomInteger(min, max) returns a random integer from the range specified by the two arguments. The range includes the top number. So **randomInteger(1,6)** is a die.

randomPick(1, 2, ...) takes up to 20 arguments. It picks one of its arguments at random to return. This is an unexpectedly useful function for simulation. Thus, **randomPick("M", "F")** randomly assigns sex, **randomPick(1,2,3,4,5,6,6,6)** gives us a loaded die, and so forth.

Rolling Dice

Name(s): _____

This activity shows you how to use Fathom's random-number function to simulate rolling dice. Once you know how to do that, you'll be able to simulate other things as well. Remember, though: Using random numbers is not the only way to simulate, nor is it always the best.

We'll start by making a single die.

1. Start Fathom or get a new document. (Choose **New** from the **File** menu.)

2. Make a new case table by choosing **Case Table** from the **Insert** menu.

3. Create a new attribute (click on **<new>**) and call it **face**. This attribute will show the value of the number on the die's face.

Now we'll give **face** a formula to give us a number from 1 to 6. We'll use a random-number function. Fathom has several.

4. Click on the **face** attribute label and choose **Edit Formula** from the **Edit** menu. The formula editor appears.

5. Enter **randomPick(1,2,3,4,5,6)**. That will randomly pick one of the numbers listed. Close the formula editor by clicking **OK**. Now we have the formula, but we still need a case.

6. Choose **New Cases...** from the **Data** menu. Ask for one new case (the default) and click **OK**. A case appears, and its value for **face**.

7. Choose **Rerandomize** from the **Analyze** menu (or repeatedly press **CTRL-Y** (Windows) or **⌘-Y**(Mac)) to see the value change.

Rolling one die is fine, but let's roll more and see about their distribution.

8. Choose **New Cases...** from the **Data** menu. Enter **29** and click **OK**. Now you should have 30 cases, each with a random number from 1 to 6.

9. Choose **Graph** from the **Insert** menu. A new, empty graph appears.

10. We want to graph **face**, so drag **face** from the head of the column to the horizontal axis of the graph. The graph changes to a dot plot.

11. Choose **Histogram** from the popup menu in the corner of the graph. The dot plot changes to a histogram.

12. Press **CTRL-Y** (Windows) or **⌘-Y**(Mac) repeatedly, again, and watch the distribution change. Describe how the distribution changes each time you rerandomize.

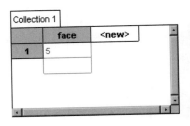

Since the numbers are discrete, you might think a bar chart would be a better graph. But Fathom thinks that the numbers in **face** are continuous, so it only lets us make a histogram in this situation.

13. Now change the simulation so that you are rolling 360 dice instead of 30. Explain how you made that change.

Make sure you have 360 dice by scrolling to the bottom of the case table.

To rescale the graph, drag on the axis or choose **Histogram** again from the popup menu on the graph.

Data in Depth
© 2001 Key Curriculum Press

Name(s): _____

14. Again, choose **Rerandomize** from the **Analyze** menu repeatedly. Describe how the graph changes. Especially, how do the graphs look different from the way they did before, when you had only 30 dice?

Two Dice Now

Time to make a second die and add them up.

15. In the case table, make a new attribute by clicking on **<new>**. Call it **face2**.

16. Give that attribute the same formula that **face** has. (You can copy/paste formulas.)

17. Make another new attribute, **sum**.

18. Give it a formula that adds the two **face**s, for example **face + face2**.

19. Graph the **sum**. Make it a histogram. Sketch the labeled graph.

20. Point to the bar for seven in the histogram. How many of the 360 rolls were sevens? Look in the status bar; in one example, as shown, there were 61. (Your number will probably be different.)

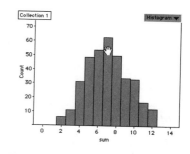

21. The fraction of the cases that were seven, for us, was 61/360, or about 0.17, a little more than 1/6 (the theoretical value). What was your fraction?

You can find how many are in a bar by pointing to it and looking in the status bar at the bottom of the window.

That fraction is the *empirical probability* of rolling a seven with two dice. It may be different every time you rerandomize.

Going Further

Seven is not always the most popular sum. With trials of 360 rolls, in about what fraction of these trials does a number other than seven come out most frequently?

Exploring Sampling

- Two structured computer activities
- Data from file and simulation
- Student pages 233–235
- Starter→guided, complex features

Sampling is a central idea in statistics. These two activities could be done in one session. *Exploring Sampling I: With and Without* introduces the mechanics of sampling; *Exploring Sampling II: Picking a Pair* uses them to investigate probability.

What's Important Here

- The mechanics of sampling. Students will need sampling when they analyze inferential situations with Fathom.

- Students explore the distinction between sampling with replacement and without it.

Discussion Questions

⮌ What kinds of real-life situations can you model with sampling with and without replacement?

⮌ Why do you suppose we collected so many samples to distinguish the probability of drawing a pair with replacement, from the probability without replacement?

Logistics Note

In *Exploring Sampling II: Picking a Pair,* in Steps 13 and 16 the handout asks students to find out how many pairs were drawn in all the samples from the entire class. You will need to facilitate this data collection in any way that is practical. We do this to increase the number of samples, and to therefore decrease the sampling error of the probability we get.

The Formula for pair

The handout doesn't tell students how to make the formula for **pair**—the Boolean formula that assesses whether the two cards in the sample are a pair or not. Any formula that accomplishes the task is acceptable. Here are two possibilities:

Straightforward   **first(number) = last(number)**

Subtle   **uniqueValues(number) = 1**

    The subtle version is important because it's the key to the "Going Further" section about poker-hand pairs. That is, a poker-hand sample of five has a pair if **uniqueValues(number) = 4**. (The equals sign—as opposed to ≤—is correct. If **uniqueValues(number) = 3**, for example, that means the hand has two pair or three of a kind.)

Topics
    sampling with/without replacement
    probability

Students need to be able to
    open files
    use the formula editor

Exploring Sampling I: With and Without

Name(s): _____

This is an introduction to Fathom's sampling capabilities—especially sampling
with and without replacement.

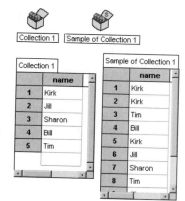

1. Make a new case table and give it one attribute, **name**. Put in five different
   names. Make yours one of them. The collection—a box of balls—appears.

2. Select the collection. Then choose **Sample Cases** from the **Analyze** menu. A
   new collection appears, probably named **Sample of Collection 1**. Make a case
   table for that collection. You'll see something like the screen shown here.

3. Double-click on the sample collection (the second box of balls, with
   an **S** on its lid) to open its inspector. The far-right tab is the **Sample** tab.
   Click on it. The **Sample** pane appears.

4. Click on the **Sample More Cases** button repeatedly. Describe what happens.

5. In the inspector, change the number from 10 to 3. Click on **Sample More
   Cases** again. Keep clicking until you see the same person appear twice in
   the same sample of three. About how many times did you have to click?

6. Now we will sample *without replacement*. Uncheck the **With replacement**
   box as shown. Click on the **Sample More Cases** button until you are
   convinced that the same person will never appear again in the same
   sample of three. Explain why not.

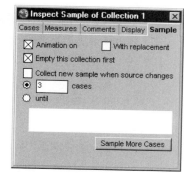

In Step 6, the **Sample** pane
should look like this.

7. Increase the number from 3 to 5—the number of people in your
   collection. Click on the **Sample More Cases** button repeatedly. What
   happens in the case table?

8. Increase the number from 5 to 10. Click on the **Sample More Cases**
   button repeatedly. Now what happens? Explain why the number of cases
   is what it is.

Exploring Sampling II: Picking a Pair

Name(s): _____

In this activity, you'll use sampling to simulate picking cards from a deck. Once you know that, you can use sampling to simulate many other things. Remember, though, that sampling is not the only way, nor is it always the best.

You need
DeckOfCards

1. Open **DeckOfCards.** Explore the document briefly; you can see that the collection in it represents a **deck** of cards.

2. Select **deck** (the collection) and choose **Sample Cases** from the **Analyze** menu. A new collection appears, called **Sample of deck.** Open up the collection by dragging a corner of the icon. You'll see the gold balls as in the picture here.

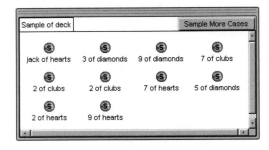

3. Click on the **Sample More Cases** button as shown in the picture. Describe what happens.

4. We want to control the way Fathom does this sampling. Double-click inside the **Sample** collection to open its inspector. Click on the **Sample** tab to go to the *sample pane.* It will look like the illustration shown here.

5. Explore what these controls do. When you're finished exploring, set the pane back to the way it was.

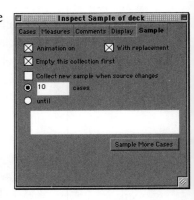

Animation takes extra time, so we'll skip it for now.

The Chance of a Pair

Now we will make a simulation to determine the chance that we get a pair when we draw two cards. A pair occurs when the **number** attributes are the same.

6. Now change the number sampled from 10 (the default) to 2. Uncheck the animation checkbox. When you press **Sample More Cases** (whether in the inspector or in the collection), you now get two cards.

7. We want to know if there's a pair. We should record the answer in a *measure.* So click on the **Measures** tab in the inspector (it may just say **Mea . . .**) to go to that pane. Click on **<new>** to make a new measure. Call it **pair.** Press **ENTER.**

8. Double-click in the formula column to the right of **pair.** The formula editor appears.

9. Give **pair** a formula that will be **true** if the two cards in the collection are a pair and **false** if they are not. Write that formula here.

Three functions that might help are **first( )**, **last( )**, and **uniqueValues( )**. They're all in the **One Variable** group in the **Statistical** category in the function browser.

10. Now we'll collect some different samples—different sets of two cards. With the **Sample...** collection selected, choose **Collect Measures** from the **Analyze** menu. A new collection appears, called **Measures from Sample of deck.** It has one attribute, **pair,** and five cases showing whether the five samples were pairs.

11. Open this collection's inspector and go to the **Collect Measures** pane. Uncheck the **Animation on** box. Increase the number to 200 and click on **Collect More Measures.** Be patient.

12. How many of your 200 samples were pairs? How do you know?

13. In the entire class, how many pairs were there? Out of how many samples?

14. Now open up the inspector for the **Sample of deck** collection, the one where you made the pairs. In its **Sample** pane, uncheck the **With replacement** box. We will now sample *without replacement.*

15. Back in the measures collection, press **Collect Measures** again. You'll (slowly) get the data on 200 samples. How many of those samples were pairs?

16. In the entire class, how many pairs were there? Out of how many samples?

17. What's the empirical probability of getting a pair when drawing from a 52-card deck *with replacement?* What's the probability *without replacement?* Explain, in words, why one is greater than the other.

Going Further

1. Find the theoretical probabilities for Step 17 above.
2. Modify the simulation to compute the probability of getting a blackjack in Twenty-one.
3. Modify the simulation to compute the probability of getting a pair in a five-card sample—that is, a pair in poker.

Getting a blackjack means that when you get two cards, one is an ace and the other is a king, a queen, a jack, or a ten.

Just You Wait!

- Structured computer activity
- Data generated in simulation
- Student pages 237–238
- Intermediate, complex features

This activity explores another kind of probability situation: one in which we ask how long it will be until an event occurs. Answers to problems like these often involve a geometric distribution (though we do not use that term in the handout).

Topics
probability
simulation

What's Important Here

Students need to be able to
make graphs and tables
use an inspector
make measures and give them
formulas

- If the probability of an event is p, the expected number of trials you need to get a success is $1/p$.

- Sampling does not necessarily involve choosing the size of the sample ahead of time. However, if it does not, you must be specific about the conditions under which sampling ceases. In Fathom, you can control sampling with a Boolean expression.

You can always stop Fathom from sampling or collecting measures by pressing **esc**.

- It is possible (though unlikely, we hope) for some sampling situations to go on forever.

- This kind of situation gives rise to a distribution that starts off big and tails off. With this kind of distribution, mean > median > mode.

Discussion Questions

- Suppose you wanted to answer the question "How many rolls does it take, on average, to get a six?" theoretically and you decided to make a tree diagram. How would that look? What problems would you run into?

- Looking back at the census data (if you did those activities), does the distribution of numbers of die rolls resemble any of the attributes you remember? (**income**.)

Extensions

Besides the "Going Further" questions, here are two more ideas for ways to extend this lesson:

- Use the Fathom random-number function **randomExponential(1/6)**—where **p = 1/6** is the probability of an event—to model this situation more quickly and get a lot of cases.

- Use **DeckOfCards.** Set up a simulation that deals poker hands until you get a flush. (For a flush, use the formula **uniqueValues(suit) = 1.**) How many hands do you have to deal before the first flush comes up? From your experience with these "wait until" simulations, what is a range of probabilities you would accept for getting a flush?

A poker hand is five (different) cards from a traditional deck. In a flush, the five cards are all from the same suit, for example, five spades.

Just You Wait!

Name(s): _____

Sometimes when you sample or collect measures, you don't know exactly how many things you want to collect. Instead, you want to sample (or collect) until some condition is met. We'll use a traditional problem as an example: On the average, how many times do you have to roll a die in order to get a six?

1. Before we do the simulation, what do you think the answer is?

You need to know how to
make graphs and tables
use an inspector
make measures and give them
formulas

2. Open the file **RollingDice.** It should have two collections: one called **Single Die** and another called **Sample of Single Die.** Make sure you can see a case table for **Sample of Single Die.**

3. Open the inspector for the **Sample** collection and click on the **Sample** tab. The sample pane is probably set to sample two dice, with replacement.

Double-click on the collection to open the inspector.

4. We don't know how many times to roll. Here's how we'll set it up: Click on the radio button marked **until.**

5. Double-click on the white rectangle below it. The formula editor appears.

6. Here we enter the expression that will tell Fathom to *stop* collecting samples. Enter **face = 6.** Click **OK** to close the editor. Your inspector should look like the one shown here.

7. Click on **Sample More Cases** repeatedly. What happens in the case table?

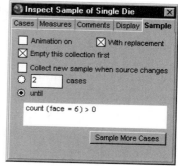

Now we want to collect the numbers of die rolls. This calls for measures and a way to collect them.

8. Press the **Measures** tab of the inspector. (It may just read **Mea . . .**)

9. Make a new measure, **numberOfRolls**, with a formula, **count( ).** That will be the number of cases in the **Sample** collection. Close the **Sample** collection's inspector.

Measures from Sample of single die

The measures collection

10. Select the **Sample of Single Die** collection and choose **Collect Measures** from the **Analyze** menu. A new measures collection appears, called **Measures from Sample of Single Die.** It may take a little while for that collection to fill up.

11. Make a case table for the new collection. You will see **numberOfRolls** for five runs of the simulation, because Fathom collects five measures by default. Open the **Measures** collection's inspector and the **Collect Measures** tab. (It may just read **Col . . .**)

12. Change the number of measures from 5 to 10. Click on **Collect More Measures.** The simulation runs 10 times, collecting the numbers of rolls in the **Measures** collection's case table.

13. Make a histogram of **numberOfRolls.**

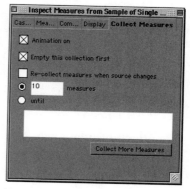

Here is its inspector, open to the **Collect Measures** pane.

Just You Wait! (continued)

Name(s): _____

14. Choose **Plot Value** from the **Graph** menu. Give it the formula mean(numberOfRolls). Close the editor with **OK** and sketch the graph at right.

15. Explain in words what the number being plotted means.

16. Collect measures again, watching the graph.

17. Continue to collect measures in order to answer the original question: What is the average number of rolls you need in order to get a six? Alter the parameters in the **Measures** pane as you see fit.

18. Based on the simulation, what do you think is the *most likely* number of rolls you need to get a six? Explain what evidence you have for your answer. Sketch or refer to a graph if you need to.

19. Explain how the most likely number of rolls can be different from the average number of rolls.

Going Further

1. The most likely number of rolls is the *mode*. We know the mean. What's the *median* number of rolls you need to get a six?

2. (Sonata) Suppose you roll two six-sided dice. How many rolls will you need, on the average, to get a seven or an eleven? Predict first, based on this activity, then design the simulation and carry it out.

3. (Sonata) Suppose a couple decide to have babies until they have one daughter and then stop. Assuming that the probabilities of the two sexes are equal, how many sons can they expect to have? Predict first, based on this activity, then design the simulation (which will create many possible families) and carry it out.

4. Suppose you changed the "middle" collection—the **Sample** collection—to sample *without* replacement. What would happen to the mean number of rolls it would take to get a six?

5. On the average, how many rolls does it take to get a five *and* a six? Predict first!

6. On the average, how many rolls does it take to get a five *or* a six? Predict first!

7. Which is more likely, a statement with **and** in it or the same statement with **or** in it? Explain your answer and give really good examples.

8. On the average, how long does it take a one-dimensional random walk (start at 0, take steps of +1 or −1) to get at least three steps from the origin?

Great Expectations

• Structured computer activity

• Data generated in simulation

• Student pages 240–241

• Guided, complex features

The simulation in this activity focuses on expected value. Here, students can see that the expected value for a random variable is the same as the average value of that variable taken over many simulations.

What's Important Here

• To find expected value with simulation, first set up a simulation to find the quantity once. If that quantity varies, run the simulation many times and average.

• Students who have done other activities in this chapter should begin to see how the use of measures collections is parallel in all these situations.

Discussion Questions

➲ How would you go about computing Sven's average income theoretically? (You could do a weighted average.)

➲ What does the simulation tell you that the simple theoretical solution does not? (The simulation tells us about the spread as well as the expected value. Though you can derive that theoretically, it's harder than finding a weighted average.)

➲ Why would you use the mean rather than the median (or vice versa) to find the average of Sven's salary? (The mean is probably better, since you could use it to figure long-term income. Also, the median will take on only a few discrete values, so its insensitivity loses information.)

➲ If your income were like Sven's, why would you want to know the standard deviation?

Topics
expected value
proportion

Students need to be able to
make a slider
make case tables
make new attributes
make graphs
use formulas

Great Expectations

Name(s): _____

Here's a question we'll explore first:

Sven works five days a week. Usually he builds fences for $100.00 per day, but sometimes he gets a job doing finish carpentry, and that pays $250.00 per day. On the average, he does carpentry 30% of the time. On the average, how much does he make in a week?

In this activity, you'll build a simulation to solve the problem. This kind of problem involves *expected value*.

We'll make a collection that simulates a week, so it will have five cases—one for each day. Then we'll make a collection to record how much Sven makes in a week, so that when we have the computer produce lots of weeks, we can take those numbers and average them.

You need to know how to
make a slider
make case tables
make new attributes
make graphs
use formulas

You'll learn
about expected value
how to use measures
how to use the inspector

1. We'll start with a slider so we can change the chance that Sven gets a carpentry job. In a new document, make a slider. Name it **p** (for probability). Set it to 0.30 (30%).

2. Make a new case table. Give it two new attributes, **job** and **income**. A closed collection will appear. Name it **week.**

3. Choose **New Cases** from the **Data** menu, and give **week** five empty cases.

4. Here are the formulas for **job** and **income**. Enter them using the formula editor. (Select the attribute name and choose **Edit Formula** from the **Data** menu to get the editor.)

job	income
if (random ( ) < p) $\begin{cases} \text{"carpentry"} \\ \text{"fences"} \end{cases}$	if (job = "carpentry") $\begin{cases} 250 \\ 100 \end{cases}$

5. Repeatedly press **CTRL-Y** (Windows) or **⌘-Y** (Mac) to get new weeks of work. About how much does Sven make?

Fathom can help us record the data. First we have to make Fathom add up Sven's week's pay. That sum is an attribute of the whole collection (the week), not of the individual cases (the days). So we need to make a *measure*.

6. Open the inspector for **week** by double-clicking on the collection or choosing **Inspect Collection** from the **Data** menu. Click on the **Measures** tab.

7. Click on **<new>** to make a new measure. Call the new measure **paycheck.**

8. Double-click on the formula box to the right of the name to open the formula editor.

9. Enter **sum(income)** as the formula for **paycheck.** Close the formula editor. You'll see the value in the inspector. Pressing **CTRL-Y** (Windows) or **⌘-Y** (Mac) will now update the sum as well as the individual days.

CTRL-I (Windows) or **⌘-I** (Mac) is the shortcut.

Great Expectations (continued)

Name(s): _____

Collecting the Paychecks

Now we have Sven's weekly paycheck, but how do we find the average over many weeks? We need what's called a *measures collection* to collect those data so we can analyze them.

It may seem odd to think of the week's paycheck as being a measure. Yet it is—in this case, a measure of how much Sven earned.

10. Select the collection called **week** (not the case table) and choose **Collect Measures** from the **Analyze** menu. A new collection appears, **Measures from week.** Make a case table for it. What do you see?

To make a case table, select the collection, then choose **Case Table** from the **Insert** menu.

11. Make a graph and drag **paycheck** from the case table onto the horizontal axis.

Close the inspector for **week** if your screen is too crowded. And save your work!

12. With the graph selected, choose **Plot Value** from the **Graph** menu. When the formula editor appears, enter **mean( )**. Click **OK** to close the editor. What is Sven's average **paycheck**?

13. Average isn't the whole picture. Sven's income fluctuates. Find the standard deviation. Use **Plot Value** again and the function **stdDev( )**. What is it?

The standard deviation is a measure of the amount of variation, or *spread,* in Sven's weekly paycheck.

14. We need more! Double-click on the **Measures...** collection to open its inspector. Click on the **Collect Measures** tab to go to the pane that controls how it collects measures. Change the number in the inspector from 5 to 50. Press **Collect More Measures**. Now what do you get for the average and standard deviation of Sven's **paycheck**?

15. Explain clearly why your statistics for 50 weeks are probably more accurate than those for 5.

Going Further

1. About how many weeks a year does Sven make more than $1,000.00?

2. How does Sven's average paycheck depend on the probability **p** of getting a carpentry job?

3. Cats weigh 12 pounds; dogs weigh 35. A truckload of 30 animals averages 55% dogs. What does an average truckload weigh? What fraction of the time is the cargo over 800 pounds?

4. Suppose an average cat weighs 12 pounds with a standard deviation of 4. Dogs average 35 with a standard deviation of 10. Same questions as above; explain why the answers are so different.

Use **randomNormal(mean,sd)** to draw random numbers from a normal distribution. Find out how to use it in **Help.**

5. Ella pays $1.00 to play a game. She rolls two dice. If she rolls a seven, she wins $2.50, and if she rolls an eleven, she wins $10.00. On the average, how much will she win or lose in 100 games?

HIV Testing

- Two structured computer activities
- Data generated in simulation
- Student pages 246–248
- Starter, medium features

This is a set of two activities about conditional probability in the context of HIV testing.

- **HIV Testing I.** This is introductory and requires only an understanding of proportions. Students need some experience with Fathom, but do not have to construct formulas or enter data. They do see and discuss how to construct such a simulation.

- **HIV Testing II: Be an Epidemiologist.** Students look at the issue in more depth and need enough mathematics experience to solve simple simultaneous equations.

Neither activity uses the traditional conditional-probability notation (A | B, etc.), but either could be a good introduction to that notation or a good application of it. One of the central questions, "If you test positive, what's the chance that you actually are infected?" is perfect for Bayes's Rule, explained in more detail on pages 244–245.

Topics
proportion
conditional probability
false positives

Materials
HIV_Simulation
Epidemiologist

Students need to be able to
make a summary table
do some algebra, possibly solving simple linear simultaneous equations

Background

A small fraction of the population is actually infected with the Human Immunodeficiency Virus (HIV). When you get an HIV test, there is a small chance that the test will give an incorrect result. That is, you may get a *false positive* if you are not infected, or a *false negative* if you are.

Suppose 1% of the population has HIV and the test is 95% correct (in both directions). If you look at 10,000 people, you expect 100 infected subjects and 9900 uninfected ones. Of the 100 infected people, 95 will test positive. Of the 9900 uninfected people, most will test negative, but 5% (495) will test positive. So of the 590 positive results (495 + 95), the majority are from uninfected people.

An important question, therefore, is "If I test positive for HIV, what's the chance that I actually have the virus?" And if you are an employer, or an insurer, or a diagnostician, you ask similar questions—about this and all similar situations, for example about results from random drug testing, consumer product testing, airline baggage X-rays, and so on.

Other issues intrude, for example, when you know you have engaged in risky behaviors or if you belong to at-risk groups. Then the numbers change—in ways that may affect the rest of your life.

HIV Testing I: Discussion Questions

In your discussion, you might introduce the terms *false positive, false negative,* and so on; they will make some of the discussion easier, and they're important vocabulary.

➲ Based on your simulated data, if you test positive for HIV, what's the probability that you're actually infected?

➲ What proportion of donors were actually infected in this simulation? (3%.)

HIV Testing

➲ Some populations (e.g., IV drug users) have a higher proportion of infected people. How would you change the simulation to model a higher proportion of infected people?

➲ Every test is wrong some percentage of the time. Suppose a test were correct only 80% of the time. How would you change the model?

➲ How does the mathematics in this activity apply to other situations (e.g., insurance, airline baggage screening, or employee drug testing)?

HIV Testing II: Be an Epidemiologist

Students have seen how it's possible to get a higher incidence of positive tests than the actual proportion of people with the infection. But medical professionals want to know the real prevalence of the infection. You can answer this question with a fairly easy solution of two simultaneous equations. (**Note:** This is a genuine use for algebra, though at the Algebra II level.)

Experienced students could zoom through *HIV Testing I* quickly to get to this activity and record their data in a single period. They could do the calculations and finish the page for homework.

HIV Testing II: Discussion Questions

➲ How did you calculate the true prevalence of HIV? (There are many ways to approach this, depending on how you look at the problem.)

➲ How do you suppose the testers know how accurate their test is? That is, if it's always wrong a fraction of the time, how can they figure out what that fraction is? (Often they use better, but more expensive, tests as a calibration. They use less expensive tests on the general population and accept the false positives in return for the lower cost. A follow-up question: What are the consequences of this policy? Is the lower cost worth the consequences?)

Philosophy

The HIV-testing problem is a counterintuitive example from probability. Understanding it will help students come to grips with many public-policy issues and to recognize ill-reasoned persuasion. And understanding the problem in its context could even help students make choices that will save their lives.

Why is it so hard? It deals with *conditional probability*, which seems to be hard for many of us (consider also the problem in *Saved by the Belt*, page 87). Some problems in conditional probability are famously perplexing (see *Monty Hall*, page 253), but such tricky puzzles are not nearly as important as the ubiquitous problem of testing and false positives.

Bayes's Rule

Here is the formula in Bayes's Rule:

$$P(B|A) = \frac{P(B) \times P(A|B)}{P(A)}$$

where the notation $P(A|B)$ means "the probability of A given that B is true."

Working on the HIV activity, you may have been struck by the form of the main question: *What's the probability that someone who tests positive is actually healthy?* Reword that and you get *What's the probability that you're healthy given that you test positive?* That's a Bayes's Rule question. In symbols, we have the answer right away:

$$P(healthy|positive) = \frac{P(healthy) \times P(positive|healthy)}{P(positive)}$$

The quantity $P(positive|healthy)$ ("the probability that you get a positive—that is, bad—result given that you're healthy") is the false positive rate, 0.05. $P(healthy)$ is (1 – the prevalence of the disease), which comes to 0.97 in the initial simulation. Finally, $P(positive)$ is the observed rate of positives, let's say 0.077 (the theoretical value).

In that case (plugging in the numbers), the answer to our question is

$$P(healthy|positive) = \frac{0.97 \times 0.05}{0.077} = 0.63$$

That is, if you get a positive result, you have a 63% chance of being healthy after all.

Derivation

Where does this formula come from? There are a lot of derivations, and here is a favorite. We'll make an area model (shown here) for the probability that's just like a Fathom ribbon chart.

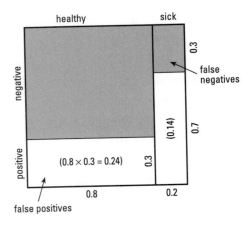

This is an excellent example of a useful mathematical formula whose very appearance can give you indigestion. We read it and it sounds like gobbledygook. If you're an adult math teacher, you once had this in some course, but you're rare if you can pull it up from memory. It's hard (the author thinks) because it's soaked in conditional probability, which defies ordinary language. It requires the subjunctive.

But it's not so bad if you approach it visually. First, though, we just use it.

Assume the square is one unit on a side, so the total area is 1.00, and the probability of each (mutually exclusive) condition is the *area* of the corresponding rectangle.

This diagram is for a disease with numbers that are easier to display. The test is good 70% of the time, and 20% of the population has the disease. The clear regions are positive tests (false positives in the left, healthy region); the gray ones are negative tests (false negatives in the right, sick region).

Bayes's Rule

The question is: If you test positive, what's the chance that you're healthy? Or, in more orthodox language, what's the chance that you're healthy *given* a positive test? That is, what's $P(healthy|positive)$?

Instead of formulas, we'll use the areas. We know we have already tested positive, so we need only consider the clear parts of the diagram. We want to know the chance that we're in the left-hand rectangle, given that we know we're in the clear area.

That's the ratio of the left clear area to the entire clear area, or $0.24/(0.24 + 0.14)$, or 63%—that it matches the answer we got previously is a coincidence. Let's generalize it with symbols.

First, the entire clear area (the denominator) is $P(positive)$, almost by definition.

We need the left-hand area. That's the width times the height. The width is the probability that we're healthy (knowing nothing about a test). That's 0.8, or, in symbols, $P(healthy)$.

The height is the chance that we test positive *given that we're healthy*. That's the false positive rate, 0.3 in the example, or $P(healthy|positive)$.

Putting it together, we get

$$P(healthy|positive) = \frac{\text{width} \times \text{height}}{P(positive)}$$

$$= \frac{P(healthy) \times P(positive|healthy)}{P(positive)}$$

which is exactly what we got before.

Can I Use This in the Epidemiologist Activity?

You may say to yourself, "Aha! In that case, I want $P(healthy)$. So I just solve the equation the other way, and get

$$P(healthy) = \frac{P(healthy|positive) \times P(positive)}{P(positive|healthy)}$$

Unfortunately, you don't know $P(healthy|positive)$.

Personally, the author prefers to write an equation for the total proportion of positive tests (since that's what we'll observe). This amounts to adding up the areas of the two clear rectangles in the diagram.

If d is the actual disease rate (so $d = 0.10$ means 10% have the disease), and a is the accuracy of the test (0.95 in our case), the proportion of true positives is da, and the number of false positives is $(1 - d)(1 - a)$. So

$$P = ad + (1 - a)(1 - d)$$

where P is the observed rate of positives. Solve that for d to get your answer. In the case of a 95%-accurate test and an observed positive test rate of 12%, the author found that 7.8% of the population has the disease.

HIV Testing I

Name(s): _____

Your data file represents 200 potential blood donors. You don't want to use blood infected with the Human Immunodeficiency Virus (HIV)—the AIDS virus. You will test the blood before you use it. The test is imperfect, however. It gives the correct result only 95% of the time.

You need
HIV_Simulation

You'll learn how to
work with formulas with randomness in them

1. Choose **Open** from the **File** menu and open the file **HIV_Simulation.** You'll see information on the 200 donors and the results of their blood tests. There is also a summary table showing the outcomes of their HIV tests.

2. Use the summary table to answer these questions:
   How many of the donors tested positive for HIV?

   What *percentage* of the donors is that?

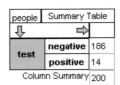

A summary table showing test results for 200 potential blood donors

3. This is a simulation; let's run it again to see how else the numbers might have turned out. Press **CTRL-Y** (Windows) or **⌘-Y** (Mac) and wait a moment; the number in the summary table will change as Fathom recomputes the HIV tests.

4. Answer the questions in Step 2 for four more runs of the simulation. You'll have a total of five runs of the simulation—a total of 1000 donors.

people		
	HIV	**test**
41	healthy	negative
42	healthy	negative
43	healthy	positive
44	healthy	negative
45	healthy	negative
46	healthy	negative
47	healthy	negative
48	healthy	negative
49	healthy	negative

5. Let's look at the guts of this simulation. Click on the **HIV** attribute label and choose **Edit Formula** from the **Edit** menu. In the formula editor, you can see the formula that determines whether each person is infected. The function **random(1)** returns a random number between 0 and 1.

6. Copy the formula here and explain, in words, how it works.

The test results (**test**) depend on the attribute **HIV**, which states whether each person really has the HIV virus. *In reality, we never know this for sure.* Some people who have the virus will test negative, and some without it will test positive.

7. Close the formula box. Select the **test** attribute label and choose **Edit Formula** from the **Edit** menu to view the formula for **test**. This is a much more complicated formula; you'll need to stretch the box just to see it all. It should look like the picture shown here.

$$\text{if (HIV = "healthy")} \begin{cases} \text{if (random (1) < 0.95)} \begin{cases} \text{"negative"} \\ \text{"positive"} \end{cases} \\ \text{if (random (1) < 0.95)} \begin{cases} \text{"positive"} \\ \text{"negative"} \end{cases} \end{cases}$$

8. Explain below what the 0.95 means in the formula in the picture.

9. Now we'll see something really strange. Drag the attribute label for **HIV** onto the column headings of the summary table. You'll get a table similar to the one shown here. Remember: In reality, we never know the true value of **HIV**; we only get the results of the test.

people	Summary Table			
		HIV		Row Summary
		healthy	infected	
test	**negative**	183	0	183
	positive	10	7	17
	Column Summary	193	7	200

S1 = count ( )

10. Of the people who tested positive, what fraction are actually healthy? Rerandomize the simulation—**CTRL-Y** (Windows) or **⌘-Y** (Mac)—five times and record this fraction here.

11. Explain in words how this can be true: *More than half the people who test positive for HIV are actually free of the virus, even though the test is correct 95% of the time.*

Going Further

1. Experiment with values different from 0.03 in the formula for **HIV**. What value makes it true that only half the people who test positive are free of the virus? (That is, when is the number of false positives equal to the number of true positives?) Explain, if you can, why that value is the one.

In our simulation, it was the same: 0.05.

2. In a real test for drugs or a disease or whatever, the chance of getting a false positive is different from the chance of getting a false negative. In practice, there's a trade-off between the two. Generally, if you have a low false positive rate, you'll have a higher false negative rate, and vice versa. Explain why that might be the case.

3. If you were making a test for HIV, which would you choose—to get a low false positive rate or a low false negative rate? Why? What are the positive and negative consequences of your decision?

4. Compare your decision for HIV with one for some other test: a sobriety checkpoint, for example, or an airline metal detector, or a high school performance evaluation required for graduation. What kinds of mis-tests do you accept more easily—false positives or false negatives? (You will have to decide what "positive" means in each case.)

HIV Testing II: Be an Epidemiologist

Name(s): _____

Suppose you don't know how many people were actually infected.

You need
Epidemiologist

You need to know how to
make a summary table
do some algebra, possibly
    solving simple linear
    simultaneous equations

You'll learn how to
estimate unknown parameters

1. Open the file **Epidemiologist.** This is a file with a secret—the true proportion of infected people. In real life you do not know this value, only the results of people's tests. Therefore, you are honor-bound not to peek.

2. Have someone *secretly* change the proportion of infected people. In this file, it's governed by a slider named **pInfected.** Your helper can find the slider by scrolling to the right. He or she should change **pInfected** to some value between 0.0 and 0.1.

3. Have the person scroll back so that the case table is visible (and **pInfected** is not).

4. Now you may look. You may make a summary table of **test**, but you may not look at **HIV** (we've hidden it because you really can't tell). You may rerandomize for a total of five runs. You know that the test is 95% correct. How many people test positive? Record your data here.

5. Estimate (by calculating, not by guessing) the actual percentage of people who are infected. Show and explain your calculations.

6. Change roles with your partner.

7. Compare your estimates to the actual slider values for the proportion of people infected.

Going Further

1. Change the simulation to add a second test with the same accuracy. Figure out how (or whether) to use the additional information. What about a third test?

2. Following on the preceding suggestion, suppose you only retested people who had tested positive. How would you set up Fathom to do that?

3. (Sonata) It's important to keep drugged truckers off the roads. Suppose you're in charge of random drug testing for truck drivers. A test costs only $10 to administer, but it's accurate only 80% of the time. There's another, better test, correct 99% of the time, that costs $100 to administer. Invent a scheme for testing that keeps the cost down and try it out in a simulation. Don't forget the human cost: what it's like to be falsely suspected.

Data in Depth
© 2001 Key Curriculum Press

Simulation Problems and Sonatas

- Numerous open-ended computer activities
- Data from simulation
- Student pages 250–253
- Independent, complex features

These pages present problems in probability that students can address using what they have learned in these activities. The first two are formatted as Sonatas; you can learn more about the Sonata form on pages xxii–xxiii.

Grubs Again?

This is an adaptation of the "pearl" problem from the 1998 AP statistics exam.

A New Birthday Problem

This problem is a variation on the old one that asks "What's the probability that out of 30 people in a room, two will have the same birthday?" The surprising answer is that the probability is better than .5. Here we turn it around a little, and ask how many people it takes until you get a match—and simulate that.

If students have trouble, suggest that they start with a collection with *one* case with *one* attribute, **birthday**, with a formula of **randomInteger(1,365)**. They should sample from that, using an **until** formula in the sample pane.

Dice Probability Problems

These problems are all versions of standard dice problems, made more complex in different directions.

Sampling Challenges

Here are a few problems about sampling with and without replacement. In solving them, students can use various Fathom tools they will have learned.

Sonata 26: Grubs Again?

Name(s): _____

Howard is the manager of a grub farm. He has received a special order for two grubs between 3.6 and 3.8 grams in weight. From past experience, Howard knows that the grubs' weights are normally distributed with a mean of 3.5 grams and a standard deviation of 0.3 grams.

Howard wants to know how many grubs he can expect to harvest in order to find two of the appropriate size for the special order.

Design

Design a simulation that will answer the question. This answer should include not only the expected number of grubs but also the distribution of those numbers if the task were repeated many (≥ 100) times. Briefly describe how you'll do it. What collections will you need? Any special formulas? Any things you don't know that you need to find out?

Construction

Build your simulation in Fathom and run it. Report your results below: Sketch the graph of the distribution and give the expected number of grubs you got.

Reflection and Extension

Do your results seem reasonable? Were they surprising? Did your simulation work as planned? Describe any modifications you had to make.

Then suppose that when Howard harvests the grubs, he actually has to climb the tree where the grubs grow, so that it's a pain to climb up and get more if there aren't enough grubs of the right size. How many grubs should he harvest if he wants a 90% probability of getting two grubs that fit the order?

Sonata 27: A New Birthday Problem

Name(s): _____

Here's a new version of an old problem.

Suppose people come into a room one at a time. Whenever a new person comes into the room, he or she announces his or her birthday. If it matches that of anyone else in the room, the door is locked. No one else is let in.

On the average, how many people will get into the room before this happens? What's the distribution of that number?

Conjecture and Design

First, what do you think? About how many people will come in before there's a birthday match?

Design a simulation that will answer the question. This answer should include not only the average number of people but also the distribution of those people if the task were repeated many times. Briefly describe how you'll do it. What collections will you need? Any special formulas? Any things you don't know that you need to find out?

Construction

Build your simulation in Fathom and run it. Report your results below: Sketch the graph of the distribution and give the average number of people you got.

Comparison and Reflection

Do your results seem reasonable? How did they compare with your conjecture? Did your simulation work as planned? Describe any modifications you had to make.

Dice Probability Problems

Name(s): _____

Use Fathom to simulate rolling dice for each of these problems. Unless we ask you to do otherwise, find experimental, empirical probabilities rather than theoretical ones.

Subtracting Dice

The most likely outcome if you roll two six-sided dice and add is seven. What's the most likely outcome if you *subtract* the second die from the first (you will get some negative numbers)? Simulate it. Explain how you set it up in Fathom and report your results. What do you think the theoretical result is, and why?

Absolute Subtraction

Do the preceding problem again, but this time, when you subtract, take the absolute difference (no negative numbers). What's the most likely outcome? **Extension:** Find the answer theoretically.

In the formula editor, use the vertical bars to indicate absolute value.

Scatter Plot of Dice

Go back to the simple sum of two dice. Imagine the graph of one of the dice as a function of the sum. Predict what that graph will look like, then use Fathom to make it. Sketch the graph and explain why it has the shape it does.

Special Dice

Imagine two special dice that you roll and then add. One of the dice has faces with the numbers {2, 4, 6, 8, 10, 12} and the other has {1, 3, 5, 7, 9, 11}. What will the distribution of the sum look like? Sketch your prediction below. Then construct the simulation in Fathom. Sketch the resulting distribution and explain how you made your simulation (especially, give any formulas).

Adding Up Dice with More Sides

Predict: How will the distribution of die-roll sums change if you change from two six-sided dice to two dice of more and more sides? Write your prediction, then make a simulation to test your prediction.

Adding Up More Dice

Predict: How will the distribution of die-roll sums change if you change from two six-sided dice to more and more dice of six sides? Write your prediction, then make a simulation to test your prediction. Then compare these results with the preceding problem's results. Explain why and how changing the number of dice is different from changing the number of sides.

Sampling Challenges

Name(s): _____

Awarding Five Prizes

Suppose you had five identical prizes to award to people in the class. And suppose you had a collection with one case for each person (maybe with the attribute **name**). How could you use Fathom—and sampling—to determine who would get the prizes? Set it up in Fathom and make it work. Be sure it works more than once! Then explain how you set it up.

Everybody's a Winner

Now suppose you had exactly as many prizes as you have people, but the prizes were all different. You decide to let Fathom pick people in a random order and let the first person choose first, and so forth. Of course, no one should be picked twice. Set it up in Fathom and make it work. Be sure it works more than once! Then explain how you set it up.

Simulating 50 Animals

Create a fictional population of 50 animals. Use sampling to make it roughly 40% dogs and 60% cats, then use a formula (with an **if( )** function and whatever **random...** functions you need) to make the cats two-thirds male and one-third female, and the dogs half and half. Use Fathom to answer the question "If you're female, what's the chance that you're a cat?"

Collect Them All

Each box of Whole-Grain Clusters contains a Famous Fictional Detective Action Figure. There are six figures: Easy Rawlins, Adam Dalgliesh, Kinsey Millhone, Imanishi Eitaro, Jane Marple, and Sam Spade. There are the same number of figures for each character, and they are distributed randomly in the boxes. Set up a simulation that will tell you how many boxes you have to buy to get a complete set of six. In addition to explaining how you did it, run the simulation 10 times and record your results.

Monty Hall

You may already know this one. A game show host has put a desirable prize behind one of three doors. You pick a door. Before that door is opened, the host opens one of the two doors you did not choose, showing a prize you don't want. Then the host gives you a chance to switch to the remaining door. Should you switch? Even some professional mathematicians have said that since it's random, it can't make a difference. But it does. Design a Fathom simulation to demonstrate this.

Inference with Fathom

10

We use statistical inference to learn about a population from a sample. Here are some examples of inference at work:

- A legislative committee wants to know whether the public approves of its policy in Grand Fenwick. It's impractical to ask everyone, so the committee takes an opinion poll. Of 1000 people, 610 approve. We can't say for sure that exactly 61% of the public approves, but that figure is probably pretty close, because we polled so many people. When we report the results, we might say, "61% ± 3%," or we might give an interval such as "58% to 64%." This range is a *confidence interval.*

- Researchers do an experiment to find out whether Pedinix really cures foot fungus in teenagers. They have before-and-after fungal counts for two groups. On the average, the Pedinix group does better than the control group, but there is quite a bit of variation within each group. Is the difference real, or is it just due to chance? Researchers set up a *null hypothesis*—that Pedinix makes no difference—and perform a *hypothesis test* to see how likely their result would be if the null hypothesis were true. If they get a small probability, that's evidence that Pedinix really does the job.

The field of statistical inference is filled with subtlety, difficulty, and pitfalls. Whole books can be and have been written about it—we can't address it all in this final chapter. But here are some general points to bear in mind:

- When you do inference, you infer statistics about a population using data from a sample. And that's all. There's a lot more to the field of statistics than inference.

- Many courses are labeled "Probability and Statistics." Why probability? Because of inference. Inferential results are probability statements; it is always *possible* that your conclusion will be wrong. Inference tells you how likely that is. It tells you your risk.

- To make these probability statements, inference depends on everything being set up properly. For example, it generally depends on samples being *random* samples.

The activities in this chapter are designed to clarify the basic issues of inference. But these activities are only a taste. To enjoy more of the inferential feast, you will need a statistics book. If you have a strong background in inference, you will see how to take these activities further.

Finding a statistics book

Fortunately, there are excellent and humane texts; to find one, get a recommendation from an AP statistics teacher or search in **forum.swarthmore.edu**.

Level

These activities could be an introduction to inference for any students with algebra experience, but are especially appropriate for students in a statistics course.

The Activities

This chapter has three offline activities, each of which is rich enough to begin early in the year and return to as students become more sophisticated. The online part of each activity illustrates a different aspect of inference through simulation.

- **Constructivist Dice.** This is about hypothesis testing. Students make their own dice and test them for fairness, inventing their own measure. In "official" statistics, this is the chi-square goodness-of-fit situation.

- **Pennies and Polling.** This is about the confidence interval of a proportion. We use a large population of pennies to simulate a population of voters and sample from it to simulate polling. What proportion were minted later than 1994 (or whatever works with your pennies)?

- **Orbital Express.** In this activity, students compare competing designs for orbital re-entry craft. Students take measurements and devise a measure of association. We introduce scrambling (officially, a permutation test) as a technique for simulating independence. This is the "two-sample t" situation.

In addition to these three activities, there are several more that probe aspects of inference:

- **Inferring the Mean.** This is a set of two activities that introduce and explore the use of Fathom's analyses. These provide more traditional inference capability; we'll do a t-test on the mean and find its confidence interval.

- **Inference Sonatas and Other Challenges.** These are more open-ended investigations and problems.

Objectives

In this chapter, students should

- Come to understand the basic meaning of hypothesis tests and confidence intervals

- Create distributions of appropriate statistics and compare their test data to see how unusual they are

- Invent statistics that accomplish particular goals (e.g., to assess whether a die is unfair)

- Begin to connect invented, nonparametric tests with their traditional counterparts

Our Approach to Inference

We will try to be as experiential as possible in these activities, letting students construct as much of their own understanding as we can. We will generate distributions by simulating them; probabilities will be experimental rather than theoretical; and, most important, students will use statistics they design rather than picking one from an approved list.

We do not think that *z, t,* and chi-square are bad—by no means. Instead, we believe that by moving more slowly and less abstractly, some students will come to understand what those powerful tools mean in a way they did not before.

In the simulation activities, students collect data in the real world and use simulation to do inference. In each activity, making an inference has five steps:

1. First decide on a statistic that describes your data, especially one that shows how unusual your data are. This is the *test statistic.*

2. Then make a collection that simulates the null hypothesis. The data should have the same form as your real data—the same attributes, for example—but simulate a condition in which you know precisely what is going on (usually nothing). This collection will include some randomness, provided (for example) through random numbers or sampling. The key point is to make the null hypothesis real; students will compare their data to it directly.

3. Compute the same statistic in the "null" collection as you did in your data.

4. Collect these null statistics repeatedly. The randomness in the null hypothesis' definition will vary the cases, and therefore the statistic, appropriately. This process will generate a distribution of the statistic.

5. Compare the test statistic to that distribution. If it's far outside the distribution, your data are unlikely to arise from the null hypothesis, and you should reject it. If the test statistic looks pretty typical, you can't reject the null.

Here's an example. We wonder whether the average student carries less than $1.00 in change. So we choose five students at random and ask them to count the change in their pockets. The amounts are 0.45, 0.37, 1.10, 0.80, and 0.03 (the mean is 0.55; the standard deviation, using $n - 1$, is 0.41). We decide on the mean as a test statistic (Step 1). Next, we make a collection of five random amounts drawn from a population with a mean of 1.00 and a standard deviation of 0.41 (Step 2). We compute the mean of those amounts (Step 3), then repeat Steps 1 and 2 a hundred times, collecting the means (Step 4) to make a distribution. Finally (Step 5), we see how many of those are 0.55 or less. See the results on the following pages.

Only 2 of the 100 means are as small as 0.55, so we feel justified in concluding that on the average, students carry less than $1.00 in change.

We don't use the phrase "null hypothesis" in the student materials until late in *Orbital Express.* You may want to introduce it earlier, depending on student experience.

The reasoning is somewhat different for a confidence interval activity such as *Pennies and Polling,* but the principles are the same.

This example is *parametric.* Like many traditional tests, it uses parameters of the sample (its mean and standard deviation) to help make the distribution and test, and it assumes that the parent distribution is normal. That isn't necessary; in fact, the activities in this chapter are mostly nonparametric and do not use the normal distribution.

Here's a picture of the simulation with labels so you can see what it looks like in Fathom.

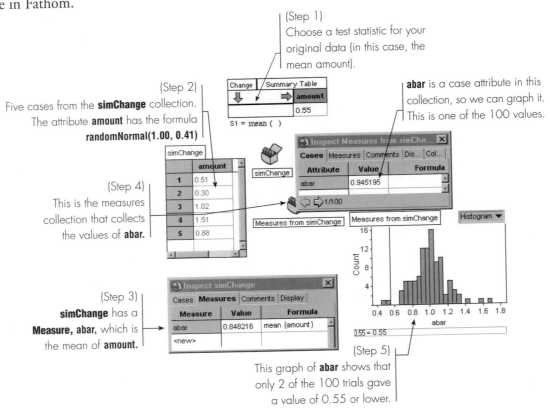

(Step 1)
Choose a test statistic for your original data (in this case, the mean amount).

(Step 2)
Five cases from the **simChange** collection. The attribute **amount** has the formula **randomNormal(1.00, 0.41)**

abar is a case attribute in this collection, so we can graph it. This is one of the 100 values.

(Step 4)
This is the measures collection that collects the values of **abar**.

(Step 3)
simChange has a **Measure, abar**, which is the mean of **amount**.

(Step 5)
This graph of **abar** shows that only 2 of the 100 trials gave a value of 0.55 or lower.

Making Formulas for the Statistic

Students may need help—all the way from understanding that a *statistic* is a single number that represents the sample to the mechanics of teaching Fathom how to calculate that number. Here are some examples of formulas, some of which work and some of which don't.

These work for measures:

This calculates the mean of **height**. (The **mean( )** function would work just as well.)

This adds **p** (a slider value) to the interquartile range.

These don't:

This generates an error. Since **height** is different for every case, it cannot give a single value for the measure.

This does not give an error, but it may not be what you want for a statistic since it always has the same value.

We use measures to compute statistics for two reasons: First, they apply to the collection as a whole rather than to individual cases. Second, they are the ones collected by the **Measures...** collections, so we can make distributions out of them.

Formulas can be more complex. Here's one a student might invent to measure spread. Note that you can use Fathom's functions on the results of calculations:

The vertical bars signify absolute value, so this is the mean of the absolute differences between the **height**s and their mean.

Sometimes an **if( )** or **switch( )** function is just what you need. This function uses different **height** standards for males and females.

Formulas can become much more elaborate. Don't forget that if a formula gets too hairy, you can break it down and use more than one attribute to compute what you need.

Using the Files

Each of the major activities in this chapter uses a file that's already set up, so students don't have to hook up all the collections and graphs. This means that you need to be careful; you don't want the class at 10 a.m. to start out with files altered by the class at 9 a.m.

Therefore, we advise you to keep these files *locked*. Students will be able to make changes in the documents they work with; but when they save their documents, they will be asked to save the file with a name of their own, e.g., **PaulAndJamie.**

Students should know, however, that there is nothing special about these files. They could make such files themselves. In fact, a good assignment after any of these activities is to have students study the files to see how they work.

Constructivist Dice

- Structured offline activity
- Data generated in simulation
- No student page

This is an example of hypothesis testing. Be sure to read *Our Approach to Inference* in the Chapter 10 Overview, page 257.

In this activity, we make our own dice. There's no reason to believe they are fair, especially since they aren't accurate cubes. But are they really *that* unfair—especially compared with real dice? What does "unfair" mean?

Collecting Data on "Unfair" Dice

Introduce the activity by explaining that we will make our own dice. Explain how to make them, then let each student do so. This can be done days in advance.

Then ask if the dice are fair. Students will say, "No." Ask how you would tell. After discussion, explain that we will start by rolling each die 30 times and recording the results. Students should do this in pairs, rolling 30 times for each of their dice. They should record the number of ones, twos, and so on that appear.

Ask if students think the dice are fair now. They probably still do not. Ask for evidence: What in their data convinces them that the dice are unfair (or fair, as the case may be)?

During this discussion, ask what you would see if you rolled a fair die. Students will say that each face should come up five times: we expect 5–5–5–5–5–5. Some may realize that this distribution will vary.

Explain that each pair will devise a way to calculate a *statistic*—a single number—that measures how unfair the die is. That number should be small if the die is close to fair, and larger the more unfair it is. Encourage students to come up with at least two different statistics. Share the various statistics in the class.

Choose one statistic and a set of data (from different students, if possible) to use as examples. Have the class calculate that statistic for the example data. Explain that this is called the *test statistic*. Ask if they think this die is fair. Ask how they know. Make sure students mention that this statistic is bigger than it would be for a fair die.

Comparing to Fair Dice

Ask (if necessary) if the faces of a fair die will always come up 5–5–5–5–5–5. Pass out fair dice and ask each student to roll his or her die 30 times and record the results. Then each student is to calculate the example statistic (whatever you chose above) for the fair die.

Discuss how to make a graph of this statistic. (What's its range? How should the numbers be binned, etc.?) Make a class graph (we've shown an example). Have all the students plot their fair dice. Note that each dot on the graph represents 30 rolls of a fair die.

Have students compare the original *test statistic* to the distribution. Is it far out on the tail, or is it in the pack? Mark the position of the test statistic clearly on the distribution. Discuss whether this is evidence that the die is unfair.

Topic
hypothesis testing (eventually, chi-square)

Materials
marker
dice
class graph (blank transparency or blackboard is fine)
materials for making our own dice (clay or wood will work)

Note: The most common statistic is the sum of the absolute differences from what we expect in a fair die.

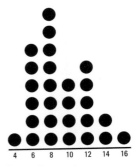

Denise's statistic

Students can also compute the statistics for their own dice and see where their dice lie relative to the class distribution for fair dice.

Constructivist Dice

Ask, based on the data that have been collected, what the probability is that a fair die would have a statistic at least as unfair as (i.e., greater than or equal to) the test statistic. Make sure students see that they should divide the number of cases in the "tail" by the total number to compute this probability.

Finally, ask whether students think that probability is low enough to convince them that the die is not fair. This completes the hypothesis test.

A more conservative ratio for probability—for more sophisticated students—is the number greater than or equal to the test statistic *plus 1* divided by the population *plus 1*. That is, it includes the test die as a candidate for fairness.

Likely Results

Quite uncubical dice can give results consistent with fairness. This should disturb students who are paying attention.

What's Important Here

- We assess our test situation by comparing it to a *distribution* of measures generated by a fair die. The fair die represents the null hypothesis—there's nothing unusual going on.

- Variability: One key understanding is that fair dice vary quite a bit. The expected distribution, 5–5–5–5–5–5, is unusual. And even a fair die often looks unfair in a set of 30 rolls.

- Be clear that the probability we get (often called the *P*-value) is the chance that a fair die would give a result like this, *not* the probability that our die is fair.

That is, when students said the dice were unfair, they were right. But our data—with only 30 rolls—may not be enough for us to reject that null hypothesis.

Making the Dice

There are a number of ways to create your own dice for this activity. Here are two:

- From an art supply store, get clay that will harden when baked. Have students mold their dice, making the dots with a toothpick or pencil point. This clay comes in many terrific colors; perhaps you could bake it in a food lab at school.

- Cut (or have someone cut) wood into strips whose cross section is not quite square. Then let students cut not-quite-cubes off the ends of these strips with hand saws. (Get help supervising students. Wood shop is one possibility.) Make the dots with permanent markers.

Don't have a food lab nearby? We know a teacher who brings a toaster oven to class and bakes the dice right there.

Always be careful about safety. Supervise any activity in which students could get hurt. And whatever scheme you choose, practice first!

Constructivist Dice

Chi-Square Connection

These data are appropriate for a chi-square goodness-of-fit test. The expected value for each possible number is 5; if x_i is the number of times the number i came up, calculate chi-square by adding

$$\chi^2 = \sum \frac{(observed - expected)^2}{expected}$$

$$= \sum_{i=1}^{6} \frac{(x_i - 5)^2}{5}, \; 5 \text{ df (degrees of freedom)}$$

For example, if the data were 7–4–5–3–10–1, you'd get

$$\chi^2 = \frac{(7-5)^2}{5} + \frac{(4-5)^2}{5} + \frac{(5-5)^2}{5} + \frac{(3-5)^2}{5} + \frac{(10-5)^2}{5} + \frac{(1-5)^2}{5}$$

$$\chi^2 = \frac{4}{5} + \frac{1}{5} + \frac{0}{5} + \frac{4}{5} + \frac{25}{5} + \frac{16}{5} = \frac{50}{5} = 10.0.$$

Is a chi-square of 10.0 unusual for 5 degrees of freedom? You can check a statistical calculator or look up critical P-values—the probabilities—in a table. You'll get a value for P between .05 and .10, so the set of rolls looks unusual, but you wouldn't bet the farm that the die is unfair.

On the other hand, if you got the same result again, and combined the samples, you'd have 14–8–10–6–20–2, which gives a chi-square of 20.0, where P is about .00125. Definitely suspicious.

Constructivist Dice Online

- Structured computer activity
- Data from simulation and preceding activity
- Student pages 264–265
- Intermediate, complex features

Assuming students have done the offline activity *Constructivist Dice,* this will be their second time through the logic of the hypothesis test in this context.

The hard part of this online phase will probably be writing the formula for the measure. We have tried, in our setup, to anticipate the measures students are most likely to invent. The **fair dice** collection already has six useful measures defined—**count_1**, **count_2**, etc.,—that count how many of each number appeared. It also has **howUnfair**, which is a placeholder for the one they will invent.

So, for example, if (as is likely) a student decided to add the absolute differences between the counts and 5 (the expected value for the count in 30 rolls), the student would use

$|count\_1 - 5| + |count\_2 - 5| + |count\_3 - 5| + |count\_4 - 5| + |count\_5 - 5| + |count\_6 - 5|.$

Discussion Question

↻ When we have a distribution of statistics, and we compare it to the test statistic, why do we calculate the proportion of that distribution which is greater than *or equal to* the test statistic and use that as our *P*-value, instead of simply greater than? (If we're making the case that our test statistic is unusual, it's only fair to include the "equal" ones in the proportion. That is, they "count" as being examples of naturally-occurring "that extreme" trials in the fair-dice situation.)

Extensions

Many additional problems appear on pages 296–297.

Constructivist Dice Online

Name(s): _____

The problem is to tell whether the die you made is fair. You'll take your data from *Constructivist Dice* (written on paper) and the measure you invented, and have the computer do a lot of the work for you. The file is already set up with 30 fair die rolls.

The plan is this:

- Tell Fathom how to compute your measure for the 30 die rolls.

- Have Fathom roll the dice and calculate the measure many times, recording the measure each time and collecting it so we can see its distribution.

- Compare that distribution to the measure for your own die to see whether your die is typical of fair dice or unusual.

1. First describe your measure and write its value for your test die.

2. Open the document **ConstructivistDice.** You'll see a collection called **fair dice** with 30 fair dice in it.

3. Press **CTRL-Y** (Windows) or **⌘-Y** (Mac) to rerandomize the dice. You can see their values change.

4. Double-click the **fair dice...** collection to open its inspector. Click the **Measures** tab to bring up that pane. You can see that we have already defined a statistic called **howUnfair.**

5. Currently, **howUnfair** is defined as zero. Double-click in the **Formula** column. Enter the formula for your measure. You may use **count_1**, **count_2**, etc., in your formula, and any of the functions you can see in the editor (especially under *statistics*). Close the formula editor when you're finished. Write your formula here.

6. Check the formula: In the space below, write one set of fair dice data and calculate the value of **howUnfair** by hand. Compare it to the calculated value that appears in the inspector.

Prerequisite
Constructivist Dice

You need
data from *Constructivist Dice* (30 rolls)
the measure you decided on

You need to know how to
open a file
write formulas
make graphs

You'll learn
to use the collection inspector
about sampling and resampling
about assessing likelihood

If the dice do not rerandomize, make sure that either (1) the **fair dice** collection is selected or (2) no components are selected.

7. What's the value of your measure for more sets of 30 fair dice? Press repeatedly **CTRL-Y** (Windows) or ⌘**-Y** (Mac) to get 10 values for your measure from different sets of random dice. Write them here.

8. Compare those 10 values from fair dice to the value of your measure for your test die. What's your first impression: Is your die fair or not? Why?

9. Now we'll collect many samples of 30 dice. We'll use a *measures collection*. Select the **fair dice. . .** collection and choose **Collect Measures** from the **Analyze** menu. A new collection, **Measures from fair dice,** appears.

10. Make a case table for the new collection. You'll see five values for **howUnfair.** (By default, Fathom collects five measures.)

11. We want more sets of 30. Open the inspector for **Measures from fair dice.**

12. Press the **Collect Measures** tab to go to the last pane in the inspector. Uncheck the boxes labeled **Animation on** and **Empty this collection first,** as shown. Then click **Collect More Measures.** Fathom collects data from five more sets of rolls—and because we unchecked that box, it adds them to the existing data file.

13. Collect more measures until you have at least 100 in your **Measures...** collection. Now make a histogram of **howUnfair** and sketch it here.

14. We'd like to see where our test statistic appears in the distribution. Select the graph and choose **Plot Value** from the **Graph** menu. Use the number from the *Constructivist Dice* offline activity (a constant) for the formula. A line appears. Include it in your sketch in Step 13.

Not all formulas need variables. This one is a constant.

15. Figure out how many samples in the graph of **howUnfair** are equal to or more extreme than your test value. Calculate a percentage. What percentage of the samples are at least that extreme? Tell how many and describe the way you counted them.

One strategy is to drag a histogram bar edge to coincide with the line. Then select the bars to the right of the line. When you point at the measures collection, the number of selected points appears in the status bar at the bottom of the window.

16. What do you think? Based on your original 30 rolls, and simulating thousands of fair dice, do you think your die is substantially different from a fair die?

Pennies and Polling

- Structured offline activity
- Data from materials
- No student page
- Guided, complex features

How well does a sample reflect the population? This activity lays the groundwork for exploring the confidence interval of a proportion; the online activity that follows develops it further.

We pretend that a population of 3000 pennies is really a population of voters, and ask whether Proposition 1994 will pass. Every penny whose date is 1994 or later votes for the proposition; all others vote against it. Of course, we don't want to look at all 3000 pennies—so we poll. We take a sample.

Preparation

Besides collecting the materials and making the class graph, be sure that the pennies are well mixed. Also, everywhere that we have "1994" in this handout, you should substitute an appropriate year (your guess of the pennies' median) to make the poll close.

And about the number of pennies: The $30.00 is not vital, but you do need a large number of pennies—large enough that the students don't run out of them and large enough that we can see it's impractical to count them all. We have also ignored the problem that we will be sampling *without* replacement, so the samples are not independent of one another. The more pennies you have to draw from, the less of a problem this is.

Taking the Samples

Each student gets a small cup containing 50 pennies. If there are not exactly 50, the student should put the extras back or take a few more—without looking at the dates, of course.

Each student

1. Counts the number, out of the 50 voters sampled, who vote for Proposition 1994 (i.e., are pennies from 1994 or later)
2. Calculates the percentage of voters in her or his sample who are for the proposition
3. Estimates a range of percentages so that he or she is *pretty sure* that the percentage from the whole population falls within the range
4. Talks with a partner about what she or he means by "pretty sure"

Discussion: Considering the "Informal" Confidence Interval

Ask the class how big their ranges are. Ask what "pretty sure" means. There may be some confusion. You can give concrete examples: How low could the proportion be? Could it be zero? Or even really small? What's the (informal) chance that almost all the pennies left in the bowl were minted earlier than 1994? (Very small.) On the other hand, what's the chance that the bowl's percentage is exactly the same as yours? (Also very small.) We will now get more precise about what "pretty sure" means.

If you were really taking a poll, you'd want to know how accurate your poll was. If we ignore bias, there's still chance error. We need a way to estimate what that is. Now we'll explain how.

Topics

sampling
confidence interval for a proportion

Materials

$30.00 in pennies in a bowl
small cups
dots or markers
class graph (one-inch chart paper is fine, marked so that each column represents 2%)

Factoid! Pennies made after 1982 weigh 2.5 grams each. The relevance is that 3000 pennies weigh 7500 grams, or 16.5 pounds—more than four full half-gallon milk cartons, though 3000 pennies fit in one.

You might begin by showing a transparency of a newspaper report of a poll with the confidence interval. Ask: What does this mean? Where do they get the numbers? Then explain that that's what this activity is all about.

Brainstorm the ways a poll—or this simulation—can give you a "wrong" answer. (Two ways: through bias—we only asked at the shopping center, or we just put in a roll of new pennies at the top—and through chance error. There may be many interesting sources of bias.)

Data in Depth
© 2001 Key Curriculum Press

Pennies and Polling

Graphing the Distribution

5. Each student places a dot on the class graph (which you have prepared), representing the percentage in his or her sample that will vote "yes."

Now you have a class graph of all the proportions. Ask the class, "Looking at this graph, in what range are you pretty sure the voter percentage is now?" (For ours, something like 48–54%.) It's probably tighter than their individual ranges.

"We can make a better estimate because we're looking at so many pennies. But here's how we can measure our uncertainty when we have only one sample . . ."

With the class to help you, look at the completed graph and determine the interval where the middle 90% (80% if you have fewer than 20 samples) of the dots (samples) reside.

6. Determine a 90% "percentile interval" based on the class graph. Then divide its full width by 2 to get a half-width.

That half-width is what each student could have attached to his or her original sample (if it had been done in isolation).

7. Each student computes the 90% interval for his or her own sample. It should be a range, from the student's percentage minus the class half-width to the student's percentage plus the class half-width. For example, if the class graph had a 90% range of (40%, 64%) (half-width 12%) and your sample was 56%, your 90% interval is (44%, 68%)—a range of 24% *centered* on your sample value.

Students formally studying statistics need to understand that the interval we have just made is an approximation to the confidence interval. Check the background information on page 269.

Approximate or no, the graph and the pennies can give students a good feel for the fact that the procedure yields intervals that fail to cover the population value 10% of the time.

8. Ask students how many of them think their individual ranges contain the true population percentage.

9. Hope for an outlier in order to impress upon students that such a result was just due to chance error and not from having done something wrong. The outlier happened to be in the 10% of the time that our estimate messes up.

Stress this: If you have only your own sample, that sample percentage is your best guess as to the percentage of people who will vote yes. Yet you know your sample may not have *exactly* the same proportion as the whole population. This activity is about how to figure out the likely range in which the "true" (population) percentage falls.

To determine a 90% interval, count inward 5% from each end. The middle 90% is *completely contained* in the interval, as in the picture below. Probably no more than one point on each end will fall outside the interval. Be sure the whole class got the full-width the same. (We choose 90% because it's easy to calculate by hand. Ninety-five percent is traditional, but you can make an interval with any percentage, even though popular poll reports don't mention it.)

Consider drawing the range on a transparency right over the dots. Label where the students think the true population proportion is (it should be a small range, not a precise number) on the same transparency. Then you can slide the range back and forth over the graph to show the range for any proportion and how it overlaps the likely true proportion from almost all the dots.

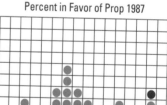

Percent in Favor of Prop 1987

Pennies and Polling

Extension: Making a Better Estimate

What could we do to make a better estimate? Of course, we could ask more people. Have students combine their numbers with their partners' (so they have 100) and quickly make another class graph. Is it narrower? You bet!

The Formula

The orthodox formula for a confidence interval of a proportion works if the sample size is large enough, where that size depends on how close P is to 0 or 1. In this case, it works fine. Here's the formula:

$$C.I. = \hat{p} \pm z^* \sqrt{\frac{\hat{p}(1 - \hat{p})}{n}}$$

where $\hat{p}$ is the sample proportion, n is the sample size, and z^* is the critical value from the standard normal distribution—1.96 for a 95% interval. For 50 pennies and a P near 50%, the interval is about ±14%.

If you have enough groups (or enough time and pennies), you can make samples of size 200, which should have half the width of the $n = 50$ case. Or you can save that work for the computer.

Help! Confidence Intervals!

There is no more confusing topic in beginning statistics than confidence intervals. Even well-prepared AP statistics teachers may get befuddled. This may be a different approach than you're used to; with topics like this, variety helps. Briefly:

Scheaffer et al., in *Activity-Based Statistics,* give an exceptionally well-rounded treatment of this subject.

For any population with true proportion p, from which you take samples of size n, you can find a range of proportions where the vast majority (the central 95%, for example) of these samples lie. Let's call these samples *plausible* samples. You can calculate (or simulate to find) the endpoint-proportions of this range. Let's call them MinPlausible(p) and MaxPlausible(p)—for the minimum and maximum plausible sample proportions.

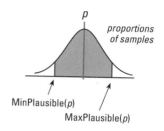

Now suppose we have a sample from a population where we don't know p. The sample has proportion $\hat{p}$. We define the confidence interval thus: It is the range of population proportions p for which $\hat{p}$ is plausible. That is, the lower bound of the interval is a proportion p_L such that MaxPlausible(p_L) = $\hat{p}$. Similarly, the upper bound p_U is where MinPlausible(p_U) = $\hat{p}$. This procedure, however tortured, is correct: Following it captures the true population proportion 95% of the time. Formulas (pages 268 and 275) and the shortcut from *Pennies and Polling Online II* (page 273) are approximations.

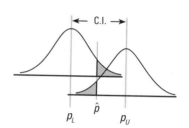

Why Is This Hard?

One problem is the way "official" confidence intervals are defined. Like hypothesis tests, they're subjunctive: *A confidence interval measures confidence in a process. We define that process so that if we were to draw a large number of samples and calculate the confidence interval for each, 95% (or the percentage you specify) of those intervals would contain the true value for the population.*

This is *not* the same as saying *There is a 95% chance that the true value is in our interval.* Why not? Since the true value is already determined—though unknown—you cannot ask probability questions of it. Either it's in the interval or it isn't; there's no chance involved in the formal sense, even though, subjectively, it does not "feel" determined.

Then, when you try to wrestle with what makes a confidence interval work, you encounter a "figure-ground" problem. The definition above (in italics) is all about taking multiple *samples* from a single, unknown *population.* Yet we use the interval to define a range of reasonable *population* values— derived from a single known *sample.* It's confusing, so we explain it by taking multiple samples from multiple *hypothetical* populations, which, while correct, can confuse students all the more.

But What's Really Important?

The tumult about confidence intervals is important for AP or college statistics. But the most important issue for everyone is this: When you produce an estimate of some parameter—a proportion, a mean, an interquartile range, whatever—for a population based on a sample, your estimate is probably wrong due to chance error. Such an estimate is misleading unless you figure out how big that error is likely to be.

Pennies and Polling Online

- Structured computer activity
- Data generated in simulation and from offline
- Student pages 271–274
- Guided, complex features

Suppose that in *Pennies and Polling* 54% of a sample favored the proposition. Does that mean the proposition will pass? It's certainly possible that fewer than half will vote yes, even though our sample has 54% in favor.

Pennies and Polling investigated this by looking at many samples from the real (unknown-proportion) population. But remember: In real life, we get one sample. So here we will take many simulated samples from known populations and compare those proportions to what we see in our single sample. (One theoretical approach is to make calculations based on the Binomial Theorem. We won't do that here.)

Prerequisite
Pennies and Polling (offline)

Topic
confidence interval for a proportion

Materials
handout
each group needs a fresh copy of **PenniesAndPolling**

Getting Oriented

Before they go to the computers, have students look at the screen shot on their handouts. It will resemble what they'll see on the screen. Be sure they understand percentiles. (They can read the margin paragraph to remind them, though it may not be enough.) These questions may orient them:

1. What percentage of the people really favor the measure? (50%.)
2. How many people are in the poll? (50.)
3. What does the histogram represent? (The distribution of 100 simulated poll results from a population in which 50% favor Proposition 1994.)
4. Ninety percent of the time, with this value for *p*, we'd get results between about 38% and 63%. How can you tell? (The 5th and 95th percentiles of **result** are 38 and 63. That means that the middle 90% of the simulated polls are in that interval.)

During the activity, make sure that students understand what we mean by *plausible*. If the true population is 50% in favor, it's *plausible* (at the 90% level) to get any poll result between about 38% and 63%. This also means that a poll with more than 63% in favor is convincing evidence that the actual percentage is greater than 50%.

The graph students make by hand (page 272) should look something like the one shown here. The confidence interval is the region where the points are up at "yes." There may be some overlap; you can discuss how that can be.

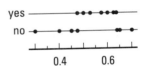

Tech Notes

- Be sure students do not confuse the **poll** collection—a single poll of 50 people—with the **Measures from poll** collection—a collection of the results from repeated (hypothetical) polling.

- Some students may need help collecting results from repeated polling. First they have to set a value for **p** on the slider. If they type it, they must press **ENTER** to ensure that the new number "gets in." Then they have to tell Fathom to collect the 100 new polls. They can click the **Collect More Measures** button on the measures collection itself, or open the inspector for the collection, go to the **Collect Measures** pane, and click **Collect More Measures.**

Under the hood: The **results** attribute is defined as a measure in **poll**. It converts to a case (normal) attribute as part of the "measures" process.

The collection has to be "open"— not iconified—for the **Collect More Measures** button to show.

Pennies and Polling Online I

Name(s): _____

In this activity, you'll use a simulation of taking a poll. In this simulation, you control the true proportion of "yes" voters with the slider named **p**. In reality, we don't know that proportion. We'll use this setup to see which values of that proportion make sense, given your poll results.

1. What percentage of people favored Proposition 1994 when you did your poll in class? Write that number here.

2. Open **PenniesAndPolling.** The window will look something like the one shown here.

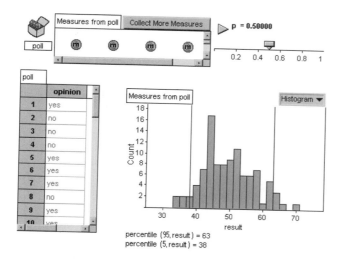

Percentiles

The 5th percentile of the result attribute is the value for which only 5% of the data is lower. That is, if the population is really split 50-50 ($p = .500$) and you take polls of 50 people, you'll get a result of 38% or lower 5% of the time.

Similarly, you'll get a result of 63% or more only 5% of the time—because that's the 95th percentile.

There are two collections: **poll,** which contains 50 opinions (either **yes** or **no**), and **Measures from poll,** which contains the results (the percentage who said **yes**) from each of 100 polls. You can see a case table of the opinions from one poll and a histogram of the percentages from the 100 polls. The histogram shows the 5th and 95th percentiles for **result**. The slider, **p**, controls the true proportion of people who favor Proposition 1994.

To use this simulation, change the value of **p** and then take a new set of samples. Just move the slider to the value you want (or type the value there and press **ENTER**) and click the **Collect More Measures** button in the **Measures** collection.

3. Look at the picture in Step 2. Is your poll a plausible result if exactly 50% of the population favor Proposition 1994? Explain why or why not.

4. Change the value of **p** and take new sets of samples. Describe, qualitatively, the way the distribution of poll **results** changes as you change **p**.

5. Work with your partner to find the 5th-percentile and 95th-percentile limits for *p* = 20%, 30%, and so on, all the way to 80%. A row for **p** = 0 is already filled in. For each value of *p*,

   • Set the slider for **p** to the value.

   • Collect a new set of measures (**results**).

   • Enter the percentile values from the histogram in the table below.

   • Enter "yes" or "no" in the third column, depending on whether your polled value falls between the 5th and 95th percentiles.

If *p* =	5th percentile of result	95th percentile of result	Our poll is in the interval
.00	0	0	no
.20			
.30			
.40			
.50			
.60			
.70			
.80			

6. Fill in the graph below. Make one point for each row in the table above. The point for (0, no) is already filled in.

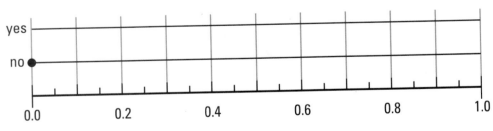

7. Figure out, as accurately as possible, where the points change from **no** to **yes** and back again. Probe in-between values for **p** such as 35%, as necessary. Enter them in the table and on the graph.

8. For which values of **p** are your poll results plausible? Explain. (Your response should be two numbers: a lower and an upper bound. This is a *confidence interval*.)

9. Ideally, your results should be in the middle of the interval. Then you can write your results as *something ± something else*. Do that here.

Data in Depth
© 2001 Key Curriculum Press

Pennies and Polling Online II

Name(s): _____

A Shortcut

You need

PenniesAndPolling

1. Open **PenniesAndPolling** (a fresh copy is fine).
2. Set **p** to the value of your poll results when you did *Pennies and Polling*. Click **Collect More Measures** again. What are the values for the 5th and 95th percentiles?

3. They ought to be close to the numbers in the confidence interval you found in *Pennies and Polling Online I*. Are they? Repeat the process a few times.

4. Here's a sophisticated issue: Why is the range we just obtained so close to the one we got by checking lots of different values for **p** and making our "yes-no" graph? Discuss this with your partner and try to explain it.

To put it another way, why are we allowed to assume that the population has the percentage we polled?

How Much Confidence?

The confidence interval we had in *Pennies and Polling Online I* is called a 90% confidence interval because at each value of *p*, the range of plausible values for **result** was the one that contained 90% of the samples—from the 5th to the 95th percentile.

5. Traditionally, researchers most often use a 95% confidence interval. What percentiles should you use?

6. Change the formulas in the histogram (double-click them to open the formula editor) so that you get those percentiles.

7. Figure out the 95% confidence interval about your poll results. (You may use the shortcut described above.) Write down the interval.

8. Is the 95% confidence interval larger or smaller than the 90% interval? Explain why.

Effect of Sample Size

Suppose you polled more than 50 people. What effect would that have on your confidence interval?

9. Increase the number of cases in the **poll** collection to 100. Compute the 95% confidence interval (using the shortcut) for your poll results here.

10. Complete the table below.

Number polled	95% confidence interval	Width of interval
50		
100		
200		
400		
1000		
2000		

11. Explain why the width of the interval gets smaller as the number polled increases.

Going Further

1. Enter the data from the table on page 272 into Fathom. Take additional data if you need them (all with 50 people polled). Does the width of the 90% interval change with the population proportion, **p**? If so, how? And why? (If you know the formula, use it by all means.)

2. A typical national poll has a "margin of error" of 3%. Usually this is the half-width of a 95% confidence interval. How many people do you think they had to poll to get that small a confidence interval?

3. Edvard says, "In my poll about opinions on the economy, 42% of the people said it was great. The 95% confidence interval was from 36% to 48%." Assuming Edvard did everything right, describe in words, as clearly as you can, what his confidence interval really means. The answer is *not* "There is a 95% chance that the true number of people who think the economy is great is between 36% and 48%."

4. Confidence interval calculations (like so much in statistics) depend on the sample's being a simple random sample of the population to be studied. Give an example showing how that could go wrong and what effect it would have on the confidence interval.

5. Perform a poll of 50 people and figure out its confidence interval.

Pennies and Polling III

- Open-ended computer activities
- Data generated in simulation
- No student page
- Independent, complex features

There is no student page for these problems and investigations. You may want to assign different problems to different groups and have them report to the class; doing *all* of these is a lot of work! You may use the Sonata form (see page xxii) for the assignments; if so, be sure that students make conjectures before they go to the computers.

Effect of Population Percentage

Set up the file with **p = .500**. Keep the poll size at 50, but increase the number of polls to 1000 (honest!). (Do this in the inspector for the **Measures from poll** collection—in the **Collect Measures** pane.) Compute a 90% confidence interval using the shortcut in *Pennies and Polling II*. (That is, find the distance between the 5th and 95th percentiles of the **results**.)

Now change *P* systematically. Record the confidence intervals you get. You can use any number between 0.0 and about 1.0.

What is the relationship between the population percentage *P* and the width of the confidence interval? Make a graph of your data (using Fathom).

Can you explain the relationship? Why is it the way it is?

If students know how to use the built-in analyses, they can use a **Measures...** collection to record the confidence intervals. We recommend this "automation" for students with more experience.

Effect of the Number of Sets

This is the most subtle of these assignments.

Set up the file with **p = .500** and leave the sample size at 50 and the number of polls at 100. Set up to find the 90% confidence interval. (This is how the file should open if it hasn't been changed.)

Now change the number of polls systematically by changing the number in the inspector (it's in the **Collect Measures** pane). You can use any number between 1 and about 10,000—you just may have to wait a while.

How does the value of that number affect what happens in the display? Can you explain that?

What's the Formula?

The official formula for the 95% confidence interval is

$$CI = \hat{p} \pm 1.96 \sqrt{\frac{\hat{p}(1 - \hat{p})}{n}}$$

where $\hat{p}$ is the sample proportion and n is the number in the sample. Compare what this formula tells you with the results you get through simulation. How do the numbers compare? Which is easier? Which is more understandable? Answers will vary!

The 1.96 is the number of standard deviations you go out on a normal curve to enclose 95% of the population. The corresponding number for a 90% interval is 1.64.

Orbital Express

- Structured offline activity
- Data from measurement
- No student page

Like *Constructivist Dice* (page 260), this activity is about hypothesis testing. Students test two competing designs for orbital re-entry vehicles. The null hypothesis is that there is no difference; the analysis will see if we can reject that hypothesis.

We bring in the computer to help in *Orbital Express Online*, page 284.

What's Important Here

- Students develop a statistic that measures how much better one design is than the other.

- They come to understand that a measured difference could result from chance variation; they also see that many genuinely random patterns look quite skewed.

- They see that by shuffling the data between the designs repeatedly, they can assess how likely it is that any difference they see is due to chance.

Materials and Preparation Notes

Be sure the paper is in similar-sized pieces (letter size is OK).

Cut the 3 × 5 cards into identically sized pieces, for instance into quarters. These will be shuffled, so it's important that they be the same size to make shuffling easier. Whole cards are too big. Each group will need at least 14 little cards; 20 is better.

About the paper. Paper towels and copier paper are so different that you may want to try something a little closer. Cheap, flimsy binder paper or scratch newsprint works well when contrasted with a crisp, strong copier paper. Ideally, some groups will get significant differences, but not so gross that there is no point in doing statistics.

Introducing the Activity

Describe this situation to the students:

> You work in the design and testing department for Orbital Express (OrbEx), the big delivery company. The company has decided to start delivering packages by dropping them from orbit onto the customers' houses. They are testing two competing designs for the new re-entry vehicle. Your job here is simply to test the two designs and report which is better. (If students ask, tell them the two designs cost the same to build.)

> "Better" means that the package gets closer to the place where it's going.

Then show them the two designs. One is regular paper, wadded up into a ball. Another is a paper towel, also wadded up into a ball.

Topic

Comparing samples of continuous random variables from two groups (the two-sample *t*-test situation)

Materials

two kinds of paper, for example, copy paper and paper towels

3 × 5 cards

tape measures at least 5 ft (130 cm) long

coins or markers (one per group)

masking tape

paper, pencils, marking pens

Location Needs

Some place (indoors, no wind) where students can drop wadded-up balls of paper. Standing and dropping is OK, but not as much fun as using stairwells or balconies. If you use outdoor bleachers, you'll need different re-entry vehicles to account for the wind.

Orbital Express

You'll test these by dropping them from orbit and measuring (hold up tape measure) how far they land from the place where they're supposed to go. The target is this penny (or whatever), and the orbit is in the stairwell (or wherever).

Discuss this briefly with the students and answer questions. Many issues will not arise until you're doing the drops. These you have to address now:

- Each group will need to keep a recording sheet.
- Each group will need to use each design more than once. Get students to agree on a reasonably small number. Seven per design (14 total) is good because it's easy to find the median and you can do a box plot easily if you decide to.
- Groups will collect data and then come back to analyze it. (You may, if you wish, ask students to brainstorm *briefly* how they plan to do that.)

The Drop

Go to the place where the students will do their drops and show the setup. They collect their data. They'll ask whether bounces count. They do. The distance is from the marker to where the wad of paper comes to rest, not where it first hits. (People aren't going to *catch* packages falling from orbit; they'll wait until the packages stop, then walk out and pick them up.)

Data Analysis

Each group now has 14 data points, 7 for each design.

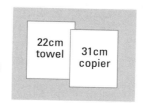

1. Have each group write the data values (with the designs) on the little cards.
2. Have the groups stretch their tape measures on a table or floor (possibly taping them down) and have them set the cards opposite the measurements; one design on one side of the tape, the other on the other:

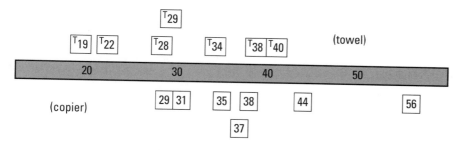

3. Ask the groups to decide which is the better design (this will be really quick) and *how they can tell* which is better.
4. Next, ask each group to come up with a way to calculate a *statistic*—a single number—that describes how much better one design is than the other (e.g., the difference of means). The statistic should be *small* if the two papers are *alike* and *larger* the more *different* they are.

Orbital Express

5. Have students share their statistics and the values they get for their test data. (This value is called the *test statistic*.) Discuss the way the procedures for calculating statistics do or do not fit the small/large rule on the preceding page.

6. Ask students whether they think their statistic shows that there really is a difference between the two papers. If it does, how small would it have to be before you were no longer convinced? If it does not show a real difference, how big would it have to be before you were convinced?

One of the points of this activity is that random variation is more varied than we expect. Consider recording these informal "critical values" so you can compare them to the distribution later.

Data Analysis, Continued: The Shuffle

Is the difference "real" or just due to chance?

If there were no relation between the design and the distance—if the designs were really the same—there would still be a difference when you did the experiment. There's some random variation. The difference of means, for example, won't always be zero. How much difference do we expect—according to the statistic? We don't know, so here's how we find out:

1. Groups take the cards and shuffle them. They deal them out, seven to one side of the tape, seven to the other. Now—because of the shuffle—there is no relationship between side-of-tape and distance. So compute (and record) your "shuffled" statistic.

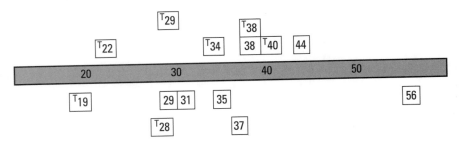

Students may be tempted simply to compute. Be sure students actually place the cards next to the measuring tape and have a chance to see one another's graphs. Again, variation is more than we might expect: Some of the scrambled graphs will be quite skewed.

2. Groups repeat this several times, recording the "shuffled" statistic each time. For example, if their statistic were difference of *medians,* our original data would produce an 8 (= 37 – 29), while these first scrambled data (above) would produce a 7 (= 38 – 31).

The question is whether groups think their original value (the test statistic) is unusual among the distribution of numbers they get when they shuffle. Discuss: How far out in the distribution would it have to be to be unusual? For some groups, the shuffled statistics will not exceed the test statistic in three tries. Ask: How many times would that have to happen to convince you that your difference was real?

Orbital Express

What's Next?

We hope students conclude that they need to shuffle many times to make a convincing assessment. For example, they might say they should do it 10 times and if they never get anything as big as their test statistic, they'll be thoroughly convinced.

But if it's within the distribution, it gets trickier. They may need more shuffles. And that gets boring. Fortunately, we have Fathom to help us. The next lesson has the computer do the shuffling.

Discussion Questions

➲ What variables affect how close to the target the vehicle lands? How did you try to control most of them?

➲ How did your group decide to measure the distance? What did you do about "interference"?

➲ Did anything surprise you in the shuffled data? What does the shuffling accomplish?

➲ (Stats students.) What is the null hypothesis in this situation? (The design of the vehicle is not related to the distance from where it lands from the target.)

Extension

Can you design a re-entry vehicle that's any better than the existing designs? Make a prototype and test it against the best "wad" design. Consider having a different researcher conduct the test. (Paper helicopters are pretty good in low-wind settings . . .)

Orbital Express Online

- Structured computer activity
- Data from measurement
- Student pages 284–286
- Intermediate, complex features

Before this session, students must have collected data in the *Orbital Express* offline activity, or from any other two-sample comparison situation. *Orbital Express* itself generates seven cases for each of two conditions (designs of the delivery vehicle)—in our examples, paper towel or copier paper.

Students have also designed a test statistic—a single number that describes how much better one design is than the other (officially, a measure of association). This number should be small if the designs perform the same and large if they're very different.

In this activity, students

- Enter their test data.
- Express their statistic using the formula editor.
- Collect many scrambled statistics in a measures collection.
- Compare their test statistic to the distribution of the test statistic from the scrambled collections.

Topic

Comparing samples of continuous random variables from two groups (the two-sample *t*-test situation)

Materials

data from *Orbital Express*

What's Important Here

- The first point is mechanical. How do you use Fathom to set up scrambling? We hope this becomes easy for students, but it seems complicated at first. This is their introduction.

- The second is more important: We use this activity to develop the central idea of creating a distribution of a statistic, given the null hypothesis introduced in the offline activity. That is, in order to see whether our statistic would likely arise by chance, we artificially make the two variables—**distance** and **paper** type—independent. We break their association through randomization (scrambling the values of one of the attributes).

Scrambling is a recognized nonparametric technique. It's called a randomized permutation test. If you used all 3432 different ways of assigning the papers, it wouldn't be randomized.

Overview of Scrambling

Scrambling was probably not part of your statistics education as a teacher. Your students have done it now with concrete materials: cards on a tape measure. Read the student materials yourself and use a computer to see how it will play out in Fathom. This section gives you additional background on the procedure and how it works on the computer.

There are two attributes, **paper** and **distance**. The values of **paper** will be (for example) **copier** and **towel**, so **paper** is a categorical attribute. The **distance**s will be continuous, measured in centimeters. Each case (each row in the table) will be *only one measurement*. Students should not put the two kinds of paper in the same row. Each collection will have 14 cases. That's the *source* collection.

Here's the key: If one design (**towel**, say) is really better than the other, there will be a relationship between the two attributes. For example, the median **distance** may be smaller for **towel** than it is for **copier**. Put another way, knowing what kind of paper is being used helps you predict the **distance**.

drop data		
	paper	**distance**
1	copier	45
2	copier	44
3	copier	49
4	copier	28
5	copier	47
6	copier	40
7	copier	34
8	towel	33
9	towel	32
10	towel	20
11	towel	30
12	towel	36
13	towel	28
14	towel	34

On the other hand, if there is no difference between the two designs, the two attributes are independent. Knowing the kind of **paper** doesn't help you predict **distance**. That's our *null hypothesis*. Even under the null hypothesis, though, one median will be smaller in a given sample of 14 drops. But that's because of chance variation, not because one design is really better.

Now suppose that the median **distance** for **towel** is 12 cm less than for **copier**. How do we figure out whether our data could be due to chance variation? Just as we did in *Constructivist Dice*, we make the null hypothesis real and generate the data many times to make a distribution. In this case, we make the null hypothesis real by forcing the two attributes to be independent—by shuffling one of them. When an attribute is randomly shuffled, *there is no relationship between its values and those of any other attribute.* There will still be chance variation, but that's what we want. By computing our measure (e.g., the difference of medians) for a slew of null-hypothesis situations, we can see how much the measure is likely to vary by chance.

Scrambling in Fathom

To do this in Fathom requires three collections. Here's a screen shot of what a document might look like near the end of the activity.

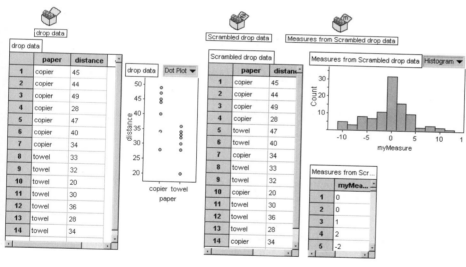

The original data are on the left. In the middle, you can see the same data with the first attribute, **paper**, scrambled. The scrambled collection itself is on the top in the middle.

At the right, you see the measures collection, **Measures from Scrambled drop data.** It has 100 values of **myMeasure**, which is the difference of medians. We defined **myMeasure** as a measure in the original **drop data** collection (it's 12). Then every time we scramble, the scrambled collection calculates its value for **myMeasure** and passes it on to the **Measures** collection, which graphs it.

Orbital Express Online

Help with Writing Formulas

Students will need help writing formulas. Listen carefully to their ideas and see if you can explain things in terms of the ideas they already have. Let them try their formulas and see what happens. Say "The computer won't understand that" instead of "That's wrong."

For example, when you ask what number they will use to describe how much better one is than the other, some students answer, "The mean." If you ask, "The mean of what?" they answer, "The mean of distance." Let them try it. The formula would be

mean(distance).

With that formula, every scramble gets the same statistic! What they really want is the *difference* of means:

mean(distance, paper = "copier") – mean(distance, paper = "towel").

Of course, we'd like to see many different formulas in the class. Here are some other ideas: difference of medians; ratio of medians; ratio of means; the mean of the **copier** paper only; and the number of **copier** measurements that are larger than the overall mean.

Don't forget the **Help** system. There's a topic called "How to define a statistic."

How It Will Probably Turn Out

For most groups, it will look as if the paper towel is better than the copier paper.

Nevertheless, when you do the test, you will probably get a *P*-value above the orthodox 5%; that is, it will look somewhat unlikely—but still plausible—that the difference could have arisen by chance. One solution is to get more samples.

Discussion Questions

Discuss the questions on the student pages. Here are additional issues you might raise:

- ⮑ Why do you suppose the directions always say "at least as extreme" instead of "more extreme"? That is, why are ties on the side against the effect's being real?

- ⮑ What makes a formula easy or hard to describe in Fathom? Does anyone have ideas for ways to express a hard one more easily?

- ⮑ (For statistics students.) Besides scrambling, how else could you test whether the two papers were different? How is that method similar to the one we used here? What are the important differences between the two techniques?

- ⮑ (Also for statistics students.) Shouldn't we be using a two-tailed test? (Probably.) How would you do that in Fathom?

Orbital Express Online

What's the Formula?

Traditionally, this is a situation in which you might do a two-sample t-test for the difference of means. You compute the t-statistic,

$$t = \frac{\overline{d}_c - \overline{d}_t}{\sqrt{\dfrac{s_c^2}{n_c} + \dfrac{s_t^2}{n_t}}},$$

where the d-bars are the sample mean distances, the s's are the sample standard deviations, and the n's are the numbers in each sample. The subscripts c and t denote **copier** and **towel**. Your P-value (two-tailed) is twice the probability that $T > t$, where T is drawn from a t-distribution with degrees of freedom equal to the smaller of the two n's minus one. (In this case, 6.)

This test assumes that both populations are normally distributed. That is not true in this case (since $d \geq 0$), but the test is not bad despite that.

If you get the t-distribution from tables or from a good calculator, you don't have to scramble at all. On the other hand, t is a perfectly good measure, so you could illustrate the distribution by entering it into Fathom for **myMeasure** and scrambling.

Orbital Express Online

Name(s): _____

You could shuffle and compute three or four times without getting too bored, but we'd like to do it at least 50 times. This requires a computer.

1. Start up Fathom and open the file **OrbEx.** It has an empty setup for doing this activity, so you don't have to build everything yourself (though you could). It has several different collections. We'll work with them all. Start with **drop data.** It has a case table already open, with 14 cases in it.

2. Enter the data. You should have 14 cases—7 with each kind of paper. Put the kind of paper (e.g., **towel**) under **paper** and the distance for each trial under **distance**.

3. Explore the data (e.g., make graphs) to see if they look right. Make a graph that compares the two types of paper. It should have **paper** on one axis and **distance** on the other. Sketch your graph here.

4. What does the graph suggest as to which paper is better?

5. Now we'll look at the second collection, called **Scrambled drop data.** Click the **Scramble Attribute Values Again** button in the collection.

6. Its case table should fill with data, but values from the first attribute should be scrambled. Make another graph (just like the first, but of the scrambled data) and sketch it below.

Entering Your Statistic

Now you'll enter the measure of association you developed—the formula that describes how different the two designs are. Because this difference is a property of the entire collection, and not of individual cases, it should be a *measure.*

7. Double-click your original "source" collection—**drop data**—the one with the real data in it. Its inspector appears. Click the **Measures** tab.

You need

   data from *Orbital Express*
   a statistical measure you've
      invented
   OrbEx

You need to know how to

   enter data
   make graphs
   write a formula
   use the inspector

You'll show that you can

   use scrambling
   use measures
   assess independence

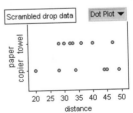

A sample graph of drop data. If your screen gets cluttered, you can hide the graph (or any component) by choosing **Hide Graph** from the **Display** menu.

The scrambled collection

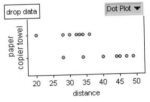

Scrambled data graph. Compare it to the original data in the illustration above. Same distances, different papers.

8. Make a new measure, called **myMeasure** (or whatever is appropriate). Press **ENTER** to accept the name.

9. Double-click in the formula box at the right of that attribute name's row. The formula editor appears. Enter your formula. Close the formula editor with **OK** when you're finished. Write the formula for your statistic here.

10. You can see the value of the statistic in the inspector. It's between the name and the formula cell. What is that value? (This is important. It tells how different your statistic says the two designs are.) Write it below and close the **drop data** inspector.

> If you have trouble getting your formula to work, look in the **Help** system under **Formulas.** Your teacher can help as well.

11. In the scrambled collection, click the **Scramble Attribute Values Again** button again and look in the scrambled collection. What's the value of **myMeasure** for that collection?

> Look in its inspector, in the **Measures** pane.

The Distribution of Your Statistic

12. We'll scramble many times, but we need a place to collect the **myMeasure**s. This will be a *measures collection* (since **myMeasure** is a measure of difference). Select **Scrambled drop data** and choose **Collect Measures** from the **Analyze** menu. A new collection appears, called **Measures from Scrambled drop data.**

> You'll have three collections: **drop data, Scrambled drop data,** and **Measures from Scrambled drop data.**

13. Make a case table for this new collection. You'll see five cases, with values for **myMeasure.**

14. Double-click the collection to open its inspector and go to the **Collect Measures** pane.

15. There you can tell it how many measures to collect. Make sure it says 100 and that animation is turned off. Then click **Collect More Measures.** You'll see 100 values of **myMeasure** appear—one from each scramble.

16. Make a new graph by dragging one off the shelf or choosing **Graph** from the **Insert** menu.

17. Graph the statistic **myMeasure** as a histogram. (Drag the name of the measure from the table to an axis of the graph, then choose **Histogram** from the popup menu. Then hide the case table if you need the space.) Sketch the histogram below.

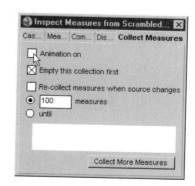

18. Describe what the three collections you have are for; that is, why do you need three?

Comparing to Your Original Data

This distribution shows how our statistic **myMeasure** is distributed for situations in which the kind of **paper** has no influence on the **distance**. It shows what it's like when the null hypothesis is true. We need to find out where our original test data stand in this distribution. Is it unusual (in which case it would not happen often if the null hypothesis were true) or right in the distribution (in which case it's consistent with the null hypothesis)? Fortunately, you wrote down your statistic in Step 10. But we want to see it on the graph.

19. Click on your measures graph—the distribution—to activate it.

20. Choose **Plot Value** (*not* **Plot Function**) from the **Graph** menu. The formula editor appears.

21. Enter the value of the statistic for your test data. Close the box. The value appears at the bottom of the graph, and a line appears showing where that value is in the distribution. Add that line to your sketch on the preceding page.

Now we want to find out how many of the 100 shuffles are at least as extreme as your source collection.

22. Drag the edge of a histogram bar so that it coincides with the line.

23. Select all the bins outside the line. (You can drag a rectangle to encompass or intersect them. Or you can shift-click to get more than one.)

24. Point at the measures collection (*not* **drop data**). Look in the status bar at the bottom of the window to see how many are selected. Write that number here, and compute a percentage.

25. Collect measures a few more times. What percentage are at least as extreme as your test statistic? Record your results below as percentages.

26. Overall, about what percentage of the scrambled collections are at least as extreme as your original data?

27. Do you think one design of a re-entry vehicle for Orbital Express is better than the other? Based on your data and analysis, explain why or why not.

The distribution of measures. We've used **Plot Value** to put a line at 12, our test statistic.

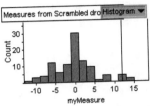

Changing the bins to match the **Plot Value** line.

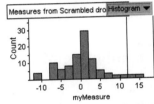

We select the cases equal to or more extreme than our test statistic . . .

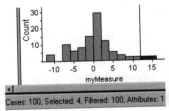

. . . and see how many are selected. In this case, we have 4 out of 100, or 4%. Of course, we haven't counted the negative ones . . .

Inferring the Mean

- Two structured computer activities
- Data from file
- Student pages 288–292
- *Complex features

Topics
Fathom's built-in tests
type I errors
probability
alpha level of tests

*Part I: starter

*Part II: intermediate

Materials
T_Simulation

These activities explore essential concepts in hypothesis testing in an abstract setting. Therefore, they are most appropriate for statistics students. You could use them as an introduction to traditional tests, but it may be more effective to wait until students have solved some straightforward problems using whatever technology is most common in your class. These activities do not, for example, explain what a *t*-statistic is, so students who already know that—even shakily—may get more out of the experience.

The first activity introduces Fathom's analyses—both hypothesis tests and confidence intervals (estimates). We explore *P*-values, critical *t*-values, and the correspondence between hypothesis testing and estimation. This activity is designed to be suitable as an introductory activity; that is, you don't have to know much about Fathom.

The second activity simulates repeated hypothesis tests; we get a chance to see, for example, that we get the wrong answer 10% of the time when we do a 10% test. This activity is much easier with some Fathom experience, although it makes few assumptions about the user's skill.

What's Important Here

- Critical *t*-values for hypothesis tests are special "edge" values of a statistic.

- Hypothesis tests and confidence intervals for the mean are closely related; we explore that relationship in Part I, Steps 13–16.

- The alpha level of a test is the chance that you will incorrectly reject a true null hypothesis (false positive). This kind of error is called a Type I error (though the student pages do not use this terminology). (Part II, Step 17)

- Type I errors are inevitable. If you get one, you haven't done anything wrong.

Discussion Questions, Part I

➲ What is the possible range of values for *P*? What about *t*?

➲ How do you compute the *t*-statistic? Verify it using numbers from one of your tests.

➲ What does it really mean for a *P*-value to be small? What if it's large?

➲ Why do you suppose Fathom's statistical tests have so many words in them? (Fathom has a non-verbose mode for when you tire of them; select the test and look in the **Test** menu.)

Discussion Questions, Part II

➲ The sample collection is a sample. But of what population?

➲ Explain why the *P*-distribution looks flat for **mu** = 0.

➲ Roughly 10% of the samples will have *P* < .10 when **mu** = 0. How will that percentage change as **mu** increases? (It will increase, asymptotically approaching 1. This leads to the power function.)

Inferring the Mean, Part I

Name(s): _____

In this activity, you'll explore Fathom's analyses and the relationship between hypothesis tests and confidence intervals. Here's the context: Imagine we're making gizmos that should have a mean diameter of 2.25 cm. We pull five from the assembly line and measure them. We get 2.23, 2.25, 2.26, 2.27, and 2.29. They seem a little high, but is that "highness" reasonable given the variation in the gizmos?

You need
  InferringTheMean_I

You need to know how to
  drag points and attributes

You'll learn how to
  use Fathom's analyses

We'll start with a hypothesis test and connect it to confidence intervals.

1. Open **InferringTheMean_I.** You'll see a collection, a dot plot of values for the attribute **diameter**, and a slider (called **diameterTarget**) that controls the mean of the population against which **diameter** is tested. It's set to 2.25.

2. Choose **Test Hypothesis** from the **Analyze** menu. An empty test appears.

3. Choose **Test Mean** from the popup menu in the analysis.

4. Drag **diameter** from the case table to the top of the analysis. The analysis changes to look like the illustration below right.

5. Point at the **0** of **is not equal to 0** and choose **Change formula for value, . . .** to open the formula editor. Enter **diameterTarget** and close the editor.

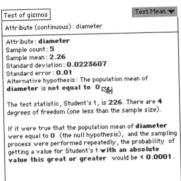

Pointing at **0** with the **f(x)** cursor.

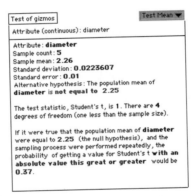

With attribute **diameter** assigned.

If you wanted, you could simply enter the number in the sample, the sample mean and standard deviation, and the null-hypothesis parameter (what the mean is not equal to—in this case zero). Fathom will update the *P*-value at the bottom depending on those parameters. You can even change the "is not equal to." Click it to see.

Once you've assigned an attribute, Fathom uses its data to compute the values. If we had real data, we'd be finished here. If *P* were less than about .05, we would probably be convinced that we could reject the null hypothesis.

6. In the illustration, the *P*-value for our sample—the last number in the paragraph—is 0.37. This is not very small. What does that mean about the gizmos? Can we say they clearly don't average 2.25 cm in diameter?

7. Drag the left-hand (lowest) point. This changes its value. Describe what happens to the numbers in the test.

8. Many people use *P* = .05 as the alpha level—the probability below which they reject the null hypothesis as implausible. Move that left-hand point until the *P*-value is as close to .05 as you can get it. Now look in the analysis: What's the value of Student's *t* in this situation?

9. This is a critical value for *t*. Verify it by looking it up in a statistics book or by using a calculator. Look under df = 4 and in a section for two-tailed tests. What do you find? How well does it match?

(df stands for degrees of freedom)

10. Put the data back where they were by choosing **Undo**—**CTRL-Z** (Windows) or **⌘-Z** (Mac)—from the **Edit** menu repeatedly.

You could also choose **Revert Collection** from the **File** menu.

11. What happens to the *P*-value if you set the **diameterTarget slider** to 2.00? What's the new value? Explain why it's smaller than before.

12. If the gizmos were supposed to be 2.00 cm in diameter (instead of 2.25 cm), what would you conclude from our data?

This changes the "null" value of gizmo diameter you're comparing the sample data to.

Making Confidence Intervals

13. Find the range of values for **diameterTarget** for which our data are plausible. That is, find the smallest and largest values on the slider for which $P \geq .05$. (Anything outside the range—such as 2.00—would be an unreasonable estimate for the diameter of the population of gizmos.) Give the range and explain how you found it.

Working with Sliders

You can drag the pointer to change the value, or edit the number itself. But sometimes you want finer control. Adjust the bounds of the axis by pushing the axis numbers off the end or pulling new ones on. You can also zoom in by holding down **CTRL** (Windows) or **OPTION** (Mac) and clicking the axis numbers.

14. Now choose **Estimate Parameters** from the **Analyze** menu. A new analysis object appears. Choose **Estimate Mean** from the popup menu and drag **diameter** into the top of the box, as you did with the test. You'll see information about the confidence interval, as in the illustration.

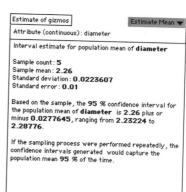

15. If everything went well, the range of values in this confidence interval (2.xxx to 2.xxx) is the same as the one you found above. Compare them. If they are not the same, figure out what to do to get these numbers as the limits when you adjust **diameterTarget**, as we did in Step 13.

16. (Hard.) Explain as clearly as you can why these two ranges are the same.

Going Further

1. As you dragged the lowest data point to the right, the *P*-value first got smaller, then got larger. Verify this (how small did it get?) and explain why it happened.

2. If we were really worried only about gizmos being too big, we could alter the test. Click the words **is not equal to**. A popup menu appears; choose **is greater than**. What does the *P*-value change to? Explain why it changes in the direction it does.

Inferring the Mean, Part II

Name(s): _____

A hypothesis test helps you infer things about the population based on a sample. In this activity, we'll begin with a file that is already set up with a sample drawn from a known population—a normal distribution. We'll see what happens when we try to use that sample to learn things about the population. Will it tell us the truth? Let's see.

You need
    InferringTheMean_II

You need to know how to
  make graphs
  use the inspector

You'll learn how to
  use Fathom's analyses
  collect measures

1. Open the file **InferringTheMean_II.** You should see a collection (**sample**), a dot plot of the sample **values**, a slider that determines the population mean **mu** (its standard deviation is 1.00), and a hypothesis test, testing whether **mu = 0**.

2. What happens when you move the slider for **mu**? Explain why this happens.

If the test is "empty," choose **Test Mean** from the popup menu and drag **value** to the top of the test.

3. With **mu** set to zero, select the sample collection and choose **Rerandomize** from the **Analyze** menu or press **CTRL-Y** (Windows) or **⌘-Y** (Mac). Write down the new *P*-value from the test. Collect five *P*-values in this way and record them here.

4. Set the slider to 2.00. Do the same—collect five *P*-values and write them here.

5. Your values for **mu = 2** should be small and close together; those for **mu = 0** should range widely between 0 and 1. Explain why.

The inspector will have five tabs—one for each of its five panes: case attributes, measures, comments, display attributes, and collect measures.

6. Now let's perform this experiment many times. With **mu** set to zero, we will collect measures. First, click the test to select it.

7. Then choose **Collect Measures** from the **Analyze** menu. A new *measures* collection appears and is selected.

8. Open the inspector for that collection by double-clicking it. Look at the case attributes and see the various attributes you have collected. They include **tValue** and **pValue**, the values for the *t*-statistic and the *P*-value, respectively.

9. Click the **Collect Measures** tab (which may just read **Col...**) to bring up the **Collect Measures** pane. Change its settings so they match the illustration. (Turn animation off and increase the number to 100.)

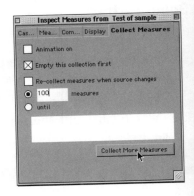

10. Click **Collect More Measures.** Fathom will rerandomize your sample 100 times, test the mean of the sample, and collect the information for each *t*-test in this **Measures** collection.

Exploring the Results

11. Now tell Fathom to make a histogram of the *t*-values. Find the attribute name (**tValue**) in the **Case Attributes** pane of that inspector (or in a case table if you made one).

12. Make a histogram of **pValue** as well.

13. Let's adjust the bins on the *P*-histogram. Double-click an axis. Some text appears; you can edit it to control the binning and the axes. Make the bin width 0.1, starting at 0, as shown in the illustration. Press **ENTER** or **TAB** after you type your numbers.

14. Now you have two histograms. Sketch them here.

To make a graph, drag an empty graph off the shelf. Then drag the name of the attribute you want onto an axis. You can change a dot plot to a histogram in the popup menu in the corner of the graph.

Histogram: Bin width: **0.10858** starting at: **0.0019600**
The number axis is horizontal from **-0.10000** to **1.30**
The Count axis is vertical from 0 to **23.000**

Before Adjusting Bin Width

Histogram: Bin width: **0.10000** starting at: **0**
The number axis is horizontal from **-0.10000** to **1.30**
The Count axis is vertical from 0 to **23.000**

After Adjusting Bin Width

Delete this special text (click it and choose **Delete Object** from the **Edit** menu) and close the inspector if you need the screen space.

Let's review what they are histograms *of.* Each shows 100 cases. Each case was a statistical test on a different sample—a test to see if the mean of that sample showed that the population's mean was not equal to zero. Each test produced a *t*-statistic—it was zero if the sample mean was zero, and became larger (or smaller) the more the sample mean differed from zero. Each test also produced a *P*-value—the probability that a sample of 5 from the null distribution (mean 0, SD 1) would have a *t* as extreme as the sample we're testing.

15. Select a tall bin in the middle of the *t*-histogram. What part of the *p*-histogram is selected? Explain.

16. Select the bottom bin (*P* < .1) of the *P*-histogram. What part of the *t* is selected? Explain.

17. The cases in this bottom bin are where *P* < .10. If 10% were our criterion, we would reject the null hypothesis for these cases. Yet in our simulation, the null hypothesis is *true,* because we built it that way (**mu** = 0). Is there something wrong with our rejecting the null when it's true? How many cases have this problem? Is that about what you would expect? Explain.

Inferring the Mean, Part II (continued)

Name(s): _____

Going Further

1. Change the t-histogram to a dot plot and be sure the bottom bin is selected on the P. Zoom in to the dot plot and decide on a value for t above which the dots are selected. What is that value? What does it represent? Add more cases if you like.

2. Do the previous problem for an alpha level of 0.05 instead of 0.10.

3. Plot **pValue** as a function of **tValue**. Sketch the scatter plot and explain it.

4. Set **mu** to .5 (or some other value) and predict what the P-distribution will look like. Graph the distribution and compare it to your prediction.

Inference Sonatas and Other Challenges

- Many computer investigations
- Data from everywhere
- Student pages 294–298
- Independent, complex features

Aunt Belinda

This Sonata is an inference problem based on a simple binomial situation.

One solution is to make a collection with 20 cases, each a coin with an attribute face controlled by a formula such as **randomPick("heads", "tails")**. Then make a measure, **nHeads**, with a formula such as **count(face = "heads")**. Now collect measures from that collection. The distribution of **nHeads** in the **Measures** collection will show that a result of 16 heads out of 20 is unusual. Students will vary in what they do with that result.

Hot Hoops

We invite students to explore the phenomenon of being "hot" or "cold" in sports. Do people get "hot hands," or are we just looking for patterns in randomness?

The key is to design an experiment in which there is an identifiable null hypothesis (there are no streaks) and you can construct a statistic to measure streakiness.

The suggestion on the student sheet leads to a 2-by-2 array that you can test for independence using chi-square or any equivalent statistic. That is, the null hypothesis is that there is no relationship between the outcome of the preceding shot and this one.

Another alternative is to look at streak length itself. The function **runLength( )** will help you investigate streaks in your data; for example, **max(runLength(shot))** will give the length of the longest string of cases in which shot has the same value. If the data are streaky, this should be large. Or **count(runLength(shot) = 1)** will give the number of streaks. In streaky data, this number is small. To simulate the null hypothesis, scramble your data so that order is random and build up a distribution of your statistic.

Beyond Constructivist Dice

These are two pages of problem prompts based on the activity on pages 260–265.

More Inference Challenges

Here are more problems that apply other inferential techniques from this chapter. Some of them use the census microdata files you may have used for activities in the first chapter of this book. If you have not, open the Census Files folder in the Samples Documents folder to choose a file with data from your area or one you're interested in. Background on census microdata is on page 6. There's also more information in the "Read Me (census)" file.

Sonata 28: Aunt Belinda

Name(s): _____

Aunt Belinda claims to have magnetized her kitchen table. She says that it makes nickels come up heads when she flips them. "Magnets don't attract nickels," you say.

"Ordinary magnets don't," she admits, "but mine is special." You supply her with 20 nickels. She sits at her table and throws the coins into the air. When they come down, 16 are heads.

Of course, you ask her to do it again. Of course, she refuses. "The energy fields in my table are exhausted," she says. "Besides, one proof is enough." What do you think?

Conjecture and Design

Without any calculations, what do you think is the chance of throwing 16 heads in 20 throws? Do you think a result of 16 out of 20 is convincing evidence? If so, evidence of what?

Now design an experiment you can do with Fathom to compute experimentally the probability of getting 16 or more heads out of 20 throws. Describe what you will do before you set hand to mouse.

Measurement

Build your simulation (possibly starting by editing the file **ConstructivistDice**) and run it. Describe below any changes you made in your experiment design above. Sketch the histogram (or whatever display you use) that finally gives your results.

If you happen to know about the **randomBinomial()** function, please don't use it except to check your work.

Comparison and Conclusion

How did the actual probability compare to what you thought it would be? Write what you think you can conclude from your experiment with Aunt Belinda. Be as clear as possible.

Sonata 29: Hot Hoops

Name(s): _____

Are there streaks in sports? Some researchers who studied pro basketball decided that, despite players' and coaches' subjective experiences of being "hot" or "cold," the streaks were illusions. That is, whether a player hit or missed a basket was independent of whether the player had hit the preceding one.

Conjecture and Design

Design a study to test whether streaks exist. One idea: Get someone to shoot 100 free throws in a row while you feed the shooter balls and record the data. Use the **prev( )** function in Fathom to make an attribute for the preceding shot. Then you can make a frequency table of (say) **shot** vs. **prevShot** to show you how many of the pairs are hit-hit, hit-miss, miss-hit, and miss-miss.

If you like this scheme, you'll have to decide what to do about the first shot—for which there is no preceding shot.

Predict: Do you think there will be streaks? If so (or if not), what will that frequency table look like if there are streaks? If there are not? What measure will distinguish a streaky data set from the (null hypothesis) independent one?

Measurement

Gather the data and enter them into Fathom. Make a graph or table that displays your data well. Sketch it below.

Analysis

Try to figure out whether your data show streaks. Use Fathom to create a collection (probably scrambled, so that the proportion of hits will be the same as in the data) in which the shots really are independent of the preceding shots. Try your proposed measure—make its distribution in the case of the null hypothesis. Sketch the distribution and show where your test data fall. If you discover that you want to improve your measure, do so and explain how and why you did. Finally, how do you feel about streaks now?

Reference: "'Hot Hands' Phenomenon: A Myth?" *New York Times,* 19 April 1988, Late City Final Edition, sec. C, p. 1.

Beyond Constructivist Dice

Name(s): _____

Here are some problems and investigations. Use Fathom to help you explore them and develop your responses.

Always Even

One of the easiest measures to devise is the one in which you add up the differences between the observed value and the expected value for each possible die roll. For example, if your die rolled 10–0–5–5–5–5, the value for m would be 10.0 because you compare those numbers to 5–5–5–5–5–5 and add up the (absolute) differences. If you roll a die 30 times, the value for this measure is always an even integer. Why?

Critical Values for howUnfair, Part 1

If you were stuck on a desert island without a computer, you could still assess whether a set of rolls was reasonably fair if you knew what value of **howUnfair** (for a particular measure) gave what value for P.

  1. Pick a measure (your own, for example).

  2. Pick a value for P that you find convincing (many scientists use $P = .05$, or 5%).

  3. Use your setup in **ConstructivistDice** to make a distribution of your measure for samples of 30 die rolls. Figure out where the $P = .05$ point is, that is, where only 5% of the sets of 30 rolls are that high or higher. That's the *5% critical value* for your measure. What is that value?

  4. Take someone else's die and roll it 30 times. Calculate your **howUnfair**. Compare it to your critical value. Explain what the result means.

Critical Values for howUnfair, Part 2

You have to have done *Critical Values for* **howUnfair**, *Part 1*.

    Be sure your formula for **howUnfair** works *no matter how many rolls you have*. For example, if you used the number 5 as an expected number of ones in 30 rolls, use **count( )/6** instead.

    What if there is a different number of rolls in your set? Do the exercise again, at least for 18, 60, and 120 rolls. Do you find that the same value of **howUnfair** gives the same value for P? What's the relationship?

    Compare your findings with those of others, especially if they have studied different measures.

What's Wrong with This?

Arthur used Fathom to decide whether his die was fair. Part of his write-up contained this statement: "Since this distribution of die rolls had $P = .005$, the chances are $(1 - P)$, or 99.5%, that the die is unfair." Is Arthur right? Why or why not? Comment on his statement.

Chi-Square, Who Cares?

The chi-square statistic is the measure "official" statisticians have used for ages to figure out whether a die is unfair. You calculate it with this formula:

$$\chi^2 = \sum \frac{(observed - expected)^2}{expected} = \sum_{i=1}^{6} \frac{(x_i - 5)^2}{5}.$$

The number of rolls that came up i is x_i. Five is the expected frequency. The summation is over all cells (all six possible die rolls). And χ is the Greek letter chi.

If you were to put in 7–4–5–3–10–1, you'd add up the square of the difference between 5 and the number and divide by 5 to get

$$\chi^2 = \frac{(7-5)^2}{5} + \frac{(4-5)^2}{5} + \frac{(5-5)^2}{5} + \frac{(3-5)^2}{5} + \frac{(10-5)^2}{5} + \frac{(1-5)^2}{5}$$

$$\chi^2 = \frac{4}{5} + \frac{1}{5} + \frac{0}{5} + \frac{4}{5} + \frac{25}{5} + \frac{16}{5} = \frac{50}{5} = 10.0.$$

Chi, the Greek letter, is pronounced "ki" with I as in *ice cream*. Chi, pronounced "chee," is the life force allegedly regulated by acupuncture.

Why would anyone invent such a bizarre statistic? One reason may become clear if you've done the two *Critical Values for* **howUnfair** investigations.

- Do them again, using chi-square as the measure. You can cooperate with others, splitting up the work. What do you find?

- Compare your results with a chi-square table. If you're rolling six-sided dice, the number of *degrees of freedom,* or *df,* is 5.

Too, Too Fair

If you roll a fair die 30 times, what's the probability that each number will come up exactly 5 times? Use Fathom to simulate it. It's really unusual to have the distribution come up 5–5–5–5–5–5. If you saw that, or something almost even, you might suspect that somebody had "cooked" the data or that the die was somehow fishy. What measure could you use to assess whether a set of die rolls was too even?

Too Many Twos

Amy thinks her die makes a lot of twos and not enough fives. Invent a measure that would be especially sensitive to Amy's conjecture.

More Inference Challenges

Name(s): _____

Gender and Income I

Using your census microdata, assuming that your file is a sample of the local population, test the null hypothesis that females earn just as much as males. Try to make your test as fair and informative as possible. For example, don't include children. Be sure to document the way you chose the data to use and what you did in your test, especially the way you computed your statistic.

One obvious statistic is the difference of means between the sexes. But is that the best statistic to use?

Gender and Income II

What proportion of people in your census microdata file earn more than $35,000 per year (or some other appropriate, comfortable figure)? Compute the value and find a 90% confidence interval for that proportion. Then compute the confidence intervals separately for males and females. What do you conclude?

Use the "percentile interval" shortcut from *Pennies and Polling* to compute the confidence intervals.

Husbands and Wives

Using the file **Couples**—with information on **height** and **age**—investigate and report on any of these questions:

- Are males generally taller than females? If so, by how much?
- Are husbands generally taller than their wives? If so, by how much?
- Are males generally older than females? If so, by how much?
- Are husbands generally older than their wives? If so, by how much?
- Assuming that the file contains a simple random sample of couples, which of the above questions can you legitimately answer? Explain.
- Assuming the first two bullets in this list are both legitimate questions, consider the first (hypothesis test) question for each. Which gives the stronger *P*-value? Why?

More Text Analysis

We have included several Fathom files with famous text: the beginning of the Declaration of Independence (**Declaration**), the Gettysburg address (**Gettysburg**), the opening of *The Old Man and the Sea* (**OldManAndTheSea**), and George Bush's inaugural address (**BushInaugural**). In these collections, each letter is a case. Pick one that interests you and analyze it. Here is a task you might tackle:

Make a new attribute that distinguishes consonants from vowels. Then look at their sequence. Show that the sequence is not consistent with randomness, even if you know the frequency of vowels (which you can determine from the data). You may need to investigate the streakiness of an attribute. Look at the statistical function **runLength( )**. It will help you.

Another task might be to investigate stereotypes. Hemingway was said to use a lot of short words. Can you use Fathom to design a test to see whether he used significantly shorter words than, say, Jefferson? The files are *not* simple random samples of their writing, but for these purposes, pretend that they are.

Solutions

1 Come to Your Census

Answers here are based on data from Berkeley, so your answers will differ in the details.

Exploring Census Data

Discussion Question

Race is usually the largest group (or tribe) of which a person is a member (Black, Chinese, Cherokee, White, etc.). *Ancestry* usually means the more specific country or subgroup (German, Polish, etc.). Answers for the other questions are in the Teacher Notes.

Answer These

1. Using the dot plot, any of the right-most dots is the case we want, which has age 90.

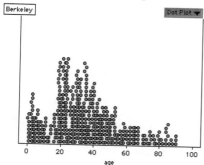

2. By pointing at the median in a box plot, we can read in the status bar that the median of the group is 32.5 years.

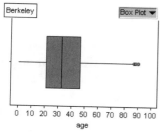

3. After constructing the graph and the histogram, the ranges of the rectangles and the number of cases in each rectangle are displayed in the status bar. If the widths of the rectangles are not appropriate to answer this question, move the cursor over the edge of a rectangle and resize it until the widths are useful. In the Berkeley data, there are 29 people in the age group from 15 to 20.

4. The median age for males is 35, and the median age for females is 30.

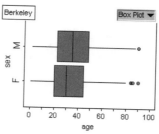

5. The mean age for the entire group is 35. Since the median age of males is 35, we know from the box plot that the mean is a little higher—about 37. The females' mean might be about 33 or 34.

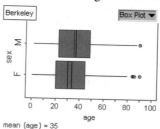

By zooming in, we see that the mean of the males is indeed 37 and of the females about 33.2.

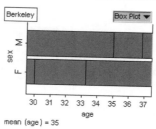

6. The population has a longer tail on the right; those high ages act like outliers and affect the mean much more than they do the median.

Two Graphs and Selection

6. "Selected" tells us that 145 people in the data set are married.

Cases: 424   Selected: 145

7. Using the **Sex** instead of the **Marital** attribute and choosing the category **Female**, we can see that there are 224 females in the data set. Since there are 424 people, the females are about 53%.

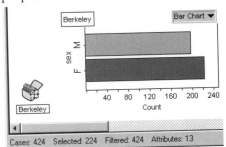

8. Taken together, these two graphs show that males make the highest salaries and that these males are middle aged—40 to 60 years old.

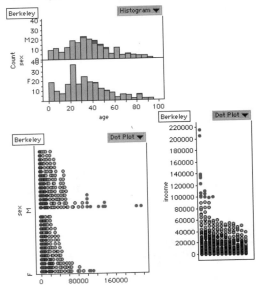

9. Estimate the median ages from the box plots. As we might expect, never-married people are younger; widows and widowers are older.

Nev = 22   Mar = 43   Div = 47
Sep = 35   Wid = 82.5

Out of Many, Fewer II

These answers are based on the data from Berkeley.

1. In this file, 45 persons earned more than $50,000 a year. Filter: **income>50,000**.

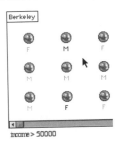

2. Retype the filter. Start with the "(" key. The status bar shows that there are 16 females in the sample who earn more than $50,000 a year. Filter: **(income>50000) and (sex="F")**. Occupations will vary. In Berkeley, there are doctors, dentists, lawyers, managers, a real estate salesperson, and even an actor/director.

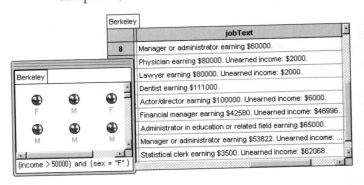

3. There are 34 teenagers in this file.
   Filter: **(age>12) and (age<20)** or **InRange(age, 13, 20)**

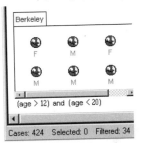

4. By looking at a box plot of income using the above filter, then zooming in on the graph, we see that the median income of teenagers is about $820 a year. (You can get this number exactly by pointing at the median and reading the number on the status bar.)

5. There are five White males over age 80 in the Berkeley data. (Filter given in text.)

6. In our Berkeley sample, there are eight Blacks who earn more than $30,000 in the data. Their median age is 42.5. Filter: **(income>30000) and (race ="Black")**

7. Answers will vary. For example, in the Berkeley data, the median income of Norwegians aged 30 and over (all four of them) is $47,959.
   Filter: **(ancestry = "Norwegian") and (age > 30)**

8. The oldest person who does not have a high school diploma, found by filtering with **educode < 10** then scrolling through the case table, is 88 years old. (If you know how to sort the case table, that makes it quicker; if not, you could use a graph.)

9. The median income of persons with a four-year college degree is $15,907.

10. The median income of those with high school diplomas but no degree from a four-year college or university is $7,000 a year.

Data in Depth
© 2001 Key Curriculum Press

11. Answers will vary; very few students will find anyone like themselves—or even very close. People are more varied than we think.

Making Categories

3. We chose $20,000 for this example.

8. The graph should look something like this.

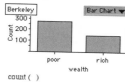

9. There are 148 **rich** people. You could point at the bar marked **rich**, then look at the status bar (at the bottom of the Fathom window).

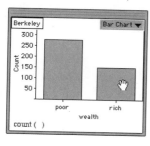

10. Approximately 35% (148 of 424) of the people in this data set are **rich**. We can calculate the percentage or simply look at the ribbon chart.

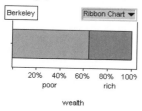

11. We could figure this out in several ways, one of which is scrolling through the case table looking under the adjacent headings of **eduCode** and **eduText** to see what the various headings mean. The easiest way would be to refer to the list of **eduCode** numbers (given on page 21).

12. if (educode > 11) $\begin{cases} \text{"degree"} \\ \text{"no degree"} \end{cases}$

13.

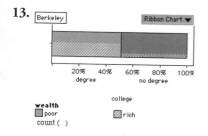

14. There is a positive correlation between wealth and whether you have a degree. One astute student's response was, "Getting a degree doesn't guarantee that you'll be rich, but if you *don't* get a degree, it's pretty sure you won't be." While this response may assign causation unnecessarily, it shows understanding of the data. The data show that the proportion of rich people among those with degrees is much higher than the proportion of rich people in the no-degree category.

15.

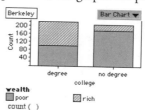

Berkeley	Summary Table	wealth		Row Summary
		poor	rich	
college	degree	99	119	218
	no degree	177	29	206
	Column Summary	276	148	424

S1 = count ( )

17. Answers may vary, but the ribbon chart produces percentages, while the bar chart produces a picture of the summary table. When choosing a presentation, the question to answer is what are you trying to demonstrate. If you need to do exact calculations, you may need the table. To visualize proportions and to persuade, the graphs are probably more effective.

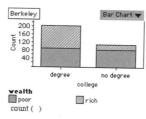

Going Further

1. **inRange(age, 18, 65)** will get the range of people from ages 18 to 64. To discuss wealth we want wage-earning people who, for the most part, are in this age range. Note that the **inRange** function includes the lower value in its interval but does not include the upper value. One clear change is that there are many fewer poor people with no degree (the now-excluded children had low incomes, so they were labeled poor). This does not change the sense of the correlation between income and education.

2. Using the above numbers, 133/310 = 43%.

3. Using the above numbers, 109/133 = 82%.

4. Using the above numbers, 109/201 = 54%.

5. One advantage is that it allows for broad statements about the data that are unencumbered by many small details. This is also a disadvantage in that it obscures many of these details.

Investigating a Conjecture

The conclusions you draw will depend upon your data and conjectures. If you have made a decision to use only a sample of data, check to be sure that your sample is not all from one category. You also need to know (as discussed in the Teacher Notes) that even your area may have some strong bias compared to state or national numbers, especially if you live in a city, a retirement area, or a rural farm area.

Features Buffet: Plot Value

7. The graph shows mean ages of 50 for Divorced, 46 for Married, 24 for Never Married, 39 for Separated, and 80 for Widowed.

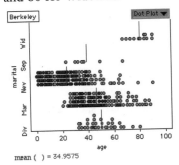

mean ( ) = 34.9575

8. The number at the bottom of the graph is the mean age of the entire data set.

10. The mean age of the entire population changes as these points are dragged (but not as fast as the points move), as do the values of the individual ages in the case table. The lines representing standard deviation will move, too, but not in simple ways. In general, though, as you move points away from the mean, the lines for **s** will move farther, too, but not as fast.

Features Buffet: Summary Tables

These answers are based on the data from Berkeley.

4. At this step, students should see something like this:

Berkeley	Summary Table
age	34.96

S1 = mean ( )

7.

Berkeley	Summary Table
age	34.96
	32.50

S1 = mean ( )
S2 = median ( )

8. The mean age of males is older by about 3.6 years, and the median age of males is also older, by 5 years.

Berkeley	Summary Table		
		sex		Row
		F	M	Summary
age		33.25	36.85	34.95
		224	199	423
		30	35	32

S1 = mean ( )
S2 = count ( )
S3 = median ( )

9. The mean earnings of males are greater by about $8660, and the median earnings are also greater, by $5000.

Berkeley	Summary Table		
		sex		Row
		F	M	Summary
age		33.25	36.85	34.95
		224	199	423
		30	35	32
income		16490	25150	20570
		224	199	423
		8000	13056	10200

S1 = mean ( )
S2 = count ( )
S3 = median ( )

10. Here is a table with all the requested other formulas.

Berkeley	Summary Table		
		sex		Row
		F	M	Summary
age		0	1	0
		90	90	90
		20.73	20.31	20.61
		25	27	26
income		0	0	0
		111000	215516	215516
		21230	33830	28210
		22550	31000	29000

S1 = min ( )
S2 = max ( )
S3 = stdDev ( )
S4 = iqr ( )

11. The difference of mean age minus standard deviation of age for males is 16.5 and for females is 12.48. (**Note:** You can use **s( )** instead of **stdDev( )** if you're estimating the standard deviation of the population.)

Berkeley	Summary Table		
		sex		Row
		F	M	Summary
age		12.52	16.55	14.34
income		-4736	-8678	-7643

S1 = mean ( ) – stdDev ( )

Features Buffet: Display Attributes

These answers are based on data from Berkeley.

6. The gold ball drops down a little.

7. The origin is in the upper left corner. The axes point to the right and down. As the *x*-coordinates increase, the balls move farther to the right. As the *y*-coordinates increase, the balls move down.

8.

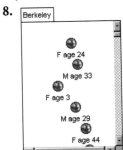

9. concat (racetext," ",sex," age ",age," earning ",income)

10. The richest person at the top is a White male, age 44, earning $215,516. The oldest are a White male, age 90, earning $16,800, and two White females, age 90, earning $20,247 and $6350.

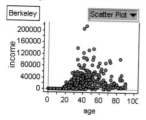

Features Buffet: Sorting

These answers are based on data from Berkeley.

4. The data sort from lowest to highest, with the lowest at the top of the table and the highest at the bottom.

5. The **race** column sorts alphabetically, starting at A.

6. To avoid scrolling through the entire table to see the oldest person, highlight the age column and sort descending. This pulls up three persons aged 90.

7. Sort the **income** attribute, then scroll to the area in question. For the Berkeley data, there are 16 persons who earned between $15,000 and $17,000.

8. The key is to sort first by income. Then when you sort by **eduText**, each category is still sorted by income. We could also sort by **eduCode**, since we want persons whose code is exactly 10. If we do so, scrolling the list lets us find the highest income (assuming we have previously sorted by income). In the case of Berkeley, the highest income for a high school graduate with no college is $47,574, which is interesting in this data, since it is unearned income.

Features Buffet: Percentile Plots

5.

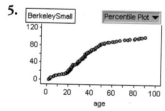

6. The 50% person in this graph is age 33.

7. The 90th percentile of **age** is at 65. To find this, we could zoom in on the vertical axis at the value 90 until some point or points are clearly at this percentage.

8. There are fewer people in the lower and higher age groups than in the middle age group. The distribution is higher in the middle than at the ends.

9. This percentile plot of income shows that the greatest number of people have incomes less than $60,000 per year, and at the low end (lower left-hand corner of

the graph) there is a vertical rise for the first 20%, indicating an income that is either very low or zero.

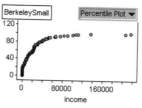

Features Buffet: Ntigrams

These answers are based on data from Berkeley.

7. There are 85 cases in each bin here (we have 424 cases).

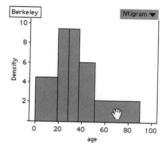

8. Depending on how you adjust the edges, it will look something like this.

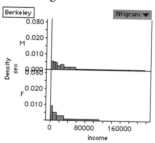

9. For these data, you would have to be earning between $46,280 and $215,516. When you point to the right-hand Ntigram box, its information is displayed at the bottom left edge of the Fathom window. (The graph will need to be stretched vertically to get the right bin large enough for the information to come up in the status bar when the hand is over it.)

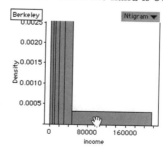

10. Again, you may need to stretch the graph vertically, since the first bin is so tall.

In this illustration, you can see that the top 10% for males starts at about $69,000 and for females at about $30,000. Note that the 90th percentile for females lines up with the 80th for males.

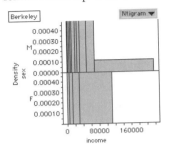

Features Buffet: The Switch Function

13. We can now read the mean incomes of these three age groups.

Berkeley	Summary Table			
		ageCategory		Row
	middle	old	young	Summary
income	25500	23810	289.9	20570
	301	43	80	424

S1 = mean ( )
S2 = count ( )

Your specific numbers will differ, of course; the most obvious observation will be that young people have much lower incomes than the two older groups. It may be surprising that the "old" group has such a large income—though for retirees, much of that may be unearned, that is, from pensions, investments, entitlements, alimony, and so forth.

2 Lines and Data

Reading the News, Part I (Offline)

Answer These

These answers will depend on your newspaper. A typical front page might have 150 column-centimeters of text. At a typical rate of 0.2 centimeters per second, that would take 750 seconds to read. Since that's over 10 minutes, 30 minutes of reading would probably not take you through the front section.

Answer These

1. If the student is not reading, there will be no amount read.

2. Slope actually represents reading speed in centimeters per second. The faster reader should have a steeper line.

3. If the rate is constant, all the points will be in a straight line. If the rate varies, some points will be above the line and some below.

4. As we saw in 2 above, this slope represents the average reading speed, so this is the average number of *vertical* centimeters per second—the actual speed your eyes move down (not across) the page.

5. The equation for this should be *centimeters = rate × time*, so multiply reading rate by 100.

6. This depends on the students and the column you are reading. Expect numbers less than one centimeter per second.

Reading the News, Part II (Online)

8. Here's a typical plot.

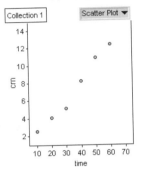

Answer These

1. The slope should be close to the slope of the hand-plotted data, less than 1 centimeter per second, probably near 0.2.

2. Yes, the ordered pair (0,0) = (no time reading, no centimeters read).

3. There may be some differences in slope and perhaps even a *y*-intercept. If there are no unusual points, this graph should look much like the movable line graph. Remember that the least-squares line is a line of best fit *for the data,* and some variance in the data may produce a line with a *y*-intercept not at zero. A typical equation is **0.19 time + 0.25.**

4. **Note:** Points can be dragged outside of the window into areas that are meaningless in this problem, such as the second, third, or fourth quadrants. If dragged points are left in the first quadrant, the smallest slope will be close to zero. While the largest depends on the data, it will probably be smaller than 1.5. If you can drag it anywhere and rescale the graph, you can get just about any slope.

5. The slope should represent the number of seconds per centimeter, or how many seconds it takes to read one centimeter. This is the reciprocal of the number found in the answer to 3 above.

The Coast Starlight II: Studying Train Speed

7. Dunsmuir, California

13. The new column for **time** shows that Seattle is listed at 34 hours. Adjust the new formula by subtracting 34 from the total. Then rescale the scatter plot by choosing **Scatter Plot** from the graph's popup menu again.

16. The movable line should have a slope in the 40 to 50 range and a *y*-intercept somewhere near zero (depending whether you did the optional Step 13).

Going Further

1. *Rate = distance/time.*
   43 miles/(50 minutes) = 43 miles/(5/6 hours) = 51.6.

2. The vertical scale represents changing distance (starting at zero in Seattle). The horizontal scale represents changing time (in hours traveled since leaving Seattle). For slope, the vertical change is taken over the horizontal change, so this means that *miles* divided by *time* gives *rate*, or miles per hour. Reversing the axes gives *time* per *miles*, or how long it takes to go some distance.

3. We need to edit the formula. Remember that **time** needs to be in hours, so we'll make it **day * 24 + hour + (minute / 60)**. We divide **minute** by 60 to get hours; after all, if **minute** is 30, we want 0.5 and so on.

4. One strategy is to lay a movable line over each area separately. You can also calculate: Students can highlight two points and find them in the table. For example, Tacoma is at distance 40 and time 0.95, and Kelso is at distance 137 and time 2.87. That gives an average rate of 50.5 mph. Compare this with Santa Barbara at distance 1286 and time 32.28 and Los Angeles at distance 1389 and time 35.08. That gives an average rate of 36.8 mph.

5. A new point will appear when you insert the new case. It will be directly to the right of the first point, since no distance has been added, only time. This makes steeper (faster) slopes for the two segments taken separately (pre-Portland and post-Portland) than we saw taking the two segments together.

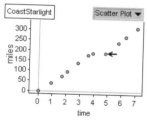

Rehearsal: The Prisoner Sonata

1. Conjectures will vary. See the Teacher Notes (page 51) for some ideas about the level of model you might encounter.

2. This figure should correspond to the model above.

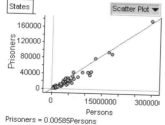

10. (first bullet) To get incarceration rates, create a new attribute named **PercentInPrison**. Then give it a formula, such as **Prisoners/Persons*100**.

Sonata 1: The Prisoner Sonata

The Question. A final answer between 55,000 and 60,000 would be fine, but do not expect the predictions to be in that range. The answer based on the least-squares regression line is 50,400. **Prediction.** Most students will predict a linear relationship, but a higher rate of incarceration than actual unless they have already done the least-squares line.

Sonata 2: Tall Buildings

Prediction. We might predict that the **height** is proportional to **stories** with a constant of proportionality of 10 to 12—the number of feet per story. **Measurement.** Make the graph and place a movable line on it, fitting it to the data. The equation appears below the graph.

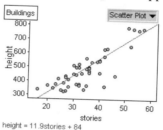

Comparison. The slope of the line (depending on your line, between 10 and 12) is the number of feet per story, but the relationship is surprisingly muddled, and, in addition, there's an intercept we can't neglect. It's fun to speculate on the reasons for these observations. We think the intercept is due to two causes: the extra height of lobbies and the height of radio masts and other gewgaws on the tops of buildings. Perhaps the spread of the points is due to different codes, styles for different purposes, and ages of buildings. **Extras.** It is worth taking the time to use a filter to look at Minnesota buildings and Florida buildings separately. Notice that Fathom changes scales automatically to fit the filtered data. Also, if students have a good idea of what least-squares lines do, this would be a place to add them to your graphs and discuss the differences in the slopes that the Minnesota versus Florida lines represent.

Sonata 3: Airliners and Fuel Cost

It makes sense that the more fuel a plane burns per hour, the higher its fuel cost per hour will be. We'd expect a linear relationship, and that's what we get: The cost is about 2.1 times the fuel use in gallons—so jet fuel (purchased in bulk) probably cost about $2.10 a gallon when these data were recorded. Note that the movable line in the illustration has its intercept locked at zero.

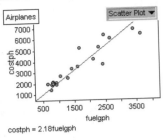

costph = 2.18fuelgph

Sonata 4: Batter Up!

We expect the horizontal axis to run from zero to 162 (the number of games in the 1996 season). And we find the slope of the limit line to be about 4, since you can't get more than about 4 at-bats per game on the average. Players below the line include pinch-hitters and people who get a lot of walks.

Sonata 5: What R π?

The value of the slope should be somewhere near the value of π.

Sonata 6: The Book Cover

If students have seen similarity in figures, they should predict that the slope of the line that they will draw will be the ratio of their vertical attribute (*y*-axis) to their horizontal attribute (*x*-axis). This ratio should be somewhat near the actual ratio of the two dimensions of the book. Real people, however, don't always work proportionally. Some people tend to make the smaller covers more square than the larger ones.

Sonata 7: Everybody's Favorite Rectangle

See the Teacher Notes, page 59.

3 Per Portions

Introduction to "Per" Quantities

1. David: 1950/8700 = $0.224, or 22.4 cents per mile
   Thalia: 1675/6950 = $0.241, or 24.1 cents per mile
2. David: 8700/50 = 174 miles per week
   Thalia: 6950/40 = 173.75 miles per week
3. David: 1950 − (1000 + 300) = 650.
   650/8750 = $0.07 per mile
   Thalia: 1675 − (800 + 500) = 375.
   375/6950 = $0.05 per mile.
4. David: 1.40/.07 = 20 mpg
   Thalia: 1.40/.05 = 28 mpg
5. Such an answer might involve time spent driving, insurance based on distance traveled, tire wear or other maintenance issues, and so on.

6. Such an answer might involve weekly rentals on cars, average time spent away from the office per week, and so on.

A Return to Prison

6. The states with the highest and lowest *rates* are Nevada (0.70) and Vermont (0.13).
7. The states with the highest and lowest *numbers* of prisoners are California (177,949) and Vermont (745).
8. The state with the highest rate is not the same as the one with the highest number, since the populations of the two states are so different.
9.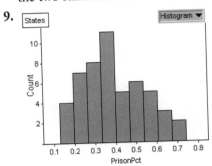

A typical incarceration rate is near 0.4 percent; the distribution is high there, and it looks like it's in the middle. (You could also compute a median.)

10.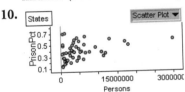

11.

	Low Population	High Population
High Incarceration Rate	D.C. Nevada	California Florida
Low Incarceration Rate	North Dakota Vermont	

There are no states that have a high population and a low incarceration rate.

12. Brenda can look at California and Florida as examples supporting her view, but states like Illinois and Pennsylvania are contrary to this.
13. Its formula is **Age85Plus/Persons**.
14. Alaska is the only outlier.

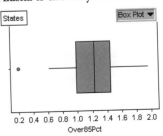

Data in Depth

15. Maybe it's the ruggedness of life there, or the climate. Perhaps people die younger in Alaska or are inclined to leave as they get older. Or maybe older Alaskans hide from census takers—or lie about their age. Alternatively, maybe there are just so many young people in Alaska that the percentage of older people is less.

Going Further

1. We use the attributes **MedHousIncome, Persons,** and **Prisoners.** In this possible solution, we create a new attribute, **rateCategory,** that depends on the incarceration rate. You can see that the high-rate states have a *higher* median income than the low-rate states, contrary to what HTI thinks.

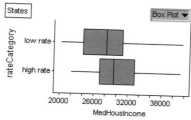

2. Many things could be wrong with this argument. One challenge is to think of as many as possible. Here are some: We're looking at entire states; crime may well be worse in low-income areas within each state. We're using median household income for income. That doesn't take cost of living into account (families in high-income states may still be relatively poor and thus—according to HTI—prone to crime). It also lumps households together. Number of prisoners doesn't necessarily reflect the crime rate. Maybe the states with lower incarceration rates have *more* crime because they haven't caught the criminals.

The Geography of U.S. Cars I

2. Guesses will vary. California is a natural (but wrong) guess for one of the most.

7. The highest percentage of licensed drivers is in Ohio (83.23), followed by Oregon (81.49) and Florida (78.13). The lowest percentage of licensed drivers is in New York (57.18), preceded by Minnesota (58.59) and D.C. (59.76).

8. Construct a dot plot of the **PctDrivers** attribute, then select the highest and lowest three dots. Sorting and scrolling the original case table will reveal the states and their percentages.

9. For the highest states, perhaps distances to travel (Oregon, Ohio), freedom of movement, or age of population (Florida) are considerations. For lowest states, high density and congestion in large cities (New York, D.C.) might be factors, while Minnesota—hard to say. Perhaps young children are another issue.

10. These predictions will vary. It makes sense that low-driver states would have fewer vehicles per person.

11. Highest number of vehicles per person was Montana at 1.13. The lowest was D.C. at 0.44.

12. The attribute can be **VehPerPerson.** A possible formula is **VehThou/PopThou.**

13.

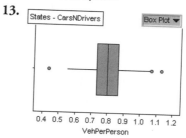

14. With many farmers having several vehicles for work, Montana has a high ratio of vehicles per person. Because of urban congestion and poverty, D.C. has a low ratio.

15. The average number of miles per vehicle ranges from Arkansas at 15,234.98 to Alaska at 7728.37.

The attribute can be **MilesPerVeh.** One formula is **MilesDrvMill*1000/VehThou.** (**MilesDrvMill** must be multiplied by 1,000,000 to get the actual number, and **VehThou** must be multiplied by 1000. The formula makes this adjustment.)

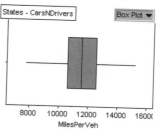

Alaska clearly has fewer roads to drive. Arkansas drivers might like to drive a lot.

16. In a scatter plot, you can see that these two quantities are negatively correlated. Maybe this is because, if there are more cars per person, each car would be driven less.

The Geography of U.S. Cars II: Total It Up

6. Sum ÷ Mean = 51, which is the number of states (counting D.C.).

7. The table will look like this.

States - CarsNDrivers	Summary Table	
	RoadMiles	**VehThou**
	76600	3812
	3906537	194423
S1 = mean ( )		
S2 = sum ( )		

8. The number, 194,423, is still in thousands of vehicles, so there are 194,423,000 vehicles in the United States. We know because this was a sum of **VehThou,** or vehicles in thousands.

9. **VehPerMile** is **VehThou*1000/RoadMiles**.

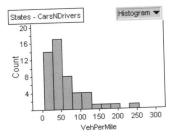

10. This number represents the sum of a collection of averages; as such, it is not an average itself.

11. The mean number of vehicles per mile is 59.144. It is the mean of the state values.

12. The calculator value is 49.77.

13. The calculator value of 49.77 is probably more reasonable since the earlier value of 59.144 is an average of averages and is better at representing roads in a typical *state* than a typical mile of road nationwide. In general, averaging ratios doesn't get you what you want, because ratios can't be added in any meaningful way. For example, one out of 4 is 1/4, two out of three is 2/3, and the average of 1/4 and 2/3 is (1/4 + 2/3)/2 = 11/24, but 1 plus 2 out of 4 plus 3 is 3/7. Other answers that the students suggest should be considered as well.

14. The average of state averages is larger than the calculator value. Many states are packed closely together in the lower end of the distribution, and the mean is greatly influenced by the larger values.

15–17. See the summary table, and make appropriate adjustments for the attribute definitions in thousands or millions. The area is 3,540,000 square miles; there are 173,126,000 drivers; we drive 2,239,828,000,000 miles per year—more than two *trillion* miles.

States - CarsNDrivers	Summary Table				
	RoadMiles	VehThou	DriversThou	AreaSqMi	MilesDrvMill
	76600	3812	3395	69420	43920
	3906537	194423	173126	3540000	2239828

S1 = mean ( )
S2 = sum ( )

Going Further

Weighting **VehPerMile** by miles of road is the same as taking the nationwide sum of the vehicles and dividing by the nationwide sum of the roads: 49.77. That is, a typical mile of road in the country has 50 cars on it.

Weighting **VehPerMile** by vehicles gives you 71.61; by drivers 73.35. Taking the vehicles as an example, this means that a typical vehicle nationwide is on a mile of road with 71 other cars. That these two ways of taking the average can seem so different (the typical mile has 50 cars but the typical car is on a mile with 71 others) yet both be correct is an important realization.

The Geography of U.S. Cars III: Unsafe in Any State

The Assignment
Fatal92 and DriversThou

4. Let's use **DeathsPerMillDrivers** (i.e., per *million* drivers) with formula **Fatal92*1000/DriversThou**. (Other definitions are possible, of course.) The other attribute could be **DriversPerDeath**. Its formula is **DriversThou*1000/Fatal92**.

5. **DeathsPerMillDrivers** is the number of fatal deaths per million drivers. **DriversPerDeath** is the number of drivers per each death.

6.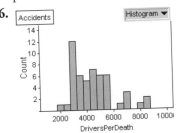

7. The best state is Rhode Island with 8671 drivers per death. The worst state is Mississippi with 2125 drivers per death.

8. Speculations will vary.

9. Choosing drivers per death gives a feeling of the number of persons who would be in a group before one of them would be killed in a car accident. Deaths per million might be useful thinking about a large city.

Fatal92 and VehThou

4. One attribute: **VehPerDeath**. The formula: **VehThou*1000/Fatal92**. The other attribute: **DeathsPerMillVeh**, defined by **Fatal92*1000/VehThou**.

5. **VehPerDeath** is the number of vehicles on the road for each death that occurs. **DeathsPerMillVeh** is the number of deaths that occur for every million vehicles on the road.

6.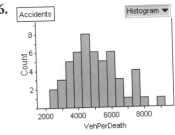

7. The best state is Connecticut, at 8848 vehicles per death. The worst state is Arkansas at 2576.5.

8. Speculations will vary.

9. Again, the size of the numbers make vehicles per death easier to use than deaths per vehicle, although deaths per *million* vehicles makes comparisons of the states easier to make (i.e., Arkansas has a death rate three times that of Connecticut).

Data in Depth
© 2001 Key Curriculum Press

Fatal92 and RoadMiles

4. One attribute: **DeathsPer100Miles**, which is **Fatal92*100/RoadMiles**. The other attribute: **MilesPerDeath**. Its formula is **RoadMiles/Fatal92**.

5. **DeathsPer100Miles** is the number of deaths per hundred miles of roadway. If you spread the fatalities uniformly over the state's highways, there would be one every **MilesPerDeath** miles.

6.

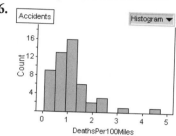

7. The best state for this attribute is North Dakota, with 0.10 deaths per 100 miles. The worst state is D.C., with 4.52 deaths per 100 miles of roadway.

8. North Dakota is best because there are few drivers per mile in that state. D.C. is probably the worst because it has no long highways; the number of miles of road is smaller per car. (See next problem.)

9. Miles per death (i.e., for North Dakota this would be 985.6) would mean that on average, there is about one fatality for every 1000 miles of road. This may be meaningful, but deaths per 100 miles may be more understandable.

DriversThou and RoadMiles

4. One attribute: **MilesPerDriver**. Its formula: **RoadMiles/(DriversThou*1000)** [see #9 below]. The other attribute: **DriversPerMile**. Its formula: **DriversThou*1000/RoadMiles**.

5. **MilesPerDriver** is the number of miles of road for each driver in the state. **DriversPerMile** is the number of drivers for each mile of road in the state.

6.

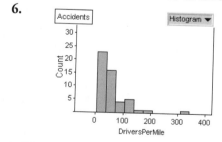

7. If we assume less crowded is better, the best state would be North Dakota with 4.99 drivers per mile. The worst is D.C. with 318.6 drivers per mile.

8. North Dakota is a very lightly populated state, so has few total drivers for the many miles of road. D.C. is very densely populated.

9. Drivers per mile is easy to grasp, but miles per driver is also useful. In North Dakota, with 0.20 miles per driver, each driver has on average $(0.20)(5280) = 1056$ feet of space. In D.C., with 0.003 miles per driver, this would only be $(0.003)(5280)=16.5$ feet per driver—very crowded.

Saved by the Belt

Warm-Up

1. $618*0.6910 = 427$

2. $618*0.055 = 34$

3. $34*0.42 = 14$

4. $4,136,000*0.42 = 1,737,120$

5. $441/1,737,120 = 0.000254$

The Problem

There are many ways to come to a good answer to this complex problem. The answers will vary somewhat depending on your assumptions—for example, how you deal with the missing data in Wyoming. But these differences should not amount to more than a few hundred lives either way. Our solution gives an answer of 14,516 lives saved. If you follow the path set forth on page 85 (*Saved by the Belt: Two Ways to Think About It*), anything between 14,000 and 15,000 is reasonable.

You might create several new attributes, representing the actual numbers of people killed wearing belts and not wearing belts. With those quantities, you can calculate the proportion of the belted and unbelted *population* that was killed wearing and not wearing belts. Then the proportion of belted people that are saved is the *difference* in these proportions. From that, you can calculate the number of people saved in each state and add those for the national total. **Note:** If you mistakenly calculate national averages for the relevant proportions and calculate from those, you get an answer more like 12,000.

For example, in Alabama,

Killed, wearing belts	177

   (157+20, using the unknown assumptions from the hints page)

Killed, beltless	441
Proportion of belted killed	.00007
Proportion of beltless killed	.00025
Proportion of belted saved (= .00025 – .00007)	.00018
Number of belted people (= population * **BeltUsePct**)	2,400,000
Number of saved people (= 2,400,000 * .00018)	432

Here is a diagram that may help with the logic.

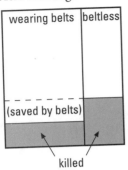

Sonata 8: Counting the Cars

Since **MilesDrvMill** is in millions of miles per year, and **RoadMiles** is in miles, if we take **RoadMiles/(MilesDrvMill * 1000000)**, we'll get an answer in years. That will be very small, of course, so multiply by $\pi*10^7$ (seconds per year) and you get a value in seconds. This ranges from less than 10 seconds (D.C.) to more than 400 (North Dakota).

Additional considerations: This solution is an average over a 24-hour day; we have no information on the maximum traffic time, and so forth. In the absence of additional information, this still gives an interesting and comprehensible summary statistic.

Sonata 9: Extreme Capital

Using **CarsNDrivers**, there are several ratios that are extreme. Any attribute per **RuralRoads** will produce a quantity divided by zero, extreme to be sure. However, within the finite numbers, consider **PopThou/AreaSqMi**, where the ratio of D.C. to the next smallest value (New Jersey) is about nine to one. The ratio of the largest value for D.C. (**MilesDrvMill**) to the smallest value for D.C. (**AreaSqMi**) compared with the next smallest value (also New Jersey) gives a ratio of a little better than seven to one. Using **States-Accidents**, one of the ratios that produces an extreme case is **PopThou/RoadMiles**, where the ratio is about 1.9 to one compared with the next smallest value, Hawaii.

Sonata 10: The Best Drivers

The question of what best means may need some elaboration on the part of the students. Some possible comparison areas might be to create new attributes such as **MilesPerAccident**, **DriversPerAccident**, **PeoplePerAccident**, **CarsPerAccident**, or other "pers" that might reflect how well people drive. Each per will probably show different states as better or worse than others, though New England comes out well in many comparisons, which may surprise anyone who has ever driven in Boston.

Sonata 11: The Wide-Open Spaces

Create two new attributes, such as **PeoplePerSquareMile** (formula **PopThou*1000/AreaSqMi**) and **CarsPerMile** (formula **VehThou*1000/RoadMiles**). We assume that population and vehicles are uniformly distributed throughout the state.

The serious outlier is D.C.

To consider deleting D.C. from the cases, we must remember that this is an area where population is extremely dense and roads are exclusively urban. Since this does not represent the majority of the states, it could be deleted for the rest of the Sonata.

If a least-squares line is now put on a graph, we get an equation such as **CarsPerMile = 0.134*PeoplePerSquareMile + 33**. The intercept is to make the equation fit the data, not to suggest that a state with no population has 33 cars per mile of road. The graph is dense at the left end and has some unusual points that might be worth further investigation. The slope suggests that on the average it takes eight more people in a square mile to add another car.

More Car Stuff

Percent Paved

Create a new attribute, perhaps **PercentPaved**. Assuming a road width of 30 feet, one formula is **100*RoadMiles*5280*30/(AreaSqMi*5280*5280)**. This gives the percentage of paved area. Should your assumed width be different from the 30 feet used here, just substitute that number in the formula. You will need a summary table to find the totals needed for national averages. This example gives a national average of 2.0898 percent paved. Intersections would bring the total percentage down a little, but parking lots and wide roads (arteries and highways) would add more to the total. Pavement also includes interchanges, playgrounds, rest areas, and so on. Note that you cannot simply use the average value for **PercentPaved** for the national average—you have to calculate the national figure from the total area and the total road miles.

An interesting extension is to use the data to try to estimate the percentage of the country covered by buildings—and compare it to the paved area.

Acres of Cars

Create a new attribute, perhaps **CarsPerAcre**. An assumption here is that **VehThou** is all cars, since we have no more specific data. A formula for this attribute could be **VehThou*1000/(AreaSqMi*640)**. This shows Alaska to be the state with the smallest number with 0.0014 cars per acre, and D.C. to be the state with the largest number with 6.57 cars per acre. The overall national average is 0.085 cars per acre.

Dropping a Meteor

First, we calculate the area of a vehicle. For this example, use 2 by 6 meters as an average, which would take care of most cars. If you wish to include trucks, buses, and vans, change 12 to some higher number in the formula. An acre contains 4047 square meters. So we could create **CarAreaPerAcre**. The formula would be **VehThou*1000*12/(AreaSqMi*640*4047)**, but these numbers are very small. Multiply by 1,000,000 and the numbers become large enough to discuss—and the units are parts per million covered by cars.

The largest value is in D.C., of course, where about 2% of the area is covered in cars (about 20,000 parts per million). Alaska is the least car-covered state, at about four parts per million. These are the probabilities of a car being hit, given a meteor strike in that state.

Now for the tricky question. The chance of a meteor falling on *your* car is the same no matter where you are (ignoring geometrical-astronomical effects, that is, assuming the location of a meteor strike is random). So it doesn't matter what state you're in. To calculate the relevant probabilities, consider the ratio of the area of your car to the area of Earth. The radius of Earth is 6.37×10^6 meters, so its area is $4\pi(6.37 \times 10^6)^2$, roughly $= 5.1 \times 10^{14} \text{m}^2$, so the chance of being struck is 12 m^2 divided by that, or about one chance in 42,500,000,000,000. Even this is the chance of being struck *if* a meteor strikes Earth. We should really calculate the chance of being struck over a specific period of time, say, a year. To do this, we would need to know the number of meteors that strike Earth in one year and multiply the above answer by that.

4 Straighten Up!

Fitting a Curve to the Planets

1.

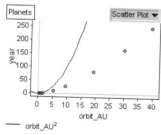

4. The parabola appears with the data below. The curve does not fit the points.

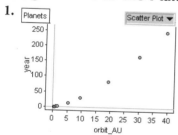

6. Notice that the value **V1** changes as the slider is moved to the left or right.

10. Your window in Fathom should look something like the following:

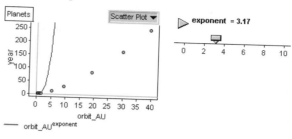

As the slider gives bigger numbers, the curve gets steeper. As the slider gives smaller numbers, the curve gets flatter.

11. The values will differ, but somewhere between 1.4 and 1.6 would be good first efforts.

13. The scale on the residual plot is different.

14. Given patience and judicious zooming, the following graph and an exponent of 1.50 will result.

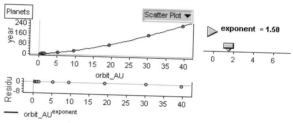

Going Further

1.

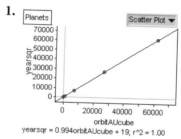

yearsqr = 0.994orbitAUcube + 19; r^2 = 1.00

2. No matter what we do with the coefficient, two or three planets never lie on the curve. An example is pictured below.

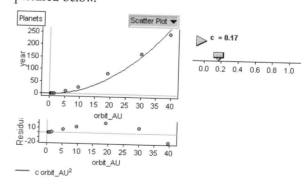

3. As before, no matter what we do with the coefficient, the curve does not match the data well. An example is below.

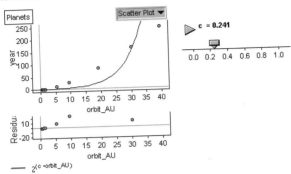

Straightening the Planets with Logs

1.
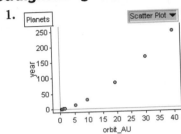

5. In this illustration, Earth is at the origin and Saturn is selected.

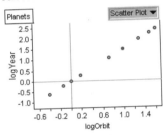

6. **LogYear = 1.5*logOrbit + 0.000044.** The correlation coefficient is 1.0

7. **log(Year) = 1.5 * log(orbit_AU).** Let's ignore the .000044.

$$\log(year) = 1.5\log(orbit\_AU)$$

$$\log(year) = \log(orbit\_AU^{1.5})$$

$$10^{(\log(year))} = 10^{(orbit\_AU^{1.5})}$$

$$year = orbit\_AU^{3/2}$$

8. The slope is the exponent in the power-law equation.

9. If it's twice as far, then **orbit_AU = 2.** So **year = $2^{1.5}$**, or 2.83 years.

10. If its year is 20 Earth years, then $20 = $ **orbit_AU$^{1.5}$**. Solving for **orbit_AU** (by taking the 2/3 power of both sides), we get **orbit_AU** $= 20^{(2/3)} = 7.37$ AU.

Going Further

1. The gap is the asteroid belt. Ceres—the largest asteroid—goes around the Sun in 4.6 years at a distance of 2.56 AU.

2. The mathematics of the situation guarantees that Earth is at the origin, but fitting a least-squares line does not guarantee that the line goes through a particular point. The intercept is due to small variations in the actual data and other effects, such as round-off error.

3. The equation is **logYear = 1.5log(Orbit_Mkm) – 3.26.** This becomes **Year ≅ (Orbit_Mkm$^{1.5}$)/1820** (because $10^{3.26} \cong 1820$). The reason for the nonzero intercept is that we're using millions of kilometers instead of astronomical units. The Earth's orbital radius, 149.6 Mkm, has to give you a year of 1.0. So we need 1820 in the denominator, or about $149^{1.5}$. Another way of looking at it is that it's the *x*-intercept that you can make sense of—and that is the log of the orbital radius of Earth.

Moore's Law Logs

2.
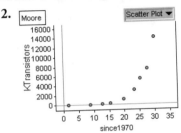

4.
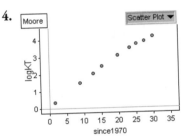

5. The graph could look like this (with lines anything like either of these).

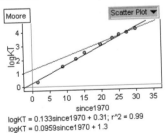

logKT = 0.133since1970 + 0.31; r^2 = 0.99
logKT = 0.0959since1970 + 1.3

6–7. Depending how you place the line, you can get a different answer. The illustration above shows a least-squares line, which predicts a value for logKT in 2005 of 4.965, which corresponds to 92,000,000 transistors.

The graph also shows a movable line, set to fit the last four points, which predicts a value of logKT of 4.673, which corresponds to about 47,000,000 transistors. Any answer near these values is

Data in Depth

reasonable. Students may be distressed by the differences in the possible solutions, which will appear as variation within the class. So a good follow-up question is, "When it gets to be 2005, what numbers of transistors-on-a-chip would you find surprising?" That is, reinforce the idea that even if we can't predict an exact answer, we can predict something *about* the answer.

Moore's Law Redux

2.

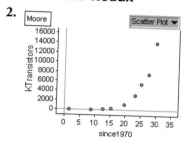

4. Here is one possibility.

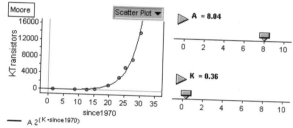

5. The above equation would be Ktransistors = $8.035*2^{(0.3636*\text{since}1970)}$. This equation would give 54,437,000 transistors in 2005.

6. Invert the coefficient in the exponent (here, 0.36) to get the right value for **T**, in this case, about 2.75. A possible graph appears below (these parameters can vary pretty widely and still give plausible graphs).

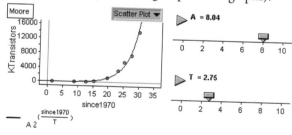

7. **T** is the doubling time because if the time (**since1970**) increases by that amount, that quotient (**since1970/T**) will increase by one. Since that's in an exponent with 2 as the base, the total amount will double when that happens.

8. Not quite. Our doubling time is greater than two years.

Area and Perimeter: A Study in Limits

8. One such table appears below.

	length random (10	width random (10	area width·length	perimeter 2 (width + le
1	9.22271	7.83248	72.2366	34.1104
2	3.84747	3.77678	14.5311	15.2485
3	4.86493	4.07526	19.8259	17.8804
4	6.097	6.30396	38.4353	24.8019
5	5.18698	0.262421	1.36118	10.8988
6	3.50465	7.25857	25.4387	21.5264
7	6.40247	4.48595	28.7212	21.7768
8	6.66227	3.10527	20.6882	19.5351
9	0.410455	4.69663	1.92776	10.2142

9. The graph appears below.

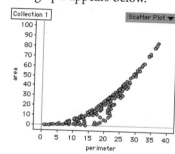

10. There are several ways to discuss this phenomenon. An intuitive approach would be to say that such a rectangle would have to have a big area and a teeny perimeter, which is impossible. A more elaborate (and revealing) response would be to say that for a given perimeter there's only so much area you can enclose. For example, with a perimeter of 20, the most area we can enclose is a five-by-five square—an area of 25 square units. Therefore everything above this limit is blank. Another response is that for a given area there's a *minimum* perimeter you need to enclose it. For example, with an area of 25, 20 units is the smallest perimeter possible by configuring a five-by-five square.

15. Here is a graph. Note that **denom** is about 16.

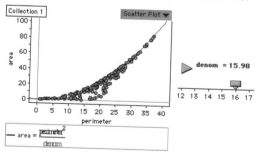

16. These rectangles are nearly squares.

17. Among rectangles, squares have the greatest area for a given perimeter—or the least perimeter for a given area. We're connecting to Question 10 above.

Going Further

1. The area of a square is **Area = length²**. However, the perimeter of a square is **4*length**. If we use perimeter in the formula for area, it would be **Area = Perimeter²/16**. This gives us the correct value for **denom**.

2. The empty region below the points exists because the limits of **length** and **width** limit the sizes of the rectangles. For instance, if the perimeter were 30, the area could not be zero since the **length** (or **width**) would have to be 15, and no values are available above 10. This means there is a lower bound, or minimum, on the area for any given perimeter.

   The derivation of the limiting line is on page 111. Plot that equation in the Fathom graph to see what it does.

How Much Tape Is Left?

Discussion Questions

Here's one response: The function is curved because the same change in **D** requires different changes in **L** depending on the current diameter of the roll (because it takes more **L** to go around the roll). So, since rise-over-run changes, the slope changes: The function curves.

The data look pretty straight because the curvature is surprisingly small over that range of diameter. It would appear to curve a lot more if you could unroll the tape all the way to zero diameter.

Student Pages

1. Depends on the tape you use.

2. Will vary. The key is that it is a decreasing graph in the first quadrant, with **L** on the vertical axis and **D** on the horizontal. The domain of the function does not extend all the way down to **D** = 0.

7. Will vary. Students should attend to the curvature of the graph, which should have a downward curvature (i.e., it's always decreasing, but more steeply on the right).

Making the Fit

9. The residual plots (from a least-squares line) on these graphs are shown below. The best one is clearly **L** as a function of **Dsquared** (or **DD**, if you use the naming in the text).

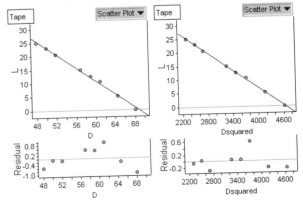

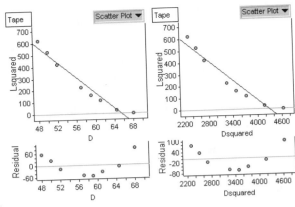

10. The equation for this graph is
    L = −0.0109 Dsquared + 50.5

11. Suppose **D** = 20 mm. Then **Dsquared** = 400.

12. **L** = −0.0109(400) + 50.5 = 46 meters. Given our accuracy, this is probably a 150-foot roll of tape. Subtract the latest value of **L** to get how much is left.

13. Since we are using cross-sectional areas, there will be a square involved in the computations. Details appear on page 115, the Algebra section.

Sonata 12: The Great Toilet Paper Mystery

This works exactly like *How Much Tape Is Left?* The difference is the nonstandard measurement (squares) and the squish factor of the roll.

Sonata 13: Printing Paragraphs

Students should predict that as length increases, width decreases. If they predict the curvature, all the better. Here's a graph with a curve fit using a slider for area, as suggested in the Teacher Notes.

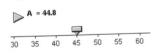

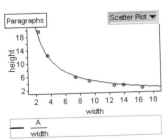

To take the ragged right into account, see *Estimating Parameters Using Residuals*, page 183.

Sonata 14: Incredible Shrinking Text

Here are two possible graphical approaches.

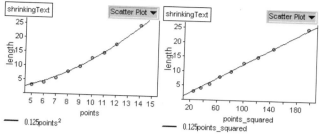

As we predicted in the Teacher Notes, the relationship is roughly quadratic. Some systematic deviation from that model is present, however; could that be a ragged right effect as well?

As for lines of text, the graph below shows this (linear) relationship.

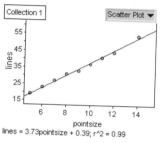

Sonata 15: Measuring the Bass

See the Teacher Notes (page 118). You have to measure carefully to distinguish the exponential decay of a guitar's frets from being simply linear. Basses are much better, but you still need care.

Sonata 16: Puff Puff Puff Puff Pop

See the Teacher Notes (page 118). Even reasonably careful puffing (and a prestretched balloon) gives a pretty good result.

5 Lines and Leverage

Introducing the World Population Clock

Discussion Questions

The estimate from Step 7 is probably better because it represents a measurement taken over a longer period of time. One way to look at it is that, with a larger number to divide by, you have more possibilities of different numbers coming up. If you only divide by a few, you can't get "as many different decimals." (This is the source of round-off error.)

People got different rates because they connected at slightly different times. Since there is always an integer number of people on the World Population Clock, the exact observed rate will wiggle around some.

If you switch the axes, instead of being people per second, it would be its reciprocal—seconds per person. If it had been 2.5 people per second, the reciprocal would be 0.4 seconds per person.

Student Pages

3. A sample of what this data looks like is below.

	Hours	minutes	seconds	pop	da
1	11	55	41	5934782465	1
2	11	56	46	5934782627	1
3	12	14	57	5934785343	1

5. Based on the first two points, the population is increasing at (627 – 465)/(46 – 41 + 60) = 2.49 persons per second. This would give 2.49*60*60*24 = 215,136 persons per day.

7. Using the first and third data points in the example, population is changing at a rate of (85,343 – 82,465)/(18*60*11) = 2.64 persons per second.

8. There are various reasons, such as rounding errors or changes in estimates.

9. These will depend on the class data. The values could reasonably vary by tens of thousands if you have a fast Internet connection. (The longer it takes students to get the data, the smaller the range will be.)

14. A formula could look like

TotalSeconds = Hours*60*60+Minutes*60+Seconds.

The table will look something like this.

	Hours	minutes	seconds	pop	day	totalseconds
1	11	55	41	5934782465	1	42941
2	11	56	46	5934782627	1	43006
3	12	14	57	5934785343	1	44097
4	12	27	50	5934787267	1	44870
5	12	28	19	5934787339	1	44899
6	12	29	42	5934787546	1	44982
7	12	30	48	5934787710	1	45048
8	12	31	34	5934787825	1	45094
9	12	34	35	5934788275	1	45275
10	12	35	51	5934788464	1	45351

17–21. Below is a scatter plot of these 10 points, with a least-squares line.

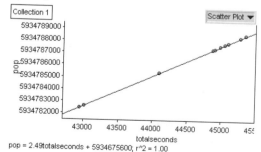

pop = 2.49totalseconds + 5934675600; r^2 = 1.00

The slope of the line is the rate of change in population per second, 2.49; that is, the number of people increases by 2.49 every second.

22. The residuals come from round-off error. Students may also suggest that people are not being born at a constant rate due to time of day, weather, wars, and so on, but looking at the source of data, how would the U.S. Census Web site get this information? They can't. They just have a model.

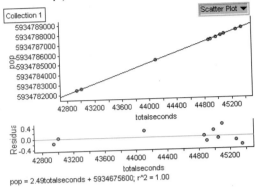

pop = 2.49totalseconds + 5934675600; r^2 = 1.00

Predict-a-Pop

Discussion Questions

Each student could have a different formula for **totalDays**, depending on how they constructed it. Basically, the formula is doing unit conversions, and it doesn't matter what order you do them in. You might see any of a number of other formulas, all algebraically equivalent.

Student Pages

4. One formula is **Totaldays = Day + Hours/24 + Minutes/(24*60) + Seconds/(24*60*60)**

or **Day + ((Second + (Minute + (Hour * 60)) * 60) / 86400)**.

6. The least-squares line will change similar to the following:

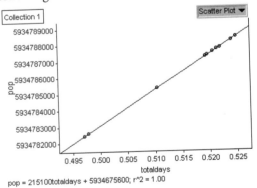

pop = 215100totaldays + 5934675600; r^2 = 1.00

In this example, which follows the previous day's work, the slope now is the average world population increase per day.

15. The formula for **time** will be something like **DayP + HourP/24 + MinuteP/(24*60) + SecondP/(24*60*60)**.

16. The exact value will differ from day to day, but all the values in the class should be close to one another. "Reasonable" might be "because we did this Wednesday afternoon, and now it's Friday at about 10 a.m., so it should be a little less than 2."

19. Here is a sample table.

	name	slope	intercepts	predictedPop
=				slope*timeP + intercepts
1	Albert	215000	5934675600	5936382700
2	Barrie	214000	5934674500	5936373660
3	Carrie	216000	5934676300	5936391340
4	Debbie	213000	5934673200	5936364420

This works because the regression lines are linear and because the **slope** and **intercept** define the regression line predicted from our original points. The linear function transforms any value for **time** into a predicted population based on those data.

22. The graph for this example is below.

23. For this example, a range from 5,936,360,000 to 5,936,390,000 would be reasonable.

World Population: A Little Leverage

The specific responses in this activity depend greatly on the particular data students have saved from previous activities.

5. Distributions should look about the same throughout the class. The true value should be within the range of the distribution.

6. Students can select their own line in the case table and it will highlight in the histogram.

10. To zoom, use **CTRL** (Win) or **OPTION** (Mac) and click at the point you wish to investigate. For example, you might get an answer like **Pop = 215073.4Totaldays + 5934675573.2**. Fathom will add extra significant figures as you zoom in (and they become relevant).

12–13. **Slope2** should be tighter because its line was based on points taken over a longer period of time. Slope is difference in population ÷ difference in time. So the differences between groups' populations get divided by a larger time-baseline—resulting in a smaller difference in slope.

16. **predictedPop2** should be tighter.

17. Unlike the question in Step 13, when the points we are predicting are further from the points used to find the least-squares line, a given difference in slopes produces a greater difference in predictions than when the predicted point is closer to the original data. That is, the change in population is equal to **slope *(change in time)**. Small differences in slope, multiplied by large changes in time, give larger differences in population.

Going Further

1. The experiment might have a large number of closely spaced points (and therefore have a short baseline for calculation), contrasted with a few widely spaced points.

2. The formula for **EightBillion** is **Days = (8000000000 – intercept)/slope**. This gives total days to reach eight billion population. To convert this to years, divide by 365.25 (the 0.25 accounts for leap years). At the time of this writing, we predicted reaching eight billion in about 2025. We assume that the population growth rate will stay linear and neither flatten out nor become more exponential.

The predictions might look like the following.

	name	slope	intercepts	predictedPop	EightBillion	EightBilYears
=				slope•timeP + intercepts	(8000000000 –	EightBillion
1	Albert	215000	5934675600	5936382700	9606.16	26.293
2	Barrie	214000	5934674500	5936373660	9651.05	26.4159
3	Carrie	216000	5934676300	5936391340	9561.68	26.1713
4	Debbie	213000	5934673200	5936364420	9696.37	26.5399

Collection 1

Jupiter's Moons

Be sure to look at the Teacher Notes, page 139.

3. This should be a rough but plausible estimate. For example, using the Ganymede graph on the student page, anything from five to nine days is reasonable for a single period. So seven plus or minus two days is reasonable for this moon.

6. See the Teacher Notes for a good formula.

8. Different segments of the graph jump around, seemingly at random. That is, a small change in the slider makes a big change in each point on the graph.

11. Below is one possible graph for Ganymede.

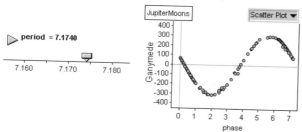

12. The value of **period** here is approximately 7.174. The plus-or-minus will be smaller than in Question 3 above, since it will be clear in a fraction of a day that the points no longer line up.

17. The estimate will be even more precise.

18. It is more accurate because the new points are much more sensitive to the slider parameter. They nail it down more tightly—simply because they are so far away in time.

Going Further

1. You can actually tweak the slider so the July points are on a different part of the curve. But when you do, it's so far off that other segments (like the ones you lined up for the question in Step 12) are no longer lined up. So we aren't a whole cycle off.

4. You should find the same relationship that we did for the entire solar system in the *Planets* activities (page 102). That is, the square of the period is proportional to the cube of the radius.

6 Describing and Modeling Change

Mauna Loa

The Tasks

The data increase pretty linearly, with a seasonal variation superimposed on it; that seasonal variation has a period of one year and an amplitude of about 7. The overall increase is at a rate of about 1.0 to 1.5 parts per million (ppm) per year. The extrapolations will depend on when you do the task.

Carbon Dioxide: The Whole World

2. The scatter plot is displayed in the Teacher Notes, page 147.

3. Here are the six scatter plots. Most (except **solid**) have some dip in the 1980 range.

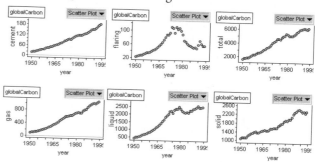

4. Other than the decline in the early 1980s, the graph tends to go up, sometimes with more acceleration than at other times, such as in the 1960s and 1970s. Also there is a peak again near 1990. The overall curve does not appear to be exactly linear.

As an example of another graph, the **flaring** graph is considerably different in shape from the **total** graph. There is definitely a peak (maximum) in the mid-1970s, with an initial drop, followed by another quick rise to a peak, followed by a gradual decline for the next 10 years. Though **flaring** rises in the early 1990s (the Gulf War?), it is short-lived.

Other graphs can be discussed in a similar way. It might be of interest to research historical background on oil production and distribution to see if these fluctuations in graphs have global causes or are just anomalies.

5. The graphs are different in that they clearly have different directions: While **solids** are continuing to go upward, **solidProp** is going downward. This says that burning of solid fuels is decreasing as a proportion of the total.

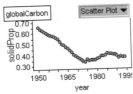

6. The formula to use is **total/(percap*1000)**. **Percap** is total **CO2** divided by total population to get the per person value. Dividing **total** by **percap** gives the population total. Dividing by 1000 changes the results from population in millions to population in billions. It has taken about 37 years for the population to double from about 2520 million to 5032 million.

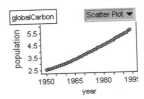

Carbon Dioxide by Region

5–6. Specific numbers and intervals of years should support these arguments if possible. Some of the charts may be hard to follow if the graph is not made large enough. Students who enjoy historical research might find some of these data interesting to correlate with world events. Another interesting feature of the graph is that as U.S. CO_2 levels were declining slightly in the late 1980s, levels of CO_2 from Centrally-Planned Europe (CPE) were rapidly increasing to levels as high as the United States, then dramatically dropped off. What happened? The collapse of former Soviet industry after 1989? It might be of interest that the graph for Germany actually stays flat for most of the graph, then begins a slow downward turn after 1990. Perhaps this shows the gradual industrial decision by the united Germany to shut down East German industry that was highly inefficient and outdated in favor of high-tech, environmentally clean production facilities. Also, the Middle East (MDE) graph stays close to the graph for AFR throughout all the years shown (except for 1991 when, during the Gulf War, the Iraqi Army blew up hundreds of oil wells in Kuwait).

Change Playground

Exploring

6. First, the value can only change up and down since its horizontal position (3 in this case) is the **caseIndex**, not a data value. As the point is dragged lower, the difference between it and point 2 decreases, but the difference between it and point 4 increases. Therefore, in the second **B** plot, point 3 decreases and point 4 increases. The directions reverse if point 3 is dragged higher.

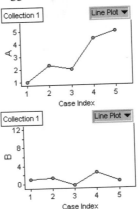

7.

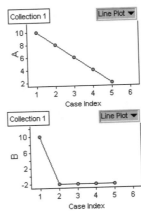

8. The points in **A** determine the values of the differences that are graphed in **B**. The first point chosen for the difference in **B** is 10, since a missing value (previous **A**) is assumed to be zero.

Exercises

1.

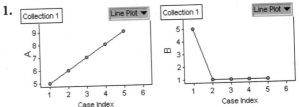

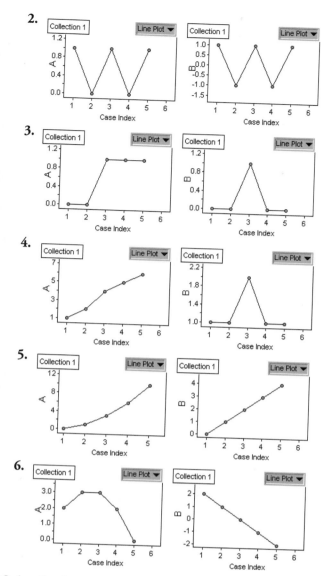

2.

3.

4.

5.

6.

Going Further

1. You can't drag the points in the **B** graph because they are determined by the differences between successive points in the **A** graph. Since this is determined by formula, the **B** graph points are not movable.

2. If **B** is flat, **A** is straight. The higher the value of **B**'s points, the steeper **A**'s line.

Consumer Price Index

Discussion Questions

The first point is strange because in the first case (1913), **prev(CPI)** is defined as zero. So **CPI–prev(CPI)** does not give the difference between 1913 and 1912, but rather the total value for 1913.

To change **CPI** from being based on 1967 to being based on 1990, divide by 3.914 (since **CPI** in 1990 is 391.4, this converts it to 100). Note that you have to use the number itself, unless you use a convoluted formula such as **sum(CPI, year=1990)**.

Student Page

3. 1980 (or thereabouts) looks like the steepest year.

7. By pointing to the highest point in the graph, we can read its year and its increase in the status bar. It was 29.4 in 1980.

8. One formula to calculate the percentage change of the **CPI** from one year to the next is **deltaCPI/prev (CPI)**. The results are shown below, and the highest point in this graph occurred in 1918 when the change was about 17.5%. Contrast this with 1980 when the **percentChange** was only 13.5%.

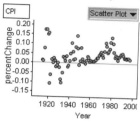

9. A typical **percentChange** overall is about 3%. For the past 10 years, the guess might be about 3.5%. As stated above, the highest **percentChange** was in 1918.

Radiosonde

Discussion Questions

(second bullet) Moving at four meters per second is about the same as running at 9 miles per hour. Running a four-minute mile is the same as running at 15 miles per hour, so four meters per second is speedy, but a believable pace if you're in shape. Fast marathon runners move at about 12 miles per hour.

Student Page

2. The graph should look something like this. The equation is below the graph, and the slope is the coefficient of time, in this case 4.27.

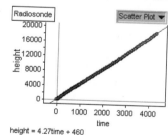

height = 4.27time + 460

3. The above estimate says the balloon is rising at 4.27 meters per second.

7.

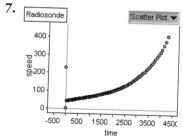

Data in Depth
© 2001 Key Curriculum Press

8. First there is no speed at time zero, so the first speed value is actually the altitude of the field. The second is also misleading, since the second value recorded was so close to the first one. This is because the first reading is taken (in this case) 33 seconds before launch, probably to provide baseline readings.

11. The units for *speed* are currently in meters (height was in meters, so this represents a change in meters).

12. For one thing it does not include any reference to time. It represents changing altitude but no change in time, hence does not represent rate or acceleration.

The Right Way

15. The scatter plot looks like this.

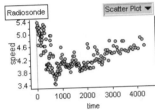

16. Make a summary table. The mean of the speeds is 4.31. Also, scrolling through the table shows numbers running from about 3.4 to greater than 5.3. This is consistent with the estimate of the slope we had in Step 3.

Going Further

1. If we interpret the equation correctly, the intercept should be the altitude at time zero, which would mean that the balloon was released at a site 810 meters above sea level.

2. By examining the times, we see that the intervals increase as the balloon ascends. Also, the height itself is not uniformly changing. We want snapshots of speed, not the average speed; besides, **height** includes the altitude of the field.

3. The average of the values in **speed** is 4.31, the mean that can be found from a summary table. The slope of the least-squares line in the graph of **height** as a function of **time** is 4.17. One of the reasons for this difference is that the speed values are calculated for different amounts of time. A weighted average would give a closer result.

4. This gives the graph below. The rate of change is usually negative, since temperature goes down as altitude goes up. However, this is subject to a variety of atmospheric conditions, such as sunshine, clouds, rain, inversions, and so on. When it changes sign the temperature actually is going back up.

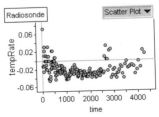

5. Here is the graph. Values appear mostly near -5 degrees celsius per km. This would be of interest if you were climbing up a mountain or going up in a hot air balloon and needed to know what to wear for the altitude you were visiting.

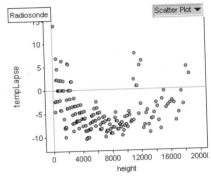

Generation by Generation

Student Pages

8. The graph now has a definite curve to it (exponential perhaps?).

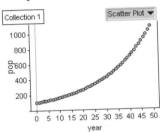

Making a Function to Fit

12. As the value of **A** goes toward zero, the curve gets flatter near the origin. As the value of **A** gets larger, the curve gets steeper close to the *y*-axis. The value of **A** also controls the *y*-intercept.

13. The crucial value for **B** is 1. At 1, the curve becomes a straight line, since we are graphing A(1)^year. For values just slightly larger than 1, the curve begins to move upward on the right end very quickly. An example is below.

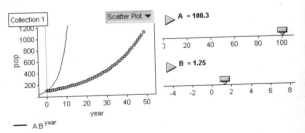

Data in Depth
© 2001 Key Curriculum Press

14. Since the graph goes through the ordered pair (1,100), the formula AB^{year} must be equal to 100 when **year** = 1. But **year** has a value of **caseIndex–1**, so **A** must be 100. Move the slider for **A** to 100. This raises the *y*-intercept of the graph to where it must be. Now adjust the **B** slider to see what value makes the graph of the new function lie on top of the original **POP** graph (try values around 1.05). Zooming in on the slider scales eases some of the slider's sensitivity.

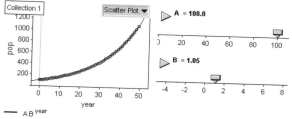

15. **A** is the initial population, and **B** represents the (1 + *rate*) term seen in the compound interest formula.

16. **A** could be initial population, and **B** could be rate of increase.

Making the Simulation More Realistic

18. One possible formula under **Functions/Arithmetic** is the use of **floor**, which returns the greatest integer less than or equal to the argument (this is the greatest integer function). Another possibility is **round**, which returns the correctly rounded integer value. These would be inserted at the beginning of the **births** and **deaths** formulas.

20. The rate at which the curve will go up will change, that is, the population should not increase quite so quickly, so the curve from Question 14 above will flatten slightly.

21. We need to subtract the **deaths** from the previous **pop** formula we had created, so the formula for **pop** reads **prev(pop)+prev(births)–prev(deaths)**.

22. Here is the new graph; it has flattened out to the right.

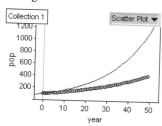

25. Here's one way to do it.

let **deaths** be

floor (pop•deathRate)

let **births** be

floor (pop•birthRate)

26. If the **birthRate** stays the same, increasing the **deathRate** will make the graph drop on the right rather dramatically as the value of the **deathRate** slider increases. If the **deathRate** slider moves toward zero, the population curve moves upward much more rapidly.

27. If **deathRate > birthRate**, the graph becomes an exponential decay going downward toward zero population or extinction.

Going Further

Both the **floor** and the **round** functions change the data and hence the curve. The **floor** choice will make the overall graph curve upward less quickly; hence the graph will drop below the real numbers originally in the table.

Generation II: Limits to Growth

3. The population levels off at about 1000.

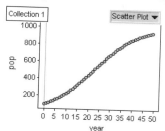

4. As the population increases, so do the number of deaths—and the death rate.

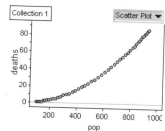

5. The population stabilizes at close to 1000. If we omit the **floor( )** function, the algebra is clear: stability occurs when

births = deaths or **0.10 pop = 0.02 pop (pop/200)**. Solving this gives **pop = 1000** (or **pop = 0**).

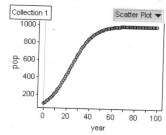

6. If **birthRate** increases to 0.2, the population will stabilize at about 2000. Do the algebra in the formulas to set **birthRate** and **deathRate** equal in order to see the reason for this.

7. The graph shows a stabilized population at 1998, or nearly 2000.

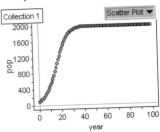

A Plague

10. Collections of some of the graphs using **Rerandomize** are pictured below.

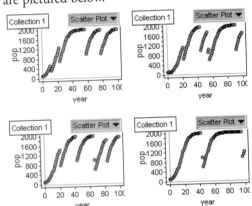

11. The formula uses a random number generator that is reset each time it is rerandomized. When the random number is less than 0.05, half of the population is killed off in the plague.

Going Further

1. **Pop/200** causes the value of the **deathRate** to drop when the population is relatively low, below 200. However, as the population grows above 200, the value of **pop/200** rises above 1, and hence the value of **deathRate** begins to increase, ultimately reaching the same value as **birthrate** unless some other factor (**plague**) alters the values.

2. Look again at the **births = deaths** formula. Let's let the denominator equal D.

$$birthRate \times pop = deathRate \times pop \times \left(\frac{pop}{D}\right)$$

$$pop = D \times \frac{birthRate}{deathRate}$$

So the stable population (where *births = deaths*) is proportional to the denominator D.

3. The complicated graph below is an example of this plot. As a plague hits, the population goes down because **deathRate** increases dramatically and **birthRate** immediately decreases dramatically (there are fewer people to give birth to children). Each time the plague hits, there is a point far to the right of the gradually sloping curve that connects to the next point back and down toward the curve.

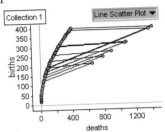

4. Below is a scatter plot using a plague formula that will cause the random number generator to be applied more frequently as population increases. Though the population does not stabilize as it did without the plague, we can use plagues to keep the population from getting too large.

$$\text{if } (\text{random } (\ ) < 0.05\cdot 0.05\text{pop}) \begin{cases} \frac{pop}{2} \\ 0 \end{cases}$$

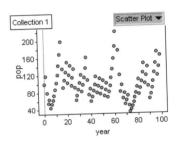

Building the Weather Machine

15. A ribbon chart might be useful to see the percentage of sun versus rain. Other graphs will show the data in other ways.

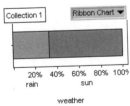

20. An example is below. This helps us to see the strings of sunny and rainy days. Students might be surprised that some streaks are so long.

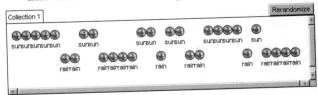

Data in Depth
© 2001 Key Curriculum Press

Sonata 17: Sequences of Squares

The differences are odd numbers; to be precise, if the number is n^2, the difference between it and the next square is $2n + 1$. Algebraically, students can see that $(n + 1)^2 - n^2 = (n^2 + 2n + 1) - n^2 = 2n + 1$.

Geometrically, you can draw overlapping squares with a common corner, like the one below.

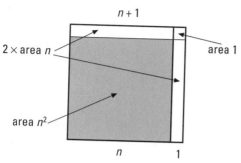

The difference between the gray (n by n) square and the clear, outer ($n + 1$) by ($n + 1$) square is two strips of size n and one of 1, or $2n + 1$.

Sonata 18: Fibonacci

The key expression is `prev(F) + prev(prev(F))`. The full formula appears on page 170.

Changing the first two elements changes the sequence, often to a remarkably similar sequence.

The sequence of ratios converges to the golden ratio, about 1.618.

Since the sequence of ratios converges to a constant, a good function is exponential. It should have the form $A*1.618^{(caseIndex)}$. Some experimentation yields $A = 0.45$ as a reasonable coefficient.

You get the Lucas numbers, which are the Fibonacci-like sequence that begins with (1, 3) instead of (1,1).

7 What to Do with Leftovers

Residuals Playground

4. The points show up on the curve because they're calculated using the official formula, just as the curve is.

5. For each case, **area** is the vertical position of the data; **areaP** is the vertical position of the curve. So the difference in the positions is the vertical distance.

7. The points move in tandem; if you move the data up, the residuals go up too.

9–10. Residual plots will vary. Points will not appear exactly on the curve when the plot is rescaled because you can't get them all exactly on the line (by dragging) and the scale in the residual plot is so much finer.

Heating Water

2. Below is what the graph looks like. Differences between student predictions and this graph should be noted and discussed—especially when students think it ought to be curved. (The point is that it *is* curved but we need residual plots to see it.)

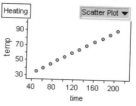

3. The graph and equation are below. The slope is the rate of change in temperature (in degrees Celsius) per minute of heating; that is, the temperature increases at 0.351 degrees per minute.

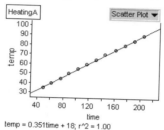

temp = 0.351time + 18; r^2 = 1.00

4. Here is an example of the point on the line at (103, 55). The line predicts that the coordinates should be (103, 54.673), so the data point is actually a little above the line, hence the residual would be +0.327.

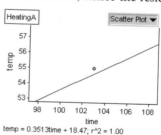

temp = 0.3513time + 18.47; r^2 = 1.00

5. The points in the middle are slightly above the least-squares line, and they all are together. The ones on the ends are below the line.

8. The formula is the standard formula for residuals that assigns positive values to distances from points above the line to the line and negative values to distances from points below the line.

9. The curve shows that the water heats more quickly at the beginning than at the end; that is, it's harder to heat hot water 1 degree than cold water 1 degree. Note that it is *incorrect* to say that the water heats more slowly at the beginning of the graph (near $t = 50$) because the residuals are low. Look at the *slope:* it's highest at the beginning. (Students may say that this graph shows that it takes a while for the water to "get started." This is wrong; that effect takes place at lower temperatures. You can see it if you look at the complete data set, **HeatingAndCooling**.)

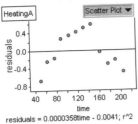

residuals = 0.0000358time – 0.0041; r^2

A Great Shortcut

10. Both the original graph and the residual graph appear in the same window.

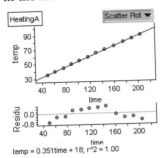

temp = 0.351time + 18; r^2 = 1.00

11. All graphs and the table reflect the changes made. In particular, the residual plot shows clearly which side of the line the point is on and how far from the line it has been dragged.

Going Further

1. The residuals are smaller than 1 degree in absolute value. This could be due to errors in reading the scale on the thermometer. However, the *pattern* of the residuals is too regular to be due to chance.

2. In the original data, time measurements are to the nearest second, but it takes time to read the scale and the watch, and even with a stopwatch, catching the exact moment when the temperature reached 30, 35, and so on would be inexact with a mercury thermometer. So the time measurements are probably good to within three seconds, but certainly not within one second.

3. The time measurements would have to be relatively late at the beginning and end of the experiment and early in the middle—by up to about two seconds.

4. If the delay were the same every time, it would have no effect on the slope of the line or the residuals. There would be a difference only in the intercept of the fitted line.

Introduction to Residuals III: Radiosonde Residuals

3. The points at the far right end of the graph appear to diverge from the least-squares line.

5. After one anomalous point at the beginning, the residual curve increases fairly steadily from launch until about 500 meters, then decreases fairly steadily until about 2500 meters, crossing from positive residuals to negative residuals near 1200 meters. After 2500 meters, the curve increases fairly steadily again through the end of the graph, crossing from negative to positive near 3200 meters. The residuals at the right end are clearly increasing and are larger than the residuals elsewhere.

6. The balloon is not going down, but its rate of rise is lower than the least-squares line has predicted it would be for the corresponding time. This could be due to any number of reasons—the important thing is to recognize that the balloon is just rising more slowly.

7. If you choose the very first hump near the top of the left side of the graph, the residual plot is at (365, 119.75). The point in the original data is at (365, 1967).

8. This means that the data point is 119.75 meters above what the line predicted it would be, or that the line has predicted that the point should be at 1847.25 meters.

Estimating Parameters Using Residuals

Discussion Questions

(first bullet) People who set type care about lengths of text—for example, newspaper layout people, advertisers, book publishers, magazine editors, and so on.

(fourth bullet) Students will probably get tighter results with the residual plots.

Student Pages

5. A value somewhere near 45 is reasonable, as in the graph below.

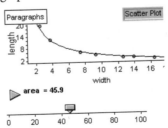

6. The area is in square centimeters, and the value is consistent with the size of the paragraphs.

7. The range 42 to 48 is a fairly good interval.

8.

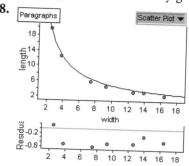

9. One reasonable value is 45.5, which leaves the first two points high and the rest low but flat. The first point of the graph has a large residual near 1.5, while the rest of the residuals are small.

10. Values depend on what choices are made for "acceptable" values, but if students use the same criteria for a good fit, the range should be smaller.

Improving the Model

15. As before, the whole curve moves.

16. The first points move more than the later ones.

17. In our fit, the **area** is near 38.5, and the slider for **dw** is near 0.56. Student answers may vary, depending on what they like in a good fit.

18. The value for **area** was smaller after adding **dw**. The reason is that we are now accounting for the white space in the ragged right edges of the paragraphs, subtracting it.

19. The left-hand points were those with shorter lines; hence the word wrap had a larger effect on their adjustment than on the paragraphs with longer lines.

Going Further

1. (algebraically) As the value of the x-coordinate gets smaller (toward zero), the effect of the subtraction of **dw** makes the denominator smaller (proportionally), much more so than when the value of x is larger. The smaller the denominator, the more effect this value of **dw** will have on the formula.

2. Again, the first points are the most problematic, though these are actually from the other end of the data; an area in the low to mid-40s is reasonable. The relationship is still **area = length * (width-dw)**, but this time we solve for **width**, to get **(area/length) + dw**. Then the same values give a reasonable fit.

Exercises: Inverting Residual Plots

Each exercise has multiple solutions; the test of a solution is whether it makes the relevant graph in Fathom. Here are examples:

6. V = 20H + H2/100

7. V = 20Hf (1/100(H + 1/2))

8. V = 20H + (2H/50)

9. V = 20H + randomNormal(0, .1)

10. V = 20H + (sgn(H + 1/2)/10)

11. V = 20H + (cos(H)/10)

British Couples

Discussion Questions

(second bullet) The slope is the number of millimeters taller the average husband is for a wife one millimeter taller.

(third bullet) We might have chosen a steeper slope to align with the major axis of the cloud of points.

Student Pages

2. In general, the taller the wife, the taller her husband.

3. It's really just $y = kx$, but transformed up and across to the means. Adding **hbar** raises the function up by that amount. Subtracting **wbar** from **W_Height** translates it to the right by that amount.

4. **hbar** is simply **mean(H_Height)**, similarly for **wbar**.

7. When you drag **m**, the line rotates around the intersection of means. The best slope depends on how you look at the points. Anywhere between 0.4 and 1.0 is plausible; encourage students to explain why they like one slope over another. (Larger slopes, incidentally, minimize the slanted—as opposed to vertical—distance from points to the line.)

8. Now the best slope is likely to be closer to the least-squares slope, between 0.4 and 0.5.

Goodness of Fit

11. **HHPred** is the vertical position of the line itself, so the difference is the distance from the line.

14. The mean residual stays incredibly close to zero no matter what you do. (In fact, it's theoretically zero.) The margin hint wisely suggests not to analyze the tiny number too closely. It's a bad measure because you can't use it at all to find a best value.

16. You try to minimize the mean of the absolute residuals. That value will depend on the specific data you're using. In the file on the CD, it is about 45.

17. Again, it depends; in our file, it is about 0.45.

18. An advantage is that it's objective. A disadvantage is that it requires computation and it may not be clear that you're making the *right* computation.

Going Further

1. It is close, but not exactly the same. (This is the least-squares line.)

2. Both are quite close to the least-squares line. In our file, the median-median line was quite different.

3. The key is that the equation for the line goes through the means. Using conventional notation with subscripts we modify the equation for **HHpred** to x's and y's. If we let δ represent a residual, a demonstration complete with big sigmas might look like this.

$$\delta_i = y_i - \text{pred}_i$$

$$= y_i - m(x_i - \bar{x}) - \bar{y}$$

Now take the mean of both

$$\frac{\sum\limits_{i=1}^{n} \delta_i}{n} = \frac{\sum y_i}{n} - m\frac{\sum x_i}{n} + m\frac{\sum \bar{x}}{n} - \frac{\sum \bar{y}}{n}$$

$$= \bar{y} - m\bar{x} + m\bar{x}\frac{\sum 1}{n} - \bar{y}\frac{\sum 1}{n}$$

$$= \bar{y} - \bar{x} + \bar{x} - \bar{y}$$

$$= 0$$

Modeling Mauna Loa

2. year + (month − 1)/12. Since we don't want the formula to jump to the next year in December of the present year, the "minus 1" takes care of that. So January 1980 is 1980.0.

3. The lowest value for **CO2** is 328.17 and the highest is at 351.66, so the range is 23.49.

4. The data look periodic, with periods of one year. There is also an upward trend.

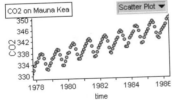

6. The residuals have a lowest value of about −4 and a highest value of about 3.3, so the range is 7.3.

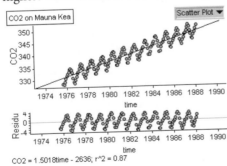

CO2 = 1.5018time − 2636; r^2 = 0.87

Seasonal Variation

9. The graph of **afterLine** looks like this.

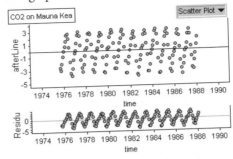

13. The **amp** slider changes the height of the red curve in the graph, and the **phase** slider moves the red curve to the left or right.

14. Here is an example in which **amp** = 3.5 and **phase** = 3.99.

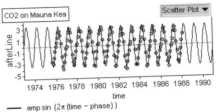

amp sin (2π (time − phase))

15. The values go from −2.5 to 1.3, so the range is 3.8.

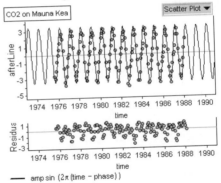

amp sin (2π (time − phase))

16. Here is **1.5018time − 2636 + 3.5sin(2*pi(time − 4))**.

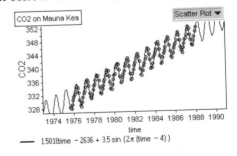

1.5018time − 2636 + 3.5 sin (2π (time − 4))

Going Further

1. It depends on the values of **amp** and **phase**. For our values, the greatest residuals are during the early months of the year—January or February.

2. The residuals could also be periodic if the oscillation is not perfectly sinusoidal, but still periodic. That is, higher-order Fourier terms remain.

Data in Depth
© 2001 Key Curriculum Press

3. There are many possible strategies and various combinations of the parameters. Using just the data set, **MaunaShort**, you might improve slightly (but not much) over an eyeball fit.

4. One clear feature of the larger data set is that the increase in **CO2** slowed down in the 1960s, then climbed again at its earlier rate in the 1970s and 1980s, but the increase is slowing down again in the 1990s. Students might try piecewise fits to the trend or higher-order polynomials.

Sonata 19: Cooling Off

The curve decreases, approaching an asymptote (the ambient temperature). Students may interpret this as a hyperbola, though cooling is usually an exponential. Either curve-fitting will do in a mathematics class; if this is physics or chemistry, insist on the exponential. Even so, things aren't perfect, perhaps because the pan itself is cooling along with the water and the stove remains hotter than the room.

If the function has the form **temp = A * e^(−(time/k)) + ambient**, you'll need sliders for **A** (related to the initial temperature), **k** (a cooling rate), and **ambient** (the position of the asymptote). Using a transformed time attribute (so that the cooling starts at **time** = 0) helps.

Sonata 20: Out on a Limb with Jupiter

The angular size of Jupiter is inversely proportional to the distance from Earth to Jupiter. If the two planets' orbits around the sun are circular, you can use the lengths of years in **Planets** as their periods (Earth's, one year, is 365.25 days).

So set up parametric equations for the x and y positions of Earth and Jupiter and use the Pythagorean theorem to find the distance. Because you know the periods and radii, you won't need sliders for those. You will need one for **phase** and one for a constant relating the distance (probably in astronomical units) to the angular size.

Unmodeled effects include the ellipticity of the orbits.

The author's solution is on the CD-ROM, so you can see how he modeled these effects. Note especially transforming time to years, the use of measures to record Jupiter's parameters, and how he handled **phase**.

8 Under a Cloud

Random Walk: Inventing Spread

Discussion Questions

The horizontal axis in a line plot (if your attribute is on the vertical) is **caseIndex**, the number of the case.

The histogram of **final**s shows the distribution of final positions for many random walks.

In general, the more steps you take, the farther you are from the start. For one thing, you have the *possibility* of being farther from the start—as many as n units in n steps. For another, suppose you're some distance already. In the next step, you'll be either one step closer or one step farther away—so that evens out *unless* you happen to be at the origin, in which case you'll definitely be one step farther away. So with every (even) step, the average distance increases.

But this is not linearly additive; if you've taken twice as many steps, you are *not* generally twice as far away. It goes as the square root; on the average, you have to take four times as many steps to be twice as far from the start.

Student Pages

7. The starting value is either 1 or −1, but the remaining values vary each time you rerandomize, with the final values usually between −6 and 6.

Finding the Averages

13. In one such example, scores ranged from −6 to 6 with these totals: −6 (2 times), −4 (four times), −2 (six times), 0 (four times), 2 (no times), 4 (three times), 6 (once).

14. The above average is −1.1.

15. One would expect the average to be zero because of symmetry.

16. The average of the absolute values above is 2.9.

17. The first average represents the location on the number line where the average walk ended. The second average represents the distance of the final point from the starting point.

Collecting Measures

30. The bars represent the number of times the walk ended at each of the values. The line represents the mean (average) of those end values.

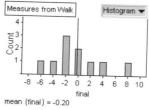

31. This value is bigger because it is averaging in a different way—it is ignoring the direction from zero; hence the value of the numerator of the fraction used to calculate the mean will be larger.

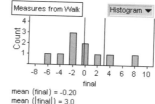

34. We expect a value near zero for **final**. Several trials for the mean of absolute value for **final** produced values near 2.5.

Going Further

1. You could do this with sums and combinations, but let's use Pascal's triangle instead. Each additional row represents the possibilities after an additional step. After 10 steps, we have 11 numbers, representing the possibilities from −10 to +10 (even numbers only). Looking at only that row of Pascal's triangle, we see:

Pascal	1	10	45	120	210	252	210	120	45	10	1
Location	−10	−8	−6	−4	−2	0	2	4	6	8	10

Each of the *Pascal* numbers is the number of ways you can get to that location. Since there are 10 steps, there are $2^{10} = 1024$ possible routes—and that is the sum of the *Pascal* row.

To find the expected absolute value, we find the mean of the absolute value of *Location,* weighted by the number of routes in *Pascal.* So we add the absolute values of the *products* of the top and bottom rows of that table:

$10 + 80 + 270 + 480 + 420 + 0 + 420 + 480 + 270 + 80 + 1 = 2520.$

That's the total distance for all the "walks," so we divide by the number of walks, 1024.

$2520/1024 = 2.461$, which is our expected value.

2. The mean of the absolute value will not change value for 400 or for 40 trials, since each walk consists of 10 steps. But the observed mean will probably be closer to the theoretical value with 400 trials than with only 40 samples.

3. If the walk were 40 steps instead of 10, we could extend Pascal's triangle further or use combinations or estimate that since there are four times as many steps, we're likely to be twice as far away— about 5 units. The exact answer is

$$expected\ value = 4 \cdot (0.5)^n \sum_{i=1}^{n/2} i \cdot \binom{10}{\frac{n}{2} - i} \approx 5.015,$$

where *n*, the number of steps, is 40.

SATs and GPAs

1. The mean **math** score for males is higher than the mean **math** score for females, but the first-year grade point average for females is higher than that for males.

8.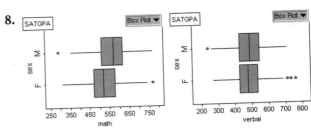

9. The median for the males' **math** scores is significantly higher than the females', and it would appear that the median for females' **math** scores is closer to the first quartile for males', which would indicate that while 50% of the females score above 522, nearly 75% of the males score above 522. Contrast this with the **verbal** scores, which are nearly identical.

Making It Quantitative

12–13, 16. (We have filled in the table.)

SATGPA	Summary Table		
⬇ ⇨	**math**	**verbal**	**FYGPA**
	110	110	1.04
	50	10	−0.18
	0.45454545	0.09090909	−0.17307692
	0.50498999	0.078359643	−0.20058607

S1 = iqr ( )

S2 = median (?, sex = "M") − median (?, sex = "F")

S3 = $\dfrac{\text{median (?, sex = "M") − median (?, sex = "F")}}{\text{iqr ( )}}$

S4 = $\dfrac{\text{mean (?, sex = "M") − mean (?, sex = "F")}}{\text{stdDev ( )}}$

15. The difference in the **math** scores is larger compared to the difference in the **verbal** scores or the GPA.

17. $\dfrac{\text{mean (?, sex = "M") − mean (?, sex = "F")}}{\text{stdDev ( )}}$

18. The difference in the **math** scores is bigger (proportionally) than the **verbal** or the **FYGPA** scores, and though females have better average **FYGPA** scores, the proportional difference is less than the difference in the **math** scores.

19. These scores show that the males tend to score higher than the females do even when SATs are totaled, but only by one quarter of an IQR or one third of a standard deviation. The males' "superiority" in SAT scores is now similar to the females' "superiority" in GPA.

20. The numbers indicate some differences, but the range in values for the **FYGPA** scores is very small compared to the range in scores for the SATs. The averages we have found put the differences fairly close together, though the **math** difference still is more than the others.

Going Further

1. By plotting graphs of both **totalSAT**s and **HSGPA**s against the **FYGPA**s, we can find the least-squares regression line and see that neither graph is an excellent predictor of success in college. The differences in r^2 suggest that high school GPA may be a slightly better predictor than the combined SAT score.

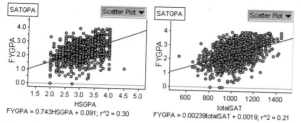

FYGPA = 0.743HSGPA + 0.091; r^2 = 0.30   FYGPA = 0.00239totalSAT + 0.0019; r^2 = 0.21

2. The slope of the least-squares line in the above graph tells us that for each increase of 1 in the **HSGPA** there should be an increase of 0.743 in the **FYGPA** at college.

Exploring the Normal Distribution

Discussion Questions

The first two questions probe basic ideas about random variables and standard deviation. If you double **a**, its standard deviation doubles because each value is doubled: Extreme values become twice as extreme. But if you add **a** to **b** (an attribute *like* **a** but not equal to **a**), it's like going on a random walk. Some extreme values will become more extreme, but in general, extreme values will not be added to values that are as extreme as they are. So the standard deviation does not double.

The Problems

1. In one trial, we had 72 cases within one standard deviation from the mean. So the empirical proportion is 72%. Answers will vary somewhat around the theoretical (68%) value.

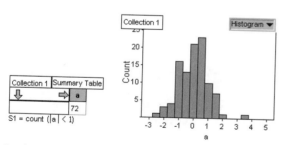

2. In the example from above, we could create a slider to represent standard deviations and find where the count goes to 50. The table and chart below show this method, which produces a value of 0.715 to enclose half of the cases. (Theoretical value: 0.67 standard deviations enclose 50%.)

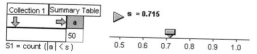

3. If we rounded it off to 2, we'd expect to enclose more than 95% of the cases. But how much more? We did 30 trials of 1000 cases; of those 30,000 cases, 95.5% were within 2.0 standard deviations. The theoretical value is 95.45%.

4. In general, the mean and standard deviation will be doubled: 0 and 2, respectively.

5. The standard deviation of **(a + b)** will be about 1.4 times that of **a** alone. If the cases truly had standard deviations of 1, then we would need to add four of them together to get a standard deviation of 2.

6. First, we needed to make a new attribute, **game**, which is **win** if b>a and **lose** otherwise. For this example, **c**, the mean of **b**'s distribution, only needed to be 0.607 for **b** to win twice as many as **a**.

$$\text{if } (b > a) \begin{cases} \text{"win"} \\ \text{"lose"} \end{cases}$$

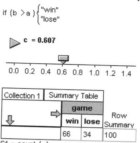

7. As **b**'s standard deviation gets larger and larger, the difference between the means of **a** and **b** will be less and less significant compared to the spread of **b**, so the probability that **b > a** approaches 50%.

8. Here is a typical result with the standard deviation of **b** equal to 100.

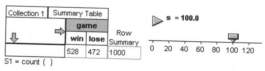

9. There is a spike toward the middle of the distribution and it tails off more slowly than a normal distribution does. Here are two ways to assess how non-normal it is: 1) Make another distribution with the same mean and standard deviation and compare their box plots; 2) Plot the data on a Normal Quantile Plot, and see how far it is from straight.

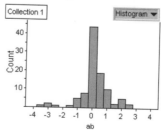

10. Here are two examples of different distribution samples, one where the histogram of **a** is oddly shaped (though it is still a **randomNormal(0,1)** sample) and **ab** still shows the spike in the middle. The right pair shows a more obviously normal histogram for **a** but the spike for **ab** is still present. Summary tables are below each set.

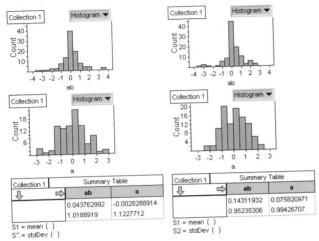

Exploring Correlation

2. The value of r^2 will be very close to +1.

3. The value of r^2 will be very close to +1.

4. The value of r^2 will be close to 0.

8. As the points in the **x-y** graph are moved, their corresponding points in the **zx-zy** graph are moving in similar directions. Other points move as well, often, but not always, in the opposite direction.

9. The origin of the **zx-zy** graph is the point that represents the mean of the **x**'s and the mean of the **y**'s.

12. For the **prod** to be positive, the point must have both coordinates larger than their respective means or both coordinates smaller than their respective means. This is the same as saying that the points must lie in the first or third quadrants of the **zx-zy** graph. For the results to be negative, one of the coordinates must be larger than its respective mean, and the other must be smaller than its respective mean. This is the same as saying that the points must lie in the second or fourth quadrant of the **zx-zy** graph.

14. The mean of the **prod**s is +1.

14a. (the margin question): Because the coordinates in the **zx-zy** graph are determined by a formula.

15.

Point Slant	r^2	Mean of the prods
Upward	1.00	1.00
Upward	0.64	0.80
Upward	0.25	0.50
Upward	0.09	0.30
Downward	1.00	-1.00
Downward	0.49	-0.70
Downward	0.25	-0.50
Downward	0.0625	-0.25

16. The relationship is that r^2 is the mean of **prod**-squared.

17. If the mean of **prod** is negative, the data slope downward. If the mean of **prod** is positive, the data slope upward. The more tightly linear the points are, the closer this mean will be to +1.00 or −1.00.

Building a Cloud from Scratch

Discussion Question

(first bullet) It means that the errors are normally distributed with a mean of zero and a standard deviation of **SD**.

Student Page

7. As **SD** gets closer to zero, the graph returns to the straight line $y = x$.

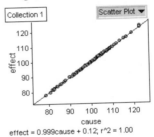

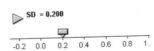

8. As **SD** gets larger, the error increases and the points become more scattered about the original line, resulting in the r^2 value decreasing.

9. While the slope bounces around more (due to sampling variation) it remains the same on the average. The mean value of **effect** in a given vertical swath is the same as it always was.

11. Now both slope and r^2 go to zero as **SD** increases.

12. The least-squares line—unlike the correlation coefficient—is not symmetrical. In this situation, as **SD** increases, the mean value for **cause** in a vertical swath where **effect** is low actually *increases*. One explanation is that with horizontal errors and normally distributed data, more points will move into the swath as a result of error from above than from below. The reverse happens for large values of **effect**, lowering the slope of the regression line.

Straight or Curved?

11. The points are decreasing with respect to the least-squares line, that is, they start out above it and wind up below it. Another way to say it is that they are decreasing on the residual plot, but the least-squares line—the function from which they are residuals—is increasing more quickly, so the net effect is that the values are increasing.

Adding Randomness

16. A value at about 0.10 makes the residual plot become flat. Answers vary.

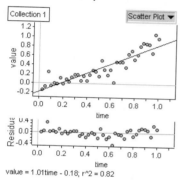

value = 1.01time − 0.18; r^2 = 0.82

17. One example looks like the one below (still with **SD** = 0.10).

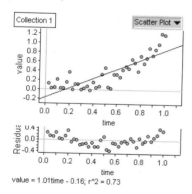

value = 1.01time − 0.16; r^2 = 0.73

18. Some value smaller than 0.10 but larger than 0.04 (depending on how much imagination you have) is where the plot will show the curvature most of the time.

Going Further

1. The graph looks different because the scale is now much larger, going from 100 to 121, so the range of *y*-values is 21 compared to the earlier graph that had a range of *y*-values only from 0 to 1. The residual plot, however, looks about the same.

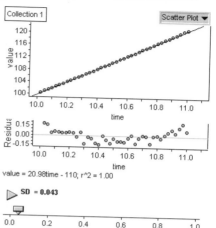

value = 20.98time − 110; r^2 = 1.00

SD = 0.043

2. It makes no difference. Use **random( )** for **time**.

3. The more cases that are added, the more error the curve can endure and still show the curvature.

4. Including more cases can help reduce the effect of the error. If you suspect curvature, increasing the size of the interval (cf. *Leverage*) is very effective.

Sonata 21: Predicting Spread

Conjecture. Especially if they have done *Random Walk*, (pages 200–203), students should have enough experience to realize that the expected distance from the origin increases with number of steps. Astute students will realize that it should have negative curvature, that is, it should be less than linear. In fact, the expected distance is proportional to the square root of the number of steps.

Measurement. First, students must decide what they want to measure, whether it is the final spot or the absolute value of the final distance. Then they need to build a series of steps by which they collect the data for various tests at various numbers of steps. One cool way to do this is to make a random walk collection and collect measures to get many walks (with a measures collection) so you can get the mean absolute distance. Then, with that mean as a measure, collect measures from that collection (to get **Measures from Measures from steps,** say). The tricks are (a) to make sure that the number of steps gets transmitted appropriately so you have that *n* in the final collection and (b) to set the final collection to collect one measure at a time, but not to empty the collection every time.

Sonatas 22–23: The Yahtzee Sonatas

See the Teacher Notes, page 220, for suggestions on these tasks.

Sonata 24: The Error in the Sum

One way to do this is somewhat like *Exploring the Normal Distribution,* pages 210–211. Make a collection with two normally distributed attributes, **a** and **b**. Let **a**'s standard deviation be 1, but let **b**'s be connected to a slider. Add them to get **s** (for sum), and calculate the standard deviation of **s**.

Record the data in a separate collection, either by collecting measures or by typing them in. Compare your results to predicted values based on the formula. The graph below shows the standard deviation of **s (ssd)** as a function of the standard deviation of **b (bsd)**. We have left **a**'s standard deviation fixed at 1. The curve is the predicted function based on the formula. The residual plot helps convince us that the model is good.

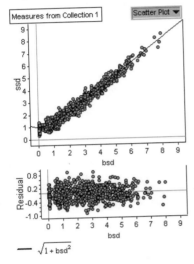

$$\sqrt{1 + bsd^2}$$

Sonata 25: Combined SAT Scores

Conjecture. In the case of the SAT scores, where correlation is very likely, the combined standard deviation should be larger than the Pythagorean answer, as Isabel suggested. Her reason, however, is weak. Suppose they're perfectly (positively) correlated. In fact, suppose the two scores are identical. Then the standard deviation (SD) would be the arithmetic sum of the two SDs. As the correlation decreases from perfection to none (i.e., independence), the sum of the SDs will decrease from the arithmetic sum (roughly twice each component) to the Pythagorean one (roughly $\sqrt{2}$ times each component). If they were negatively correlated, the SD would be smaller than you would expect from independence. Another way to look at it is that if the scores are positively correlated, two big scores will tend to go together, making a combined score that's farther from the combined mean— thereby increasing the SD.

Calculation. Below are the data from the freshman class, shown above simulated data as suggested. You can see that the total SAT score in the simulated case has a smaller standard deviation than in the real data, as advertised.

SATGPA	Summary Table		
	verbal	math	totalSAT
	489.34	543.95	1033.29
	82.298022	84.458851	142.80223

S1 = mean ( )
S2 = stdDev ( )

sim SAT	Summary Table		
	vsim	msim	tsim
	490.77757	541.2767	1032.0543
	81.699229	83.688091	114.03445

S1 = mean ( )
S2 = stdDev ( )

9 Probability Through Simulations

Rolling Dice

Discussion Questions

There are more ways (six) to make 7 as the sum of two dice than there are ways to make any other number.

If you feared a loaded die, you might record many rolls and see if the distribution of numbers was flat.

Student Pages

12. The distribution shows the frequency of each of the face numbers for each rerandomized trial. These trials show quite a bit of variation from one to the next, but overall the distribution is flat.

13. By using the **New Cases** choice from the **Data** menu, we can put 330 into the dialog box to create 330 more cases, for a total of 360. The graph (histogram) will need to have the popup menu chosen again, or the axis dragged, to reset the scales for the bars.

14. First, the scale on the left is different, since there are more tosses. Second, the tops of the bars tend to stay more uniform across than when there were only 30 tosses.

Two Dice Now

19.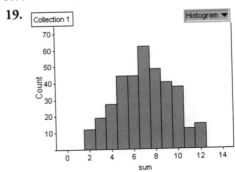

20. By reading the status bar, you see that there were 61 tosses producing a 7 in this example.

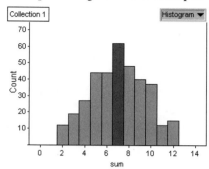

21. The fraction for the above case was 61/360 = 0.169, slightly above the theoretical value of 1/6.

Going Further

In 20 trials, 7 came out on top 15 times. With a larger numbers of trials (using a measures collection—see **RollingDiceContest**) the proportion of 7-winners is clearly between 3/5 and 2/3.

Exploring Sampling I: With and Without

4. The **Sample** case table produces 10 names from the list in the original case table; it will repeat one or more names.

5. About every second time we chose **Sample More Cases,** two names were the same. In one, all three were the same. Theoretically, you will see a match 13 times out of 25. One of those times will be a triple.

6. With the box now unchecked, we get samples without replacement, which means that once a name has been selected it is no longer in the pool of names to be chosen for the next slot in the collection.

7. All five names appear, but in different orders. (**Note:** These are *permutations.*)

8. The number of cases sampled "sticks" at five. When sampling without replacement, the number of cases cannot be larger than the number of names in the list. Once the name is chosen, it is removed from the pool of names to be placed in the collection. When all the names are placed, there are no more names to select.

Exploring Sampling II: Picking a Pair

3. The collection of 10 cards changes as the **Sample More Cases** button is pressed.

5. When **With Replacement** is checked, there may be duplications of the cards in the sample, since each card chosen could be any of the 52 in the deck each draw. However, when **With Replacement** is unchecked, the 10 cards will always be different. If the **Empty Collection First** button is checked, the collection will be 10 cards each time, but if the button is unchecked, the total collection will increase by the number of chosen cases each time.

9. Two possibilities: **first(number) = last(number)**, and **uniqueValues(number) = 1**.

12. Answers will vary, but in this sample trial, the author had 13 cases true, 187 cases false.

13. This will vary with class size and computers available.

15. The author had 10 samples out of 200 that were pairs.

16. Again, answers will vary depending on class size and computers available. But in general, 1/13, or about 15/200 of the trials will show pairs.

17. To get these values, add up the total true cases, then divide by the total number of cases gathered in the above exercises. Here, we would get 13/200 and 10/200, or .065 and .050.

Going Further

1. A good way to think about this problem is to consider only the second card. With replacement, the chances are 4/52, or about .077, that you draw a card of the same number. Without replacement, however, there are only three same-number cards left (you're holding the fourth) and only 51 cards in the deck, for a probability of 3/51, or about .059.

2. There are a number of ways to accomplish this. For example, in the original collection, make several new measures.

hasAce   **(first(number) = 1) or (last(number) = 1)**

hasFace   **(first(number) > 9) or (last(number) > 9)**

blackJack   **hasAce and hasFace**

You can find **and** and **or** on the calculator keypad. In 500 trials, we got 20 blackjacks (4%), slightly lower than the theoretical 8/169, or about .047.

3. Again modifying the sampling pane in the Inspector for the sample collection, the number of cases now must be five, and the formula for the pair can be changed to **uniqueValues(number) = 4**. This will return those cases where four numbers are unique and the fifth is not, thus making a pair. The author had 89 of 200 cases true, so 89/200 = .445.

Just You Wait!

Discussion Questions

A tree diagram can get messy because of the possibility that the process will go on forever. You end up summing an infinite series.

Student Pages

1. Many students will say six, which is correct.

7. As the sample is collected, the case table fills until a 6 is obtained, sometimes on the first sample, sometimes not until much later (20 samples or more).

13. The graph looks something like this.

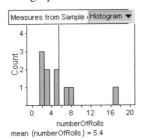

mean (numberOfRolls) = 5.4

15. The mean value in the illustration tells us that approximately five rolls would be needed to obtain the first six. A second experiment produced a mean value of 6.4.

17. We could simply collect measures from more trials, increasing the number to 10 or unchecking the **Empty This Collection First** box. Below we have 100 trials that (fortuitously) give a mean value of 6.0, the theoretical result.

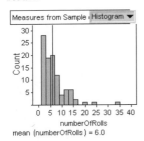

mean (numberOfRolls) = 6.0

18. The most likely number of rolls, surprisingly, is one. With sufficient trials, students should see that the distribution of numbers of rolls decreases monotonically from one (it's a geometric distribution).

19. This is the same as asking how the mode can be different from the mean. In this case, the mode is at one end of the distribution; the long tail pulls the mean to the right.

Going Further

1. The median is four rolls. A box plot helps.

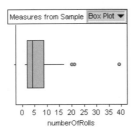

2. The best guess might be between four and five rolls because there are eight ways to get a seven or an eleven out of the thirty-six total outcomes (6 on first die times 6 on second die). Theoretically, the mean is the reciprocal of the probability (4.5). The simulation can be carried out by adjusting the collections in *Just You Wait!* Add another face to the first collection, and add another column to add those two faces together. Each face has the formula **randomPick(1,2,3,4,5,6)**. Run the rest of the simulation with similar adjustments. One set of 100 trials gave a mean of 4.5 and a median of three rolls.

3. This is analogous to the dice problems. Use a collection with one attribute, **sex**, and two cases with values **girl** and **boy**. Then sample from that collection until **sex = "girl"**. One simulation with 100 trials gave a mean and a median of two children in the family (one boy). The mode is zero boys.

4. The mean number of rolls would go down, since there will not be any possibility of getting repeated rolls of any value. Besides, it becomes impossible to have to roll more than six dice to get a six!

5. The average number of trials to get a five *and* a six for one experiment was 4.7.

6. The average number of trials to get a five *or* a six for one experiment was 2.4.

7. A statement with **or** in it is more likely than with **and**. The basic reason, as seen above, is that the probability is greater that one of the conditions will be met before both of the conditions are met.

8. On the average, it takes about 10 steps. You can build a simulation to study this, especially if you have done the random walks activity.

Great Expectations

Discussion Question

(last bullet) Knowing the mean is not the only thing you need if you're planning. A small standard deviation means that income is steady and reliable. With a large standard deviation, you have to be ready for bad weeks (or prepared to enjoy good ones).

Student Pages

5. Sven generally makes between $500 and $950 per week.

10. The case table should show his income for 5 weeks.

12. In this example, $710.

13. The standard deviation in this example is $180.

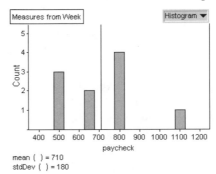

mean ( ) = 710
stdDev ( ) = 180

14. This is for a collection of 50 cases ($720 mean; theoretically, $725).

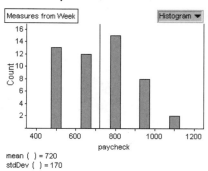

mean ( ) = 720
stdDev ( ) = 170

15. As the number of cases goes up, the fluctuations will tend to smooth out. Technically, as the number of trials increases, the proportional standard error decreases, making our estimate of the population mean more accurate.

Going Further

1. In several trials, Sven earned more than $1000 in only about two or three weeks out of each year.

2. As the value of *p* increases, Sven's total weekly income will move upward because he will get fewer lower-paying jobs and more higher-paying jobs. A more ambitious student would try to find the expected value as a *function* of *p;* theoretically, that function is $E = 5(250p + 100(1 - p))$, which is linear.

3. By using a setup similar to Sven's income, we can assign **animal** to be one attribute and **weight** to be another attribute, and use a measure (use the Inspector) and a measures collection to collect the weight of 30 animals in a truck. *In several experiments, the proportion by which the weight exceeded 800 pounds was 0.20.*

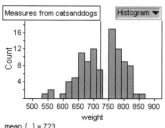

mean ( ) = 723

4. Though the graph is much different, the mean weight in these two experiments is the same. The number of animals chosen by the random picks would stay about the same as well, with dogs occurring about 55% of the time and cats about 45%. But because of the standard deviations, there's more slop in the weights, increasing the total standard deviation and increasing the number of times the total weight exceeds 800 pounds.

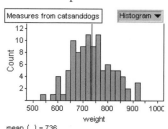

mean ( ) = 736

5. This problem has a delicious ambiguity. Ella pays $1 to play. If she rolls a 7, does she win back $2.50 or $2.50 *plus her dollar?* Worldwise teachers know that ambiguity always favors the house, but accept student responses in either category. If she gets her dollar plus the prize, Ella would win about $0.19 per game in the long run in this simulation (a huge return on investment).

To simulate this, make a collection with two dice and add them; make a lot of cases (100, say) and then collect measures, repeating your 100-game experiment, perhaps 100 times. This histogram is for 100 trials of 100 tosses of two dice, with each die having a formula of **randomPick(1,2,3,4,5,6)**, and the formula for winnings is below the histogram.

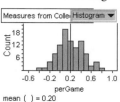

mean ( ) = 0.20

$$\text{if } ((\text{totalRoll} = 7) \text{ or } (\text{totalRoll} = 11)) \begin{cases} \text{if } (\text{totalRoll} = 7) \begin{cases} 2.5 \\ 10 \end{cases} \\ -1 \end{cases}$$

On the other hand, if they don't refund your dollar when you win, things are not as rosy. On the average, Ella will lose about $0.03 per game, but there is a good chance of having a set of, say, 100 games that show a win. This demonstrates the importance of looking at a really long "long run" to assess whether you want to play.

Here is another formula for winnings tuned to the pessimistic rules (but using the elegant **switch** function).

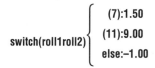

$$\text{switch}(\text{roll1roll2}) \begin{cases} (7):1.50 \\ (11):9.00 \\ \text{else:}-1.00 \end{cases}$$

Incidentally, to do this theoretically, compute a weighted average as you would with any expected value problem. If you focus only on winnings, you see

$$E = P(7)(\$2.50) + P(11)(\$10.00)$$

$$= \frac{6}{36}(2.5) + \frac{2}{36}(10)$$

$$\approx .41 + .56$$

$$\approx .97$$

That is, you get back 97 cents for every dollar you put in.

HIV Testing I

2. The number in this simulation was 14. This represents 7% of the donors.

people	Summary Table	
test	negative	186
	positive	14
Column Summary		200

S1 = count ( )

4. In four more simulations, the numbers were 17, 22, 11, and 9 for a total of 73 donors who tested positive. This represents 7.3% of the total donors.

6. Random( ) returns random values between 0.0 and 1.0. Each time a value below 0.03 is returned, Fathom labels the donor "infected." Otherwise Fathom labels the donor "healthy"—so only 3% of the population is infected.

if (random (1.00) < 0.03) $\begin{cases} \text{"infected"} \\ \text{"healthy"} \end{cases}$

8. Since the test is accurate 95% of the time, when the person is healthy there should be a negative return on the test 95% of the time. When the test returns any decimal below 95%, the response for this healthy person is accurate. If not, then for the remaining 5% of cases, the return is positive, which would be an inaccurate response. Similarly, for the second cases, with the label infected, the results are switched.

10. In the illustration in the Student Pages, 10 of 17 (59%) labeled positive were actually healthy. In the illustration below, eight of 13 (62%) were healthy.

people	Summary Table	HIV		
		healthy	infected	Row Summary
test	negative	186	1	187
	positive	8	5	13
Column Summary		194	6	200

S1 = count ( )

In a sample of rerandomized groups, returns were 12 of 19 (63%), six of 19 (32%), nine of 14 (64%), and 12 of 15 (80%).

11. In a group of 1000 persons, suppose 1% of the population has HIV. That would mean that 10 persons are infected and 990 persons are free of the disease. In 95% of the tests, results would be accurate, but that would mean that 5% of the healthy persons would be classified as infected, or that about 50 cases of false positives would be reported. If 10 persons were infected, this could mean that 60 cases of positive results were found, but 50 of the 60 results (83%) would be healthy persons. (See also the discussion in the Teacher Notes.)

Going Further

1. The table below shows the results when the value of .05 is used in the formula. Repeated rerandomization of the list gives some values where healthy is larger than infected, some where infected is larger than healthy, and some where the results are exactly equal.

people	Summary Table	HIV		
		healthy	infected	Row Summary
test	negative	184	0	184
	positive	9	7	16
Column Summary		193	7	200

S1 = count ( )

We will choose some number t for the infection rate. With 200 in the sample, $200t$ represents the number of persons actually infected with HIV. In the simulation, we started with this value at 0.03. To make the number of false positives equal the number of true positives here, we need to solve the equation $0.95(200t) = .05(200 - 200t)$. The left side is the actual number of true positives. The right side is the 5% of the healthy population in which a false positive occurs. Solving this equation gives $t = 0.05$, which makes intuitive sense.

2. Think of it this way: The HIV antibody test—or any test—tests the level of some chemical in the blood. Infected people generally have a higher level of this chemical than noninfected people, but two factors conspire to muddy the waters: First, infected or not, people vary in the amount of this chemical that they have. Second, there is variation in how the test performs. These factors add spread to the observed levels of the chemical. So if we plotted a histogram of the amount of the chemical across the population, we would not see two disjointed spikes, but rather two distributions that overlap in their tails. The border between a positive and a negative test result is a line in that diagram, separating the two humps. But there are some from the left distribution that are in the right-hand tail (false positives) and some from the right that have leaked over into the left (false negatives). We get to pick the location of the line; but when we move it to the left to decrease false negatives, we add to the number of false positives.

3. There is no definitive answer, and people will be affected no matter what choice is made. One opinion put forward is that low false negatives prevent those who are infected from thinking they are not. Presumably, this results in their seeking treatment and more quickly. And although those who falsely test positive would experience trauma, they could be retested. One could argue just as forcefully for making the other choice.

4. Discussion of these various tests should include what would be evaluated and what would not. For example, an airline detector should detect explosives in luggage. A false positive would mean more baggage being opened (very carefully), which could mean delays in loading the luggage and boarding the passengers. False negatives could mean that luggage with some sort of explosive could get through the detector.

HIV Testing II: Be an Epidemiologist

4. Sample totals were 24, 19, 30, 27, and 20 for a total of 120 out of 1000 donors.

5. The equation for this should be:

$120 = truepositive + falsepositive$

$120 = 0.95(1000x) + 0.05(1000)(1 − x)$

Solving this equation gives the result 0.0778. The true infected population is somewhere near 7.8%.

7. For the above simulation, the slider had been set to 0.08, a value that produced results very close to the calculated value.

Going Further

1. With a second test, the chance that a healthy person will test positive a second time is pretty low. People whose test results in one false negative risk not getting needed help. A third test might help (you have to get two out of three to be clear). We should point out that a false positive on an HIV test usually occurs for a reason: a recent flu shot or an abundance of antibodies in the blood. So follow-up tests are different and are designed to be independent of the first.

2. By adding a filter to the collection, or an **if( )** statement to a new attribute, only those who test positive can be re-evaluated. Ninety of 1000 persons tested positive the first time the test was run, and only five of those 90 tested positive the second time. Results like this indicate that a second test could be very useful. Retesting only positive results, rather than retesting everyone, could help reduce expense.

3. At the 80% level, assuming a 5% drug-use rate and a policy of retesting positives with the 80% test, the average number of positive tests will be about 46 out of every 200 tests. Of those, approximately 15 will retest as positive—only half of whom will be drug users. The cost here would be $20 per individual

tested twice and $10 for each tested once, for a total of $2460. Of course, the cost to test all 200 at the 99% level would be $20,000. However, the decision to incur this higher expense might be influenced by how often someone who tests positive should be subjected to the 80% level of certainty. Perhaps two positive tests at the 80% level should qualify someone for the more expensive test—which would cost $1500 more but might acquit all of the false positives. Meanwhile, however, two or three drug users will have slipped through the net.

Sonata 26: Grubs Again?

Design and Execution. Our first step would be to generate a case table with one grub. It will have a **weight** attribute, with formula **randomNormal(3.5, 0.3)**. We then give the grub a value to tell us whether it is useful in this order or not. We set up an attribute labeled **Useful** using the formula **inRange(weight, 3.6, 3.8)**, which is **true** when the **weight** is in range and **false** otherwise.

Now use **Sample Cases** from the **Analyze** menu to set up a sampling mechanism to find how long it will take to get two useful grubs using this sampling. To do that, set up the inspector's sample pane as follows:

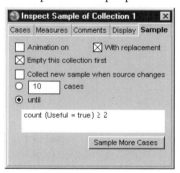

Now click the **Measures** tab in this inspector and create a measure, such as **n_Grubs**. Give this the formula **count( )** so that it will count how many grubs are inspected before two useful ones are found. Choose **Collect measures** to collect the distribution of **n_Grubs**. Here are the results from 100 trials; the mean number Howard had to harvest was 10.

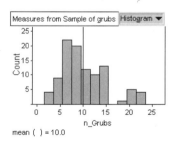

Reflection and Extension. For a 90% chance of getting two grubs, use a percentile plot or an Ntigram or compute the 90th percentile. We can see that Howard should harvest 17 grubs.

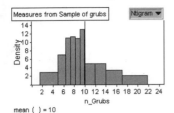

mean ( ) = 10

Sonata 27: A New Birthday Problem

Conjecture and Design. Make a collection called **people** with one attribute, **birthday**, with formula **RandomInteger(1, 365).** We'll ignore leap years. Put one case into this collection. **Sample Cases** from this collection **with replacement** and **until uniqueValues(birthday) < count( ).** Make a measure **number** with formula **count( ). Collect Measures** from the sample collection and make a histogram of the result. **Execution.** 100 trials produced these results.

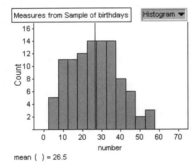

mean ( ) = 26.5

The expected number of people entering the room until two had the same birthday was 26. (The median was also 26, and the standard deviation was 13.4.)

Dice Probability Problems

Subtracting Dice

A good guess for this is that the most likely outcome is zero. The simulation has two attributes, one for each die, with the formula **RandomPick(1,2,3,4,5,6).** Then a third attribute is created for their difference, **first – second.** By creating a histogram for this difference and filling the case table with 500 cases, we can watch what happens to the mean of the histogram, as shown below.

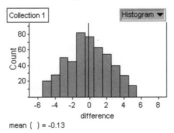

mean ( ) = -0.13

The largest category above happens to be at –1, but the mean is close to zero.

Absolute Subtraction

The distribution of values is from 0 through 5. The simulation's histogram (with 1000 cases) and mean value are below.

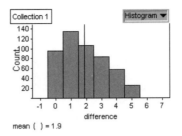

mean ( ) = 1.9

The most likely (absolute) difference is 1. Theoretically, the mean (expected value) should be the sum of the values of each difference multiplied by its probability.

mean = 0*(6/36) + 1*(10/36) + 2*(8/36) + 3*(6/36) + 4*(4/36) + 5(2/36) = 1.94.

Scatter Plot of Dice

First, the set will be made up of ordered pairs of integers, since whichever die we choose uses integers and the sum is an integer. Second, the set will have values of 2–12 for its domain and 1–6 for its range. Therefore the graph should be a stripe of values going upward to the right.

The picture for 400 cases is below.

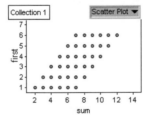

Special Dice

The distribution should be of sums that are all odd integers. The values should range from 3–23 with most of the sums in the low teens. By using **randomPick( )** for these two sets, the case table can be developed quickly and the graph for the sum derived. Below is the graph for 1000 cases.

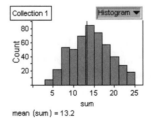

mean (sum) = 13.2

Adding Up Dice with More Sides

We already know that the mean value for rolling six-sided dice is 7. Below are consecutive cases where the dice have seven, then eight, then nine, then 10, then 12, and finally 15 faces (each with 1000 cases).

Seven faces

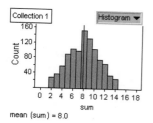

mean (sum) = 8.0

Eight faces

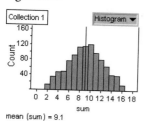

mean (sum) = 9.1

Nine faces

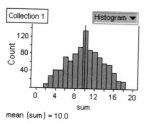

mean (sum) = 10.0

Ten faces

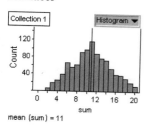

mean (sum) = 11

Twelve faces

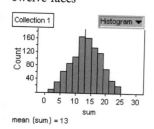

mean (sum) = 13

Fifteen faces

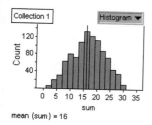

mean (sum) = 16

A good guess for the mean is **faces** + 1.

Adding Up More Dice

Below are the histograms for the sums of three, four, five, six, eight, and ten dice (each with 1000 cases).

Three dice

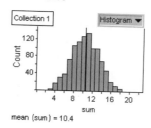

mean (sum) = 10.4

Four dice

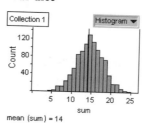

mean (sum) = 14

Five dice

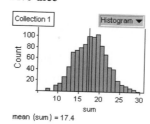

mean (sum) = 17.4

Six dice

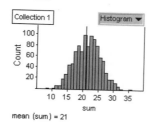

mean (sum) = 21

Eight dice

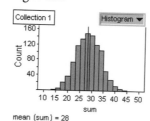

mean (sum) = 28

Ten dice

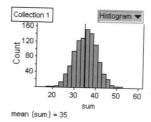

mean (sum) = 35

Chapter 9

A good prediction here might be that adding an additional die would add 3.5 to the mean of the sum since the mean of tossing one die is 3.5.

Adding more dice changes the range of the sums by more than just simply adding an additional face. The distribution is approaching normality; we are essentially engaging in a random walk. This is also a demonstration of the Central Limit Theorem.

Sampling Challenges

Awarding Five Prizes

Set up a case table with the names in it, in any order. Then go to **Sample Cases** and open the inspector. In the **sample** pane, change the number to 5, and collect samples.

Everybody's a Winner

Again, list the names in a case table and go to **Sample Cases.** With the inspector open, click off the **With replacement** box (we're sampling *without* replacement) and be sure that the sample number is equal to the number of persons in the list.

Simulating 50 Animals

By setting up a case table with two attributes (**sex** and **pet**), we can easily simulate this, and repeatedly resample. A sample of the summary table used as well as the formula for the attribute **sex** is below.

Collection 1	Summary Table	sex		Row Summary
		F	M	
pet	cat	7	22	29
	dog	9	12	21
	Column Summary	16	34	50

S1 = count ( )

$$\text{if } (pet = \text{"cat"}) \begin{cases} \text{randomPick ("M","M","F")} \\ \text{randomPick ("M","F")} \end{cases}$$

If you are female, your (empirical) chance of being a cat is 7/16.

Collect Them All

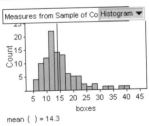

mean ( ) = 14.3

If we put the names of all six persons into a case table with the attribute **Name** and sample from that list, we need to sample until **UniqueValues(Name) = 6.** At that point we have collected all the figures. Using **Collect Measures** we can count the numbers of boxes we need each time to collect all six. We need to be sure that the **Sample** inspector has a measure (**boxes?**) set up with the formula **count( )**. The histogram shows 50 samplings. The theoretical answer is

14.7 (adding the expected values for the wait times, 6/6 + 6/5 + 6/4 + 6/3 + 6/2 + 6/1).

Monty Hall

There are a number of ways to do this—one is in **MontyHall.done** on your CD. It uses a collection of three prizes that's sampled three times without replacement to assign the prizes to doors. Assuming we start by choosing Door 1 (since where we start doesn't matter), the data set determines which door the host will reveal and records (in a measure) whether we would win or lose if we stayed or switched. A measures collection attached to a summary table completes the picture.

The result is that switching gives you a 2/3 chance of winning, whereas staying gives you the 1/3 chance you would expect.

10 Inference with Fathom

Constructivist Dice Online

1. This formula could be the class's decision or an individual student's own formula. For this example, we will use the sum of absolute difference. If we use data of 7-4-5-3-10-1, we'll get a statistic of 2 + 1 + 0 + 2 + 5 + 4, or 14.

5. The formula for this particular measure appears on page 262. Student measures may be different, of course. You can even build the chi-square statistic. Some formulas will have to be pretty elaborate—but they only have to be made once. Students should save often.

6. For the example below, our absolute-difference statistic is 8.

fair dice	Summary Table	
	1	5
	2	4
	3	7
face	**4**	3
	5	4
	6	7
	Column Summary	30

S1 = count ( )

7. Individual results will vary. In this example, we got 16, 8, 10, 4, 16, 10, 8, 12, 6, 10.

8. Answers will vary depending on what the individual statistics are. Generally, we would expect the values for the homemade dice to be larger. In practice, the values are not very much larger. If the die is anything like a cube, its statistic will probably be within the distribution of 10 fair-dice trials.

13–14. Histograms for 100 measures of chi-square and our absolute-difference statistic appear in the next solution.

15. Since answers will vary depending on the class statistic, this example will use the test statistics of 10.0 for chi-square and 14 for **howUnfair** the absolute difference sum. All of the cases in the **howUnfair** tail are selected—there are 16 of them. Note some are in the body of the chi-square distribution. That is, the empirical *P*-value using the user-constructed measure is 0.16; that for chi-square is less, 0.10.

In this case, we counted them by selecting them, pointing at the collection, and looking at the number in the status bar. We could also have made a summary table and installed a new formula such as **count(? > 13)** to get a numerical answer.

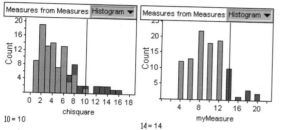

10 = 10

14 = 14

Note that we select those cases with statistics that are greater than *or equal to* our test statistic. This gives a higher, that is, less exciting, *P*-value.

16. Opinions will vary depending on individual cases. A reason should be given for the conclusion drawn. In the case of the value of chi-square = 10 and *P* = .10 from above, we might conclude that the dice used had some problem, though there are cases where the fair dice also were unusual. Traditionally the cutoff is *P* = .05 and a chi-square (5df) closer to 12, but in reality it depends on what is at stake. Depending on students' experience, you might insist on an assessment of the risk or simply a seat-of-the-pants decision about what is unlikely enough to reject the null hypothesis that the die is fair.

Pennies and Polling Online I

1. These answers will vary by individual. For this discussion assume the group had a value of 42%.

3. These answers will vary depending on the sample for each person. The 42% value would be a plausible result in the graph where *P* = 0.50.

4. The graph tends to shift to be centered (or nearly so) at the value of *P*. The illustration shows what it looked like when we chose *P* = .20.

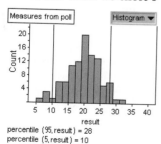

percentile (95, result) = 28
percentile (5, result) = 10

5. For our trials, we got these results (still assuming our group's poll was 42%—student results will vary).

.00	0	0	no
.20	10	30	no
.30	21	42	yes (barely)
.40	30	51	yes
.50	40	60	yes
.60	48	72	no
.70	56	80	no
.80	70	87	no

6.

	0.0	0.1	0.2	0.3	0.4	0.5	0.6	0.7	0.8	0.9	1.0
yes				x	x	x					
no	x	x					x	x	x	x	x

The nos change to yesses here at 0.30. The yesses change back to nos at 0.52. Note that there is some uncertainty in these values, since repeated trials will give slightly different results.

8. The sample value of 42% would be plausible from 0.30 through 0.52.

9. Reasonable responses include 42 ± 10 or 42 ± 12 or 41 ± 11 (in that ballpark).

Pennies and Polling Online II

2.

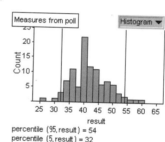

percentile (95, result) = 54
percentile (5, result) = 32

3. The first histogram is the first trial using 42% for *P*. The results are close but the lower one is further from our last test than the upper. The second histogram (below) is after resampling four times without emptying the collection first, so it represents 400 trials. Here the results are much closer at the lower end.

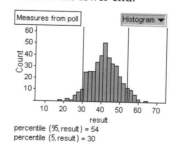

percentile (95, result) = 54
percentile (5, result) = 30

4. This is really a question for sophisticated statistics students. The 90% intervals are approximately the same width (call it w) and are approximately centered around p, for all values of p that are not too extreme (too close to 0 or too close to 1), including the value of p that we found in our sample (let's call that value **poll**). Thus the distance from any p to either end of its interval is approximately $\frac{w}{2}$. So if **pLeft** is the smallest value whose interval contains **poll**, **pLeft** is approximately **poll** $-\frac{w}{2}$, and if **pRight** is the largest value whose interval contains **poll**, **pRight** is approximately **poll** $+\frac{w}{2}$. Therefore the interval from **pLeft** to **pRight** is approximately centered around **poll** and has width approximately w—just like the 90% interval around **poll**. Note that these are approximations because the width w does change as p changes.

How Much Confidence?

5. We should use the 2.5% and 97.5% percentiles.

7. The interval is from 28 to 56, or 42 ± 14 ($n = 50$).

8. The 95% interval is *wider*. Since the distribution is the same regardless of the strength of the interval, the fewer cases excluded, the wider the interval must be.

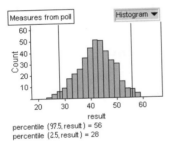

percentile (97.5, result) = 56
percentile (2.5, result) = 28

Effect of Sample Size

9. (The assumption is that **p** is still set at your sample value, in this case 42%.) For 50 cases, the interval was 28 to 56. The graph appears below. When we add another 50 cases to the poll collection (for a total of 100) and collect 100 measures, the interval gets narrower (the second histogram)—this time, it's 32% to 53%. Again, the limits fluctuate a little due to sampling error.

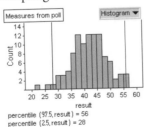

percentile (97.5, result) = 56
percentile (2.5, result) = 28

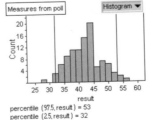

percentile (97.5, result) = 53
percentile (2.5, result) = 32

10.

Number polled	95% confidence interval	Width of interval (%)
50	28 to 56	28
100	31 to 53	22
200	36 to 49	13
400	38.2 to 47	8.8
1000	39.2 to 45.5	6.3
2000	39.5 to 44.25	4.75

11. The interval should be getting smaller because as the number of cases increases it becomes more unlikely that the poll will give a result far from the population proportion. As the results cluster more closely to the population value, the percentiles move in as well.

Going Further

1. Using the standard confidence interval notation, if the number of cases polled stays constant and the confidence value stays constant (90%, 95%, etc.), then only the value of p is changing in the formula. So the relevant quantity is $\sqrt{p(1-p)}$. As p moves away from .5, this value declines, so the width of the confidence interval gets smaller as the value of p decreases toward zero or increases toward 1. If we did not know the formula, we could see this effect in the data, especially where p is large or small. This illustration shows the width of the 90% confidence interval as a function of p, for various values of that parameter. Each point represents 50 trials of a sample of size 50.

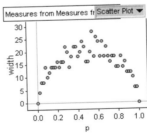

2. With 50 people, we got ±14, with 100, ±10. The full width of the interval was about 6 with 1000 cases. So that would give us ±3.

3. This means that if he did surveys repeatedly the same way he did the poll, we would expect the proportion of people who think the economy is great to fall in this interval 95% of the time. Of course, we would not know *which* surveys captured the true proportion.

4. If you have a biased sample—for example, if you polled people coming out of a grocery store when you were studying national opinion—you would not only bias your estimate of the population, but you might make the confidence interval narrower if your sample

were so homogenous that $\hat{p}$ (the sample proportion) was close to 0 or 1. On the other hand, if the measured $\hat{p}$ was still middling, a bad sample might give you a wrong answer—but the same-sized confidence interval.

5. Results will vary depending on practically everything.

Pennies and Polling III

Effect of Population Percentage

This is the more formal version of the first "Going Further" question on the page 274. Students carefully measure confidence intervals and can find that the width is indeed proportional to $\sqrt{p(1-p)}$. See the solution for the first "Going Further" question of the previous activity.

Effect of the Number of Sets

The more measures you take, the less fluctuation there is in the confidence interval values you get. This is quite complex and requires a lot of layering. That is, we have the 50 voters; a measure of the 50 is the percentage in favor. If we repeat that 100 times, we get a "measure of measure," the distribution of those percentages. From that we can calculate the width of an interval. But we're interested in the fluctuations in that interval, so we recompute again (say, 10 times), collecting the widths as measures, and compute the standard deviation of the interval widths. Having done that, we vary the 100 above and see how the standard deviation depends on it. In Fathom, that means you may have a "Measures from measures from measures from poll" collection!

Orbital Express Online

2. Here are some data for this simulation.

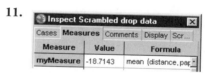

	paper	distance
1	copier	39
2	copier	8
3	copier	40
4	copier	34
5	copier	88
6	copier	24
7	copier	65
8	towel	11
9	towel	18
10	towel	43
11	towel	13
12	towel	16
13	towel	19
14	towel	15

3. A graph for these values is below.

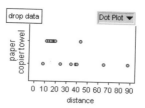

4. The graph suggests that the paper towel is better, since most of the values are very low and close together.

6.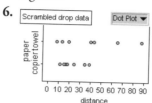

Entering Your Statistic

9. Student statistics will vary. Here's one we'll use.

mean (distance, paper = "copier") − mean (distance, paper = "towel")

10.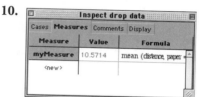

11.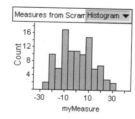

The Distribution of Your Statistic

17. The graph for this simulation looks like the one below:

18. The first collection is just the data from the original drops. We need this to hold the values from the drops and to separate them by paper quality. The second collection is the scrambled data, and this will be used to discover if our measure is due to chance or shows a real difference in the paper quality. The third collection is recording a large number of scrambles so we can find out if the **myMeasure** value tells us what we need to know.

Comparing to Your Original Data

24. Note: The solutions given here are for a one-tailed test. You can easily extend this activity to cover the two-tailed condition — which is probably more appropriate to this context.

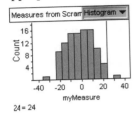

24 = 24

In this graph the value of the simulation test statistic was 24. There is only one case larger than this value, so only 2% of cases (1 of 50) is larger than this statistic.

25. Let's collect different numbers of trials.

Number of trials	% larger than 24
100	5
200	4
400	3.25
1000	3.1
2000	2.05

26. Overall 2% to 3% of the trials exceed the value 24.

27. From this we conclude that the copier re-entry vehicle really is worse than the towel vehicle; it's unlikely that the observed difference is due to chance. The difference between the means in our samples is usually less than 24, the test statistic. If there were no difference in the two paper stocks, then the value 24 should be more toward the middle of the cases than out at an extreme. A possible explanation is that if the drop is at least several feet, the towel will generally bounce less than the harder copier paper, thus making its mean value usually less than that of the paper.

Student conclusions can legitimately vary, depending on their data. In a typical class, only half or fewer get a significant difference at the 5% level. This activity also lets you bring the 5% convention into question. Or suppose the worse vehicle cost less; *then* how would you decide which one to use?

Inferring the Mean, Part I

6. No. With a P-value that high (and given the assumptions for the t test), it's completely plausible that the true diameter is 2.25 cm.

7. As you drag the point to the left, t decreases and P increases toward 1. As you drag the point to the right, the opposite happens for a while, then it reverses. So as you drag to the right, the P-value first decreases (more significant) then increases (less significant).

8. When P is .05, t is 2.776, and there are 4 degrees of freedom. We zoomed in to get a more accurate value for t.

9. A textbook (Rossman et al., *Workshop Statistics*, 1997) lists 2.776 as the .025 critical value for 4 df. Since ours is a two-tailed ("not equal to") test and P is 5%, this is appropriate.

11. When we set **diameterTarget** to 2.00, P gets very small. (The exact value will depend on where that left point is, but we have .000002.) It's smaller because (we'll give several types of responses): All of the points are separated from 2.0; it's much clearer that they don't come from a population with that mean; they straddle 2.25 but not 2.0; and so on.

12. If gizmos are supposed to be 2.00 cm, we would conclude with considerable certainty that our procedure is messing up—the gizmos are too big. Maybe some machine is poorly calibrated.

Making Confidence Intervals

13. 2.232 to 2.288. Adjust the slider until $p = .05$; then go the other way and do the same thing. If students have not put their points back, their answers will vary, but the correspondence between the plausibility interval and the confidence interval should be the same. (See next question.)

15. 2.2322 to 2.2878

16. Many capable students will make weak arguments here. Except for the most experienced students, this should be an exercise in simply addressing a problem of this complexity, not mastering it. Put another way, consider giving credit to any reasonable response!

Going Further

1. It got down to about .0308. It decreases because the standard deviation is decreasing, which makes the (increasing) difference between the sample mean and the null mean more significant. Later, the sample standard deviation increases (for example, when the point is far off to the right of the other points), which makes the difference less significant (because we're using the sample mean to estimate the population mean).

If you drag the point in the other direction, the opposite happens: P increases to 1 (when the sample mean equals the hypothesized mean), then slowly decreases as the declining sample mean (which pushes P down) slightly outpaces the effect of increasing sample standard deviation (which pushes P up).

2. Be sure to reset the data to get these answers! The P-value decreases from .37 to .19. We're asking how likely is it, if the population mean is 2.25, that we get a statistic as extreme as this one? In the two-tailed ("not equal") test, there are two ways this can happen—it can be too big or too little. In the new, one-tailed ("greater than") case, there's only one way—too big. So the probability is *less*. This also shows how, if you know in advance the direction you want to test for, the one-tailed test can give you significant results while with the same data you will fail to reject with a two-tailed test.

Inferring the Mean, Part II

2. The points jump around. Each time you move the slider, you get a new sample of points drawn from the distribution with a mean of **mu**. So if you move the slider up, the points jump, but they generally get higher.

3. Your specific values will vary. Here are ours: .057, .515, .474, .639, .282.

4. .119, .021, .052, .005, .042

5. We're testing whether the mean is zero. When the actual mean is far from zero, the *P*-value will be generally small (rejecting the null hypothesis). When the actual mean is zero, the *P*-value will be all over the place. (**Note:** *not* generally large. As we shall see, *P* is distributed uniformly.)

Exploring the Results

14. Note: When Fathom makes the *p*-graph, the bins may make one bin near the ends look much less populated. In fact, the distribution is *flat* in the interval (0, 1). (Think about this: It *has* to be in the case where the null hypothesis is true by construction.)

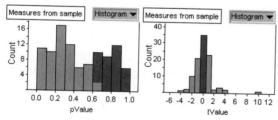

15. Selection shown in above illustration. Note that the high *P*-values (close to 1) are selected when you select the *t*-bar near zero.

16. With the bottom 0.1 selected in the *p*, the *t* graph will show both tails selected.

17. Nothing is wrong. It follows exactly from the meaning of the test and the *P*-value: It's the chance that even if the null hypothesis were true, we would get a value this extreme. Well, the null hypothesis *is* true, so if our criterion is $p < .10$, we expect 10% false rejections (Type I errors). The graph above shows 11/100 in the lowest bin. We expect it to be close to .10.

Going Further

1. We've selected $p < .1$. In the zoomed-in *t* dot plot, the point on the left is selected and the one on the right is not. So the "critical" value of *t* (in this situation) is somewhere between them—between about −2.13 and −2.08. If we look up the *t* critical value, we see 2.132 for df = 4 and 90%.

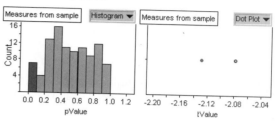

2. We've increased to 200 trials and made the bins smaller in the histogram—so we can select just 0.05. Now we zoom into the dot plot, this time on the positive side, near the place where the points change from unselected to selected. This is between $t = 2.7$ and $t = 2.8$. A table gives 2.776 as a critical value for 95% with df = 4.

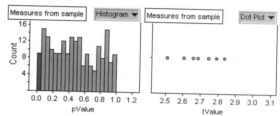

3. We have kept $p < .05$ selected. The graph shows how, when *t* is zero, *p* is 1, and that the farther *t* gets from zero in either direction, the more *p* decreases. That is, the more unlikely it is to get a value of *t* that extreme.

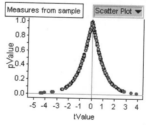

4. Predictions will vary, but here's **mu** = 0.5. You can see that the *P* distribution is now skewed towards zero. That is, it's more likely that we reject the null hypothesis (that's good, because the null is *false*). The *t* distribution (not called for in the prompt) is asymmetrical as well. This is the noncentral *t* distribution—the distribution of the *t* statistic when the null hypothesis is not true.

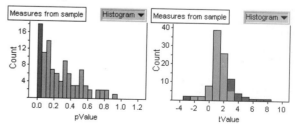

Sonata 28: Aunt Belinda

Conjecture and Design. Throwing 16 heads in 20 throws is extremely unusual. One way to see this is to set up a case table with one attribute, **side**, and two cases, **heads** and **tails**. Sample this table 20 times and count the **heads**. Then repeat the process many times, recording how many times **heads** (or **tails**) comes up 16 or more times. That is, we have a collection called **coin**. Then we make a sample of **coin** with 20 cases. We create a measure in this collection, called **sixteenOrMore**, with a formula such as **count(side="heads") > 15**.

Now we collect measures from that sample as many times as we can stand it. In that **Measures from Sample** of **coin**, we have one attribute, **sixteenOrMore**, which is either true or false. We count the trues. (You can see an alternative procedure in the file **AuntBelinda**.)

Measurement. We construct the simulation and count how many times we get 16 or more in 2000 tosses. There were seven cases out of 2000 here (.0035). The theoretical answer is .006—which is close enough, given these low probabilities.

Comparison and Conjecture. We can see that Aunt Belinda had a very unusual toss. It *could* be purely by chance. But most statisticians would reject the null hypothesis based on that low probability. Whether it's table magnetism or some other cause has yet to be established.

Sonata 29: Hot Hoops

Conjecture and Design. If there are streaks, we'd see more hit-hit and miss-miss, in comparison to hit-miss and miss-hit, than we would in the "independent" case. So we could make a 2-by-2 table and invent a statistic, such as the sum on the main diagonal minus the cross-sum, and collect that, using scrambled real data as a null hypothesis.

Another strategy is to compare percentages—if you get a hit, what's your empirical chance of hitting next time? How does that compare to your chance of hitting if you previously missed? That difference could be a statistic. Or, you could use chi-square and do a test for independence. There are other suggestions in the Teacher Notes, page 293.

Beyond Constructivist Dice

Always Even

If all observed values are the same as expected, the measure is 0. Changing the count of one value by 1 (either way) forces the count of some other value to change by 1 (the other way). Since we are adding *absolute* values, the net change is 2, so the measure is still even.

Critical Values for howUnfair, Part 1

1. We could use chi-square or any other suitable measure, such as the sum of the absolute differences.

2. Let's use the value $p = .05$.

3. In this distribution (of 100 cases, using chi-square), we can move the left edge of the last rectangle until we have five cases in the last box. This simulation has the .05 value at 11.07, which we can find in the status bar. In this case, this is the same as the theoretical chi-square value. We don't expect this to happen every time. We'd get a different critical value using a different measure.

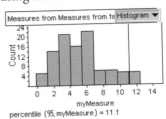

4. This will vary by individual. But if the value for the statistic is more extreme than the critical value, you would probably reject the null hypothesis (at least at the level specified).

Critical Values for howUnfair, Part 2

Most measures (such as the sum of absolute differences) will have a different critical value for every sample size. The relationship depends on the measure. More sophisticated students can try to find a function that will let them estimate the critical value based on the sample size. For a few measures (such as chi-square), the critical value is independent of the sample size.

What's Wrong with This?

Arthur is confused. The statement that the value of P or $(1 - P)$ produces a probability value for predicting the fairness or unfairness of the die is a misstatement. What this means is that, if he performed his experiment or sampling many times with a fair die, he would get a value as extreme or more extreme than he had only 0.5% of the time. Though this gives good evidence that his die is unfair, it is not a probability estimate for the die, only for the statistic he created to test it. Many statisticians say, "either the die is fair or it is not; it is not a suitable subject for a probability statement."

Chi-Square, Who Cares?

A comparison might help. The table below lists 10 samples from *Constructivist Dice*. The left column in the table uses the sum of the absolute differences while the right column uses the chi-square formula. You can evaluate the chi-square number using standard tables, while the numbers for **myMeasure** do not afford us that luxury (though we could make these tables ourselves, as in *Critical Values for* **howUnfair**). Second, chi-square gives us a wider variety of values, which helps us get a smoother distribution (and a better assessment of percentiles).

Finally, as mentioned in *Critical Values for* **howUnfair** Part 2, the same chi-square value corresponds to the same significance level independent of sample size (given the same degrees of freedom).

Measures from fair dice Table		
	myMeasure	chiSquare
1	10	6
2	10	8.4
3	12	7.2
4	14	7.6
5	8	4
6	8	3.2
7	10	4
8	12	8
9	4	0.8
10	10	4.4

Too, Too Fair

We could use the setup for *Constructivist Dice*. The question is, how often will chi-square (or the sum of absolute differences) be zero (or whatever value for the measure uniquely indicates all fives). This is very unlikely!

Chi-square would be one test to use to assess whether a set of die rolls was too even. If the chi-square test produced very small numbers most of the time, or if the numbers themselves had some sort of pattern, one would have to consider that the die were crooked. In this case, since the chi-square distribution is steep near zero and has a long tail (which makes it easier to distinguish large values), we might do better to use a statistic that is shallower at the start—such as the sum of absolute differences.

Too Many Twos

Amy could invent a statistic that concentrated on 2s and 5s. One is:

Count(face = 2) – count(face = 5).

This might work wonderfully given her *a priori* suspicion about the die. A word of caution: There might be other things wrong with the die that this test would never pick up. An interesting challenge would be to test this measure against chi-square given simulated, slightly biased data to see which gave lower *P*-values.

More Inference Challenges

Gender and Income I

Assume that the population to be considered is all over age 17 (use a filter to produce this restriction in the collection). Also, using the Berkeley data, the difference of the means of men and women is 9441. The null hypothesis would be that there is no difference in income based on gender. To test this, scramble the **sex** attribute. Then see where the value we had from the total data set (9441) appears in the distribution of the differences of the means of the scrambled data. The formulas and the distribution for this appear below. Note that 9441 lies

above the distribution of differences, giving very strong evidence that there is some bias regarding income based on gender.

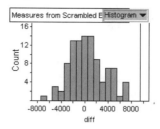

This is the formula for **diff** that was collected in the histogram.

mean (income, sex = "M") − mean (income, sex = "F")

Gender and Income II

For the Berkeley dataset, there are 101 persons who have incomes over $35,000. If we define a new attribute, **rich**, as **income > 35,000**, we can make a summary table.

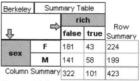

From this we can derive all of the proportions of richness by the attribute **sex**. We can get 95% confidence intervals either as we did earlier in the chapter or by using an analysis (choose **Estimate Parameters** from the **Analyze** menu, then choose **Estimate Proportion** from the popup menu). We get these results for Berkeley:

Who	Rich Proportion	95% c.i.
Total	0.239	(.198, .280)
Females	0.192	(.140, .244)
Males	0.291	(.228, .354)

We can see that the males include a larger proportion of "rich" individuals, though the 95% confidence intervals overlap.

Husbands and Wives

(first bullet) Using a summary table and the **mean** formula already there, the difference in the mean heights of men and women is 120.1 mm.

(second bullet) By entering a new attribute in the collection called **diff** with a formula **ht_husband – ht_wife**, we can look in a summary table and find that 28 of 30 husbands are taller than their wives, one is the same height, and one is shorter. The mean of the difference of these heights is 120.1 mm. If the two not-taller cases are excluded, then the mean becomes 129.8 mm.

(third bullet) Using a summary table again, the difference in the mean ages of men and women is 1.89 years.

(fourth bullet) In 22 of the 30 cases the husband is older than his wife, and the mean of this difference is 2.346. One issue here is that there are several cases where age for one or both is missing.

Each figure we get is a valid estimate for the population from which ours is a simple random sample, and each hypothesis test is valid. But if our population is *couples,* the results for the first and third questions are misleading, because a population of men and women is not the same as a population of couples. If taller men tended to stay single, for example, they would be underrepresented in our sample, and we'd get a smaller answer for the height difference than we would if we had a better-designed study.

The stronger *P*-value comes from comparing husbands' heights to the heights of their wives. This is because a paired test is more powerful; the variation within the sexes tends to obscure the general difference between them.

More Text Analysis

This can go in many different directions.

The key task in the suggested direction is to develop a statistic that measures streakiness. A simple one is to make a new attribute, **Vowel**, that is **true** if **char** is a vowel and **false** otherwise. Then make **RL**, with the formula **runLength(Vowel)**. Then make the measure, **MaxRunLength**, with the formula **max(RL)**. Use this for your statistic. You'll find that text has shorter run lengths (less than 10, being a bunch of consonants, punctuation, and spaces between two vowels) while a scrambled version of the same text will have a longer **maxRunLength**. That is, genuine randomness is streaky.

Activities Index